OBJECT-ORIENTED DATABASES

1951-1991
40 YEARS OF SERVICE

IEEE COMPUTER SOCIETY
A member society of the
Institute of Electrical and Electronics Engineers, Inc.

OBJECT-ORIENTED DATABASES

BY EZ NAHOURAII AND FRED PETRY

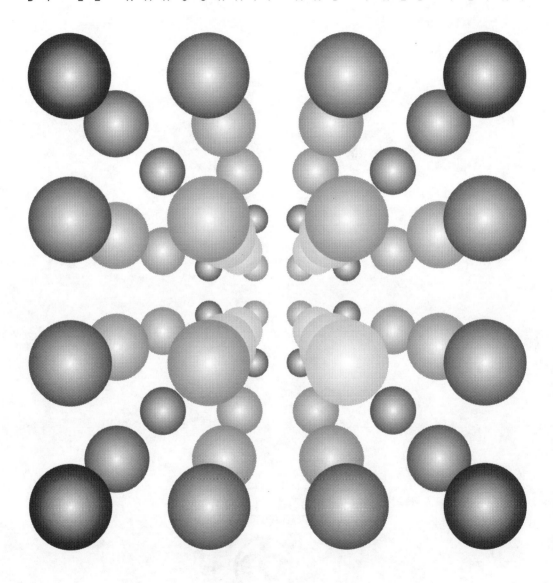

 1951-1991

 IEEE Computer Society Press   The Institute of Electrical and Electronics Engineers, Inc.

OBJECT-ORIENTED DATABASES

Edited by
Ez Nahouraii and Fred Petry

1951 - 1991
40 YEARS OF SERVICE

IEEE COMPUTER SOCIETY

IEEE Computer Society Press
Los Alamitos, California

Washington ● Brussels ● Tokyo

IEEE COMPUTER SOCIETY PRESS REPRINT COLLECTION

Published by

1951-1991

IEEE Computer Society Press
10662 Los Vaqueros Circle
P.O. Box 3014
Los Alamitos, CA 90720-1264

Copyright © 1991 by the Institute of Electrical and Electronics Engineers, Inc.

James H. Aylor, Technical Editor

Robert Werner, Production Editor

Cover design by Alex Torres

Printed in the United States of America by Bookcrafters, Chelsea, Michigan

IEEE Computer Society Press Order Number 1929
Library of Congress Number 90-86086
IEEE Catalog Number EH0332-7
ISBN 0-8186-1929-5 (paper)
ISBN 0-8186-5929-7 (microfiche)
ISBN 0-8186-8929-3 (case)
SAN 264-620X

Additional copies can be ordered from:

| IEEE Computer Society Press
Customer Service Center
10662 Los Vaqueros Circle
P.O. Box 3014
Los Alamitos, CA 90720-1264 | IEEE Computer Society
13, Avenue de l'Aquilon
B-1200 Brussels
BELGIUM | IEEE Computer Society
Ooshima Building
2-19-1 Minami-Aoyama,
Minato-Ku
Tokyo 107, JAPAN | IEEE Service Center
445 Hoes Lane
P.O. Box 1331
Piscataway, NJ 08855-1331 |

 The Institute of Electrical and Electronics Engineers, Inc.

PREFACE

This reprint collection consists of articles on object-oriented databases and is intended to provide a broad overview of current concepts, examples, and applications. This volume contains an introduction to object-oriented databases with papers organized into four sections: basic concepts, applications, design and implementation, and performance issues.

This collection should be useful for individuals wishing to obtain information about any topic relating to object-oriented databases. It could also be utilized as a supplement to either a database course or a general course introducing object-oriented programming and design if some applications to databases were to be introduced in the course. Since a brief introduction to object-oriented concepts is presented in this volume, and several papers also overview object-oriented ideas, it is possible to benefit from this collection without an extensive background in such concepts. However, for the articles contained herein it is assumed that an individual would have some knowledge of modern database management systems.

The field of object-oriented databases is presently one of great progress and diversity as many approaches and applications are being explored. It is generally agreed that existing relational database management systems are not adequate for increasingly demanding applications that require a broad variety of data elements such as graphics, sound, text, and so forth. Support for these kinds of data as needed by the use of hypertext, computer-aided design, or computer-aided software engineering can be facilitated by an object-oriented approach. However, there is currently a great deal of discussion as to whether this should be achieved by developing extensions to current relational designs[1] or promoting basically new approaches with object-oriented concepts[2]. We therefore hope this collection will prove valuable to understanding this rapidly advancing area.

---

[1]"Third-Generation Data Base System Manifesto," Committee for Advanced DBMS Function, *SIGMOD Record*, Volume 19, Number 3, September 1990, pp. 31-44.

[2]"The Object-Oriented Database System Manifesto," M. Atkinson, et al, *Deductive and Object-Oriented Databases*, Elsevier Science Publishers, Amsterdam, Netherlands, 1990.

TABLE OF CONTENTS

SECTION 1:
INTRODUCTION

SECTION 1
INTRODUCTION TO OBJECT-ORIENTED DATABASES

Very generally we perceive the clutter of the world as being "chunked" in an organized manner–as objects. In an object-oriented representation something viewed as a unified entity or item, e.g., numbers, persons, cities, components, and so on, can be represented as an object. So the object-oriented paradigm provides a natural but powerful technique for dealing with a variety of complex systems. Object-oriented concepts first surfaced in programming languages and interface design, and most recently have been utilized in a variety of new database approaches. This reprint collection will present current papers related to the use, implementation, and evaluation of object-oriented databases. In this introduction the background of object-oriented approaches and databases in particular will be overviewed.

There has been a rapidly increasing interest in the use of concepts and approaches referred to as "object-oriented." The areas of programming languages, databases, and user interface systems have successfully utilized the object-oriented paradigm with applications in areas ranging from artificial intelligence to office information systems.

However, there is a diversity of opinion about what is meant by an "object" and the degree to which an approach is "object-oriented." Typically the following terms have been used to capture various aspects of "object-oriented" approaches: encapsulation, classes, inheritance, message-passing, and persistence. Each of these terms will now be briefly discussed:

1) Encapsulation – another term for information hiding.
2) Classes – grouping of similiar objects.
3) Inheritance – sharing of properties that characterize a class by all of its
   subclasses.
4) Messages – the basic mechanism of computation is by means of messages
   passed between objects that invoke the object's procedures.
5) Persistence – refers to the idea of a long-lived or persistent entity, i.e., the
   object continues to exist after the application that created it completes.
6) Polymorphism – different objects responding differently to the same message;
   implies late or runtime binding of function calls.

With this terminology an object can be described as an encapsulation of data and the procedures which manipulate the data in the object. Typically computation procedes by message passing between objects as illustrated in Figure 1.

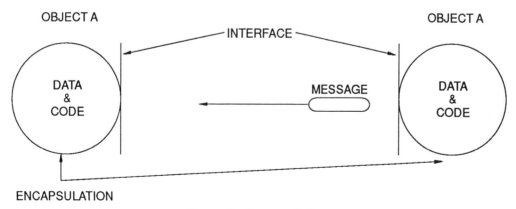

Figure 1: Encapsulation

A class is a grouping of similiar objects or instances of the class with all objects of the class using the same procedures (responding to the same messages). Classes may be organized in hierarchies in which the procedures and attributes for a class are inherited by all of its subclasses.

Concepts of object-oriented programming can be traced from roots in the programming languages Simula [1], and especially Smalltalk [2]. Simula was a language developed for computer simulation and was considered a natural for creating program constructs to represent the objects of the simulation.

In Smalltalk everything is represented as an object and all computation is expressed by message passing. There is generally one hierarchy of classes and the inheritance of functionality in classes allows the sharing and reutilization of code. With programming languages supporting an object-oriented approach we can see that inheritance should allow for easier maintenance. The use of message sending and encapsulation facilitates well-engineered software with loosely coupled and highly cohesive programs. Such features should permit greater code reusability.

Areas other than programming languages have developed approaches related to object-oriented concepts. In artificial intelligence frames [3] are related to ideas of inheritance and classes and the actor approach [4] used message passing. The use of objects design of user interfaces such as the icons in the desktop metaphor of the Macintosh computer have been proven to be a very powerful and ubiquitous facility. An object-oriented programming environment was used in the IBM System 38 and the AS/400 midrange system [5].

Relational database technolgy has emerged in a number of mature systems in many applications, especially in business-oriented data processing. However, as it is still a "record-based" data model it has difficulty in naturally representing data semantics and dealing with complex applications such as computer-aided design/manufacturing (CAD/CAM) or computer-aided software engineering (CASE).

A database approach known as semantic models [6] has a relationship to object-oriented approaches as they deal with representing complex entities by the use of abstraction. However, they are mainly static and do not use the idea of encapsulation of data and code.

The following table [7] provides an excellent summary of the properties of object-oriented databases as contrasted to conventional database models.

Table 1. Properties of Data Models

Object Model	(Conventional or Semantic) Database Model
identity	key by values of attributes
activity of objects	passivity of structures
control at object, autonomous objects	control of management
classes, specialization	rich concepts of relationships
inheritance	explicit transfer of values
objects bound to types	tuples without type
late binding of variables	strong typing of attributes
methods inside of objects (operational)	functions, procedures at structures
many types	few types
self-defined types and operations (behavioral)	–
encapsulation, information hiding	structured objects
–	efficient implementation
unified concept of manipulation	DML and DDL
adaptive, dynamic	consistent but static world
multimedia data, large data	basic data types

The papers presented in this collection are organized into four sections. In the first section there are fundamental papers about object-oriented concepts. Section 2 contains a number of applications of an object-oriented database approach as well as papers on technical issues in the area. The third section has examples of implementations and approaches to implementation issues. The papers in the final section are related to evaluation and validation of object-oriented databases.

REFERENCES

[1] G.Birtwistle, O.Dahl, B.Myhrtag, and K.Nygaard, *Simula Begin*, Auberbach Press, Philadelphia, PA, 1973.

[2] A. Goldberg and D. Robson, *Smalltalk-80: The Language and its Implementation*, Addison-Wesley, Reading, MA, 1983.

[3] M. Minsky, "A Framework for Representing Knowledge," P. Winston, ed., *The Psychology of Computer Vision*, McGraw-Hill, New York, 1975.

[4] C. Hewitt, "Viewing Control Structures as Patterns of Passing Messages," *Journal of Artificial Intelligence*, Volume 8, 1977, pp. 323-364.

[5] IBM System 38 & IBM Application System/400, *Technical Report SA21-9540*.

[6] R. Hull and R. King, "Semantic Database Modeling: Survey, Applications, and Research Issues," *ACM Computing Surveys*, June 1988.

[7] R. Cordes, M. Hoffman, H. Langendorfer, and R. Buck-Emden, "The Use of Decomposition in An Object-Oriented Approach to Present and Represent Multimedia Documents," *Proceedings of the Twenty-Second Annual Hawaii International Conference on System Sciences*, Volume II, 1989, pp. 820-828.

SECTION 2:
OBJECT-ORIENTED CONCEPTS

An Overview of Modular Smalltalk

Allen Wirfs-Brock
(503) 242-0725

Instantiations, Inc.
1020 SW Taylor St., Suite 200
Portland, OR 97205

Brian Wilkerson
brianw%spt.tek.com@relay.cs.net
(503) 627-3294

P.O. Box 500, Mail Sta. 50-470
Tektronix, Inc.
Beaverton, OR 97077

Abstract

This paper introduces the programming language Modular Smalltalk, a descendant of the Smalltalk-80 programming language. Modular Smalltalk was designed to support teams of software engineers developing production application programs that can run independently of the environment in which they are developed. We first discuss our motivation for designing Modular Smalltalk. Specifically, we examine the properties of Smalltalk-80 that make it inappropriate for our purposes. We then present an overview of the design of Modular Smalltalk, with an emphasis on how it overcomes these weaknesses.

Introduction

Modular Smalltalk is an evolution of the Smalltalk programming language and system designed to support teams of software engineers developing production application programs that can operate under the control of standard operating systems and display environments.

"An Overview of Modular Smalltalk" by A. Wirfs-Brock and B. Wilkerson from *Object-Oriented Programming Systems, Languages, and Applications (OOPSLA) Proceedings*, 1988, pp. 123-134. Copyright © 1988 by The Association for Computing Machinery, Inc., reprinted by permission.

The Smalltalk programming language and system was originally intended to be the software component of the Dynabook, a portable personal information management tool [Kay77a, Kay77b]. As described by one of its developers, its purpose was "to support children of all ages in the world of information" [Inga78]. Smalltalk is a uniformly object-oriented system which integrates a programming language and its implementation, development tools for the language, a window-oriented user interface manager, and other system software services. The development of Smalltalk was an evolutionary process which took place over an extended period [Inga83]. Its developers typically built a version of the system, experimented with it, and finally used what they learned to build the next version upon the base of the current version. The final result of this process was the Smalltalk-80™ system [Gold83, Gold84].

As Smalltalk became available to a broader group of users, it first found acceptance as a rapid prototyping system. The fact that Smalltalk proved to be an excellent prototyping tool should not be surprising, as Smalltalk's developers had themselves used the system in this manner. However, outside of research laboratories, prototypes are not viewed as ends unto themselves but rather steps on the path towards the development of a final product or solution. The success of prototype applications developed using Smalltalk has led many Smalltalk programmers to look for ways to develop and deliver the final production versions of applications using Smalltalk. These attempts have so far had only limited success.

While we have have found the Smalltalk language a very effective tool for building complex systems, we believe it is currently unrealistic to expect that an excellent rapid prototyping system can also be an excellent application delivery system. If Smalltalk is to be widely used to develop production applications, then the language, its development environment, and its implementations need to be re-engineered for that purpose. Modular Smalltalk is an offshoot of the Smalltalk language which is specifically designed to support the engineering of production application programs. Modular Smalltalk will ultimately consist of a formal language specification, an essential module and class specification, an incremental development environment, and a production-quality compiler. This paper addresses the architectural features of the Modular Smalltalk language.

In the following section we will discuss specific difficulties of conventional Smalltalk implementations for producing production applications. We then present the design goals of Modular Smalltalk. Finally we present a general overview of the Modular Smalltalk language.

Smalltalk-80 as a Production Tool

As a tool for software development, Smalltalk-80 has some serious drawbacks. These include

- the image paradigm,
- a confusion between the language and its programming environment,
- a confusion between the language definition and its implementation,
- the ability to learn the system, and
- its performance.

The Image paradigm

Conventional Smalltalk systems are built around a virtual image [Gold83]. A *virtual image* is the dynamic data structure representing all code and data for the running Smalltalk system. This includes not only the application data, but the application programs themselves. It also includes the tools (compiler, editors, debuggers) for building programs, and for basic system support facilities such as window and file management. All code and data are represented as objects described by classes which are themselves objects. Both application and system objects share

common class definitions. Applications are built by incrementally adding or modifying class definitions within a running image. A Smalltalk application "program" is in effect a set of edits to some baseline virtual image.

However, applications are not best defined as a set of incremental changes to some base environment. Other programmers may have also made a set of changes to their environments. In practice, it proves impossible to predict when two applications, two sets of independently made changes, will conflict. Conflicts can also occur during the engineering of a single application. Engineers working together can never be sure when the changes made by one will conflict with the changes made by another. The ability to refine existing programs is similarly hampered.

Furthermore, because any application can access and modify any class or object in the entire system, all dependencies between an application and other features of the system are implicit. It becomes difficult to prove that any given feature of the system is not used. It therefore becomes very difficult to extract the application from the surrounding system.

Also, every aspect of the system is open to inspection and modification. Changes made by an application for its own purposes can effect the operation of the system. For example, an application can modify a class in such a manner that it unintentionally introduces errors into the compiler or the debugger.

This can also cause problems for the distribution and continued support of applications. If users may change anything about their own systems, it becomes impossible to support an application that depends upon certain features of that system remaining stable. Similarly, user applications are vulnerable to the effects of system revisions by the system developer.

Another result of the image paradigm is that applications may rely upon a part of the state of the image for which there is no code to reproduce the state. For example, a programmer might execute code in a workspace to initialize the state of an object without including that code in the application. If the application was loaded into another image, there would be no mechanical means to perform the appropriate initializations

Confusion between language and programming environment

With conventional Smalltalk implementations, no clear distinction exists between the language and the environment in which programs are written. No distinction is made between the language and the standard set of abstractions (classes or components). No distinction is made between the standard set of abstractions and the implementation of the environment.

Because of these confusions, it becomes effectively impossible to build a new implementation optimized for a different purpose, for example the delivery of stand-alone applications instead of a system for rapid prototyping. Features implemented for the sake of the programming environment are used by programs, compounding the confusion so that neither implementor nor programmer can say which features of the environment are essential to the language, and which are just quirks of the implementation of the environment. If implementors need to reimplement the system anyway, they are forced to guess. For example, is the ability to dynamically add a method to a class a convenience of a programming environment designed for rapid prototyping, or is it an essential feature of the language definition?

Confusion between language definition and implementation

One of the main principles of object-oriented programming has been said to be separating the "what" from the "how" [Robs81]. But the Smalltalk-80 language fails to make this distinction at the grossest level. If the "what" is taken to be the language specification, and the "how" is taken to be the language implementation, Smalltalk-80 fails to separate these. For example, one would like a clear distinction between what it means to send a message, and a particular implementation of message-sending. No such distinction has ever existed for Smalltalk-80. This confusion even extends to the terminology used by Smalltalk programmers to describe the behavior of programs. Smalltalk programmers may be frequently heard speaking of "message lookup" but seldom, if ever, use phrases such as "message binding" or "message resolution" to describe the activity of sending a message to an object. Because of this confusion between language definition and implementation, a programmer can write an application that depends upon representational or algorithmic details of the canonical implementation of the virtual machine. All implementations of

Smalltalk-80 must mimic these details, regardless of the effect upon the efficiency of the implementation. At best an implementation may "cheat but not get caught" [Deut86].

The Smalltalk-80 system was originally designed as a self-hosted, incremental online program development environment. As such, not only was it required to support dynamic modification of a running program but the image implementation model required such modification be accomplished using reflective operations upon the running system. A program may make use of these same operations to dynamically modify itself. While a handful of experimental applications have made effective use of the reflective characteristics of Smalltalk-80 [Born81], the vast majority of applications do not. Should reflectiveness be considered an essential characteristic of Smalltalk, or an implementation detail? Must all implementations, including those targeted for ROM-based embedded systems, support reflective operations?

Learnability of the system

The Smalltalk-80 system is notably difficult to learn [Born87]. The size and complexity of the system (hundreds of classes and thousands of methods) alone serves as a formidable impediment. In addition, various conceptual difficulties can hamper the novice, such as metaclasses, or the distinction between methods and blocks. Other conceptual difficulties spring from the confusions discussed above. If Smalltalk is to become a widely used system, these problems need to be addressed.

Performance

Existing Smalltalk-80 systems are slower and less efficient than more conventional languages, even other dynamic languages such as LISP. Present systems are optimized for incremental rapid prototyping systems, but they are not optimized for execution speed.

While the poor performance of Smalltalk implementations is frequently attributed to the dynamic binding of procedure names to procedure implementations (message send overhead), commonly known techniques allow dynamic message binding to be only slightly more expensive than a standard procedure call. A much more severe performance problem comes from the inability of a Smalltalk compiler to perform *any* significant local or global optimization. This is a direct consequence of the reflective nature of the language. Given the possibility of reflective operations, it becomes impossible for a compiler to reason definitively about a program and hence perform any optimizations.

For example, it might be reasonably expected that the binding of message-sends to self could be statically resolved since the class of self can be determined at compilation time*. Given such a static binding, it should be possible to inline expand the target method and then apply standard local optimization techniques. Unfortunately, such optimizations prove to be impossible since the program may arbitrarily modify any of its methods. At best, an implementation could attempt to maintain both optimized and unoptimized representations of each method and switch representations if a reflexive operation is performed.

As another example, consider that it is impossible analytically to remove classes or methods from an image. Even if there are no lexically apparent references to a class or a message selector, a program may dynamically construct a new method which references them.

Modular Smalltalk Design Goals

To correct these deficiencies, we are designing a new generation of Smalltalk that we call Modular Smalltalk. Modular Smalltalk departs from Smalltalk-80 with the addition of a module facility and the elimination of all reflexive operations. In addition, we have sought to clarify and modify the definition of Smalltalk-80 to make it more semantically consistent. The module facility supports the encapsulation and hiding of classes. Modular Smalltalk is designed to support the development of separately deliverable applications — an implicit goal of most software engineering efforts.

Modular Smalltalk is an object-oriented programming language. Using Modular Smalltalk, programs can be developed within an interactive development environment similar to that of Smalltalk-80. Programs developed within the Modular Smalltalk environment, however, can then be delivered as stand-alone applications.

Modular Smalltalk differs from other proposals to modify or extend Smalltalk-80 such as Deltatalk [Born87] in that it specifically addresses the problems of building stand-alone production programs instead of enhancing Smalltalk's utility as an exploratory programming system. A principal goal of Modular Smalltalk is to maintain a clear distinction between the language specification, its implementations and its development environment. In addition Modular Smalltalk seeks to:

- support the development of application programs that execute independently of their development environment,

- allow for team engineering efforts,

- provide consistent and explicit semantics, independent of any implementation,

- allow for the possibility of efficient implementation,

- be a recognizable descendant of Smalltalk-80, thereby allowing existing Smalltalk programmers to master it quickly, and

- be simple enough for new Smalltalk programmers to learn easily.

The Modular Smalltalk Language

Modular Smalltalk defines a language with a specification that is independent of its implementation. The semantics of Modular Smalltalk allow for many varying efficient implementations. Modular Smalltalk follows the commonly understood syntax and semantics of Smalltalk-80, but differs in the following major respects:

- The language is oriented towards the construction of programs, which are stand-alone entities.

- Programs consist of modules. Modules provide the units to divide the functional and organizational responsibility within a program.

- Modules encapsulate class definitions and other constants.

- Class definitions are static, declarative syntactic structures.

- Modular Smalltalk is not reflexive.

---

* This requires the additional optimization that all inheritance issues be resolved at compilation time, and this optimization is itself greatly complicated by Smalltalk's reflectiveness.

In addition, Modular Smalltalk augments Smalltalk-80 in several ways. It provides explicit syntactic support for practices that have heretofore been merely commonly used programming conventions. It also addresses several commonly recognized deficiencies, especially the absence of multiple inheritance.

Programs

A program in Modular Smalltalk is the unit that defines an independent application. A program defines the classes of all objects used within an application. It also defines the sequence of actions performed with instances of those classes when the program is executed.

A program is a collection of modules. One module is the main module of a program. For example, a program to play the game of blackjack might consist of modules implementing the blackjack game itself, playing cards, user interface components, graphics packages, data structures, random number generators, and the kernel classes required by all Modular Smalltalk programs.

Modules can depend upon definitions from other modules, but no module can depend upon the main module. The dependencies of modules within a program form a directed, acyclic graph with a single root node (the main module). In the blackjack example above, the blackjack module would be the main module and would depend on definitions from the playing card module, among others.

When a program is executed, modules are initialized in the order given by a depth-first traversal of the dependency graph. No module is ever initialized more than once.

The objects upon which a program operates exist only within the context of the executing program. That is, independent executions of the program would operate upon distinct sets of objects. The classes that a program defines or uses and the objects that a program manipulates are separate and distinct from the classes and objects used to construct the development environment for Modular Smalltalk.

Modules

Modules are program units that manage the visibility and accessibility of names. A module defines a set of constant bindings between names and objects. Modules are not objects and have no existence (representation) during the execution of a program. A module typically groups a set of class definitions and objects to implement some service or abstraction. A module will frequently be the unit of division of responsibility within a programming team.

A module provides an independent naming environment that is separate from other modules within the program. A module consists of a sequence of *named object* definitions. A named object definition introduces a static binding between an identifier (a name) and an object. Because the binding is static, the named object may be used as a constant value within expressions. Named objects may not be the target of an assignment statement. Modular Smalltalk has no global variables. All mutable global state is encapsulated within objects. Where Smalltalk-80 makes extensive use of global variables to name the classes and utility objects that make up a program, Modular Smalltalk uses named objects.

In the blackjack example, the playing cards module might define the classes Card and CardDeck, as well as the constant collections of Ranks and Suits. An example implementation is given in the appendix.

Names must be uniquely defined within a module: no name clashes are allowed. Because a naming conflict is one form of conflict possible when teams of engineers work together on a program, modules support team engineering by providing rigorously isolated name spaces.

A module controls the visibility of named objects. Principles for the management of names follow the commonly accepted principles for the management of separate name spaces, as exemplified by languages such as Modula-2 [Wirt84] or Ada [Booc83].

Definitions

There are two ways to introduce a named object binding into a module.

- The binding may be defined locally by the module, or

- it may be imported from another module.

A local definition consists of either:

- an expression whose value is the object to which the name is bound, or

- a class definition.

Imports

Modules can import other modules. Imported modules introduce additional bindings. Imported bindings are specified by naming the module in which the binding is available, and the desired named object.

Modules must specify explicitly which other modules, and the bindings within them, they wish to import. When a module imports another module, it implicitly limits which object names are imported. Unless a module specifically requests an object named Belshazzar, for example, it will not import that object. A module, therefore, consists of:

- a set of bindings between names and objects, and
- a declaration of other bindings to import.

As stated earlier, all names, whether local or imported, must be unique within a module. Nevertheless, sometimes a module may require the import of an object with a duplicate name from another module. A renaming mechanism allows for the resolution of such name clashes. When a module imports another module, it may rename any object it imports. It may specify, for example, that it import an object named Joe as Joseph.

The management of libraries of modules is considered to be outside of the scope of the Modular Smalltalk language definition. Modules will be the most common unit of code reuse by Modular Smalltalk programmers. A typical implementation would include a module library manager that would manage a repository of a wide selection of modules and versions of modules. In order not to place undue constraints on the design of such library managers, Modular Smalltalk module names are literal strings whose interpretation is implementation defined.

Visibility

A module also incorporates a mechanism to make named objects selectively available to users of the module. Each named object, in addition to binding an object with a name, includes a visibility attribute allowing the programmer to specify whether the binding is to be public or private.

Names defined in a module are visible throughout that module. Names defined in a module are not visible outside that module unless the programmer explicitly specifies otherwise. If a named object is specified to be public, it is exported and may be made visible to another module. Even so, the named object is not visible to another module unless the other module specifically imports the module containing it, and the named object itself.

The ability to specify that a given name is private to a module provides explicit syntactic language support for information-hiding. This enhances the maintainability of an application by making explicit all dependencies.

Because all dependencies of a program must be explicit to support its delivery as a separate application, Modular Smalltalk has no global object naming space. No objects are implicitly available to all modules. Objects are available to a module by name from two sources only:

- the named objects defined within the module itself, and
- named objects declared public within imported modules, and explicitly requested by the module.

Modules control the accessibility of the *names* of objects, not the objects themselves. Objects may be freely passed as values between methods defined in different modules regardless of whether the object's name or its class name is visible in either module. While modules restrict the visibility of class names they do not restrict the use of message selector names. A program includes a single program-wide name space for message selector. A mechanism other than modules, discussed in the section entitled **Methods**, is provided to restrict selector usage.

Classes

In many ways, classes in Modular Smalltalk are quite similar to their Smalltalk-80 counterparts. There are certain crucial differences, however.

- Class definitions are static.
- Multiple inheritance is supported.
- Modular Smalltalk has no metaclasses.
- Encapsulated state is uniformly accessed using message selectors instead of variable names.

Class Definitions

A class definition is not an object and has no existence during the execution of a program. A class definition is also not an expression. New classes cannot be created using message-sends.

Instead, a class definition is a static description of the behavior* of a group of objects. Naturally, class definitions can be manipulated within a development environment. However, because Modular Smalltalk is not a reflexive language, a running program may not modify its class definitions.

A class definition defines two sets of behavior:

- the behavior of instance objects, and
- the behavior of a unique class object.

A *class object* is a named object introduced by a class definition. It is the object bound to the name associated with the class definition. Class objects in Modular Smalltalk provide a place to define behavior such as instance creation methods.

A class definition is considered to define the behavior of the associated objects completely. There are two ways a class definition may specify its object's behaviors:

- the behavior may be inherited, or
- the behavior may be locally defined as part of the class definition.

Behavior may be inherited from zero or more other class definitions (the class' superclasses). Even though behavior is inherited, it is still considered to be part of the inheriting class' definition. Modular Smalltalk does not imply or require any sort of dynamic superclass message lookup algorithm. Dynamic lookup remains a valid implementation technique, one that is especially useful in incremental development environments. Modular Smalltalk specifies the effect of sending a message, not the mechanism for sending a message.

Local behavior definitions consist of a set of mappings between message selectors and their implementations. A local definition may mask or override an inherited definition. Each selector has a visibility attribute; it may be declared public or private to its class.

Encapsulated state is declared and inherited as a special case of method definition.

Variables

Instance variable names do not exist within Modular Smalltalk. Instead, instance variables are referred to using accessing or modifying messages. For each instance variable defined by a class, two accessing methods are defined: one to set the value of the variable, and one to retrieve to value of the variable. Variable state can only be accessed or modified using message sends that invoke the accessing methods.

An accessing method only stores or retrieves the value of its associated variable. It performs no other computations. For example, one could use the unary selector getY to access an object's instance variable. One could also use the keyword selector setY: to modify the instance variable. The accessing and modifying protocols need not be lexically similar.

Referring to variables entirely through the use of accessing protocol makes it easier to reuse existing code by subclassing [Wirf88]. It also simplifies the semantics of multiple inheritance, as the semantics of variable inheritance is exactly the semantics of method inheritance.

Unlike Smalltalk-80, which defines six or more different types of variables that may appear on the left hand side of an assignment operator, Modular Smalltalk defines exactly one type, block temporaries. All other variable state is modified using message syntax.

Multiple Inheritance

Modular Smalltalk supports multiple inheritance. Multiple inheritance provides the ability to break free of a rigid, hierarchical view of the world. It allows programmers to specify that instances of a given class behave a great deal like instances of another class, but also share aspects of their behavior with a third, unrelated class. This mechanism is sufficiently compelling that Smalltalk-80 has tried to incorporate it [Born82, Wilk86]. Problems arise with multiple inheritance, however, when a class tries to inherit from two or more superclasses that contain conflicting method or variable definitions.

---

* By *behavior* we mean the complete set of message selectors recognized by an object and their associated method definitions.

Modular Smalltalk addresses the problem of conflicting methods in the following manner. A class may have any number of superclasses, including none. A class inherits behavior equally from all of its immediate superclasses (some of which may itself be inherited behavior). There is no order dependency among superclasses.

It is an error for a class to inherit two different definitions for the same message selector. Such an error can be avoided by explicitly redefining the conflicting selector in the class itself. Notice, however, that inheriting the same method definition (one defined in a single lexical location) from multiple superclasses is not an error. Because instance variables are specified in terms of message selector definitions, the rules for variable inheritance and conflict resolution are exactly those that apply to any other methods.

Metaclasses

In Smalltalk-80 all objects must be an instance of some class. The class defines the behavior of its instances in terms of the message lookup algorithm. Since classes are themselves objects, they too must be instances of a classes. Metaclasses are the classes of which each class is an instance.

In Modular Smalltalk, the behavior of every object is specified by a class definition. This includes both instance and class objects. Class definitions are not objects. Therefore the behavior of an object is not dependent upon any other object and hence an object does not need to be an instance of a class. Specifically, class objects do not need a class. Therefore, Modular Smalltalk needs no metaclasses.

Class objects have the ability to instantiate the instance objects described by their class definition. Class objects are instantiated as part of the module initialization process. The standard definition of the class message in Modular Smalltalk is to return the class object defined by the class definition that describes the behavior of the receiver. Thus the message class sent to an instance object will return its associated class object and the class message sent to a class object will return that same class object.

Metaclasses are one of the features of Smalltalk-80 that make it difficult to teach and understand [Born87]. The Modular Smalltalk model of class and instance objects is a direct reflection of the class behavior/instance behavior model presented by the standard Smalltalk-80 browser. Metaclasses are one implementation of this model, one that is difficult to

understand. Because the semantics of classes and instances are defined independently of any implementation, Modular Smalltalk is easier to learn and use.

This model of a syntactic class definition which defines the behavior of both class and instance objects is essentially the same as used by the Objective-C language [Cox86]. Objective-C uses the term *factory object* for class objects.

Class Extensions

Class extensions provide the ability for a module to add protocol to existing classes defined outside the module. This mechanism is another case where the

Modular Smalltalk programming language provides explicit syntactic support for a common object-oriented programming convention, that of specifying a default behavior for all objects.

Extensions provide the ability to encapsulate behavior supporting a function that may be common to many classes, spread across several modules. For example, an application might require that objects of a wide variety of classes be able to store themselves in a file. Just such a system has been implemented for Smalltalk-80 [Vegd86]. It is reasonable to assume that most of these classes are defined in modules other than the module of the application requiring this ability. Let us further assume that none of these classes have the desired ability.

Because this ability is required for a wide variety of classes, very different methods must be used to store the different kinds of instances. Using the mechanism of class extensions, it is possible to define a module to provide the needed storage functionality. This module could define extensions to all the classes that require the functionality. Each class extension would consist of the small number of methods required to implement the functionality. In this way, the storage module becomes a component that can be included in any application requiring this functionality.

Class extensions can only add behavior. They cannot modify or remove behavior.

Methods

Method definitions associate a message selector with an implementation.

Unlike Smalltalk-80, Modular Smalltalk message selectors are not instances of class Symbol (for example, they are not synonymous with their textual representation). Instead they are instances of class MessageSelector. Message selectors may not be dynamically constructed and specifically, strings may not be dynamically converted into message selectors. Message selectors still have a literal representation, so that one can, for example, use:

anArray perform: (#(#first #second #third) at: n)

Disallowing the dynamic construction of message selectors allows an implementation to compute for a program the set of defined but unused selectors. Code need not be generated for such selectors.

Implementations

The implementation of a method can be either

- a literal block,
- the keyword primitive,
- the keyword abstract, or
- the keyword undefined.

The ordinary implementation of a method in Modular Smalltalk is a block which is evaluated when a message is sent. Modular Smalltalk thus simplifies Smalltalk-80, unifying the semantics of block and method evaluation.

Because methods are blocks, the default value returned from a method is the value of the last expression in the block. The default value returned from a method is not self, as it was in Smalltalk-80.

Blocks in Modular Smalltalk can declare temporary variables. Blocks can be lexically nested with properly nested variable scope, and blocks are re-entrant. This means that separate invocations of the same block do not share the same state for block arguments and temporaries, thus allowing two or more executions to overlap in time.

The implementation primitive means that the associated method definition is fully specified by either the language definition or the implementation. The method is not specified by Modular Smalltalk code. Unlike Smalltalk-80, a primitive number is not associated with a primitive specification. The class name along with the message selector is sufficient to uniquely identify the primitive. A special primitive failure mechanism and associated Smalltalk code is not used. Instead, each primitive's specification fully defines its behavior, including error conditions. This behavior may include sending other messages. For example, an integer division primitive specification might specify that if the divisor is zero, the message zeroDivide would be sent to the receiver of the divide message.

Whenever possible, the syntax of Modular Smalltalk seeks to support what have up to now been only programming conventions. The method implementations abstract and undefined are an example of this support.

Defining a selector as abstract means that subclasses must provide a definition for the method. It is the equivalent of the Smalltalk-80 convention self subclassResponsibility. A class that includes abstract methods, either locally or through inheritance, is an abstract class and cannot be instantiated.

If a class inherits an abstract method from one of its superclasses, the abstract implementation will not conflict with any nonabstract implementation inherited from any other superclass. Abstract methods cannot cause method definition clashes.

Defining a selector as undefined removes the inherited selector from the behavior of the object. It is the analog of the Smalltalk-80 convention self shouldNotImplement.

Visibility

Each method includes a visibility attribute; it is either a public or a private method. The default is public. Information-hiding, the encapsulation of implementation details private to an object, is a key principle of object-oriented programming. Therefore, private methods have long been a convention of Smalltalk-80. Modular Smalltalk provides support for this convention by building it into the semantics of the language.

When sent to an object, a private selector is understood if the class description of the receiver is the same as the class description of the sender.

Private selectors are inherited by subclasses, which can therefore use them. The visibility of a message selector (whether it is public or private) is inherited separately from the body of the method. Subclasses can inherit a method body while overriding its visibility attribute.

Conclusion

We believe that Modular Smalltalk will prove to be an effective tool for the construction of complex applications. It is easier for novices to learn, while remaining similar enough that current Smalltalk programmers will be able to learn it swiftly and easily. In addition, it supports current software engineering practices for the following reasons:

- It allows the delivery of stand-alone applications.
- It allows the protection of proprietary source code.
- It supports change management and version control, so that teams of programmers can work together on a large project without collisions.
- It allows for varying implementations, each of which can be optimized for different purposes.

Acknowledgements

Many of the ideas incorporated into Modular Smalltalk grew out of a long series of language design discussions with Will Clinger, Ralph London and Steve Vegdahl. Mark Ballard was a major contributor to the initial language design and along with Brian Wilkerson built the first experimental implementation. Kit Bradley has provided continuing managerial support for what has often appeared to be a radical project. Finally, Lauren Wiener helped us make this paper and the preliminary language specification real.

References

[Booc83] Booch, Grady, *Software Engineering with Ada*, Benjamin/Cummings, Menlo Park, CA. 1983

[Born81] Borning, Alan H., "The Programming Language Aspects of ThingLab," *CM Transactions of Programming Languages and Systems*, 3(4), pp. 353-387, Oct. 1981.

[Born82] Borning, Alan H., and Daniel H. H. Ingalls, "Multiple Inheritance in Smalltalk-80," *AAAI Proceedings*, 1982, pp. 234-237.

[Born87] Borning, Alan, and Tim O'Shea, "Deltatalk: An Empirically and Aesthetically Motivated Simplification of the Smalltalk-80 Language," *ECOOP Proceedings*, 1987.

[Cox86] Cox, Brad J., *Object-Oriented Programming An Evolutionary Approach*, Addison-Wesley, Reading, Massachusetts, 1986.

[Deut86] Deutsch, L. Peter, private communication

[Gold83] Goldberg, Adele, and David Robson, *Smalltalk-80: The Language and Its Implementation*, Addison-Wesley, Reading Massachusetts, 1983.

[Gold84] Goldberg, Adele, *Smalltalk-80: The Interactive Programming Environment*, Addison-Wesley, Reading, Massachusetts, 1984.

[Inga83] Ingalls, Daniel H. H., "The Evolution of the Smalltalk Virtual Machine", *Smalltalk-80: Bits of History, Words of Advice*, ed. Glenn Krasner, Addison-Wesley, Reading, Massachusetts, 1983.

[Kay77a] Kay, Alan C., "Microelectronics and the Personal Computer," *Scientific American*, September 1977, pp. 230-244.

[Kay77b] Kay, Alan C. and Adele Goldberg, "Personal Dynamic Media," *Computer*, March 1977, pp. 31-41.

[Robs81] Robson, David. "Object-Oriented Software Systems", *Byte*, August, 1981, pp. 74-86.

[Vegd86] Vegdahl, Steven R. "Moving Structures between Smalltalk Images," *OOPSLA Proceedings*, 1986, pp. 466-471. Also published in *SIGPLAN Notices*, vol. 21, no. 11, November 1986, pp. 466-471.

[Wilk86] Wilkerson, Brian C., *Inheritance Mechanisms for Smalltalk-80*, Technical Report CR-86-57, Tektronix, Inc., Beaverton, Oregon, August 1986.

[Wirf88] Wirfs-Brock, Allen, and Brian C. Wilkerson, *Variables Limit Reusability*, Technical Report SPT-88-07.

[Wirt84] Wirth, Niklaus, "Programming in Modula-2", *Texts and Monographs in Computer Science*, 2nd ed. David Gries, Springer-Verlag, Berlin 1984.

Appendix

This appendix contains example code for the module PlayingCards. The code below is formatted in an informal publication syntax.

Module 'PlayingCards'
    "*This module defines four named objects – CardSuits, CardRanks, Card and CardDeck – that are used to implement the functionality of a deck of playing cards. Only the class CardDeck is exported.*"

    imports Object from 'Kernel'
    imports List from 'Collections'
    imports UniformDistribution from 'ProbabilityDistributions'

    CardSuits -> #('heart' 'club' 'diamond' 'spade')
    "*The symbol '->' means 'is defined as'.*"

    CardRanks -> 1 to: 13

    Card -> Class
      refines Object

instance behavior

  accessing

    variable **suit suit:** (private)
      "*Answer and set the suit of the receiver. The suit should be an element of <CardSuits>.*"

    variable **rank rank:** (private)
      "*Answer and set the rank of the receiver. The rank of jacks, queens and kings is 11, 12 and 13, respectively.*"

    value
      "*Answer the face value of the receiver.*"

      ↑self rank min: 10

  testing

    = aCard
      "*Answer <true> if the receiver represents the same card as <aCard>.*"

      ↑self suit = aCard suit
        and: [self rank = aCard rank]

class behavior

  instance creation

    suit: suitName rank: rankIndex
      "*Answer an instance of the receiver whose suit is <suitName> and whose rank is <rankName>.*"

      | card |
      card := self new.
      card suit: suitName.
      card rank: rankIndex.
      ↑card

CardDeck (public) -> Class
    refines Object

instance behavior

  accessing

    variable **cards** (private) **cards:** (private)
      "*Answer and set the ordered collection of cards remaining in the receiver.*"

    initialize (private)
      "*Initialize the receiver.*"

      self cards: List new

    addCard: aCard (private)
      "*Add <aCard> to the receiver.*"

      self cards add: aCard

    deal
      "*Deal the top card off of the receiver.*"

      ↑self cards removeFirst

    shuffle
      "*Shuffle the cards remaining in the receiver.*"

      | random |
      random := UniformDistribution from: 1 to: self cards size.
      1 to: self cards size
        do:
          [:source |
          | target temp |
          target := random next.
          temp := self cards at: source.
          self cards at: source
            put: (self cards at: target).
          self cards at: target put: temp]

instance creation

new
"*Answer an instance of the receiver
containing all 52 standard playing cards.*"

```
| deck |
deck := super new initialize.
CardSuits
  do:
    [:suit |
    CardRanks
      do:
        [:rank |
        deck addCard: (Card suit: suit
rank: rank)]].
  ↑deck
```

OBJECT ORIENTED APPROACH: SYSTEMS, PROGRAMMING, LANGUAGES, AND APPLICATIONS

Prof. C.V. Ramamoorthy, University of California at Berkeley, California.
Prof. Phillip C. Sheu, Rutgers University, New Jersey.
Pratap Chillakanti, Hewlett Packard, Cupertino, California.

Abstract :

Object oriented approaches in analysing, designing, and developing complex systems offer significant and wide spectrum of benefits such as natural and consistent decomposition of an application, powerful means for controlling access to a shared database, data abstraction, structural knowledge representation, and reusability. The paper clarifies the terms used to describe the various aspects of object oriented approach such as object oriented programming, object oriented analysis, object oriented design, object oriented languages, and object oriented databases. A survey of some of the analysis and design methodologies that are used in object oriented software development is also included. The applicability as well as the affect of object oriented approach on expert systems and database systems is investigated. The paper concludes with a discussion on some of the research issues in the realm of object oriented systems.

Keywords: Object oriented systems, Object oriented analysis, Object oriented design, Object oriented programming, Expert systems, Database systems.

1. *Introduction*:

A new approach advocated in analysing, designing, and developing complex systems is the object oriented approach. It differs from the traditional approaches; such as procedure oriented and logic oriented; and provides certain desirable features and significant benefits. Our objectives in this paper are to clarify the terms used to describe the various aspects of object oriented approach; to demonstrate some of the perceived benefits of object oriented approach; to survey some of the object oriented analysis and design methodologies; to investigate the applicability as well as the affect of object oriented approach on expert systems and database systems; and to discuss a few research issues pertaining to object oriented systems.

A system can be defined as a complex unity formed of many often diverse parts subject to a common plan or serving a common purpose [Webster's Dictionary]. Some examples of systems in the realm of computer science and engineering are CASE (Computer Aided Software Engineering) systems and Database systems. A CASE system consists of many parts such as user interface, editors, compilers, debuggers, analysis and design tools. All of these parts play a unifying role to perform the intended function, i.e., building software. Similarly, a database system is a collection of parts (or components) including a data manager, data definition language, data manipulation language, a user interface, and, ofcourse data.

The design and development of software systems has evolved over a period of time; beginning with adhoc (artistic !) approaches, continuing to structured approaches based on function decomposition, and currently adopting object oriented approaches based on object decomposition. They evolved from small and simple systems to large and complex systems today. It is this nature of changing complexities of systems that necessitate a change of thinking in order to easily comprehend, design and develop these large and complex systems.

Object oriented approaches in analysing, designing, and developing complex system offer significant and wide spectrum of benefits such as natural and consistent decomposition of an application, powerful means for controlling access to shared database, data abstraction, structural knowledge representation, and reusability. Object oriented approach is based on some fundamental concepts that we have first learned in kindergarten : objects, and attributes, classes and members, wholes and parts [Peter Coad et.al.].

A natural consequence of this approach is the plethora of terms used to describe its various aspects. It is often the case that these terms are misused, mis-interpreted and given new meaning. Some of the terms related to object oriented approach are object oriented programming, object oriented systems, object oriented analysis, object oriented design, object oriented languages, and object oriented databases. In this paper, we will attempt to clarify these terms as we think it is absolutely important to have a clear understanding of the terms used in any approach. Section 2 defines an object oriented system and discusses the distinguishing features of object oriented systems. Object oriented programming forms the basis for object oriented development of software systems and this is defined and discussed in section 3. Also included in section 3 is a discussion on object oriented languages which provide the primitives that correspond to the concepts of object oriented programming. The essential steps in developing any system are analysis and modeling of the problem space, and the design of a solution to the problem. In section 4 we will define object oriented analysis and object oriented design. This section also includes a survey of some of the analysis and design methodologies that are used in object oriented software development. Object oriented approach is applicable to various domains of computer science and engineering. Two of these domains are expert systems and database systems. Section 5 discusses the affect of object oriented approach on expert systems and section 6 considers the affect of object oriented approach on databases. The paper concludes in section 7 where we discuss some of the research issues in the realm of object oriented systems. Figure 1. shows the development process of object oriented approaches. Note that the analysis and design in an object oriented approach are iterative as reflected in the figure.

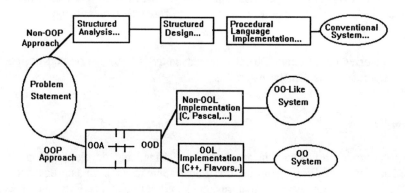

Figure 1. Development process of object oriented approaches.

2. *Object Oriented Systems*:

An object oriented system can be viewed as a collection of objects interacting and communicating through message passing in order to accomplish a goal. The three key concepts associated with the object oriented systems are : object, message, and class. An "object" consists of data (attributes) and the operations that act on the data. There is a strong coupling between the data and the operations. The operations are often called "methods" in Smalltalk, "member functions" in C++ etc. Objects communicate with each other through "messages". A message from object A to object B corresponds to invocation of a method/member function in object B. Objects are categorized into "classes". A class defines a template from which objects are created. The template contains a general description that is shared by one or more objects. The description includes the data and the operations associated with objects of that class. As an example, consider a university that consists of employees and departments. Here, the objects could be individual employees such as Tom, Joe, Dawn etc., and individual departments such as Electrical Engineering, Computer Science etc. We categorize the individual employee objects into a class "EMPLOYEE" and categorize the individual department objects into a class "DEPARTMENT". Figure 2. shows the templates for the class EMPLOYEE, and DEPARTMENT.

```
CLASS EMPLOYEE :

Operations : Print_Name( );
             Print_Dept( );
             Print_Rank( );
                 :
Data        : EMP_NAME;
              EMP_DEPT;
              EMP_RANK;
                 :
                 :
```

```
CLASS DEPARTMENT :

Operations : Print_Name( );
             Print_Num_Of_EMP( );
             Print_Chairman( );
                 :
Data        : DEPT_NAME;
              NO_OF_EMPLOYEES;
              CHAIRMAN;
                 :
                 :
```

Figure 2. Template for the class EMPLOYEE, DEPARTMENT.

The individual employee objects are created from the template class EMPLOYEE. Every employee object that is created will have its values initialized for the data : EMP-NAME, EMP-DEPT, EMP-RANK etc. Similarly, the individual department objects are created from the template class DEPARTMENT and will have the corresponding values for data. Figure 3. shows an example of employee objects : employee1, and employee2 with the corresponding values initialized.

```
EMPLOYEE        employee1;

Operations :    Print_Name( );
                Print_Dept( );
                Print_Rank( );
                    :
Data : EMP_NAME : "Joe";
       EMP_RANK : "Professor";
       EMP_DEPT : "EE";
           :
           :
```

```
EMPLOYEE        employee2;

Operations :    Print_Name( );
                Print_Dept( );
                Print_Rank( );
                    :
Data : EMP_NAME : "Mary";
       EMP_RANK : "Asst. Prof.";
       EMP_DEPT : "CS";
           :
           :
```

Figure 3. A visual picture of Employee objects : employee1, and employee2.

This figure demonstrates the creation of objects from class templates and how the data and operations defined in a class template are associated with objects of that class. Note that it is not necessary to initialize the values of data at the point of creation of objects. Objects can be created first and values for the data can be defined later. Figure 4. shows and example of department objects : department1, and department2 with the corresponding values.

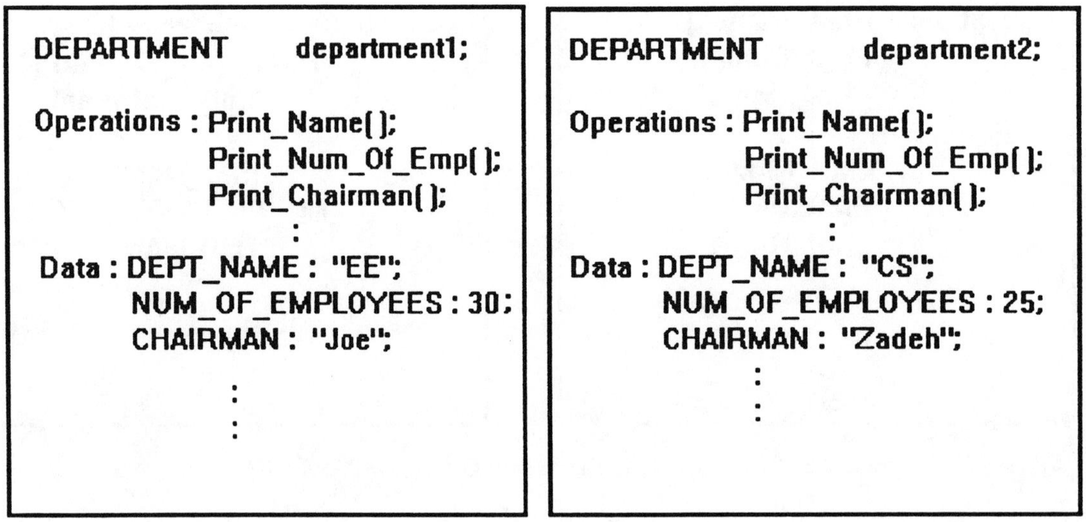

```
┌──────────────────────────────────┐  ┌──────────────────────────────────┐
│ DEPARTMENT      department1;      │  │ DEPARTMENT      department2;      │
│                                  │  │                                  │
│ Operations : Print_Name( );      │  │ Operations : Print_Name( );      │
│         Print_Num_Of_Emp( );     │  │         Print_Num_Of_Emp( );     │
│         Print_Chairman( );       │  │         Print_Chairman( );       │
│                  :               │  │                  :               │
│ Data : DEPT_NAME : "EE";         │  │ Data : DEPT_NAME : "CS";         │
│        NUM_OF_EMPLOYEES : 30;    │  │        NUM_OF_EMPLOYEES : 25;    │
│        CHAIRMAN : "Joe";         │  │        CHAIRMAN : "Zadeh";       │
│                                  │  │                                  │
│                  :               │  │                  :               │
│                  :               │  │                  :               │
│                  :               │  │                  :               │
└──────────────────────────────────┘  └──────────────────────────────────┘
```

Figure 4. A visual picture of department objects : department1, and department2.

Figures 2, 3 and 4 demonstrated the concepts of class and creation of objects of a class. "Class" is a key concept of object oriented systems. It enables capturing of the common characteristics shared by many similar objects at one place, i.e., the class template. In this respect a class is like the concept of "set" in mathematics. All members of a set have the same properties. Similarly, all objects of a class have the same characteristics (same functions and same data). The concept of a class, therefore, provides the ability to manage a large number of objects efficiently. Note that in the class template the formal parameters for the operations and the type of data are not shown but it is certainly a necessary activity in defining a class template. Now, to demonstrate the concept of message passing among objects consider the following scenario. An employee object Joe who is the chairman of EE department (see Figure 3.) wishes to know how many employees are in EE department. He/She will send a message "department1.Print_Num_Of_Employees" to department1 object (see Figure 4.). This message will invoke the operation Print_Num_Of_Employees() in the object department1. This shows the concept of message passing among objects in an object oriented system.

A system or a language has to have certain features for it to be called an object oriented system or object oriented language. There is yet some debate as to what those features should be, associated with object oriented systems/languages. In this perspective, two terms : object-based, object oriented have been proposed [Peter Wegner]. Object-based systems/languages support the notion of objects whereas object oriented systems/languages support the notion of objects, classes, and inheritance.

Object oriented systems enforce the sound software engineering principles such as abstraction : the principle of ignoring those aspects of a subject that are not relevant to the current purpose in order to concentrate more fully on those that are [Oxford Dictionary]; modularity : decomposing a problem into a set of well defined units, each of which is a collection of several related procedures and declarations; cohesion : the tight binding among the various pieces of a module; and information hiding : hiding the implementation details of a module. Additionally, the object oriented systems provide features over and above the traditional systems. These features are the following:

(i) *Data Abstraction* : This is a feature provided by both the object-based systems as well as object oriented systems. The concept of packaging the data together with the operations on the data is called data abstraction. Object-based languages like Ada, Modula-2 and object oriented languages like C++, objective-C, Flavors support the concept of data abstraction. The principle of data abstraction distinguishes the user of an object from its implementor. The implementation of the object is not visible to the user of an object. The users operate on the object by means of the operations which are made visible by the implementor. The concept of data abstraction provides a significant benefit in that the implementor can change the implementation of an encapsulated object without affecting the applications using it.

(ii) *Encapsulation* : Encapsulation is the mechanism to realize (implement) the concept of data abstraction. It means to enclose in or as if in a capsule [Webster's Dictionary]. As applied to object oriented systems; an object is said to encapsulate both its data (state representation, attributes of the object are synonymous terms for data) and the operations on the data. Stated differently, data plus the operations on the data are enclosed in an object. Encapsulation describes the visibility of the data as well as the visibility of the operations on the data. This principle is called "information hiding".

In general, an object is said to have a public interface and a private part. The public interface determines the interaction of the other objects with this object and the private part constitutes the information hidden (both the data as well as operations on the data). An object can read and modify all of its own attributes. Information hiding allows one to restrict the freedom of other objects to retrieve or replace its attribute value. An object can provide accessor functions which will enable other objects to inquire about its attribute values or to modify them. Accessor functions facilitate access control to preserve privacy and integrity of attribute values by allowing them to be read and replaced only when appropriate and by those authorized [Dyke Ten et.al.].

(iii) *Inheritance* : The concept of inheritance allows the creation of a new class from an existing class but perhaps with some changes (in terms of adding new operations and data, redefining existing operations etc.). So, inheritance provides a very powerful mechanism that allows the sharing of resources (data + operations) among classes. As an example of inheritance consider the EMPLOYEE class discussed in the previous section. All employees of the university have common attributes like name, sex, age, and rank. Figure 5. shows the template for the class EMPLOYEE.

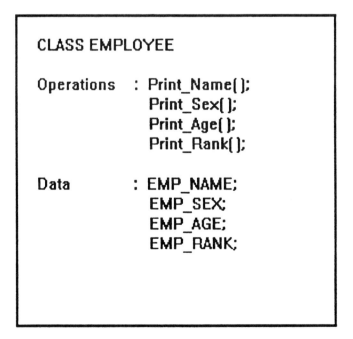

Figure 5. Template for class EMPLOYEE.

In the university there are different classes of employees such as teaching faculty, research faculty, administrative faculty, each of which have some special characteristics associated with it. However, all of these different types of employees have the common characteristics of the class EMPLOYEE shown in figure 5. Hence, all of these new special classes can inherit from the class EMPLOYEE. This concept is captured in Figure 6.

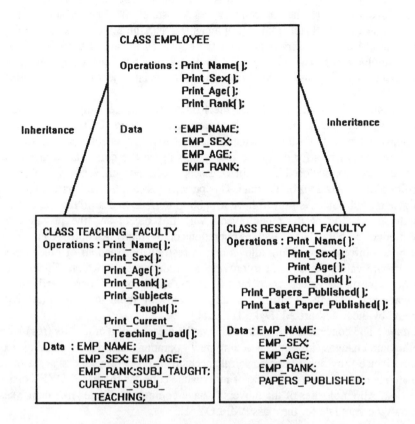

Figure 6. Inheritance Hierarchy.

Notice that both the classes TEACHING_FACULTY and RESEARCH_FACULTY have inherited operations and data from the class EMPLOYEE. In addition to these, each of the new classes have their own set of operations and data. This example demonstrates the usefulness of inheritance. It allows the reuse of existing data and operations, defined for an existing class, when defining new classes. One could say that inheritance facilitates differential programming, i.e., programming by modification.

(iv) *Polymorphism* : In object oriented programming systems, polymorphism is defined as the ability of different objects belonging to different classes to respond differently to the same message. Consider the following example. Let us assume there are two graphic objects : a square object and a triangle object. Sending a draw message to these objects would invoke different "draw" operations.

Polymorphism, like inheritance, facilitates differential programming, i.e., programming by modification. It easily enables the addition of new objects into an existing system if they respond to the same messages (perhaps differently) as the existing objects of the systems.

3. *Object Oriented Programming And Languages*:

Different software development paradigms decompose a problem in different ways. For example, structured software development paradigm decomposes a problem in terms of functions (functional decomposition); goal-oriented paradigms decompose a problem in terms of goals, facts, and rules; constraint-oriented paradigms decompose a problem as a set of invariants. Object oriented programming paradigm decomposes a problem in terms of objects, classes and relationships among them. This decomposition includes activities such as the identification of data and functions of each class, determining the inheritance relationships between classes, and identifying the objects of each class. Let us consider an object oriented system Smalltalk [A. Goldberg]. Smalltalk has applied perhaps the most uniform object oriented viewpoint to software system design and production, and is almost identical to processes having no shared data. Like a process, an object in Smalltalk is an active entity. As an example, for the object model introduced above, let us assume that a class matrix-2 defines a class of matrices of size two by two. Also, let us assume that it contains an operation : add. Objects a, b, and c are of type matrix-2. To compute the expression :

$$a:=b+c$$

users send the message "*add:c*" to the object denoted by b, where "*add*" is a method inherited from class matrix. When it receives that message, the object creates (in co-operation with the object denoted by c) a new object that results from adding the matrices. Then it sends the new object's name back to the caller. Figure 7. illustrates this computational mode. Because communication is done between the objects, and because each object is an active entity, high concurrency can be achieved.

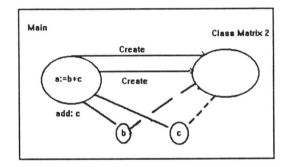

Figure 7. An Object as a computational entity.

The guiding patterns observed in object oriented software development methodology are [K.C Kang and L.S Levy]

    1. Program decomposition is based on objects but not functions.
    2. Data abstraction and Encapsulation are the key concepts used in program design.
    3. Information hiding is the principle used in implementation of the program.

It must be noted that object oriented software development methodology is a continuing and evolving methodology.

An application system development using the object oriented software development methodology will focus on decomposing the application based on the objects that are manipulated by the application. The identified objects are categorized into object types (classes) and the attributes of each object type are defined. For every class; the operations applicable to objects of that class are defined. This is followed by establishing the interfaces to each class and then implementing the operations. The steps involved in object oriented programming can therefore be summarized [G. Booch] as :

    1. Identify objects and types (classes).
    2. Identify operations on objects.
    3. Establish interfaces to each object type.
    4. Implement operations.

This approach has the following benefits [D. Paranas]:

1. It shortens the development time by facilitating concurrent work.
2. It makes the product more flexible.
3. It makes the product comprehensible, easily maintainable.
4. It facilitates correctness proofs for programs by providing a relatively simple statement of what we expect modules to do.

The object oriented software development methodology is best illustrated for an application software of a fully automated small-electronic-parts manufacturing company. Similar examples are presented in a paper by Reenskang [T.M.H reenskang].

An example:

For simplicity, let us assume a company has two departments - Stock and Production. The stock department must maintain a set of small-scale integrated (SSI) parts needed for all company-made products. The Production department must assemble each product from the parts as cheaply as possible while maintaining a specified quality level. The factory accepts product requests on a first-come-first-served basis. Requests are serviced (that is, manufactured) if all needed resources are available.

These departments are organized as follows: First, the Stock department has only one agent. Second, the Production department has two managers: the assembly planner, and the process scheduler. Product assembly comprises a job sequence performed by different work cells; each work cell may have different tools and an industrial robot. Given a product identifier, the process scheduler must obtain the product's assembly plan, and the process scheduler must allocate appropriate resources (work cells) for product assembly. Figure 8. shows the overall factory organization.

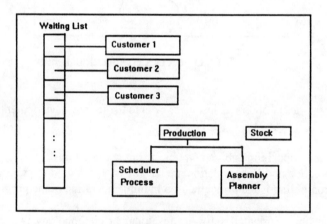

Figure 8. The factory's internal organization.

To map this factory into an object oriented system, we could represent each department as an object. We could also represent the assembly planner, the process scheduler, customer orders, resources, and products as separate objects. We can program an object oriented system to resemble the actual processing of a manufacturing order.

Let us assume the following (depicted in Figure 9). A customer submits an order specifying the name and the quantity of a medium-scale integrated (MSI) part to be assembled. The Production department creates an order object for the request, determines the SSI parts needed, and consults the Stock department to confirm that these parts are available. If parts are insufficient, the Stock department issues an order for resupply, and the customer's order is put on a parts waiting list; otherwise SSI parts are reserved and the Production department determines the resources (machines, robots) required and their availability through message communication. If resources are not available, the request is put on a resources waiting list; otherwise, the necessary resources are allocated, job objects are generated and sent to the appropriate resource object, and the assembly begins.

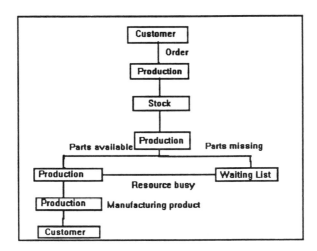

Figure 9. Processing a customer's request.

After the product is assembled, resources are released. The Production department then examines the resources waiting list to see if any request can now be served due to the recent release of resources. The process is then repeated. In parallel with production department, the stock manager examines the parts waiting list whenever new parts arrive; it then moves those customer orders whose required parts are now all available to the resources waiting list to be scheduled for assembly.

Now, let's examine the production manager's internal functions. A method called "product_request" could be associated with the production manager. A customer could activate this method by sending a message to the production manager, specifying the method as selector and product identifier and quantity as arguments. Upon receiving this message, the production manager creates an order object asking the assembly planner to define necessary SSI components and the needed process sequence. The production manager then requests the stock manager and the process scheduler to determine if the factory can currently manufacture the product. If all SSI components and the resources are available, the process scheduler reserves appropriate work cells and develops the assembly flow path. If resources or SSI components are unavailable, it puts the order object on a waiting list.

At the next level down, the assembly planner determines the assembly job sequence. Let's assume that each product the factory can manufacture is implemented as an object class. Associated with each product class is a defined operations set; for example, the operation "retrieve_assembly_plan" develops the product's assembly plan, and the operation "tools_required" reports the tools required for product assembly. Consequently, when a product is identified, a message with the selector "retrieve_assembly_plan" is sent from assembly planner to the product object, and the resultant assembly process for that object is returned. Many classes are similar in that they share operation use - "tools_required", for example. Therefore, it's possible to organize product classes into families and to let class objects enlist the services of superclass objects whenever class objects are called upon to execute methods they share with other classes.

Object Oriented Languages provide a set of primitives in the language for conveniently applying and enforcing the object oriented software development methodology. Note, however, that one could use any programming language to implement an object oriented software design. The affect of such an approach is to simulate the object oriented features in a language which does not provide the primitives corresponding to object oriented concepts. Consequently this may have some ramifications on the performance of the application system.

Simula67 was perhaps the first programming language that introduced the concept of class, which is the implementation of a data abstraction through the principle of encapsulation. Simula67 also introduced the concept of a class hierarchy that permits the inheritance of operations. Smalltalk [A. Goldberg] further normalized the concept of objects and message passing between objects. Object oriented programming has merged more uniformly with Artificial Intelligence (AI) programming languages including LISP and PROLOG. A partial list includes Flavors [D. Weinveb et.al.], Loops [D.G. Bobrow], Common Loops, and Concurrent Prolog. Existing procedural languages have also been embellished with object oriented constructs. A partial list includes C++ and EIFFEL which are extensions of the C language.

Object oriented programming and object oriented languages provide numerous advantages over traditional approaches and have an impact on programming. Object oriented programming is based on application domain oriented concepts and therefore mapping problems in the application domain to solutions becomes easier. The identification and the definition of modules is more consistent with object oriented approach. This is because the object oriented development approach facilitates the identification of fundamental concepts in an application domain. The other benefits of object oriented software development are the following :

- easy comprehension of the design because the design models the real world entities.
- provides a high level specification of the application.
- has the ability of a telescopic language i.e; the modeling constructs can be used all the way from specification to implementation. In other words, it provides one consistent model for all the activities of product development: specification, design and implementation.
- promotes reusable software development through the principle of data abstraction, information hiding, inheritance and loose coupling between objects. A vast object library is developed over a period of time. In the process new operations can reuse much of those that have already been developed obviating the need to write code from scratch. The inheritance mechanism facilitates the creation of generic program modules that can be reused in several parts of the system.
- promotes easy extension of application system because the addition of new objects to the system is accomplished without modification of existing code. That is, it allows incremental development.
- the effect of modification of code inside of an object is localized because of the principle of information hiding. This feature provides the flexibility because the internal representation of an object can be modified without affecting the interface with other objects. This is very important because improvements that can be made within a class will not affect the users of the class.
- one consistent model for analysis, design and implementation of an application implies that the testing effort at various stages of the product development is reduced. Also, since the object oriented approach allows for reuse of code; the testing effort is not replicated for those modules that are reused.

4. Survey Of Current Approaches To Object Oriented Software Development:

Any development effort must first begin with a thorough understanding of the problem domain. The study of the problem domain results in requirements specification. The requirements specification will form the basis for subsequent activities of the software development: design, development, testing and the final product.

The traditional structured software development methodologies use structured analysis and structured design approaches. The modeling constructs of these approaches are different from the modeling constructs of the object oriented software development approaches. The focus of this section is on discussing several different object oriented software development methodologies.

Sidney Bailin proposed an object oriented methodology for studying the requirements of the application domain [S. Bailin]. The analysis methods based on procedure oriented paradigm study, decompose, and articulate the functional requirements of a problem. The requirements will typically state the system must accept certain inputs and produce certain outputs. The transformation of inputs to outputs is represented using the "notion of processes". Processes are decomposed into sub-processes to easily understand what is being accomplished by the transformations. The steps involved for each transformation of inputs to outputs become the sub-processes. Hence, a step becomes the sub-process of the higher level process. Thus the principle of aggregation in structured analysis is that functions are grouped together if they are constituent steps in the execution of a higher level function. The constituent steps may operate on entirely different data abstractions. This is different from the aggregation principle of an object oriented standpoint. The principle of aggregation in object oriented approach is that functions are grouped together if they operate on the same data abstraction.

The difference in aggregation principles makes it rather cumbersome to go from structured analysis to object oriented design. The effort involved in proceeding from structured analysis to object oriented design may require significant recasting of the data flow diagrams. To avoid this painstaking process; Bailin proposed an object oriented viewpoint during the analysis phase.

The two key concepts defined are the notion of entity and the notion of function. The emphasis is on the "content" of the entity rather than on the transformation of inputs to outputs. Note that a process in structured analysis may be a valid entity but with a different semantics. The method retains the data flow diagram representation of inputs and outputs. Entity Data Flow Diagrams (EDFDs) are defined to specify the data flow between entities. EDFDs are similar to DFDs with a few exceptions; the nodes in EDFDs are categorized into entities and functions. Any function must occur within the context of an entity. This implies that a function must be preformed or act on the entity.

Bailin proposed an object oriented specification that consists of a hierarchy of EDFDs and a set of E-R diagrams to serve as a context for the specification. The seven steps of object oriented specification are :

(1) Identify key problem-domain entities.
(2) Distinguish between active vs passive entities.
(3) Establish data flow between active entities.
(4) Decompose entities (or functions) into sub-entities and/or functions.
(5) Check for new entities.
(6) Group functions under new entities.
(7) Assign new entities to appropriate domains.

Steps 4 through7 are iterative. Steps 1-3 may be reconsidered at any time.

The author has identified some aspects of requirements that are as yet not captured with ERDs and EDFDs. These include identification of passive entities under successive transformations; expression of end-to-end response time requirements.

Edward Yourdon and Peter Coad proposed an object oriented analysis technic based on the concepts of objects and attributes; classes and members; wholes and parts [Edward Yourdan et.al.]. Their approach to object oriented analysis builds on three methods of organization that are generally used by humans to perceive the real world [Encyclopedia Britannia]. These methods of organization are the following :

(1) the differentiation of experience into specific objects and their attributes. For example, distinguishing a person from an animal based on attribute "feet".
(2) the distinction between whole objects and their component parts. For example, when a house is constructed with its component rooms, and
(3) the formation of and the distinction between different classes of objects. For example, the formation of the class of all persons and the class of all animals and distinguishing between them.

Yourdon et.al. proposed five major steps of object oriented analysis model :

(1) Identifying objects (data + functionality).
(2) Identifying structures -- Represent the problem space complexity using the methods of organization discussed above.
(3) Defining objects -- A mechanism for controlling how much of a model one considers at a time. The subjects are identified corresponding to structures and objects.

(4) Defining attributes (and instance connections) for instance of an object or classification structure.

(5) Defining services (and message connections).

The model so constructed using the above steps is presented and reviewed in terms of five major layers :

(1) Subject layer.
(2) Object layer.
(3) Structural layer.
(4) Attribute layer.
(5) Service layer.

The review of the constructed model will result in a precise characterization of the problem space in terms of subjects, objects, complexity of problem space, identification of the position of attributes at the appropriate level in the classification structure, and the processing that needs to be performed by various objects on receiving a message.

The author's formulation of object oriented analysis is based on integrating the useful concepts of E-R diagrams, semantic data modeling and object oriented programming languages.

Both of the object oriented analysis techniques presented here provide a way of decomposing the problem space based on the concepts of objects oriented programming. However, the requirement specifications produced using these approaches are likely to be too detailed. Consequently they may not be the most appropriate techniques to serve as a good communication tool between the users and the designers of the system. There is a need for a simple technique that will allow the preliminary analysis of the problem space in terms of objects, attributes, classes, and relationships between them. The preliminary analysis will serve as a good communication tool and will serve the purpose of articulating the requirements of the user sooner. The result of this preliminary step may then serve as the input to any of the above analysis techniques. Also, one gets the impression that the analysis techniques proposed by Bailin and Yourdan et.al. respectively are actually doing a preliminary design of the problem space. This is a general characteristic observed in object oriented approach to problem solving. The distinction between analysis and the preliminary design appears to be fuzzy. This is unlike the traditional waterfall model of structured software development where there is a clear demarcation between analysis phase and design phase.

Several people have proposed object oriented design methodologies. Responsibility-Driven approach [Rebecca Worfs-Brock et.al.] is proposed as a design technique that will ensure object oriented design with a higher degree of encapsulation.

The emphasis is on higher degree of encapsulation because it is the primary form of abstraction for dealing with the complexity of the application domain. The paper shows why the data-driven approach to object oriented design falls short of maximizing encapsulation of the data and operations on the data.

In the data driven approach, the structure of the object is used in the definition of the object. That is the definition of the operations reflects the data structure of the object. This implies that any implementation changes in the object will not be localized t the object itself but instead will ripple through to the objects of other classes that rely on that structure. From this discussion it is clear that data driven approach to design may lead to a design that violates the goal of encapsulation.

The responsibility driven approach is based on the client/server model which describes the interaction between two entities: the client and the server. The client/server model focuses on what the server does for the client rather than how the server does it. The server implementation is encapsulated and the client is not affected by changes in implementation of the server.

The interaction between the client and the server is defined in terms of a "contract". The question asked in this approach to design are : (1) what actions are this object responsible for ?. (2) What information does this object share ?. Responsibility-driven approach facilitates polymorphism, and the design of inheritance hierarchy. These translate to generic function development and code reuse.

Jackson system development (JSD) methodology has an object oriented design basis. The applicability of the JSD specification methods for development of object oriented concurrent software systems has been explored by M. Elizabeth et.al. JSD specifications are inherently parallel and non-determinate in nature. However they lack the features to explicitly represent process synchronization and mutual exclusion in accessing their local data. In order to address the issues of synchronization and mutual exclusion; the processes in the JSD model (a process corresponds to an abstraction of a system object, called entity, and has local data structure plus its own internal structure of sequences, selections, and iterations denoting the functional activities of the object concerned) are transformed into asynchronous, concurrently executing processes which communicate but with some constraints on synchronization. It is shown that JSD method enables the development of graphic object oriented specifications that can be applied for concurrent software development using Ada and similar languages.

Grady Booch has defined a comprehensive methodology for object oriented design of systems. The emphasis of this methodology is on well-defined notation and the process. The essence of the design methodology is captured in Figure . The design consists of the following :

(1). Identifying the class structure of the system through class diagram. A class diagram shows the existence of classes and their relationships. The relationships include uses relationships, inherits relationship and instantiate relationship. The classes are documented in a class template and operation template state transition diagrams are used to represent the state space of a class and also the events that cause a transition from one state to another and actions that result from state change.

(2). Object diagrams that show the existing of objects and their relationships in the logical design of the system. The object diagram also captures the message synchronization. Object templates and message templates are also part of this step.

(3). Module diagrams that depict the allocation of classes and objects to modules in the physical design of the system.

(4). Process diagrams that show the allocation of processes to processors in the physical design of the system. The process diagrams are of interest only if applications are going to run on multiple processors.

So, in essence the object oriented design includes sets of class diagrams, object diagrams, module diagrams, and process diagrams. The top-most class diagram module and process diagram presents the highest level view of the system. The requirements can be traced from implementation by making use of the end-to end connectivity among diagrams.

One can observe from this methodology and the previously discussed methodologies that the essence of object oriented design process can be summarized as :

1. Identify the classes and objects at a given level of abstraction.
2. Identify the semantics of these classes and objects.
3. Identify the relationships among these classes and objects.
4. Implement these classes and objects.

The discovery of classes and objects is an important aspect of any object oriented design process because these form the vocabulary of the problem domain. As Grady Booch points out, the object oriented design stops when any of the following conditions occur :

1. When no new key abstractions or mechanisms exist, or
2. When the classes and objects we have already discovered may be implemented composing them from existing reusable software components.

Booch also gives a list of activities involved with the four stages of the object oriented design process.

All of the design approaches clearly demonstrate the iterative process of the software development unlike the traditional software development life cycle (the waterfall model). New classes/objects are identified at various stages of the object oriented development cycle which necessitates the iterative process of the object oriented development cycle.

5. Object Oriented Systems And AI : Cooperation and Abstraction:

Although the AI community has studied knowledge representation separately, many ideas presented here relate closely to work on frames theory and implementation of frames in knowledge representation languages including KRL, KL-One, KEE, FRL, and UNITS. Recently, object oriented programming has merged more uniformly with modern AI programming languages including Lisp and Prolog: A partial list includes Flavors, Loops, CommonLoops, and concurrent Prolog. Many of these languages have extended basic concepts in Smalltalk with some other features; for example, multiple inheritance and incremental method specification, composite objects, and perspectives.

The availability of these object oriented AI programming languages has extended traditional AI systems, adding two additional desirable features - object abstraction for hierarchical reasoning, and expert cooperation for distributed problem solving. Fikes and Kehler present a typical example of integrated distributed experts to achieve a common goal. Briefly, in the context of our factory example, we can create objects (called observers and monitors) that model diagnostic experts for each resource type (class) in the factory. When operational, each observer observes the behavior of its associated resource; based on forward-chaining rules, it can detect resource problems or malfunctions. When an observer determines that a problem has occurred, it creates a monitor whose function mimics an expert for that problem. The invokes monitor applies backward-chaining rules to analyze and fix the problem.Clearly, this modular structure makes it much easier for domain expert to write and debug rules. The following example, employing hierarchical reasoning, illustrates the power of object abstraction and expert cooperation.

A *further example*:

Assume that our automatic factory has a third department - Service - that tests and repairs faulty products customers have returned for service. For simplicity, let's assume the Service department has only one service expert; naturally, we can implement the Service department as an object.

To identify malfunctioning product faults, the Service object works in conjunction with a tester that can manipulate and observe a malfunctioning product. The diagnostician accepts from the tester, descriptions of observed malfunctions, prescribes tests, accepts the results, and ultimately identifies faulty components responsible for the malfunction. Most likely, the service expert will use the information about a product's intended structure (product parts and their interconnection) and its expected behavior (equations, rules, or productions that relate the product's inputs, outputs, and state).

Because the service should work independently of any particular product, required information must be stored independently. To achieve this, we can include design knowledge (intended structure and expected behavior) and diagnostic rules as part of the class definition. Figure 10. shows a typical product. At the top level, we can describe the product in terms of adder and multipliers. Until we reach the level of gates, we can describe adders and multipliers separately in terms of their subcomponents. A full adder stage (can add two operand bits together with an input carry) is normally used as one of n elements in an n-bit adder (Figure 11. presents a graphical representation of its design). it has three inputs, two outputs, and comprises two XOR gates (X1 and X2), two AND gates (A1 and A2), and an OR gate (O1).

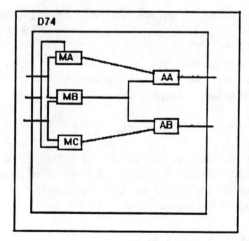
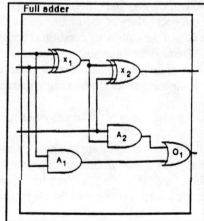

Figure 10. A typical product.   **Figure 11.** A typical adder.

Ofcourse, any product's structure can be expanded and laid out at gate level. However, most existing diagnostic expert systems employ structural abstraction. In structural abstractions of design descriptions, much structural detail has been suppressed; structural hierarchy most commonly exemplifies this. The advantage of structural abstraction for diagnoses is that it enables systems to diagnose faults in a hierarchical way.

For example, we can diagnose the Figure 10 product at a higher level of abstraction to determine major subcomponents in which faults lies (that is, the adder AA). This subcomponent can then be diagnosed to identify the fault at the next lower level (the full adder) and so on until the lowest level failure is determined (X1's output stuck "off"). By diagnosing hierarchically, we can minimize the number of components under consideration at any one time and even though higher level components are often quite complex, the cost of test generation remains manageable.

To facilitate abstraction, Figure 12. shows one possible object representation of D74. When a d74 product is to be diagnosed, the service expert associated with object a will need to identify which subcomponents of b,c,d,e, and f may be faulty. It then sends diagnosis request to service experts associated with those candidate faulty components - say b and c. Likewise, b and c will determine (concurrently) which subcomponents may be faulty. This process repeats until all faulty gates are identified. At different abstraction levels, service experts need to exercise different test patterns and diagnostic rules. In all cases, a service expert at one abstraction level (a, for instance) only sees its subcomponents at the next level and only talks to service experts at that level. Figure 13 shows communication channels among different service experts.

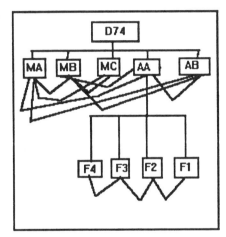 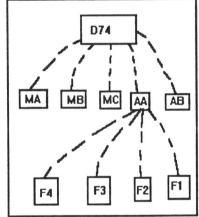

Figure 12. An object representation of D74.   **Figure 13.** Communication channels among different experts.

6. Semantic Databases And Knowledge Bases:

So far, we have assumed that all objects are core resident in object oriented systems. This assumptions may not be realistic if numerous objects are involved. For instance, the types of MSI parts a factory manufactures can become numerous; some of them may need to be put in secondary storage. Furthermore, more than one user may need to access the same object oriented system simultaneously - and some customers may specify parts by attribute rather than by name. to support intelligent systems characterized by these requirements, recent research has concentrated on developing object oriented databases.

There have been two general approaches to implementing object oriented databases. The first is to extend the relational model - a partial list includes Postgres, Genesis, Starburst, and Probe, and the other is to support object oriented programming with permanent storage (as with GemStone, and Jasmine). In addition to providing an organizational principle for data, many researchers have been concerned with database consistency; consequently they have emphasized integrity constraints (rules used to define static and dynamic application properties that are not conveniently expressed using a data model's object and operational features).

Due to their nature, compared with relational database, object oriented databases directly address information retrieval. Another important advantage of object oriented semantic data models is the availability of organizational principles, which are important for (1) application domains with highly structured components, and (2) application domains in which different levels of abstraction are desired. The two most noticeable applications of object oriented databases are computer-aided circuit design and knowledge-based software development.

The appropriateness of applying object oriented data models to computer-aided circuit design is obvious. As our factory example has shown, circuits are usually highly structured, with interrelated components. Furthermore, we find abstraction levels in most complicated circuits. In addition to modeling complicated circuits by object data models, current research concentrates on the dynamic behavior existing in design projects. Typically, researchers develop appropriate integrity constraints to ensure design database consistency.

The advantages of applying object oriented databases to knowledge-base software development may be seen more clearly if we think of our programming entities as objects. Typical objects might be combinatorial algorithms, loops with no exit tests, or mappings from integer to real. By storing these objects in a database, we may use them to synthesize a new program.

7. *Conclusion* :

The paper clarified most of the commonly used terms related to object oriented approach. We have demonstrated the simple but powerful basis that object oriented programming provides for software development and knowledge representation. We have also discussed some of the analysis and design approaches related to object oriented development. Object oriented technology is still evolving. As is the case with any new approach, object oriented approach opens the door for a variety of research problems that need to be addressed if one were to exploit the full benefits of this approach. We will briefly summarize some of these issues.

The need for object management systems.

Very large and complex systems developed using object oriented programming concepts will consist of a huge collection of objects and complex relationships among them. Object management becomes a key aspect of such a complex system. For example, an object oriented system should maintain a consistent state and not produce any harmful side effects. Also, an object management system should provide efficient mechanisms for the following functions:

(1) Query Processing -- Includes query language, and optimization mechanisms for evaluating queries.

(2) Crash Recovery -- The ability to detect faults and recover when some data or knowledge is lost.

(3) Concurrency Control -- The capacity to allow concurrent access and the ability to lock shared objects efficiently.

(4) Disk Management -- Efficient disk management is important in the context of a complex system with a large collection of objects because some of these objects have to be stored in secondary storage.

Object oriented database languages are being proposed to address some of the issues of query processing in object oriented system. One such example is the Object oriented Functional Data Language (OFDL) [Michael V. Mannini et.al.]. OFDL is a strongly typed database programming language. It provides primitives for inheritance and encapsulation and uses a functional notation for message expressions. It incorporates some system defined functions that provide a succinct and convenient notation for filtering, aggregating, and combining objects. The power of OFDL lies in the fact that it combines the object oriented and functional paradigms and provides a notation for both database and general purpose programming tasks.

ROSE data manager is one more example of an object management system [Martin Hardwick et.al.]. It is an object management system for interactive engineering applications including mechanical

CAD and VLSI design. It applies object technology for management and clustering of data. Associated with the ROSE system are : Inheritance manager tool that manages inheritance hierarchy depending on the application requirements, and back-end tools for manipulating and maintaining a database.

The need for simple, precise, and clear programming methodology.

There has been substantial progress in the area of rigorous analysis and design methodologies. This will allow programmers to map an object oriented design into implementation using any existing object oriented language. However, there still exists some confusion as to the granularity of the concept of an object. The problems that need to be addressed are :

(1) What target system element is to be an object, and what is not ?
(2) What is the best way to decompose the system into a set of classes ?
(3) What is the best set of message protocols ?
(4) Which class provides methods that realize required functions ?
(5) No automated tool support for analysis and design of object oriented systems.

These problems are practical and severe; for example, from around 5000 messages -- using no semantic-based tools -- a Smalltalk programmer must pick the best message. Programmers cannot keep all classes and message protocols in mind, apparently. We hope that programming tools will be soon available.

The need for good architectural support.

Object oriented architecture has been studied for some 20 years. It began with descriptor-based architectures aimed at supporting the segmented virtual memory concept. Next came capability-based architectures, where "capabilities" are access authorizations for particular objects.

Recent related research (for example, IBM System/38, iAPX4, Soar, and Xerox Dorado) has concentrated on the following issues : First, the creation and use of certain objects (for example, context objects) is managed partly by hardware and partly by the operating system's kernel modules. Second, the processor's instruction set includes operators that perform or facilitate the creation, deletion, and alteration of certain basic objects including queues, procedure activation contexts, and their subcomponents.

Unfortunately, the consensus is that current implementations of object oriented architectures are too slow. Although many factors should be counted, two reasons for this are obvious. The first is object granularity. In Smalltalk, for example, an integer is an object; adding two integers involves sending a message to one of the two arguments. When the number of objects in a system is huge, overhead is considerable. The second is the number of procedure calls involved in a computation. When hardware resources are limited, the time spend on context swapping is also considerable. Again, we hope such difficulties can be overcome in the future.

We have described characteristic features of object oriented systems and indicated how they can provide a foundation for various computational tasks. In particular, we have addressed the impact of object models on programming environments, expert systems, and databases. Although we used a relatively simple example for illustration, we believe that the same concepts and techniques can be applied to general applications.

We have also discussed related problems, and have highlighted important research directions. Although object oriented systems have provided us with many desirable features, their ultimate success will require significant joint efforts from disciplines including software engineering, databases, AI, and computer architecture. Only through such efforts will "object oriented programming" be in the 1990s what structured programming was in the 1970s.

Acknowledgements

We thank Charles A. Fritsch of AT&T Bell Labs and Farokh B. Bastani for reading through an earlier version of this article and giving us many helpful suggestions. We also thank Hewlett Packard for the support provided to Pratap Chillakanti for collaboration on this research.

References

1. Edward Sciore, "Object specialization", ACM Trans. on Information Systems, April 1989.
2. Martin Hardwick and David L. Spooner, "The ROSE Data Manager : Using object technology to support interactive engineering applications", IEEE Trans. Knowledge and Data Engineering, June 1989.
3. Peter Coad and Edward Yourdon, "Object oriented analysis", Prentice-Hall, 1990.
4. Sidney C. Bailin, "An object oriented requirements specification method", Comm. of ACM, May 1989.
5. K. C. Kang and L. S. Levy, "Software methodology in the harsh light of economics", Butterworth & Co (publishers) Ltd., 1989.
6. Dave Thomas, "What's in an object", Byte, March 1989.
7. M. Elizabeth C. Hall et.al., "Object oriented design, Jackson system development (JSD) specifications and concurrency", Software Engineering Journal, March 1989.
8. Rebecca Worfs-Brock et.al., "Object oriented design : A responsibilty-driven approach", OOPSLA 1989 Conference Proceedings.
9. Peter C. Lockemann, "Object oriented information management", North-Holland, Decision Support Systems, 1989.
10. R. P. Ten Dyke and J. C. Kunz, "Object oriented programming", IBM Systems Journal, Vol. 28., No. 3., 1989.
11. G. Booch, "Object oriented design -- Relational", Tutorial in SCOOP West Conference 1990.
12. A. Goldberg, "Smalltalk-80: The language and its implementation", Addison-Wesley, Reading, Mass., 1983.
13. R. Fikes and T. Kehler, "The role of Frame-base representation in reasoning", CACM, Sept. 1985.
14. G. Booch, "Object oriented development", IEEE Trans. Software Engineering, Feb. 1986.
15. D. Parnas, "On the criteria to be used in decomposing systems into modules", CACM, Dec.1972.
16. T. M. H. Reenskaug, "User-oriented description of Smalltalk systems", Byte, Aug. 1981.
17. M. Stonebraker and L. A. Rowe, "The design of Postgres", Proc. SIGMOD Conf., ACM, New York, N. Y., 1986.
18. U.Dayal et.al., "Probe -- A research project in knowledge directed DBMS", Tech. Report CCA-85-03, Computer Corporation of America, Cambridge, Mass., 1985.
19. D. Maier et. al., "Development of an object oriented DBMS", Proc. ACM OOPSLA Conf., ACM, New York, N. Y., 1986.
20. P. Deutch, "The Dorado Smalltalk-80 implementation: Hardware architecture's impacts on software architecture", in Smalltalk-80, Bits of History, Words of Advice, G. Krasner, ed., Addison-Wesley, Reading, Mass., 1983.
21. C.V. Ramamoorthy and Phillip C. Sheu, "Object Oriented Systems", IEEE Expert, Fall 1988.
22. Merriam - Webster, "Webster's ninth new collegiate dictionary", 1988.
23. Oxford University Press, "Dictionary of Computing ", 1986.

SECTION 3:
OBJECT-ORIENTED DATABASE APPROACHES

An Object-Oriented VLSI CAD Framework

A Case Study in Rapid Prototyping

Rajiv Gupta, Wesley H. Cheng, Rajesh Gupta, Ido Hardonag, and Melvin A. Breuer

University of Southern California

Reprinted from *IEEE Computer*, May 1989, pages 28-37.
Copyright © 1989 by The Institute of Electrical and Electronics Engineers, Inc. All rights reserved.

Example is more efficacious than precept.
— *Samuel Johnson*

Perhaps the most difficult part of constructing a large software system is deciding exactly what to construct. Requirements analysis, as software engineers call it, is the most crucial phase in the life of a project. An error in this phase can not only add to the time required for completing the project, but also lead to a delayed product that was not required in the first place.[1]

The difficulty arises from two sources. Typically, the would-be users do not quite know what they want, at least not until they have tried out some version of the program. Compounding this difficulty is the fact that the planner of any software design activity does not have an exhaustive repertoire of questions that will yield him the necessary information. Neither can he be sure that the specifications he has derived are complete; chances are, they are not. Rapid prototyping has been touted as a way out of this deadlock.[2]

For any software effort with more than a few thousand lines of code, some form of prototyping is a must. As noted by Brooks, "The management question, therefore, is not whether to build a pilot system and throw it away. You will do that. The only question is whether to plan in advance to

Object-oriented database management systems eminently support rapid prototyping, letting programmers gradually refine a subset of objects and operations instead of specifying and developing a complete application.

build a throwaway, or to promise to deliver the throwaway to customers."[3] The inception of the National Test Facility, with its explicit charter to build a national testbed for prototyping and simulating Strategic Defense Initiative command, control, and communications (C^3) software and other battle management software, indicates the

growing recognition and importance of rapid prototyping as a critical part of software development.

Some researchers claim that object-oriented programming in general, and object-oriented database management systems (OODBMSs) in particular,[4-9] offer several features that promote rapid prototyping. In this article, we study the suitability of OODBMS concepts for rapid prototyping in the realm of VLSI computer-aided design systems. CAD systems typically involve much user interaction. Hence the development of CAD software benefits greatly from user feedback, making rapid prototyping a desirable approach.

This article illustrates, with the help of an actual prototype VLSI CAD framework called Cbase,[10] how concepts such as data abstraction, property and operation inheritance, object specialization/generalization, data hiding, method/trigger combination, code reusability, and polymorphism offered by OODBMSs support rapid prototyping. We conducted our work on Vbase, a commercially available OODBMS from Ontologic, but the results and conclusions apply to any database with comparable capabilities. To implement the prototype user interface, we used the X11 toolkit, a windowing package from the Massachusetts Institute of Technology that is also built around the object paradigm.

EH0332-7/91/0000/0041$01.00 © 1989 IEEE   41

Rapid prototyping: the basics

Despite progress in prototyping tools, the basic steps involved in rapid prototyping have not changed. The programmer implements the key portions of a large application that provide basic system functionality, along with sample interfaces. The user "test drives" and critiques the prototype. The recommendations are incorporated, and these two steps are iterated. In this manner, the prototype evolves gradually. If the performance is satisfactory at each stage, and no major design changes are warranted, development continues. Otherwise the prototype is abandoned, although it might serve as an executable specification for future versions.[2]

This approach to large software development has several advantages, not the least of which is the early involvement of users.[11] While software developers like to design software with respect to a set of formal specifications, users evaluate it against actual functional requirements. Early, realistic validation by the user can prevent a lot of rework and redesign. In addition, less obvious effects and problems often surface during prototyping, and several prototypes can be tried. Most important, however, is rapid prototyping's accommodation of the stream of changes requested by the users once they have seen a working version of the program (i.e., it supports time-varying specifications).

A programming environment that promotes rapid prototyping must provide powerful data modeling features to ensure the fidelity of the prototype. Substantial savings in modeling and programming time can accrue if the data model mimics the real-world objects. The environment should encourage gradual evolution so that the prototyping phase can begin without a detailed formal specification of the system. Also, since a prototype is only a partial system, the programmer should be able to assign default behaviors to each object. For example, a system might start with a very simple display routine for all the objects. Once a first-cut user interface has been developed, the environment should let the programmer make it more sophisticated by implementing specialized display procedures for each object type. In addition, the environment should encourage code reusability, to extract maximum work from a minimum of code, and generic programming, to avoid reprogramming as the system evolves.

The tools and environment

Cbase[10] is an object-oriented framework for computer-aided VLSI circuit design. It provides a common repository of both circuit objects and their associated operations, a tool interface for writing new applications, an object bag that holds any type of object for ease of reference, and a user interface for invoking applications or viewing objects in the database. Cbase provides a platform for creating, displaying, manipulating, and maintaining large digital designs.

Cbase uses Vbase[5] as the object manager and the X11 toolkit for graphics and window management. Both packages offer several up-to-date features that have evolved from such diverse disciplines as artificial intelligence, programming languages, compiler theory, and database theory.

Vbase provides a type definition language (TDL) for object schema definition, and a C object processor (COP) for object manipulation. A programmer can use a TDL to specify types of complex objects, their properties and interrelationships, and associated operations. The object type definitions can be arranged in a type hierarchy that determines property and operation inheritance among them. Only single inheritance is currently supported. The TDL compiler compiles the user-defined types into the database, where they supplement the system-defined types.

COP is an object-oriented extension to C that provides constructs for accessing and manipulating objects. Several specialized constructs are also provided, such as those for iterating over aggregates or collections and those for handling exceptions. Perhaps most significant is COP's mapping of database objects into the C process space. Once the database is opened, database objects can be accessed in much the same way as C variables, and they observe all the conventions followed by C variables. This frees the programmer from the chores associated with bringing objects to and from disk. Vbase also provides a source-level debugger, an object browser, and Object SQL for querying the database.

With the advent of multiwindow systems built on a bitmapped display, users expect much more from a user interface than they did when only CRTs were available. A good user interface is generally time-consuming to build because it has to deal with low-level tasks such as I/O, as well as provide such constructs as pull-down menus, pop-up dialog boxes, and mouse-pointing capabilities. Programming all this from scratch requires a substantial amount of design, coding, and debugging.

The Cbase user interface is implemented using the X11 toolkit package, which is available as a library of standard C subroutines. The X toolkit provides predefined widgets (window objects) that a programmer has only to instantiate and organize once he or she has decided on the look and feel of the user interface. Our system uses primitive X operations for graphics operations such as drawing buses and ports. (We do not necessarily advocate Vbase or X11 in CAD software development. The concepts discussed in this article are true of any software development using the object-oriented paradigm.)

Evolution of Cbase

Cbase grew out of the need for a common platform for integrating various CAD applications under development at the University of Southern California. The initial requirements called for a persistent data structure versatile enough for most CAD applications. In addition, the system had to allow different applications to work on and update the same circuit design.

The development of Cbase took place through the construction of two successive prototypes, Cbase 1.0 and Cbase 2.0. When the first version of Cbase was reviewed by the "customer," it not only successfully demonstrated the feasibility of the project goals, but also led to a review of the original goals, based on the programming team's experience with the first working prototype. The resulting specifications for Cbase 2.0 were better defined, and the corresponding system became much more powerful than originally envisioned.

We conceived Cbase 1.0 as a layered structure, whose layers would evolve as more functionality was added to it. Figure 1 shows the organization of various layers and the languages/packages upon which they were implemented. Cbase 2.0 uses the same organization. It is a tribute to the object paradigm that the same basic organization can support the increased complexity and extra functionality of Cbase 2.0 over Cbase 1.0.

Core (CAD Object Repository), the innermost layer of Cbase, consists of schema or type definitions for circuit elements. The object schema has been defined

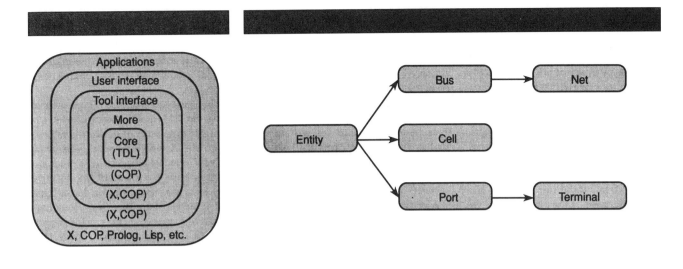

Figure 1. Layered organization of Cbase.

Figure 2. Cbase 1.0 is-a hierarchy.

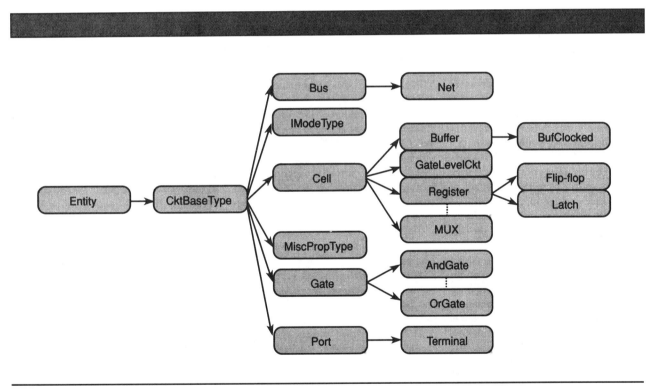

Figure 3. Cbase 2.0 is-a hierarchy.

in Vbase's TDL. Cbase 1.0 implemented the is-a hierarchy shown in Figure 2. We used a very simple but extensible model of circuits in this version. The basic object types employed in modeling a circuit were cells, ports, and buses. Bus was further specialized into net, with bit-width constrained to 1, and port was specialized into terminal, with bit-width 1. The topology of the circuit was represented by dynamic links between these objects, which were stored as properties of the corresponding objects. Each cell could be associated with several I/O ports, and each port could be connected to a bus (or wire). Cells could also be organized hierarchically.

In Cbase 2.0, we have considerably enhanced the Core layer and introduced several specialized refinements of the cell object type, such as register, adder, and multiplexer. Figure 3 shows the Cbase 2.0 type hierarchy.

More (Method Object Repository) is a collection of methods associated with cir-

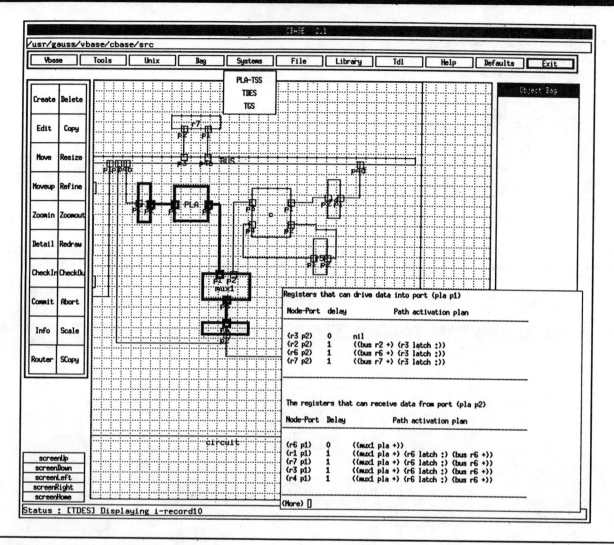

Figure 4. Cbase 2.0 user interface.

cuit object types. It insulates the application developer from internal changes in Core through an OODBMS-supported mechanism called polymorphism. Methods in More are written in COP, and methods for creating, deleting, and maintaining the object types in the Core have been implemented. The primary difference between Cbase 1.0 and 2.0 is the addition of methods catering to the new object types.

The Cbase tool interface is a library of object-independent access/maintenance routines that define the protocol through which all the applications access the database. While methods in More are tightly bound to the objects in Core, no such restriction is placed on the operations defined in the tool interface. The Cbase 1.0

tool interface was virtually nonexistent, as that version was designed to develop working prototypes, not new applications.

The Cbase 2.0 tool interface has procedures that application programs and the user interface can use to manipulate circuit objects in a generic, type-independent manner. It uses a file-based protocol to communicate with applications written in alien languages such as Lisp. For example, using the tool interface, applications can request Cbase to highlight certain circuit objects on the graphic display, as shown in Figure 4. The tool interface also contains procedures for exporting and importing circuits to and from files.

The most visible enhancement to Cbase 2.0 is in the user interface. To access cir-

cuits and predefined subsystems in the database, Cbase 1.0 had a multiwindow user interface based on the X10 windowing package. Access to several utilities, such as the Vbase Object Browser, Object SQL, Unix operations, and primitive help features, was built into the interface. Cbase 2.0 adds a structural view editor so that a user can interactively create and manipulate circuits in the database by working with a schematic display. All circuit objects have been given image properties, and data entry forms have been added so that nongraphic properties of objects can be displayed and edited. A user can work with a hierarchical circuit by moving up and down the hierarchy. The Cbase 2.0 user interface provides a convenient sche-

```
define Type Cell
    ........
    hasPorts: distributed Set[Port]
        inverse $Port$isOnCell;
    ........
end Cell;

define Type Port
    ........
    isOnCell: distributed Set[Cell]
        inverse $Cell$hasPorts;
    ........
end Cell;
```

Figure 5. TDL segments showing many-to-many relationship between cell and port.

matic capture facility and has hooks for further enhancements.

The main purpose of Cbase is to provide a framework for integrating diverse VLSI CAD applications. Cbase 1.0 supported three CAD applications. Since these systems primarily used files for I/O, a file-based interface was used. These applications migrated directly to Cbase 2.0 with little change. Currently, several applications that work directly off the database are being developed.

Several features of Cbase's evolution are noteworthy. A working version was available at all times during the development of both prototypes, allowing enhancements to be added incrementally. Instead of starting with a formal requirement specification document, specification was an ongoing process.

OODBMS features that aid rapid prototyping

Several OODBMS features helped us build the Cbase prototype. In this section we illustrate each OODBMS concept with examples from our code and show how the feature's absence would have resulted in more design effort, more code, or both.

Modeling power. One of the major advantages of the object-oriented paradigm is increased modeling power. The objects and their interrelationships in OODBMSs can be aligned very closely to the real-world objects and their interrelationships. On the other hand, conventional data modeling paradigms such as file formats or relational data models require considerable effort to force real-world objects into fixed programming constructs. Thus, a semantic gap exists between the way information is stored and the way it will be used. Relational databases, in particular, are inadequate for storing complex information structures such as those in CAD.[12]

Consider, for example, the task of modeling many-to-many relationships. To make the example concrete, consider cell and port object types. In general, a cell can have many ports, and a port can be on many cells. (In Cbase 1.0, a port can be shared between a cell and its subcell.) The TDL segments in Figure 5 show the relevant parts of the definitions of the port and cell object types. The inverse clause helps maintain the two-way pointers between ports and cells. Thus, the insertion

SetInsert(aPort, aCell.hasPorts)

where aPort and aCell are port and cell objects respectively, would include aPort in the set aCell.hasPorts, and aCell in the set aPort.isOnCell. In the relational model, the port and cell definitions would roughly correspond to a relation for each. However, to model this relationship, a programmer would have to introduce an extra relation (or an intersection record). Furthermore, a join over these relations might be required to retrieve combined information. The gain in both modeling power and object access time in the case of OODBMSs is substantial.

OODBMSs typically provide a set of predefined system types, such as set, queue, stack, list, and ordered dictionary. Vbase provides many of the routinely used data structures and their associated operations, such as insert, push, and pop. This simplifies the modeling effort, as the designer can concentrate on the problem at hand and not clutter the solution with data-structure-specific routines.

Another advantage of storing a powerful data structure directly on the disk is that most applications do not need a local, memory-resident data structure. When accessed, the relevant information about an object is automatically cached into memory. No code for loading and mapping disk information to memory data structures is needed. If the same information were stored using a file format such as EDIF (Electronic Design Interchange Format), the front end of every application would have to be a parser/loader utility. Note that this advantage does not apply to object-oriented languages that lack object persistence, such as C++, SmallTalk, and Objective-C.

To clarify this point, consider the task of drawing a circuit consisting of cells, ports, and buses. A programmer need only iterate over those circuit objects in the database and draw each one of them. This is exactly how one would like to think of drawing a circuit, that is, without building a set of queries to extract the data from the database, loading them into local data structures, and then displaying them.

Object specialization/generalization, classification, and aggregation. Using a limited set of constructs to model several concepts inevitably leads to a loss of exact meaning. OODBMSs provide several mechanisms to model different relationships among objects.

Object specialization/generalization refers to the ability to organize objects in an is-a hierarchy. For example, in Cbase, register is a cell, which in turn is a CktBaseType, which is an entity (see Figure 3).

Classification is the ability to relate an object to a group of objects via the is-instance-of relationship. To check the class (or type) to which an object O belongs, one simply checks O.DirectType. The function TypeOf(O) (which is defined on entity, and hence inherited by every object) also returns the type of object O.

Aggregation allows the programmer to model an object as an aggregate of its constituent objects. This type of relationship is known as the is-part-of relationship and is specified in TDL by defining an object's properties. For example, the constituent objects in a cell are given in the properties clause of the cell TDL, as shown in Figure 6.

Research in artificial intelligence and semantic data modeling has shown that these three relationship classes are sufficient to model many real-world situations.[5] Also, the ability to represent different relationships directly without overloading any single construct (as must be done in conventional models due to the small set of fixed types of a particular language) leads to a clearer model and cleaner code. This, in turn, helps rapid prototyping by reducing development time.

Data abstraction and data hiding. The advent of third-generation programming languages (such as CLU) pointed out the need for a clear distinction between the storage structures associated with data and the logical structure of the information. Data abstraction refers to the extreme case of this separation, where the only access to the storage structure is through a set of predefined operations. TDL defines a set of operations for each VLSI object in Cbase. Data hiding insulates the programmer from the actual structure in which the data are stored.

For example, the cell definition in Figure 7 lists some of the allowable operations on a cell — delete, CreDrawEdit, Display-Form, etc.

Even conventional programming languages promote data abstraction and data hiding as good programming practices through defining record types, giving meaningful names to variables, and writing routines to manipulate fields in a record. But there is no way to enforce these practices in conventional languages. In OODBMSs, completely encapsulating an object with its data and operations forces the programmer to use the correct operations on all objects. In addition, a programmer needs only to know about the objects that his or her code uses.

Interface modeling. We also found the object paradigm useful in modeling the Cbase user interface. Building the interface was a simple task of using the predefined widgets in the X11 toolkit. Programming with widgets consisted mainly of declaring several types of widgets (such as label widget and command widget), attaching them to an appropriate parent widget, setting the size and position of the windows, and linking the routine that should be invoked (the call-back routine) when a particular widget is selected. Dynamic creation or destruction of a widget is performed with a single call to the create/destroy procedures. The toolkit provides mouse-pointing facilities, text widgets with editing functions based on the Emacs text editor, and several other features that make implementing a user interface easier.

We saved considerable time when we switched from using X10 primitive calls in the library of C calls to the toolkit in X11. Even the simple user interface in Cbase 1.0 (which used X10) required a lot of design and coding. Cbase 2.0 used primitive X calls only for the graphics portion, which required interactive drawing and modification of objects on the screen. The rest of the user interface consisted of toolkit commands. We easily implemented com-posite objects such as pull-down menus by declaring several command widgets and attaching them to the parent menu widget. We estimate that using the toolkit cut the code needed by more than two-thirds.

Code reusability. Given a choice, nobody would want to write more code than needed to implement a certain function. Any reduction in code reduces the number of bugs to fix. Object-oriented languages allow the programmer to write less code and implement the same functionality by reusing code modules. This is not just a matter of changing parameters to a procedure: Vbase lets programmers paste modules together as required to form larger modules. In addition, OODBMSs also support the porting of objects from one version to another. Types are automatically migrated to a new database, thereby eliminating the task of updating and copying the object definitions.

The simplest form of code reusability is to use any predefined routines that already exist on the system. OODBMSs typically provide a wide set of predefined types and their associated operations. For instance, the predefined stack object in Vbase has a set of routines that can be used directly, such as $Stack$Push, $Stack$Pop, and $Stack$Delete.

Property/operation inheritance. Property/operation inheritance implies that an object type automatically has all the properties/operations of its parent type. This is one of the fundamental differences between OODBMSs and relational databases.

From the standpoint of rapid prototyping, operation inheritance is perhaps more valuable than property inheritance. Note that all the cell operations in Figure 7 are refinements of the operations on cell's parent type. Thus, a programmer does not need to reimplement the behavior that a type shares with its supertype. More importantly, this allows a programmer to assign default behavior to objects. For example, we have not yet implemented most of the operations for register in our system. However, we can create or delete a register, or invoke several of the operations defined for cell that have been inherited by register, since cell is the supertype of register. In fact, once the subtype-supertype link is established in the is-a hierarchy, a large amount of code automatically becomes available to the object, even before a single line of code specific to the new object type has been written.

```
define Type Cell
   supertypes = {CktBaseType};
      properties = {
         name:          String;
         subCells:      distributed Set[Cell]
                        inverse $Cell$isCellOf;
         interconnect: optional Set[Bus];
         image:         optional DisplayImage;
         ...................
      };
end Cell;
```

Figure 6. The properties clause of the TDL description of cell.

```
define Type Cell
   supertypes = {CktBaseType};
      operations = {

         refines Delete (c: Cell)
            raises (CannotDelete)
            triggers (CellDeleteTrigger);

         refines CreDrawEdit (c:Cell)
            method (CellCreDrawEdit);

         refines DisplayForm (c:Cell)
            method (CellDisplayForm);

         .........
      };
end Cell;
```

Figure 7. The operations clause of the TDL description of cell.

Method and trigger combination. Method and trigger combination involves writing several small modules of code and using them in different combinations to form methods for different types and situations. Other disciplines such as hardware design have succesfully used such a building-block approach. In software engineering, however, the use of replaceable software modules is still not common, partially because of our inability to make code generic enough. In conventional programming, this would involve many checks,

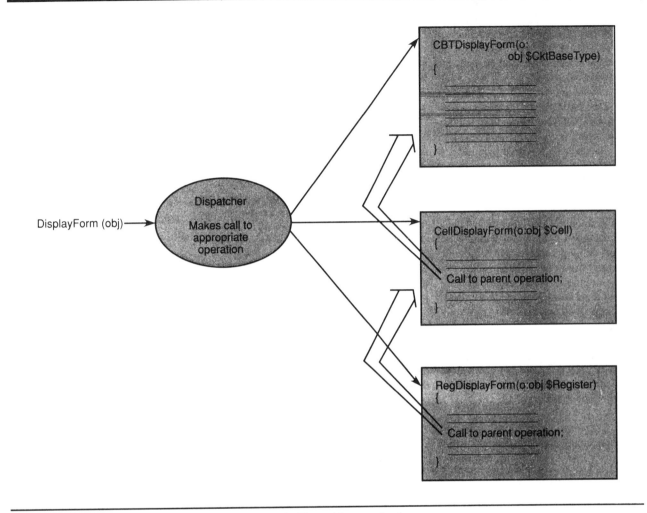

Figure 8. Combination of methods using the automatic dispatching mechanism.

which would make the code inefficient.

However, with OODBMSs, the automatic dispatching mechanism (see the next section) allows programmers to combine modules by triggering them at the appropriate places. Each object-specific operation module is designed to handle its additional set of properties and then invoke the corresponding module for its supertype. Note that all modules are invoked using the same generic call, irrespective of the argument type. Figure 8 illustrates this for the operation of displaying data entry forms on the user interface for register, cell, and CktBaseType objects.

Generic programming. In generic programming, programmers write code modules as general as possible so they can be used by different types of objects. Two essential features of the object paradigm — polymorphism and access to metainformation — help generic programming.

Polymorphism. Polymorphism is the ability to automatically dispatch a call to an appropriate routine according to the type of parameters passed. This feature makes code upwardly compatible and resilient to modifications.

Consider the call back routine createsub(), shown in Figure 9, which is invoked when a user clicks on the "create" option in the user interface. The procedure GetType displays the "is-a" hierarchy and prompts the user to select a type. An object of the selected type is then created, and the user draws the object and fills in its nongra-

phics properties using a data entry form for objects of this type. The CreDrawEdit routine does all this. Note that the createsub() code in Figure 9 is completely generic and will not change no matter how the Core grows. The generic call to CreDrawEdit is automatically dispatched to the appropriate method, such as CellCreDrawEdit, based on the type of the object. The binding between the generic call and the object-specific routine is done in the TDL, as shown in Figure 7. We have found that the whole user interface can be developed in such a generic manner.

Polymorphism is also evident in the trigger and method combination example (Figure 8). A call to DisplayForm is automatically dispatched to either CBTDisplayForm, CellDisplayForm, or RegDis-

```
createsub()
{
    /* Get the type to be created by clicking in the type hierarchy tree. The function
       GetType displays the type hierarchy rooted at its argument and prompts the
       user to select a subtype. */

    aType = $CktBaseType$GetType($CktBaseType);

    /* Call the Create, Draw and Edit routine. This call is automatically dispatched
       to the appropriate routine according to the type of "aType". */

    $theObject = $CktBaseType$CreDrawEdit(aType);
}
```

Figure 9. Generic subroutine for creating any circuit object.

playForm according to the type of object passed.

Accessibility of metainformation. Another characteristic of OODBMSs that makes a program resilient to the addition of new types is the accessibility of metainformation. The user-defined types are actually objects compiled into the database. They are therefore available to a program just like any other object.

The direct availability of metainformation in the database alleviates the need to hard-code it in the programs. The is-a hierarchy display routine is a case in point. The routine reads the types from the database at the start of each session and creates an internal data structure for graphical display. This ensures that the information displayed by the program is consistent with the current is-a hierarchy in the database.

Language and environment features. Several language features accelerate programming by catching errors early in the code-compile-test cycle. Both TDL and COP comply with some of these features.

Although C itself is a weakly typed language, the COP compiler ensures that database objects can be manipulated only by procedures attached to them. Such strict type checking eliminates several hard-to-catch bugs early.

The advanced exception-handling capability of OODBMSs comes in handy in rapid prototyping. Typically, a large amount of code in an application's final version deals with erroneous input data or other anomalous situations. Programmers

would like to avoid such detailed error handling in early prototypes. If exceptions are also treated as objects, a programmer can initially write a simple exception handler for the most general type of exception. The programmer can then gradually refine this default exception handler as the prototype grows. We did this in Cbase 1.0, where most exception handling was restricted to a print statement when an exception of the type "failure" (the most general type of exception in Vbase) was caught. Several of these exceptions handlers have since been refined to perform context-sensitive error handling.

Drawbacks and limitations

While the above discussion might lead one to believe that the object paradigm is a panacea for all the woes of software engineering, the paradigm does have drawbacks.

One of object technology's disadvantages is the long learning curve. Most programmers trained in conventional programming can pick up a new language fairly quickly. However, object programming seems to require longer gestation. We have found that programmers normally need several months before they are skilled enough to start a project.

Another problem that is expected in the initial stages of any budding technology is the unavailability of robust and reliable tools such as source-level debuggers and fast compilers. With packages such as X11,

which are based on the client-server model and process client requests asynchronously, there is an associated problem in dealing with bugs. Error latency can camouflage the real bug, since the source line at which a program fails might not be the line in error. Even synchronous packages such as Vbase often report errors in user code as some abstruse error in system code.

Yet another potential problem lurks in the nature of abstraction. While it shields applications from low-level details, it also makes them dependent on the reliability of the abstraction layer. A well-hidden bug in this layer will show up as a rare malfunction in the application layer. Since the application programmer does not have implementation-level knowledge of the lower layer, the bug can be almost impossible to isolate and eradicate, especially if it is disguised by asynchrony.

Programmers must also consider performance carefully. The emphasis in rapid prototyping is typically on proof of concepts rather than performance. However, a programmer should consider performance as early as possible if the prototype is to evolve into the final system. OODBMSs occupy more space and are generally slower than the file-based systems in widespread use in the CAD industry. Files offer the rawest form of data access, while an OODBMS requires more storage space for the same data because a considerable amount of semantic information is also stored. Compile-time performance is also poorer in OODBMSs because of strict type checking (with respect to a persistent data structure).

Our experience with Vbase shows that default object creation/manipulation operations provided by the environment might not deliver the desired level of performance. Fortunately, since OODBMSs are generally open systems, most default operations can be substituted by user-defined, object-specific operations. In addition, access performance can improve via provisions for clustering objects on the disk.

Prototyping can have an adverse impact on maintainability, since the finished product might consist of code that has been patched and modified several times. However, with the object-oriented paradigm, the system expands primarily by the addition of specialized object types. The problem is automatically partitioned so that, as the system grows, the major changes consist of new code rather than modified old code.

Cbase 2.0 culminates about seven months of effort by two graduate students with no prior experience in object-oriented programming. When we first embarked on Cbase 1.0, we were still learning about Vbase and the X window system. Building the system as envisioned took approximately four months. We completed Cbase 2.0, which is much more detailed and sophisticated, in about six more months. We are adding more functionality and integrating existing programs in Cbase 2.0, though we have completed most of the structural modeling.

By far the most important contribution of object-oriented technology was its modeling power. Complex CAD structures and concepts were implemented exactly as perceived in the real world, without the need to force them into predefined constructs. In addition, the gradual refinement and evolutionary approach forwarded by OODBMSs particularly suited rapid prototyping of an application such as Cbase due to the application's ill-specified nature. Features such as generic programming and code reusability also shortened the time needed to complete the prototype. However, the environment is not perfect; some special problems exist due largely to the newness of the technology and the lack of user education and experience with this new paradigm.

With the increasing complexity of software systems, rapid prototyping is fast becoming an indispensable part of the software development life cycle. Our experience in this project has convinced us that the object paradigm will be a leading candidate for rapid prototyping environments in the coming years. □

Acknowledgments

The authors are grateful to Ellis Horowitz for help with the initial specification of Cbase, and to Abhijit Khale and Sheng Y. Lin for help with system integration and maintenance. This work was supported by the Defense Advanced Research Projects Agency and monitored by the Office of Naval Research under contract number N00014-87-K-0861. The views and conclusions in this article are those of the authors and should not be interpreted as necessarily representing the official policies, either expressed or implied, of the Defense Advanced Research Projects Agency or the US government.

References

1. F.P. Brooks, "No Silver Bullet," *Computer*, Vol. 20, No. 4, Apr. 1987, pp.10-19.

2. R.S. Pressman, *Software Engineering*, McGraw-Hill, New York, 1987.

3. F.P. Brooks, *The Mythical Man-Month*, Addison-Wesley, Reading, Mass., 1982.

4. J. Banarjee et al., "Data Model Issues for Object-Oriented Applications," *ACM Trans. Office Information Systems*, Vol. 5, No. 1, Jan. 1987, pp. 3-26.

5. T. Andrews and C. Harris, "Combining Language and Database Advances in an Object-Oriented Development Environment," *Proc. OOPSLA 87*, ACM, pp. 430-440.

6. D.H. Fishman et al., "Iris: An Object-Oriented Database Management System," *ACM Trans. Office Information Systems*, Vol. 5 , No. 1, Jan. 1987, pp. 48-69.

7. D. Maier et al., "Development of an Object-Oriented DBMS," *Proc. OOPSLA 86*, ACM, pp. 472-482.

8. D.S. Harrison et al., "Data Management and Graphics Editing in the Berkeley Design Environment," *Proc. ICCAD 86*, CS Press, Los Alamitos, Calif., Order No. 744, pp. 24-27.

9. W.D. Smith et al., "Flexible Module Generation in the FACE Design Environment," *Proc. ICCAD 88*, CS Press, Los Alamitos, Calif., Order No. 869, pp. 396-399.

10. M.A. Breuer et al., "Cbase 1.0: A CAD Database for VLSI Circuits Using Object-Oriented Technology," *Proc. ICCAD 88*, CS Press, Los Alamitos, Calif., Order No. 869, pp. 392-395.

11. B.W. Boehm, *Software Engineering Economics*, Prentice Hall, Englewood Cliffs, NJ, 1981.

12. W. Kent, "Limitations of Record-based Information Models", *ACM Trans. Database Systems*, Vol. 4, No. 1, Mar. 1979, pp. 107-131.

Rajiv Gupta is a research assistant professor at the University of Southern California, where he was previously a postdoctoral research fellow in the VLSI Test Group. His research interests include object-oriented frameworks for VLSI CAD, VLSI testing, system-level fault diagnosis and reconfiguration, and fault-tolerant computing. He has published numerous research articles on subjects ranging from system reconfiguration, fault diagnosis, VLSI testing, and logic programming to object-oriented databases for VLSI CAD. He is the coeditor of *Object-Oriented Databases with Applications to CASE, Networks and VLSI CAD* (Prentice Hall).

Gupta is a recipient of the National Science Talent Search Scholarship awarded by the Government of India. He received his BE and MSc, both with honors, from Birla Institute of Technology and Science, Pilani, India, in 1982. He received his MS and PhD in computer science from the State University of New York at Stony Brook, where he was a research assistant from August 1982 to July 1987.

Wesley H. Cheng is a software development engineer at Hewlett-Packard. His current interests include windowing systems, object-oriented technology, and architectures for parallel processing. He completed his BS at the University of the Pacific and his MS at the University of Southern California, both in computer engineering.

Rajesh Gupta is a research assistant in the Department of Electrical Engineering at the University of Southern California. His interests are in VLSI design automation, design for testability, and design applications of artificial intelligence. He received the B.Tech. degree in electrical engineering from the Indian Institute of Technology, Madras, in 1985, and the MS degree in computer engineering from the University of Southern California in 1987. In 1979, he was awarded the National Science Talent Search Scholarship by the Government of India.

Ido Hardonag is a graduate student and research assistant in the Computer Science Department at the University of Southern California. His technical interests are research and development in CAD, user interfaces, and object-oriented databases. Hardonag received his BS in mathematics and computer science from Tel Aviv University in 1985.

Melvin A. Breuer is a professor of electrical engineering and computer science at the University of Southern California. His main interests are in CAD for digital computers, fault-tolerant computing, and VLSI circuits.

Breuer has published over 100 technical papers and is the editor or coauthor of several books on design automation and hardware description languages. He was editor-in-chief of the *Journal of Design Automation and Fault-Tolerant Computing*, coeditor of the *Journal of Digital Systems*, and program chair of the Fifth International IFIP Conference on Computer Hardware Description Languages and their Applications.

Breuer is a member of Sigma Xi, Tau Beta Pi, and Eta Kappa Nu, a fellow of the IEEE, and was a Fullbright-Hays Scholar in 1973. He received his BS in engineering with honors and his MS in engineering from the University of California at Los Angeles in 1959 and 1961, respectively. He received his PhD in electrical engineering from the University of California at Berkeley in 1965.

Readers can contact Rajiv Gupta at the Dept. of Electrical Engineering Systems, University of Southern California, Los Angeles, CA 90089.

An Object-Oriented Design for Distributed Knowledge-Based Systems

David A. Carlson   Sudha Ram

Department of Management Information Systems
College of Business and Public Administration
University of Arizona
Tucson, AZ 85721
(602)621-2748

Abstract

Many management information systems have requirements that are inherently distributed, either logically or physically, however, no adequate architectures exist which allow multiple knowledge bases and databases to be shared and integrated. An architecture for Distributed Knowledge-Based Systems (DKBS) is presented which satisfies these requirements. A Distributed Knowledge Base Management System (DKBMS) is described which manages the meta-knowledge necessary to coordinate multiple local Knowledge-Based Systems (KBSs). We propose an object-oriented design for implementing the DKBMS structure and the communication protocol which connects the DKBMS with each of the local KBSs. An example is described where the DKBS architecture is applied to planning research projects within a university. The resulting architecture is compared with previous research in related topics, and directions for future research on the DKBS architecture are described.

1 Introduction

This paper presents an architectural design which facilitates the implementation of information systems supporting knowledge-based decisions made by groups of individuals or business entities. This architecture allows both knowledge-based and data-based information to be shared and integrated by semi-autonomous sites in order to achieve common global objectives.

A Distributed Knowledge-Based System (DKBS) consists of several Knowledge-Based Systems (KBSs) that may be logically or physically distinct from one another. The KBSs are linked together and managed by a single Distributed Knowledge Base Management System (DKBMS) which coordinates global inferencing to resolve goals that span multiple KBS sites in the network. A significant requirement of this global inference process will be to resolve the inevitable conflict which arises between the autonomous KBSs. A global knowledge base component of the DKBMS will contain meta-knowledge describing the entire distributed network of knowledge-based systems. User goals may be directed at either the DKBMS or at a specific local KBS. We propose that an object-oriented model be used to implement the DKBMS structure.

We present an application for a distributed knowledge-based system which assists research personnel in planning research projects and their funding. Although our DKBS architecture supports any knowledge representation paradigm at each local KBS, we will present an object-oriented design for the research planning system. Object-oriented programming (OOP) supplies a powerful control mechanism for organizing the KBS; rule-based and logic-based representations may be used to store the knowledge within the system.

Section 2 describes our motivation for research on Distributed Knowledge-Based Systems and reviews previous research in related areas. Section 3 presents a conceptual design of the DKBS architecture and details of the DKBMS specification. Section 4 describes a knowledge-based system for planning research projects and proposes an object-oriented approach for implementing the prototype design. Finally, we discuss open research issues and present conclusions.

2 Motivation for Research in DKBS

This section describes our research goals, provides a brief overview of knowledge and data integration, and reviews prior research which is relevant to the architecture.

2.1 Research Goals

Our goal is to design an architecture which facilitates the implementation of information systems supporting decisions made by groups of individuals or business entities. This group decision process requires a network of databases and knowledge bases with coordinated communication among them. Cooperative action needs to be stressed. Performance of the integrated information system may be enhanced by allowing parallel processing of sub-tasks by individual knowledge-based systems. When cooperative decisions are required, each knowledge-based system must have access to multiple external sources of data and knowledge. No adequate architectures exist in the current literature to integrate multiple distributed knowledge base *and* database systems.

The knowledge-based component of this integrated system would contain meta-knowledge describing decision heuristics and empirically established relationships between data items. These relationships would infer information from conflicting or partial data, or manage uncertainty associated with the stored data. Information management problems require procedural knowledge for determining acceptable solutions, and control knowledge in terms of strategies for making efficient use of the procedural knowledge. The meta-knowledge would direct the global inferences and resolve conflict among multiple autonomous knowledge-based systems.

In order to establish an effective communication between knowledge base and database systems, each component must depend on its own representation structures and inference methods. A simple interface between the two components will not suffice. In an integrated system the strengths of each system must be exploited [32].

Manola and Brodie [21] present a hypothetical Knowledge Base Management System (KBMS) architecture, which the authors hope will stimulate further research into formal architectures for a KBMS. The authors state that "knowledge sharing" will be new to both databases and knowledge base systems. Knowledge provides the controlling and general information, typically complex and relatively small in volume, whereas, data represent the manipulated and factual information, typically regular but voluminous [33]. The KBMS will require unified control schemes for consistency, semantics, and knowledge content (i.e., what knowledge resources the KBMS has) as well as for redundancy, reliability, and security. Several requirements are outlined which will allow a KBMS to manage the "knowledge resources" of a collection of knowledge based applications. The solutions to a series of objectives for KBMS architectures are left for future research.

2.2 Previous Research

Our architectural design represents a synthesis of four major areas of research: distributed database systems, distributed problem solving, object-oriented programming, and strategic planning.

Distributed Database Systems. Many issues discussed in the Distributed Database Systems (DDBS) literature are also relevant to DKBS, namely, the global schema definition, communication among local databases, heterogeneity, fragmentation, and allocation. The three-level architecture described by Ceri and Pelagatti [3] defines a conceptual schema which contains relations and attributes for the global network of distributed relational databases. The second and third levels of Ceri's architecture define fragmentation and allocation schemas which distribute the conceptual schema to the various sites in the network. All of these schemas are represented using consistent global semantics. Finally, the site schemas are mapped to the data definition language used by the DBMS at each particular site. Several architectures have been proposed for distributed database systems [23, 20], the most accepted of which is the three-level architecture described by Ceri, et al [3].

Distributed Problem Solving. Distributed problem solving requires an architecture for a network of independent knowledge-based systems that may cooperate to solve a problem faced by one individual node or a subset of the nodes. A survey of research in this field is described by Gasser [12], Smith [24], and Sridharan [25], and specific research topics can be found in [4, 5, 6, 7, 8, 10, 11, 15, 18, 19].

Partial global plans are discussed by Durfee and Lesser [7, 8] as a method for coordinating distributed problem solvers. A network plan is described as containing a *local plan* representing the detailed plan maintained by a node that is pursuing the plan, a *node-plan* representing the less specific plan that nodes use to communicate their intentions, and a *partial global plan* that represents how several nodes are actually working toward a larger goal. The partial global planner scans models of other nodes to find cases where several nodes are working on parts of some larger *partial global goal*. The partial global planner forms *partial global plans* to achieve the partial global goals. A partial global goal is global in the sense that it may (but does not necessarily) encompass the local goals of several nodes, and is partial in that only part of the network might participate in it.

Object-Oriented Programming. Objects are entities that combine the properties of procedures and data since they perform computations and save local state. All activity in object-oriented programming (OOP) results from sending messages between objects: a form of indirect procedure call. A set of class messages is designed to provide the complete user interface with an object. This related set of messages (or operators) forms a protocol for the object. The term polymorphism is used in object-oriented programming to refer to the capability for different classes of objects to respond to exactly the same protocols [26, 14, 31, 29].

The object-oriented paradigm appears to be an appropriate choice for designing a global knowledge base which will integrate a variety of distributed, heterogeneous knowledge bases. The object-oriented approach does not favor any particular "knowledge paradigm" such as logic, frames, semantic nets, or productions systems. Therefore, the object-oriented approach may be used to provide not only external views, but also internal representation of the knowledge base so that specialized interpreters can be used for reasoning about the knowledge [34].

DSS for Strategic Planning. Various approaches have been described for developing information systems to support the strategic planning domain. Goul, et al [13] describes a knowledge-based Decision Support System (DSS) that guides, instructs, and provides reasoning to identify strategic opportunities, problems, and crises. The authors examined the effects of using a knowledge-based DSS on performance in the "problem-finding" or initial stage of the strategic planning process. Applegate, et al [1] describes the requirements for knowledge management in organizational planning, and presents a knowledge-based planning system that has been implemented within a Group Decision Support Systems (GDSS) environment. McIntyre, et al [22] describes knowledge-based techniques using Semantic Inheritance Nets for view integration and for providing a flexible, dynamic, automated model of the Information Systems (IS) planning environment. A frame-based system is described by Carlson and McIntyre [2] to enhance modeling and inferencing in certain strategic planning tasks, and a strategic planning process is described for identifying organizational needs in order to increase the organization's effectiveness.

3 Architecture for Distributed Knowledge-Based Systems

This section describes the architectural design for the overall Distributed Knowledge-Based System and for the Distributed Knowledge Base Management System which integrates the network of independent Knowledge-Based Systems.

3.1 A Distributed Knowledge-Based System

A Distributed Knowledge-Based System consists of several Knowledge-Based Systems that may be logically or physically distinct from one another. The Knowledge-Based Systems (KBS) are integrated and managed by a single Distributed Knowledge Base Management System (DKBMS), as depicted in Figure 1. Each KBS consists of an inference engine, one or more knowledge base(s), database(s), and user interface(s). A Knowledge Base Management System (KBMS) provides a mechanism and a syntax to define and access the knowledge bases and databases. The databases may also be accessed directly by interfacing with a Database Management System (DBMS), or with a Distributed Database Management System (DDBMS). Each

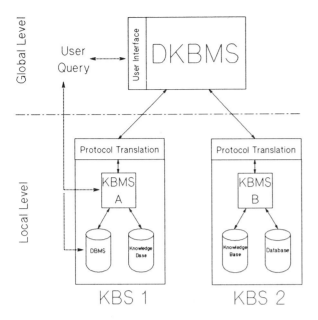

Figure 1: Distributed Knowledge-Based System Architecture

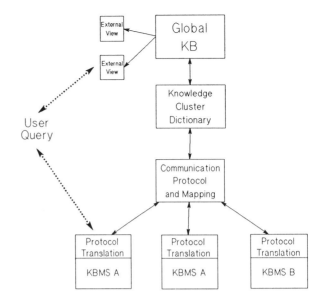

Figure 2: Distributed Knowledge Base Management System

KBS may be implemented using a different KBMS. Thus, the DKBMS must be capable of communicating in a heterogeneous system where queries and inference goals are translated between the representational languages used by the DKBMS and by each local KBMS.

Users may interact with the DKBMS or directly with any one of the local KBSs. In a direct query to a local KBS, if the local inferences require the use of other KBSs, communication must take place between the local KBMS and the DKBMS. The DKBMS passes messages to the relevant KBS(s), consolidates the results, and passes results back to the requesting KBMS. Inferences for queries issued directly to the DKBMS are decomposed into inferences at one or more local KBSs, the results of which must be returned to the DKBMS for integration and formulation of a user response. Thus, the inferencing process can take advantage of parallelism, while minimizing communication between local and global levels of the architecture.

3.2 A Distributed Knowledge Base Management System

The DKBMS is composed of three components: the Global Knowledge Base (GKB), the Knowledge Cluster Dictionary, and the Communication Protocol (see Figure 2). The global knowledge base contains knowledge describing the overall system organization and meta-knowledge defining the scope of the knowledge managed by each individual KBS. The meta-knowledge would also resolve conflicts between local KBSs through heuristics and through authority relationships established within the KBS organization. User queries may be directed at either the DKBMS, or at a specific local KBS. When a user submits a goal to the DKBMS, the global knowledge base will use the Knowledge Cluster Dictionary to determine which, if any, local knowledge bases contain the knowledge required to address the goal that was stated in the query. Several local KBSs may be solicited by the GKB in order to complete a single query. The GKB should contain the meta-knowledge necessary to select the local KBSs which are most likely to resolve the user's goal. Absolute delineation of a knowledge base's capabilities is still an active field of research. Thus, the GKB must be designed to maximize resolution

of its goals by local knowledge bases through a careful design of the GKB meta-knowledge.

External views of the GKB may be defined to facilitate or to control user queries. The actual external view definition will be determined by the particular knowledge representation paradigm selected for implementing the GKB. Our prototype system uses frames to segment the inference processes within the GKB. An external view may be limited to one or more of these knowledge frames. Defining several external views would allow knowledge to be segmented for different categories of users, e.g., confidentiality of specific goals for a business plan.

The second tier of the architecture defines a Knowledge Cluster Dictionary which groups the GKB subgoals into logically related clusters, which we will refer to as *knowledge clusters*. The GKB subgoals are the most detailed goals resolved from the initial user goal and the GKB meta-knowledge. The knowledge clusters are defined as part of the design of a particular DKBS application. The Knowledge Cluster Dictionary is composed of two parts: assignment of the GKB subgoals to a particular knowledge cluster, and assignment of each knowledge cluster to one or more local KBSs. By assigning a knowledge cluster to a local KBS, the cluster subgoals are also implicitly assigned to that KBS. Therefore, the KBS is expected to contain the knowledge needed to resolve those subgoals. The architecture accommodates redundant knowledge among the individual sites by allocating a knowledge cluster to multiple sites.

The third tier of this DKBMS architecture consists of the communication link between the DKBMS and the local KBSs. The local KBSs will communicate with the DKBMS via a standard message protocol, and the local sites will use the DKBMS as a liaison to either instruct or query other local KBSs. Depending on the message sent by the initiating local site, a specific node may be requested as the message target, or the GKB may use its organizational knowledge to select zero, one, or many sites as targets. Zero sites would be selected when the GKB meta-knowledge is unable to identify a local KBS capable of resolving the original goal.

Heterogeneous knowledge representations will be supported at

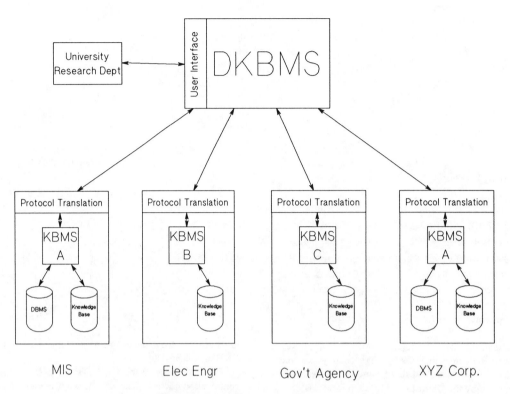

Figure 3: A DKBS for Research Planning

the local KBSs by providing a common communication protocol and argument mapping function between the GKB representation and each local KBS representation. Inherent in the communication protocol is a mapping algorithm which translates message terms between languages. For example, if the local KBS is located in Japan and the DKBMS is located in the U.S.A., then Yen must be translated to US Dollars, meters to feet, etc.

A significant benefit provided by this three tier architecture is that a logical separation is achieved between the DKBMS and the local KBSs. If the KBSs are added or deleted from the network, subdivided, or extended within the original application domain, then only the Knowledge Cluster Dictionary must be modified; the GKB is unaffected. Conversely, if the GKB meta-knowledge is reorganized, then the subgoals may need to be reassigned to knowledge clusters in the Knowledge Cluster Dictionary, but the KBSs are isolated from the changes.

The conceptual design of this architecture may be implemented with any knowledge representation paradigm; the actual representation selected for a particular application should be determined by the specific information requirements. For example, the Knowledge Cluster Dictionary may be implemented by either an object-oriented data structure, or by an external relational database. The next section discusses the design proposed for our prototype system.

4   A DKBS for Planning Research Projects

We now present an application domain which would benefit from a distributed knowledge-based system, and propose an object-oriented prototype design.

4.1   A Research Planning Domain

Most research personnel, especially those in a managerial role, devote considerable effort to managing a portfolio of research projects. Of these management tasks, planning future research projects and coordinating these projects with other organizations presents the most difficult information management problem. Most plans, whether for research or strategic business planning, must integrate the resources and requirements of numerous organizational units. The individual plans of these autonomous units must be linked between hierarchical levels, across departments and functional areas, and among outside organizations.

Consider a DKBS to support research planning at a university. This environment might have four local KBSs: Management Information Systems department, Electrical Engineering department, a government funding agency, and a private corporation (see Figure 3). An administrative Research Planning department has the charter to plan and coordinate university-wide research. This research planning department does not maintain its own KBS, however, it accesses the four local KBSs through the DKBMS interface.

Typical planning tasks would include:

- Establishing goals for the direction of research projects

- Establishing goals for total research funding in an organization

- Reviewing progress toward established goals

- Searching for sources of funding for new or continuing projects

- Submitting funding proposals

- Coordinating several independent, but related, projects

Goal 1: Develop a research plan for the next five years.

Goal 2: Plan new faculty recruiting efforts to match research objectives.

Goal 3: Plan computer facility requirements needed to support research plans.

Table 1: Goals resolvable by an individual KBS

Goal 1: Establish a joint center for collaborative research with industry.

Goal 2: Prepare a research grant proposal for a government agency to support a multi-department project.

Goal 3: Establish a task force to design a campus-wide computer network.

Table 2: Goals requiring input from multiple KBSs

- Investigating prior and current research in related areas

- Reviewing the progress on research projects

This planning problem provides an interesting domain for showing the feasibility of our research, in several respects. First, the problem is inherently distributed; the planning entities are logically and geographically dispersed. Second, the planning agents are semi-autonomous. Third, atomic data are not an adequate representation for modeling the interaction of the planning agents, thus knowledge-based paradigms are required. Fourth, the representational requirements of the individual agents are not uniform. The agents vary in size, complexity, deterministic characteristics, and stability, hence, heterogeneity is desirable at the site-level of the model. Finally, coordination and coherence of the global system is desirable. Therefore, these distributed, semi-autonomous, intelligent, heterogeneous planning entities must cooperate to produce a coherent plan and to resolve conflict.

The DKBS may be faced with two categories of goals: those which can be resolved by any one local KBS without input from outside sources, and those goals which require either knowledge-based and/or data-based input from other KBSs. Table 1 displays a set of possible goals falling into the first category and Table 2 displays several goals requiring input from multiple KBSs. The goals in Table 2 may not be resolved by a single KBS because it has insufficient knowledge resources, there exist potential conflicts with other KBSs, or both. These two categories of goals will be addressed again in our discussion of DKBMS and KBS integration in section 4.4.

We present an object-oriented design for modeling the above planning requirements and describe the knowledge-based support that such a model might contain.

4.2 An Object-Oriented Design for a Local KBS

This model will not attempt to represent all features that are required to effectively support research planning activities. Rather, this model describes the primary classes in the object-oriented design in order to demonstrate the feasibility and value of the DKBS architecture.

The model design specifications must be formalized in terms of an object-oriented classification structure. The object-oriented paradigm consists of two primary components: message-passing and specialization. An *object* is defined as an instance of a *class*, and the

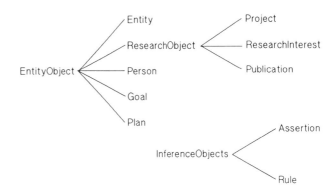

Figure 4: Object Classes for Planning Research Projects

class itself may be a subclass within a larger classification hierarchy. Each class defines its own *instance variables* and *methods* (a method is essentially a procedure which is activated by a message sent to an object), and both variables and methods may be *inherited* from higher levels of the class hierarchy. An object is a specific instance of a class, and the object encapsulates all variables and methods defined (local or inherited) for that class.

The primary classes in our prototype KBS are shown in Figure 4. Each planning entity is represented in one instance of the Entity class. This object stores pointers to all other objects required to represent the activities and plans of the single entity. An instance of the Person object is created for every member of the entity staff, and these pointers to Person objects are stored as a collection in the 'staff' instance variable of the Entity object. Figure 5 displays these object relationships, among others.

Figure 5 shows a Person object being referenced by two other objects: Entity and Project. Since the Person object encapsulates all relevant knowledge about a single person, any other object which references Person will also have access to that Person object's characteristics through its methods. These other objects would access Person's methods by sending a message to the Person object.

The Person object maintains pointers to two other classes of objects: Assertion and Rule. These objects are used to model the opinions and heuristics held by a particular individual, and these additional objects may also be available for inspection by Entity and Project to determine the knowledge-based behavior of that person. Thus, the object-oriented representation effectively models the entity's components and the knowledge-based behavior of selected components.

Although we described an object-oriented representation for the local KBS in this paper, our proposed DKBS architecture supports any appropriate knowledge base or database implementation. This knowledge representation does *not* attempt to create a system which produces "The Plan," but rather, the knowledge base will store rules and relationships which assist the plan developer in evaluating his plan's coherence with all relevant plans in the distributed system.

4.3 An Object-Oriented DKBMS Design

An object-oriented design approach was selected for our prototype DKBMS implementation. Object-oriented programming (OOP) provides an intuitively appealing environment for modeling the objects and the communication between objects in a distributed system. OOP provides a natural approach for frame-based representation in the GKB design, supports heterogeneous knowledge rep-

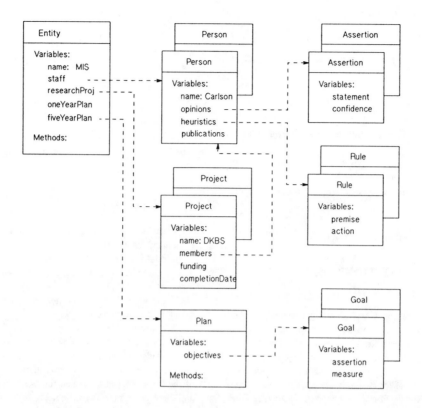

Figure 5: Example of objects for Research Planning

resentations in the local knowledge bases, and facilitates a message passing paradigm for the communication protocol which connects the components of the DKBMS architecture.

The primary classes for our DKBMS design are shown in Figure 6. Single instances of the GKB and the DKBMS classes are created to manage all objects associated with the DKBMS architecture. Similarly, single instances of the ClusterDict and LanguageDict classes are created to manage the Knowledge Cluster Dictionary and the Language Mapping Dictionary, respectively. The Frame objects are created as required to define the meta-knowledge within the GKB; the Slot class is instantiated to define the slots within each Frame object. The Cluster class describes the contents of each knowledge cluster, which is used to group subgoals within the Knowledge Cluster Dictionary. Note that the Dictionary class is provided as a standard library class within the OOP environment. Finally, the InferenceObjects subclasses, Assertion and Rule, are instantiated to describe the meta-knowledge that is stored in the slots of the GKB frames. These frames are stored in an instance variable of the GKB object [2].

A brief example of the DKBMS objects are depicted in Figure 7. The frames are used in the GKB object to organize and focus the planning meta-knowledge for the GKB inferSubGoal method. In the example shown, the knowledge associated with "Proposals" is organized within one frame. The meta-knowledge stored within the slots of this frame will derive one or more subgoals during the inference processing. These subgoals are collected, as part of the knowledge engineering process, into knowledge clusters. The granularity of these clusters relative to the frame subgoals is subject to the judgment of the knowledge engineer. The relationship between the clusters and the subgoals is stored within the Cluster objects, and

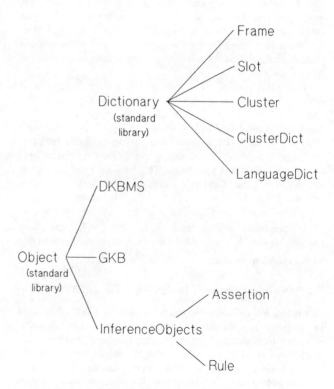

Figure 6: DKBMS Object-Oriented Class Structure

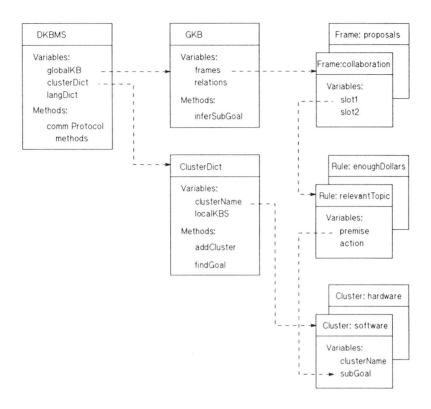

Figure 7: Example of DKBMS Objects

the Cluster objects are assigned to specific KBSs in the ClusterDict object. The LanguageDict object is used in the mapping module of the DKBMS architecture to translate the communication protocol arguments from one language to another.

Each local KBS will represent its knowledge using an appropriate paradigm, however, the local KBMSs must provide some mechanism to send and receive messages conforming to the standard protocol. We propose that the C++ language be used to implement a uniform network interface control program. The C++ language was selected for its support of object-oriented programming and for its portability across incompatible computing platforms [27, 28, 30]. The local KBMSs would customize the network interface program at their individual sites to issue system calls to their respective knowledge bases and databases. Thus, any knowledge representation paradigm, commercial or customized, can be accommodated at the local sites. Standard interfaces would be supplied for common commercial knowledge-based development tools.

4.4 Integrating the DKBMS and KBS

Refer again to the research planning goals that are listed in Tables 1 and 2. In a distributed system, the goals in Table 1 would describe possible subgoals in the DKBMS that would be delegated by metarules to one or more KBSs. Each of these subgoals would be assigned to a knowledge cluster and that knowledge cluster would be assigned to the KBS(s) which are able to resolve goals in a similar domain. The goals listed in Table 2 describe goals that would be directed at the DKBMS, which would send the necessary subgoals to one or more local KBSs.

A dialogue using the standard communication protocol may occur between the DKBMS and one or more KBSs in order to resolve a goal. For example, if Goal 1 of Table 2 were presented to the DKBMS, then the following subgoals, via appropriate protocol messages, might be sent:

1. Human operator inputs goal of total research support dollars.

2. DKBMS identifies potential participants from industry and university departments.

3. DKBMS sends a message to KBSs in XYZ Corp and Government Agency requesting research interests and dollar support available.

4. DKBMS sends a message to KBSs in MIS and EE departments requesting research topics and desired grant dollar amount.

5. DKBMS matches MIS and EE topics with the interests returned from the funding sources, and totals the potential research dollar support.

6. Iterate over this dialogue process until the financial objectives stated in step 1 are satisfied, asking the KBSs for secondary choices.

5 Research Issues

Our DKBS architecture requires the integration of knowledge bases and databases, however, discussion in the previous sections has primarily focused on the knowledge-based component. Knowledge distribution presents the most difficult unresolved problem requiring solution prior to implementing a successful prototype of this architecture. We have referred to a Knowledge Base Management System, or KBMS, which controls the integration of data and knowledge at each individual knowledge-based system (KBS) site. Research into the KBMS functionality is currently being addressed by others [9, 16, 17, 21, 33]. Our architecture allows the database at a KBS site to be accessed directly through an existing DBMS, however, when data is required by a distributed knowledge-based application, the database will be accessed through the KBMS at each local site. Thus, if the DKBMS requires data-based information while resolving a global goal, it would utilize the communications protocol to send a message to the local KBMS responsible for the required data. If the data were also distributed, then the KBMS would communicate with a DDBMS to retrieve the data.

The proposed DKBS architecture leaves several issues for further research. Although we have presented an object-oriented definition for the global knowledge base, this choice does not eliminate alternative forms of representation. The most appropriate representation will likely depend upon the application domain requirements; our future research will attempt to provide design heuristics for making this decision. The inference engine employed by the GKB deserves significant research attention to design and apply the meta-knowledge.

The appropriate determination of knowledge clusters, and allocation of local KBSs to those clusters, will also have a significant impact on the performance and flexibility of an application using this architecture.

An additional research issue is to determine the location of the DKBMS itself. The DKBMS may be located entirely at one site of the distributed network, duplicated at every network site, or selectively decomposed by distributing the DKBMS components. For example, the frames that were described in the last section to represent the GKB meta-knowledge could be split regionally or functionally between several KBS sites.

Several data communications issues require investigation for the DKBS architecture. A policy must be defined for acknowledging the communication protocol messages sent between the KBMS and all KBSs. A related issue is the system response time required to resolve global goals; communication between sites must be minimized for real-time applications of the DKBS architecture. The DKBS must maximize reliability of the overall system by ensuring that the global knowledge base is always available to the network.

6 Conclusions

We believe that this Distributed Knowledge-Based System architecture can improve the effectiveness of information management by facilitating the design of information systems which support a distributed group of semi-autonomous decision makers. This group decision process requires a network of databases and knowledge bases with coordinated communication among them. Cooperative action needs to be stressed, especially in situations where the decision makers have conflicting subgoals. Performance of the integrated information system may be enhanced by allowing parallel processing of sub-tasks by individual knowledge-based systems. When cooperative decisions are required, each knowledge-based system must have access to multiple external sources of data and knowledge.

Our research synthesizes the work from several related areas, including distributed database systems, distributed problem solving, and object-oriented design. Previous work in Knowledge Base Management Systems has focused on integrating knowledge and data at a single site. This integration is necessary for the architecture that we have described, however, many business applications require data and knowledge to be integrated from logically and geographically distributed sites. Each local site has a set of objectives implicitly incorporated into its individual knowledge-based system, but the independent sites must cooperate to produce a coherent plan which

maximizes the global objectives.

The DKBS architecture specifically supports sharing and integrating knowledge and data within the global system and allows heterogeneous knowledge-based systems to communicate through the DKBMS via a standard protocol. Generic queries, from users with system-wide goals or users having no knowledge of the network organization, will be processed by the DKBMS. The DKBMS itself may be centralized at a single node, or distributed on a few or all nodes. Thus, the DKBS architecture can be implemented with various degrees of centralization or decentralization. Partial centralization of control is desirable in many business applications to facilitate maintenance within a dynamic network structure.

A prototype DKBS for research planning is being developed to demonstrate the feasibility of the DKBS architecture functionality and to resolve or refine the research issues described above. Through this prototype, we will define the communication protocol required to minimize network communications overhead. DKBMS distribution policies will also be explored to evaluate multiple degrees of centralization. Our eventual research goal is to provide recommendations for using the DKBS architecture in a wide variety of business application domains.

7 References

1. Lynda M. Applegate, Tsung Teng Chen, Benn R. Konsynski, Jay F. Nunamaker, Jr., "Knowledge Management in Organizational Planning," *Journal of Management Information Systems*, 3, 4 (Spring 1987), pp 20-38.

2. David A. Carlson, Scott C. McIntyre, "Frame-Based Modeling Techniques for Analyzing a Strategic Planning Domain," *Proc. of the Twenty-First Hawaii International Conference on System Sciences*, Jan 1988.

3. S. Ceri, G. Pelagatti, *Distributed Databases Principles and Systems.* McGraw-Hill, 1984.

4. Daniel D. Corkill, Victor R. Lesser, "The Use of Meta-Level Control for Coordination in a Distributed Problem Solving Network," *Proceedings of the Eighth International Joint Conference on Artificial Intelligence*, pp. 748-756 , 1987.

5. Edmund H. Durfee, Victor R. Lesser, Daniel D. Corkill, "Increasing Coherence in a Distributed Problem Solving Network," *Proceedings of the Ninth International Joint Conference on Artificial Intelligence*, pp. 1025-1030, 1985.

6. E. Durfee, V. Lesser, D Corkill, "Cooperation Through Communication in a Distributed Problem Solving Network," in *Distributed Artificial Intelligence (M. Huhns, ed).* Pitman, 1987.

7. Edmund H. Durfee, Victor R. Lesser, "Using Partial Global Plans to Coordinate Distributed Problem Solvers," *Proceedings of the Tenth International Joint Conference on Artificial Intelligence*, pp. 875-883, 1987.

8. Edmund H. Durfee, Victor R. Lesser, "Planning Coordinated Actions in Dynamic Domains," Technical Report 87-130, Department of Computer and Information Science, University of Massachusetts, Amherst, Mass. 01003, December 1987.

9. Mark Fox, John McDermott, "The Role of Databases in Knowledge-Based Systems," Chapter 28 of *On Knowledge Base Management Systems: Integrating Artificial Intelligence and Database Technologies (Brodie, Mylopoulos, and Schmidt, eds.).* Springer-Verlag, June 1986.

10. L. Gasser, C. Braganza, N. Herman, "MACE: A Flexible Testbed for Distributed AI Research," in *Distributed Artificial Intelligence (M. Huhns, ed).* Pitman, 1987.

11. L. Gasser, C. Braganza, N. Herman, "Implementing Distributed AI Systems Using MACE," *Proc. IEEE Third Conference on AI Applications*, February 1987.

12. Les Gasser, "Report on the 1985 Workshop on Distributed AI," *AI Magazine* 8(2), Summer 1987, pp. 91-97.

13. Michael Goul, Barry Shane, Fred Tonge, "Using Knowledge-Based Decision Support Systems in Strategic Planning Decisions: An Empirical Study," *Journal of Management Information Systems*, 2, 4 (Spring 1986), pp 70-84.

14. Daniel C. Halbert, Patrick D. O'Brien, "Using Types and Inheritance in Object-Oriented Programming," *IEEE Software*, September 1987, pp. 71-79.

15. Ching-Chi Hsu, Shao-Ming Wu, Jan-Jan Wu, "A Distributed Approach for Inferring Production Systems," *Proceedings of the Tenth International Joint Conference on Artificial Intelligence*, pp. 62-67, 1987.

16. Charles Kellogg, "From Data Management to Knowledge Management," *IEEE Computer*, January 1986, pp. 75-84.

17. Expert Database Systems, *Proc from the First International Workshop (Larry Kerschberg ed.)*. Benjamin/Cummings, 1986.

18. Victor R. Lesser, Daniel D. Corkill, "The Distributed Vehicle Monitoring Testbed: A Tool for Investigating Distributed Problem Solving Networks," *AI Magazine*, 4(3), Fall 1983, pp. 15-33.

19. Victor R. Lesser, Daniel D. Corkill, Edmund H. Durfee, "An Update on the Distributed Vehicle Monitoring Testbed," Technical Report 87-111, Department of Computer and Information Science, University of Massachusetts, Amherst, Mass. 01003, 1987.

20. Witold Litwin, Abdelaziz Abdellatif, "Multidatabase Interoperability," *IEEE Computer*, December 1986, pp. 10-18.

21. Frank Manola, Michael Brodie, "On Knowledge-Based System Architectures," Chapter 8 of *On Knowledge Base Management Systems: Integrating Artificial Intelligence and Database Technologies (Brodie, Mylopoulos, and Schmidt, eds.)*. Springer-Verlag, June 1986.

22. Scott C. McIntyre, Benn R. Konsynski, Jay F. Nunamaker, Jr., "Automating Planning Environments: Knowledge Integration and Model Scripting," *Journal of Management Information Systems*, 2, 4 (Spring 1986), pp 49-69.

23. Sudha Ram, Clark L. Chastain, "Distributed Database Management Systems: An Architectural Survey," forthcoming in *Journal of Systems and Software*, 1988.

24. Reid G. Smith, "Report on the 1984 Distributed Artificial Intelligence Workshop," *AI Magazine* 6(3), Fall 1985, pp. 234-243.

25. N.S. Sridharan, "Report on the 1986 Workshop on Distributed AI", *AI Magazine* 8(3), Fall 1987, pp. 75-85.

26. Mark Stefik, Daniel G. Bobrow, "Object-Oriented Programming: Themes and Variations," *AI Magazine*, 6(4), Winter 85, pp. 40-62.

27. Bjarne Stroustrup, *The C++ Programming Language*. Addison-Wesley, 1986.

28. Bjarne Stroustrup, "An Overview of C++," *SIGPLAN Notices*, Vol 21, No 10, October 1986, pp. 7-18.

29. Bjarne Stroustrup, "What is "Object-Oriented Programming"?", *Proc of ECOOP*, Paris, June 1987, pp. 51-70.

30. Bjarne Stroustrup, "Design Issues in C++," *SIGPLAN Notices*, Vol 23, No 1, January 1988, pp. 33-37.

31. Peter Wegner, "Perspectives on Object-Oriented Programming," Brown University, Dept of Computer Science, Technical Report No. CS-86-25, December 1986.

32. Gio Wiederhold, "Knowledge Versus Data," Chapter 7 of *On Knowledge Base Management Systems: Integrating Artificial Intelligence and Database Technologies (Brodie, Mylopoulos, and Schmidt, eds.)*. Springer-Verlag, June 1986.

33. Gio Wiederhold, Jack Milton, "A Precis of Research on Knowledge-based Management Systems," Department of Computer Science, Stanford University, Stanford, California 94305, June 1987.

34. Carlo Zaniolo, et al, "Object Oriented Database Systems and Knowledge Systems," in *Expert Database Systems, (Kerschberg ed.)*. Benjamin/Cummings, 1986.

Object–Oriented Databases for Construction Data

Geneva G. Belford
Department of Computer Science
University of Illinois at Urbana–Champaign
1304 W. Springfield Ave, Urbana, IL 61801
(217) 333–6684; belford@m.cs.uiuc.edu

Anthony L. Santone
AT&T Data Systems Group
Rm. 4–316, 190 River Road
Summit, N.J. 07901
(201) 552–6508; ihnp4!attunix!tls

ABSTRACT

Like manufacturing (but lagging behind), the construction industry is moving towards "high–tech" and computerization. Database management systems must be designed that are able to support the various aspects of the construction process. Study of the requirements for such a database system has led us to the conclusion (suggested earlier by construction researchers but little pursued) that the most appropriate "abstract data model" for construction data is that of "object–oriented" data. To better study the appropriateness of this model for construction data, we have developed the specific example of a simple building with components specified as a hierarchy of object classes. This example shows the importance of the concepts of inheritance, aggregation, and generalization in modeling construction data.

1. INTRODUCTION

Like manufacturing (but lagging behind), the construction industry is moving towards "high–tech" and computerization. Database management systems must be designed that are able to support the construction process. A construction database must provide both horizontal and vertical integration of construction activity — horizontal meaning the support of multiple users (not only humans, but also devices such as robots and vision systems) that access the data for various purposes at the same time, and vertical meaning the support of the successive phases of a construction project over time, from the original building design through planning and materials procurement and actual construction to the creation of as–built drawings and building maintenance.

Manipulating the large volumes of data involved strains the capacity of currently existing database management systems. There are also obvious difficulties in capturing and expressing the complex relationships that exist between the data items.

Study of the requirements for such a database system has led us to the conclusion (suggested earlier by construction researchers [Ibb86] but little pursued) that the most appropriate "abstract data model" for construction data is both hierarchical and "object–oriented". Indeed, a convincing case for the superiority of object–oriented modeling of data for complex domains in general has recently been made by Blaha et al. [Bla88]. To quote from their comparison of their Object Modeling Technique with the entity–relationship (ER) model that is popularly used for ordinary database design:

"ER lacks a substructure for entities. It has no counterpart to generalization hierarchies. Generalization allows one to refine the structure of entities and add detail as needed. ER also lacks a substructure for relationships. Whereas ER only offers association, newer approaches support aggregation.... For large, complex problems ... ER lacks power."

To get a better understanding of how a hierarchical object model adapts to construction data, we have worked out the specific example of a fairly simple building with components specified as a hierarchy of object classes. The development of such a specific example demonstates more convincingly than pages of vague discussion the appropriateness of the object–oriented model for construction data. Furthermore, it has provided some valuable insights into how the concepts of inheritance, aggregation, and generalization apply to construction objects.

In the next section of this paper, we discuss the general requirements for a construction database. Section 3 then presents the example of a "building" as a hierarchy of object classes. Finally, in Section 4 we draw some conclusions from this very preliminary study and point out some of the major problems that are yet to be solved.

2. REQUIREMENTS

It is well documented that "off–the–shelf" database management systems have been developed with business applications in mind, and "fall far short of supporting" even such relatively simple engineering applications as VLSI CAD [Bat85].

To support the design and construction of even a

small–sized building with all its various details, the traditional database management system is expected to be even more inappropriate. To examine the requirements of such a system, we look first at the types of data to be stored, then at some of the usages of and necessary interfaces to those data, and finally draw some conclusions.

The types of data that must be stored are many and varied. As a first approximation the list includes:

(1) Building plans: blueprints, site data (elevations, soils, preparation required, etc.), lists of materials (analogous to the "bill of materials" familiar in the manufacturing application) and their specifications, etc.

(2) Operational descriptions of the construction process: e.g., steps in building the foundation, siting and linkages of utility lines, inspections to be carried out (and their results).

(3) Construction schedule – initial and as modified during construction.

(4) Machinery and tools (descriptions, as well as individual identifiers for large items such as cranes and earth movers) involved in the construction process. (These data would be helpful for purposes of tracking equipment utilization during construction; also to track whether equipment is on–site when needed.)

(5) Workmen – who should be (and is) on–site doing what, when.

(6) Temporal data on construction progress.

Examining this list in the context of the need for "vertical integration" (that is, over time) of the construction process, we see that data included under "building plans" are mainly (or at least initially) those generated by the architects who design the building. The architects may also provide some high–level plans for the construction process and a preliminary schedule, but both plans and schedule must be later filled in to a finer and finer level of detail by contractor and subcontractors. Some of this detail may be provided automatically by a sufficiently sophisticated Computer–Aided–Construction (CAC) system. For example, a standard "plan" detailing the steps involved in the construction of a poured concrete foundation might be stored in a large CAC support database and linked when needed into the overall plan for a particular building that includes such a foundation.

It is the contractor and the various subcontractors who contribute to the project at different times during the various phases of the construction who will be responsible for the entering of data on materials,

machinery, tools, workmen, etc., as the work progresses. Tracking progress on a day-by-day basis –– and storing this information in the database as "temporal data" –– will allow both immediate and after–the–fact analyses of problems such as schedule slippages and cost overruns. Indeed, such problems may possibly be avoided or their impact minimized if timely data analysis identifies potential trouble early enough.

A database providing vertically integrated data should support a construction project through to the maintenance stage — if not through ultimate demolition. As is well known, the original blueprints are seldom adequate for maintenance. Changes, sometimes large, in the positioning of wiring, pipes, utility lines, even of doors or windows, occur during the normal course of construction. The usual procedure for projects of any size is for "as–built" drawings to be prepared, often at great effort and cost, after a building is complete. We envision the tracking of construction progress also to include monitoring exactly where wiring, utility lines, etc.,. are actually placed, so that the original "blueprints", stored on line, are being continually updated. Then the "as–built" drawings may be generated "at the touch of a button" when the building is complete.

If a database management system is to be truly useful in any application environment, much thought must go into how it will be used – and, in particular, how it will be interfaced to the outside world. Again as a first approximation, input to a construction database might be *via* (in addition to terminals that may be located on–site as well as "in the office"):

(1) Bar–code readers to more easily and reliably input data on arriving materials and possibly also to note when they are picked up off the heap for use. Again, this is similar to the manufacturing application, in which bar-codes are used to automatically control inventory of "parts" and product. In addition, equipment, tools, workmen –– all could potentially be barcoded for automatic tracking.

(2) Vision systems, perhaps on movable tracks or linked to robots, that may be monitoring construction progress, aiding in the control of automatic operations (e.g., spray painting) or carrying out inspections. Such a vision system would be helpful, if not critical, to the data collection required for later automatic preparation of as–built drawings, as discussed above.

(3) Other sensory systems – e.g., one that measures pressure on robot arms, again in the context of facilitating automated construction.

Output should include the normal facilities to generate reports and respond to on–line queries. In addition, there should be a two–way interface to a CAD system. This would allow for easy, on–line preparation of drawings and modification of blueprints, etc., as well as permitting query responses in graphical form.

Interfacing between the data system and vision systems or robots must also be two–way in order to implement automatic operations. That is, we visualize a system in which a database contains building blueprints and construction plans to as great a level of detail as is necessary for some operations to be carried out by robots. A working robot would then get its instructions from the database as well as feeding back needed sensory control data.

Design of a database management system (DBMS) (as opposed to design of a database structure) means designing the software to store, access, and manipulate the data. A critical aspect of this is the design of the operations needed to store, access, and manipulate data in the structure supported by the system. The operations must also be designed with the applications in mind. In our case this involves looking ahead towards the interfacing required, as discussed above, as well as analyzing usage needs in general. The problem of determining the operation set of an object–oriented DBMS to support automated construction is nontrivial and is yet to be addressed.

Another aspect of DBMS design involves tackling the problem of maintaining the consistency and integrity of data. Traditional mechanisms include data locks, strictly–enforced transaction concurrency control (to prevent updates from interfering with one another), and ad hoc integrity–checking processes. It appears highly likely that somewhat different mechanisms will be appropriate for a construction database, particularly if it is implemented as a hierarchy of objects. Integrity rules might be built into the object classes (e.g., object "door" may include the fact that doors must be dimensioned so they fit into the associated door frames), or separate "constraint objects" may appear in the hierarchy to define constraints. In a parallel project, we have been examining such alternatives for constraint specification and checking in this context [Mur88].

It should be clear from this brief discussion of the requirements for a database to support the construction process — especially when automated to some extent through the use of robots or automatic tracking of materials, tools, progress, etc. — that something other than the standard business–oriented DBMS will be necessary. But before launching into a full–scale project to design an object–oriented database management system with all the features needed to meet the requirements described above, it seemed prudent to see how well the "object" concept provides the structure for construction data. To this end, we worked out an example of a simple building as a hierarchy of object classes. The major features of this example are presented in the next section. More detail may be found in [San88].

3. A BUILDING AS A HIERARCHY OF OBJECT CLASSES

3.1. Review of Concepts.

Object–oriented techniques provide for data abstraction; layers of abstraction may be used to develop a hierarchy of data. The "top" layer represents the most general view of the data. Moving down the hierarchy reveals progressively more complex views of the data. Such a data model offers information with the correct level of detail for users of differing needs [Smi77].

Two forms of abstraction useful in building such hierarchies have been defined: *aggregation* and *generalization* [Smi77, Spo86]. These two forms of abstraction define the relationship between data objects at successive levels in the hierarchy.

When a collection of related objects combine to form a higher level object, an "aggregation abstraction" exists between the higher level object and the collection of related data objects. In simpler terms, the whole (here, the higher level object) is the sum (aggregate) of its parts (here, the related data objects). In general, a building is an aggregation of many subsystems: foundation, walls, plumbing, electrical subsystem, etc.

"Generalization" refers to a mode of abstraction in which a set of similar objects is regarded as a generic object [Smi77]. The generic object includes the common characteristics of the whole group of similar objects. The similar objects can then be referred to in a *generic* manner through the higher level object. For example, doors of various sizes, materials, manufacturer, etc., can each be referred to generically as a *door*.

Combining aggregation and generalization produces data abstraction hierarchies. A well–structured information model evolves from successive abstraction applications. Information content at each level of the hierarchy is controllable by carefully choosing which abstraction method to apply in moving between layers. Regardless of whether abstraction or generalization is applied, each successive level in the hierarchy will contain a more specific view of the system data than the preceding level.

A hierarchy may also be thought of as defining a relationship between "parent" data objects and their "descendants." The descendant objects are more specific instances of their parent objects and share characteristics of their parents. Descendants are said to *inherit* the characteristics of their parents. In general the term *inheritance* describes the sharing of information between adjacent levels of the abstraction hierarchy. The type of inheritance permitted determines the style of the hierarchy, and how the hierarchy can be developed. Subclassing inheritance was used in developing the example for this paper.

The most general form of inheritance, however, is multiple inheritance. When multiple inheritance is used, objects may participate in one or more upward abstractions; that is, an object may be part of a set of objects that is generalized by a more generic object *and* the object may also be part of a collection of related objects that are aggregated to a higher level object. In this case, the hierarchy may resemble a lattice, in which an object descends from one or more parents. Although this technique allows a great amount of information sharing, it presents implementation difficulties. A given object can potentially share characteristics with every object above it in the hierarchy. As a result, every node above the given object may need to be visited to determine a characteristic that the object has inherited.

Subclassing inheritance is a more specialized form of inheritance. Subclassing is strictly hierarchical [Gol83]. In a subclassing model, each object descends from a single parent. A hierarchy developed using a subclassing model resembles a tree structure. The most general level of information is available at the root of the tree, and the most specific information is contained in the leaf nodes of the structure. Although several child nodes may descend from a single parent node, each node in the tree descends from only *one* parent node. The single means of inheritance — from no more than one parent — provides a simpler search space for locating inherited characteristics.

3.2. The Building Model — An Overview.

For a given modeling problem, a data model can be constructed using the abstraction techniques and the inheritance property outlined in the previous section. We here present such a model for the inside of a single or multistory structure.

As with most modeling problems, the data model can be constructed in a variety of ways. The approach chosen should reflect the needs of the users of the data. Data important to the users should be modeled, while that data which is not required can be omitted. Objects visible inside a building are considered required data in this model. These objects include doors, windows, ceiling fixtures and wall sockets. The motivation for this choice of level of detail was provided by a potential application to automatic spray painting. With additional levels of abstraction and more object classes, one should be able to describe the internal structure to as fine a level of detail as is necessary. The model could be expanded to define the external structure as well.

The construction domain appears to be well suited to these modeling techniques. Indeed, we found it extremely unnatural to attempt to use any technique (such as ER) that does not include generalization and aggregation to model a construction project. A structure is a natural aggregation of the substructures and materials it is constructed from. Generalization arose in that we found it very convenient to create the superclass "Volume" to encompass such functionally different objects as rooms and stairways.

The complete *Building* data model is shown in Figure 1. The notation used in this figure is consistent with that used in [Spo86]. The lines connecting nodes in the graph represent applications of data abstraction. The labels attached to these lines indicate the abstraction technique used. The label **G** indicates generalization, while the label **A** denotes an aggregation that includes exactly *one* of the specified component. The labels **A+** and **A*** indicate an aggregation involving *one or more* and *zero or more* instances of the component, respectively.

The remainder of this section contains a description of the model in breadth–first fashion.

Based on the requirements, the most general object to be represented in the system is a *Building*. As mentioned earlier, the structure may be single or multistory. A Building is defined as an aggregation of one or more stories.

A *Story* is defined as the set of rooms on the same level of a building. In most cases, the rooms on a story serve different functions and may have different characteristics based on these functions. One common characteristic of this set of rooms is that each room occupies a certain volume of space. We use the object class *Volume* to generalize all of the types of rooms that might be found on a story. From this definition, a story is an aggregation of *Volumes*. A *Volume* may also be thought of as a partitioned–off section of the story that it occupies. For simplicity, we assume that the rooms in a building divide functionally into only two groups; *Room*, and *LiftCorridor*. Thus, *Volume* generalizes the data objects *Room* and *LiftCorridor*.

Room describes those volumes that are bounded on all sides and contain floors and ceilings. Thus hallways are treated as rooms. The hallway shares partitions with the rooms that line it, as rooms share partitions with adjacent rooms. One side of a partition we decribe by the class *VericalArea*. A Room then is an aggregation of the following components: one *Floor*, one *Ceiling*, and one or more objects of the type *VerticalArea* (Figure 1b). These components define the boundaries of the Room.

A *LiftCorridor* is a volume the function of which is to provide for movement between stories. A lack of a

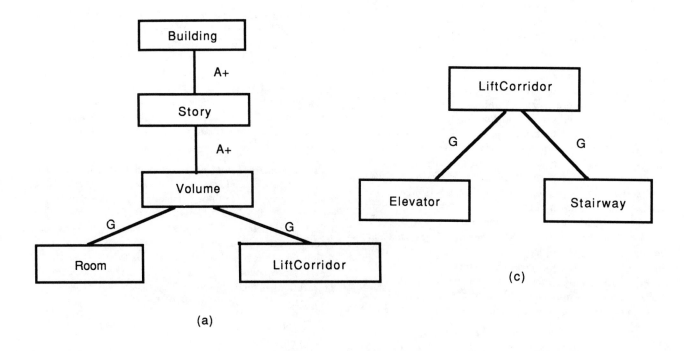

(a)

(c)

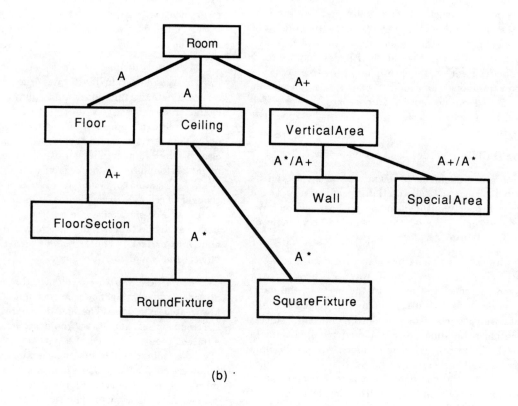

(b)

Figure 1. Building Data Model Hierarchy

Floor and Ceiling distinguishes this type of Volume from Room. Two types of these corridors are included in this model (Figure 1c). *LiftCorridor* realizes a generalization abstraction of *Elevator* and *Stairway*.

A *Floor* (Figure 1b) is a component of the *Room* class. A Floor is an aggregation of one or more instances of *FloorSection*. Modeling a floor as an aggregation of sub–sections permits the description of floors with different coverings; for example, a hall with a tiled entrance leading to a carpeted section.

Ceiling is also part of the *Room* aggregation. A Ceiling is itself an aggregation of the two types of ceiling fixtures defined in this model: *RoundFixture* and *SquareFixture*. A distinction is made between the two in order to handle the different computation methods required to compute the areas of the two fixture types.

Notice that an aggregation need not solely be the sum of its parts. Thus in describing a ceiling we may provide information on its surface material as the value of a variable associated with the ceiling instance, and only require "children" in order to specify ceiling fixtures. On the other hand, a Floor is defined to totally consist of a collection of FloorSections.

The *VerticalArea* is the final component in the *Room* aggregation. These objects partition stories into volumes. A *VerticalArea* is an aggregation of zero or more objects of type *Wall* and zero or more objects of type *SpecialArea*. (The alternatives indicated on the connector lines in Figure 1b indicate that there must be at least one Wall or SpecialArea included in a VerticalArea.) As with Floor, expressing VerticalArea as an aggregation of subsections permits the modeling of non–homogeneous vertical expanses; for example, a wall containing a window. Figure 2 shows how such a VerticalArea object would be decomposed into its homogeneous subsections.

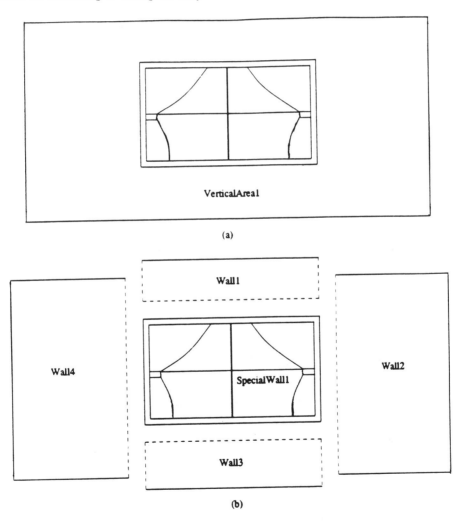

(a)

(b)

Figure 2. Decomposition of VerticalArea Object

Elevator is one child of the *LiftCorridor* generalization. No distinction is made for different types of elevator, although the model could expand to include such distinctions.

Stairway completes the LiftCorridor generalization. For this paper, a stairway is defined as a simple linear staircase. Circular stairways and stairways with intermediate landings appear to pose problems of definition that are beyond the scope of what we are attempting to do.

FloorSection represents a homogeneous section of floor. For simplicity, this model only treats regular rectangular areas of floor. A FloorSection identifies a section whose covering is of one type — tile, carpet, parquet or whatever.

Both *RoundFixture* and *SquareFixture* model objects such as heat duct openings and light fixtures that might found in the ceilings of rooms. The different shapes require different calculations to obtain their areas and boundaries. These differences necessitate the distinct data types. The precise function of a fixture was deemed to be unimportant in the context of our spray painting application; only its size and shape are of interest.

Wall represents a homogeneously covered section of vertical space inside a room. For simplicity, only rectangular areas will be considered. Note that the definition for this object refers to the space *inside* a room. The requirement that the data model be appropriate for supporting a spray painting application led to the specification that fixtures and structures visible inside a room should be describable. This specification implies that even though two Room objects may share some vertical expanse (i.e., the partition) that divides them, each must contain a reference to a Wall object that describes the vertical space visible from inside the room.

A *SpecialArea* defines a section of vertical area that provides functionality other than defining the boundaries of a volume. Examples of SpecialAreas include doors, windows, and electrical outlets. As in the case of ceiling fixtures, the only characteristics of interest are the dimensions of the area. Additional abstraction could expand the model to include details of the area's functionality.

3.3 Implementing the Building Hierarchy with Objects.

In the previous section, a data model for a construction database was proposed. This model used the data abstraction techniques of aggregation and generalization to describe a building as a hierarchy of data. The next step in making a convincing argument for the appropriateness of an object-oriented database for construction data is to define the data classes in an object-oriented implementation environment.

Numerous object-oriented environments are available for developing object-based systems. These "environments" range from programming languages that provide abstract data types, such as Simula and Ada, to complete programming environments that feature a graphical interface [Cox84]. A complete environment was chosen for this paper: Smalltalk-80.

Smalltalk-80 was chosen for several reasons. Smalltalk was the first substantial, interactive, display-based implementation of an object-oriented programming environment [Ste86]. This language, developed at the Xerox Palo Alto Research Center (PARC), is considered by many to represent the archetype of object-oriented programming [Ver87]. In using Smalltalk-80, the programmer works in a computational environment that contains only objects that the programmer creates [Cox84]. Smalltalk-80 also features an easy-to-read syntax that enables a clear presentation of the classes, objects and methods developed in this project.

Smalltalk-80 provides facilities for describing the two major aspects of the set of objects that comprise a system: the protocol description (to describe the protocols, or rules for and formats of messages passed between objects), and the implementation description (to describe the data structures and the methods, or procedures, for manipulating the data). In this paper, only the implementation description will be used, as it provides a sufficiently complete description of classes for our purposes here.

An implementation description of a class has three parts: class name, variable declarations, and method declarations. The class name section contains the names of the class and of the superclass. The superclass specifies the class's parent class in the class hierarchy. This information is necessary to support inheritance.

The variable declarations include both instance variables and class variables. The values of class variables are shared by all instances of the class, while instance variables have values that are private to the instance of the class that they are defined for. We note that this is a very valuable feature for the construction application, allowing, for example, all doors of the same dimensions and materials to form a class, while paint color, locks, etc. may be defined for specific instances.

The method descriptions include both class methods and instance methods. The class methods mostly detail the creation of an instance of the given class. The instance methods and their corresponding interface messages provide the means to set and retrieve variable values, among other things. In object-oriented systems, most of the work is accomplished by the instance methods.

Many of the methods defined in our building model

require the spatial coordinates of the objects they manipulate, which necessitated defining a coordinate system. The rectangular coordinate system chosen originates in the front of the structure, at the the lower left corner as seen when one faces the building. The positive x-axis extends across the front of the building to the right; the positive y-axis extends up the side of the building; and the positive z-axis extends to the rear of the structure.

Alternatively, we could have defined local coordinates for each substructure. That is, much like on a blueprint, the location of rooms on a floor would be given by means of a coordinate system defined for that floor. And the placement of objects on a ceiling would be defined with respect to a local coordinate system for that ceiling. Although more difficult to implement, relative coordinate systems reduce the chance of incorrectly defining the location of an object; for example, of placing a ceiling fan in the middle of a wall.

In the remainder of this section we shall summarize some of the interesting features of the *Building* hierarchy as implemented in Smalltalk. Details as well as the actual Smalltalk-80 implementation may be found in [San88].

Class *Building* is the topmost class in the data model. As such, its superclass is Class *Object* (root of the hierarchy or tree). There are no class variables, but three instance variables identify each instance (i.e., each specific building): *addressOfBuilding*, *architect*, and *nameOfBuilding*. A fourth instance variable, *collectionOfStories*, is indexed (i.e., it is an array). This variable holds pointers to the stories that make up the building (that is, to instances of the child class *Story*). Since floor plans in our application are specific to a certain level in the building, the methods that operate on this indexed variable require the users to specify the story they are interested in. One class method and eight instance methods are defined for *Building*. The class method for *Building* simply creates a new instance of the class (inserts a new building into the database). This method is inherited from the superclass, Object. Six of the eight defined instance methods set or return the instance variables used to identify a specific Building object. These may be thought of as data update and retrieval methods, or procedures for modifying and querying the database. The other two methods add a Story object to or retrieve a Story object from the given Building object. The first of these two methods corresponds to database insertion and the second provides the critical ability to navigate through the database — in this case to move down the hierarchy.

Class *Story* essentially defines objects so as to describe the floor plan of one story of a building. The superclass of Story is Building, as noted earlier. No class variables are defined for Story. (Recall that an instance method for *Building* provides for the creation of new

Stories.) An instance variable *useOfStory* was included to provide for an encoded integer value to indicate the function of that particular story. Instance variables *widthOfStory*, *depthOfStory*, and *heightOfStory* define the dimensions of the floor plan. These values cannot be shared with or stored in the superclass (*Building*), because many multi-floor structures vary their external width and depth from floor to floor. And of course heights of floors commonly vary. The remaining instance variables link in the *Volume* objects associated with the specific floor plan. Since no one conventional scheme exists for numbering the Rooms of a Story, a counter is defined and the rooms are indexed serially as they are created and inserted in the database. The methods outlined for *Story* define an instance of the class. Three of the methods set the dimensions for the Story and one sets its usage variable. Another method provides a means of adding Volume objects to a given Story object, similar to the method under *Building* that provides for the creation of Stories for a Building.

The location of stories within a building is assumed to be obvious -- stories are placed one on top of the other in numerical order. However, as soon as we must define the positions of fixtures on a ceiling, or of rooms within a story, it becomes imperative that we do this with reference to some sort of coordinate system. As indicated earlier, we decided on a global rectangular coordinate system for that purpose. To implement the coordinate system, we defined a class *SpacePoint*. It is not part of the data hierarchy, but exists to support the implementation of the data model, not unlike the system-defined class provided with a Smalltalk-80 system. The superclass for *SpacePoint* is class *Object*. SpacePoint objects define points in a three-dimensional Cartesian coordinate system by means of one indexed instance variable, *coordinate*. This variable contains the x-, y-, and z-axis values for the point the object represents. Two class methods are provided -- one for simple instance creation and the other to create a SpacePoint instance with the coordinate variable already initialized. Six instance methods are defined for the class to set and return the coordinate values, thus allowing queries as to the locations and dimensions of objects.

An example of the use of class *SpacePoint* is provided by moving one level lower is the hierarchy and looking briefly at class *Volume*. *Volume*, like *Story*, contains an integer variable *useOfVolume* to indicate its usage. And also like *Story*, *Volume* contains an integer counter and an indexed variable for adding VerticalArea objects to the given Volume instance. To specify the boundaries of a Volume, *Volume* contains the indexed variable *dimensions*, which references two objects of type SpacePoint. These objects define the minimum and maximum values for the x-, y-, and z- coordinates of the Volume; that is, the endpoints of the main diagonal of the box that forms the Volume. These values could be used to check, for example, that a given VerticalArea fits in the Volume. *Volume* then contains methods to set the usage variable and define the dimensions of the volume. The class also provides methods that allow instances to reply to queries about these values. Other methods, *addNewVertArea* and *deleteVertArea*, add and delete VerticalArea objects of the volume.

The class *Room* is of some interest. As a subclass of *Volume*, it inherits information about how it is partitioned from adjacent rooms (specifically, its dimensions and pointers to the VerticalAreas that bound it). *Room* therefore contains only two instance variables: *floor* and *ceiling* to point to the Floor object and Ceiling object, respectively, that define the upper and lower boundaries of the given Room object. *Room* contains an instance creation method, and methods for attaching a Floor object and a Ceiling object to itself. A method *computeTotalAreaOf* calculates the total area of the specific type of "wall" (window, door, wallboard, etc.) that is passed as an argument (*wallType*) to the method. In the class *VerticalArea*, an instance variable *typeOfArea* contains this information. The two classes that *VerticalArea* includes, *Wall* and *SpecialArea*, inherit this instance variable from their parent, *VerticalArea*. The method *computeTotalAreaOf* uses two control loops, one nested within the other, to calculate the total area of the given wall type that is contained in the room. The outer loop ensures that the method calculates areas for each VerticalArea object attached to the Room object. For each of the VerticalArea objects, the inner loop checks the wall areas that comprise it. If a wall object is of the type being considered (*typeOfArea* matches *wallType*), a message, *computeArea*, is sent to that object to request it to compute and return its area. The value returned by the method is then added to a running total, which is returned when all VerticalArea objects have been checked.

Notice that method *computeTotalAreaOf*, which is contained in class Room, accesses the instance variable *vertAreaCount* and the indexed instance variable *collectionOfVertArea*, which are contained in class *Volume*. These instance variables are inherited by *Room* from *Volume*, which is the superclass of class *Room*. When the method is invoked, the receiving class, here *Room*, is checked for the needed variable names. When the variables are not found, the procedure automatically searches up the hierarchy to locate the desired values. In this case, the values are found in the superclass. If the values had not been found in the superclass, the search procedure would have next checked the superclass of the superclass, in this case class *Story*. This example shows the power of inheritance. The description for the class *Room* is very simple: only two instance variables, as described above. Through inheritance, the class can describe objects with the general characteristics of class *Volume*, but use its own instance variables to realize a more specialized object description.

Another example of the power of inheritance is provided by the class *VerticalArea* and its subclasses *Wall* and *SpecialArea*. *VerticalArea* contains the instance variable *typeOfArea*, an encoded value that describes any special function of the object. This instance variable is inherited by *Wall* and *SpecialArea*. For class *Wall*, this variable encodes the type of covering or finish that is over the wall. For class *SpecialArea*, the variable encodes the type of area (window, door, etc.) that the object models. This variable is accessed by the method *computeTotalAreaOf* defined in class *Room* to allow the area of a specific type of vertical surface to be computed, as detailed above in the description of class *Room*.

The class *VericalArea* also includes indexed instance variables, *dimensions* and *collectionOfWallAreas*, to hold SpacePoint objects that define the boundaries of the object and pointers to the Wall and SpecialArea objects that make up the VerticalArea object. *VerticalArea* also contains a rich set of methods: to create instances, to set and retrieve the dimensions and the function of the object, to compute and return the width and height of the VerticalArea, to add and delete Walls and SpecialAreas that make up the VerticalArea, etc.

The subclasses inherit all of these methods and variables, so that defining them becomes very simple. No class variables, instance variables, or instance methods are defined for class *Wall*. The class contains one class method which provides simple instance creation. All variables and methods needed to define and operate on instances are inherited from the superclass *VerticalArea*. Like class *Wall*, class *SpecialArea* relies totally on inheritance to realize and operate on instances of itself.

At this point the reader should see clearly how nodes in the data hierarchy of Figure 1 may be defined in Smalltalk-80, or indeed in any implementation environment that supports the basic object concepts reviewed in Section 3.1. We have provided examples of the techniques utilized to demonstrate the feasibility of implementing the complete (or an expanded) model in an object-oriented database.

4. CONCLUSIONS

This paper represents an initial portion of a study of database support required for computer-aided-construction. We have here outlined the general requirements of a construction database system and summarized our preliminary investigation into the suitability of an object-oriented database for construction data. This preliminary investigation has been restricted to developing a data model to describe the interior of a simple building in the form of a hierarchy of objects, and then to implementing this model in the object-oriented environment Smalltalk-80. A variety of structural components were successfully modeled, and methods were readily defined for the data classes to provide such standard database operations as update and retrieval, as well as computation of areas of the structural components. The data abstraction techniques of generalization and aggregation were found to be virtually indispensable for describing a building and its components, and the concept of inheritance was useful in cutting down on storage of duplicate information and avoiding the concomitant problems of consistency maintenance. Although only a small number of methods were defined for the data classes, we believe that they are representative of those needed for an actual application. And the data encapsulation provided by the object-oriented approach makes it relatively easy to cleanly insert new methods for other operations. In summary, we believe that this example, though small, convincingly demonstrates the suitability of an object-oriented database management system for the construction application.

Work on other aspects of a DBMS for construction, including integrity and consistency controls, data manipulation operations, and user interfaces, is currently underway. We suspect, however, that because of the large amounts of data and the complicated structure required, and the need for real-time access to support some applications, efficiency will be a major issue in any implementation of a construction database.

AKNOWLEDGEMENT

This work was in part conducted as part of the University of Illinois Advanced Construction Technology Center research program sponsored by the U.S. Army Research Office under the DOD-University Research Initiative Program.

REFERENCES

[Bat85] Batory, D.S. and W. Kim, "Modeling Concepts for VLSI CAD Objects", *ACM Transactions on Database Systems*, Vol. 10, No. 3, pp. 322-346, Sept 1985.

[Bla88] Blaha, M.J., W.J. Premerlani, and J.E. Rumbaugh, "Relational Database Design Using an Object-Oriented Methodology", *Communications of the ACM*, Vol. 31, No. 4, pp. 414-427, April 1988.

[Cox84] Cox, B.J., "Message/Object Programming: An Evolutionary Change in Programming Technology", *IEEE Software*, Jan 1984.

[Gol83] Goldberg, A. and D. Robson, *Smalltalk-80: The Language and its Implementation.* Addison-Wesley, Reading, Mass., 1983.

[Ibb86] Ibbs, C.W., "Future Directions for Computerized Construction Research", *Journal of Construction Engineering*, Vol. 112, No.3, Sept 1986.

[Mur88] Muroga, E. and G. G. Belford, "Techniques for Consistency Maintenance in an Object-Oriented Database". In preparation.

[San88] Santone, A.L., M.S. Thesis, Dept. of Computer Science, University of Illinois at Urbana-Champaign, August 1988.

[Smi77] Smith, J.M. and D.C.P. Smith, "Database Abstractions: Aggregation and Generalization", *ACM Transactions on Database Systems*, Vol. 2, No. 2, pp. 105-133. June 1977.

[Spo86] Spooner, D.L., M.A. Milicia and D.B. Faatz, "Modeling Mechanical CAD Data with Data Abstraction and Object-Oriented Techniques", *Proceedings of the International Conf. on Very Large Database Systems*, Los Angeles, Feb 1986.

[Ste86] Stefik, M., and D.G. Bobrow, "Object-Oriented Programming: Themes and Variations", *The AI Magazine,* Vol. 6, No. 4, Winter 1986.

[Ver87] Verity, J.W., "The OOPS Revolution", *DATAMATION*, Vol. 3, No. 9, May 1987.

Object-Oriented Database Management Support for

Software Maintenance and Reverse Engineering

M. Ketabchi, D. Lewis, S. Dasananda
T. Lim, R. Roudsari, K. Shih, J. Tan

Department of Electrical Engineering and Computer Science
Santa Clara University
Santa Clara, CA 95053

Abstract

Computer aided software engineering systems require extensive database system support. Several industrial and academic research and development projects attempt to provide this support by using conventional database management systems or special purpose data managers.

Object-oriented database management system technology provides a set of capabilities which are required by computer integrated software engineering systems. Our objective is to take advantage of this new technology and develop computer integrated software engineering systems that support complete user-defined life cycles with uniform interface and logically centralized database support.

We have built tools to generate object-oriented databases that represent the syntax and some of the semantics of programs. We are using these tools for developing a software maintenance and reverse engineering system.

This paper presents an overview of our prototype system and tools.

1. Introduction

Our goal is to provide database system support using object-oriented database management systems for Computer Integrated Software Engineering (CISE) systems: systems which support complete user-defined software life cycle with a uniform interface and logically centralized database system. In order to achieve this objective as effectively as possible, we have developed a set of tools for generating schema and software database systems using object-oriented DBMS. We are expanding the capabilities of these tools in order to develop a sequence of progressively more powerful database systems which support applications such as maintenance and reverse engineering, reengineering, development, and design stages in the software life cycle.

Our basic assumptions are:

i. Once a faithful self-contained description of software systems, their requirements, specifications, and developments history are readily available, supporting and integrating different tools for CISE are simplified.

ii. Object-oriented DBMS technology meets the data management requirements of CISE more effectively than conventional DBMS technology does.

See reference 1 for a discussion of database system support for software engineering, reference 3 for a discussion of object-oriented DBMSs, and reference 4 for a discussion of using object-oriented DBMS for representing software.

2. Overview of the System

This section presents a high-level user-oriented description of SAMS. Section 2.1 describes the types of operations that users can perform using SAMS. Section 2.2 provides an overview of the user interface paradigm and mechanisms through which the functions of the system can be utilized.

2.1 Functionalities of SAMS

Software maintenance facilities in most environments including Unix is limited to a set of utility tools such as cref, cxref, cflow, xref, and various editors. Functionality of these tools overlap considerably, but there is no subset of the tools which provides all the operations needed for software analysis and maintenance nor integrates them in a uniform manner. These and similar tools attempt to provide important functionality for software analysis and maintenance, but they are rarely used by software engineers and programmers because the huge volume and poor representation of their outputs make them unusable. The size of output is large because the resolution of the information provided by these tools is very coarse. For example, users can not ask for all the functions called by another function; they must ask for all the functions called by all other functions. The representation is poor because the output is presented as a text stream in one format only. If the user is interested in a different part of the output and in a different format than the default one he/she must extract and reformat the desired information.

A software analysis and maintenance system should provide the required functionality through a uniform and user-friendly interface which allows users to get the information they want with the presentation format they want. For example a user should be able to ask "what are the functions called by function foo directly and indirectly" and should be able to get the results either in a textual or graphic form.

The SAMS prototype system achieves this objective in very effective way. It provides the following functionality through a uniform menu and mouse driven interface:

i. Find all the functions called by a given function directly or indirectly.

ii. Find all the functions which call a given function directly or indirectly.

iii. Construct the calling graph of a given program.

iv. Find all the functions which reference (read or write) a given variable or a given identifier (An identifier is a name and more than one variable may have the same name).

Reprinted from *Digest of Papers, COMPCON*, 1989, pages 257-260. Copyright © 1989 by The Institute of Electrical and Electronics Engineers, Inc. All rights reserved.

v. Find all the variable which are referenced, or read, or written in a given function.

vi. Find where a variable is referenced, or read, or written.

vii. Perform a global search and replace of a variable.

viii. Present an abstract view of a given program where only specifications are displayed.

ix. Present the original text of a given program or any component of it as entered.

x. Present the text of a given program or any component of it using the systems formatting options.

xi. Edit the text of the program using a text-oriented editor such as vi.

xii. Edit the text of the program using an object-oriented editor.

This functionality is implemented by a set of simple operations defined for entity types in our automatically generated object-oriented database system and is provided through a uniform interface briefly described in the following section.

2.2 Users' View

The general scenario of using SAMS multi-window menu driven interface is as follows:

i. A set of software objects is presented to a user; the user may select one of the objects as the current object.

ii. A context-sensitive menu of operations which may be performed on the current object is presented; the user may select one of the operations in the menu for execution.

iii. The results of the operation are displayed either in the same window or in a different window.

Objects in the software systems are displayed with appropriate abstractions. If an object being displayed has an embedded block, the block interface is displayed instead of the entire text of the block. A block interface is a string consisting of the block name and the names of all identifiers used but not declared in that block.

For example the C function shown in Figure 1 will be displayed as shown in Figure 2.

C Function

```
#include "defs.h"

int i=0;

main ()
{
        auto int i=1;
        PRINT1 (d,  i);
        {
                int i=2;
                PRINT1(d,i);
                {
                        i += 1;
                        PRINT1(d,i);
                }
                PRINT1(d,i);
        }
        PRINT1(d,i);
}
```

Figure 1

```
#include "defs.h"

int i=0;

main ()
{
---------
|  d   |
---------
}
```

Figure 2

If the user is interested in the details of a block then he/she may select the block as the current object and expand it. Once an object is displayed in a window, the user can use the mouse to select a component (subobject) of that object or to select the containing object of that object. Each object has a system defined identifier which uniquely identifies the object, e.g. x + 5 is an object and has an object id associated with it. x, +, and 5 are components of this object. A user can select x, +, or 5 by moving the cursor on top of them and clicking the mouse button. The containing object of these objects is object x + 5 which itself may be a component of another object such as y * (x + 5).

3. Architecture of the System

The system consists of three major subsystems:

i. Language Object Generator

ii. Software Database System

iii. Software Analysis and Maintenance Tool Set

The inputs to the system are:

i. Formal language description

ii. Programs in those languages

iii. Users' selection of the objects and operations

The output of the system is displayed results which contain the information retrieved from the software database systems in response to the users' request.

Figure 3 shows the connections among the subsystems.

Figure 3
Software Maintenance and Analysis System

3.1 Language Object Generator

This subsystem is responsible for creating a DBMS independent schema and database for programs written in the programming language described by the language description. Figure 4 shows the architecture of language object generator subsystem:

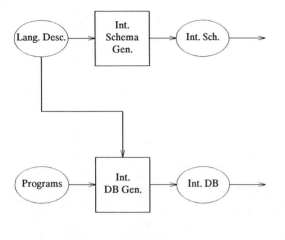

Figure 4

Language Object Generator

The intermediate database generator consists of a scanner and parser generated by using Lex and Yacc (scanner and parser generator). In order to ensure the consistency between the schema and the database we are using the same language description file as input to both the intermediate schema generator and the intermediate database generator.

The reason for generating an intermediate schema and database is to be able to use the same language object generator with multiple DBMSs.

The intermediate schema and intermediate database are DBMS independent. If the language description requires, the intermediate schema will contain such features as multiple inheritance which may not be supported by the target DBMS. It is the responsibility of the schema and database generators to deal with DBMS dependent features and limitations.

3.2 Software DataBase System

This subsystem takes the intermediate schema and intermediate database and generates schema and database for a specific object-oriented DBMS. Currently we are using GemStone and Iris. Figure 5 shows the architecture of software database systems:

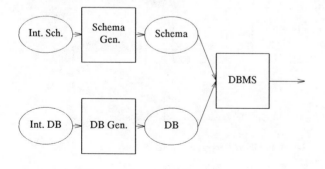

Figure 5

Software Database System

There are two cases where the intermediate schema generator attempts to simplify the task of the schema generator by extra processing which is not otherwise necessary. The first case is abbreviating the names which appear in the schema because DBMSs impose limit on the length of names. The second case is generating the type and property names in a certain order because DBMS are sensitive to the order in which new types are defined. It is reasonable for the intermediate schema generator to perform these tasks because otherwise they have to be repeated in the schema generator for each DBMS.

3.3 Software Analysis and Maintenance Tool Set

This subsystem provides a Multi Window Browser and Editor (MWB/E), a Presentation Format Translator (PFT), a Code Analysis Application Program (CAAP), and a Code Analysis Information Retriever (CAIR).

The MWB/E is a program which allows users to browse and edit software entities. MWB/E has two operational modes: text-oriented, and object-oriented

In text-oriented mode, MWB/E is used as a conventional editor such as vi with few differences. The main difference between vi and MWB/E in this mode is that before the changes are entered into the software database, an cheking the syntax and an incremental parsing must take place.

In object-oriented mode, MWB/E is used as a syntax-directed editor. In this mode only those operations which do not violate syntactic rules of the language are allowed. Changes in this mode do not require syntax cheking or parsing because they can be entered into the database directly. The user may discard them before leaving this mode. If they are not discarded the changes will become permanent. Examples of updates in this mode are syntax-directed global search and replacement of identifiers and reformatting of programs. Operations in this mode are performed via mouse and object selection. The cursor is moved on top of a character and the mouse button is clicked. If the character is not a white space then an object is selected and becomes the current object. Once a current object is selected a menu of valid operations on that object is displayed. The operations are determined by the type of the current object.

CAIR is a collection of tools used to perform operations which are not part of the object definitions stored in the database. CAIR tools do additional processing of the information retrieved from the database.

PFT is a program which takes the output of CAIR tools, reformats, and displays them, and allows selection of a displayed object for further browsing. When the information retrieved by CAIR has to be displayed in a format other than simple text representation, PFT is called upon.

CAAP is a collection of DBMS queries which provides a DBMS independent interface for CAIR and MWB/E. CAAP is DBMS dependent and must be rewritten for each DBMS.

MWB/E, PFT and CAIR are implemented as three separate programs. As depicted in the diagram, CAAP is a common subsystem of the three programs.

The tool set is a multiwindow environment whose entry point is an MWB/E process. Interprocess communication in CATS is done only once as the parent process spawns a child process. Each process will operate independently of other processes. More than one instance of each process MWB/E, CAIR, and PFT may exist simultaneously at run time. An MWB/E process is always the first process to be started. The MWB/E may spawn a CAIR process which in turn may spawn an PFT process. A PFT process may spawn another MWB/E process upon request.

The following diagram shows the architecture of software maintenance and analysis tool set.

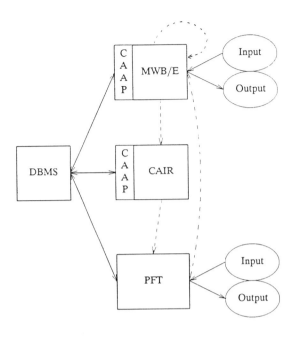

Figure 6

Software Analysis and Maintenance Tool Set

3.3.1 Software Database System and Tool Set Interface

How do software tools and software database systems interface without compromising logical independency (applications/database independence) and performance?

Ideally the analysis and maintenance tool set should not have any built-in knowledge of the database schema. By exploiting the active data capability of an OODBMS, retrieval of an object's attributes can be implemented as a message to the object. This is different from the conventional approach where the application must know about the attributes of database entities.

The most common operation is traversal of the components hierarchy of an object. Different processing may be required based on the types of properties of each component. This processing is application dependent and may vary for each program.

It is expensive to do a DBMS query for each property of an object. Furthermore if component traversal becomes a responsibility of application then each application must duplicate the component traversal logic.

We have isolated the component traversal logic from the processing required for each component.

It is more natural to delegate the traversal logic to the object itself (as object-oriented DBMS method) while the processing for each component can be implemented as part of the tool set application and passed to the DBMS methods. Therefore component processing functions are passed to the database method responsible for the traversal of the component hierarchy.

This method of interfacing applications with object-oriented DBMS seems to provide both logical independence and an efficient interface.

4. Concluding Remarks

Computer Integrated Software (CISE) Engineering systems which support complete user-defined software life cycle with a uniform interface, tools integration facilities, and logically centralized database systems will increase the productivity of software development and maintenance.

The premise of our research is that object-oriented DBMSs provide the database system support needed for the development of CISE. Object-oriented DBMS is a new technology and we have suffered from its deficiencies and immaturity in the course of our project. Nevertheless, our overall experience has been very positive and we strongly believe that the database system capabilities provided by object-oriented DBMS are essential for the development of effective CISE systems.

Automatic object-oriented software database system generation is one of the important contributions of our research project. The tools we have developed for this purpose are language and DBMS independent. We plan to enhance these tools and use them to generate software database systems which can support software tools used in different stages of software of the life cycle.

The prototype SAMS described in this paper is operational. Although currently we are storing C programs in our software database system most components of SAMS are language independent.

Acknowledgement: Work on this project is supported by US West Advanced Technologies Research Award at Santa Clara University.

References

1. "Database System Support for Software Engineering," P.A. Bernstein, Proceeding of 9th International Conference on Software Engineering, 1987.

2. "CAPS: A Computer Aided Prototyping System," Luqi, M.A. Ketabchi, March 1988, IEEE Software

3. "An Object-Oriented Semantic Data Model for CAD Applications," M.A. Ketabchi, V. Berzins, S.T. March, October 1988, Journal of Information Sciences

4. "Representing Software Using Object-Oriented Database Management Systems," M.A. Ketabchi, R.R. Roudsari, K.Y. Shih, R. Wiens, Proceedings of System Design and Networks Conference, 1988.

5. "A Matrix of CAD Applications Requirements/DBMS Capabilities," the proceedings of CAD/CIM Alert 87.

The TEIES Design and Objectives:
Computer Mediated Communications and Tailorability
by
Murray Turoff, John Foster,
Starr Roxanne Hiltz, and Kenneth Ng
Computerized Conferencing and Communications Center
New Jersey Institute of Technology
Newark, N.J. 07102
Tel: 201 596-3437

Hawaii International Conference on System Sciences (HICSS, January 1989)

ABSTRACT: This paper provides an overview of the current design of TEIES (Tailorable Electronic Information Exchange System). This system is intended to provide sufficient tailorability to allow it to support a wide range of applications in the areas of Collaborative Systems and Group Decision Support Systems. It is also intended to allow complete integration of communication and information services for users and groups.

ACKNOWLEDGMENTS: Significant acknowledgment is given to David Morris of IBM who contributed to many of the design concepts covered in this paper. Also we wish to thank Kevin Walsh, Gurinder Singh Johar, Heidi Harting, and Rana Ajaz-Ur-Rehman for their contributions to the development effort. The development of TEIES was partially supported by a grant from the New Jersey Commission on Science and Technology and by a Joint Study Agreement with the IBM Corporation. Support for Personal TEIES, referred to in this paper, was provided by the Annenberg/CPB Project.

INTRODUCTION AND HISTORICAL REVIEW

Increasing tailorability seems to be a fundamental characteristic of the evolution of technology. As individuals and groups, we use our technology to adapt our environment to a wide diversity of configurations. In the early days of a technology (e.g. cars, homes, personal computers) we are happy to have the model-T's and the log cabins. As a technology becomes more developed and offers more options we develop a diversity of versions that are tailored to different preferences and objectives and serve different functions. Hardly anyone today would be satisfied with an automobile dealer who offered only Model-T's or with living in a one-room log cabin. Even if houses all have bathrooms and kitchens, there many choices in architecture and furnishings.

While this might seem a perversity of human nature, the careful investigation of this diversity usually finds its root cause in Zipf's principle of "Least Human Effort" [1]. Humans adapt their physical environment to minimize both physical and mental efforts to accomplish their tasks and objectives.

With respect to Computer Mediated Communication (CMC), the current state of the technology is still largely one of the Model-T era where the common perception is the "message system" or "electronic mail" metaphor. However, we have always advocated that the ultimate objective of CMC systems is "collective intelligence" [2] which can be achieved through the ability to utilize the computer to create communication structures that will allow a group to act more intelligently than any one individual acting alone. The new TEIES (Tailorable Electronic Information Exchange System) has been designed specifically to facilitate that long term objective. This paper describes the design of TEIES in terms of to its fundamental objective of tailorability and the associated objective of integration with other computer based tools.

The design of TEIES has combined aspects of earlier conference systems that have been utilized and evaluated. The resulting synthesis attempts to capture the useful features and to develop a foundation design that can overcome the principal problems and limitations of these earlier systems.

In the decade following the first computerized conferencing system [3] there were only about ten general purpose systems implemented. Among the early systems were EMISARI, FORUM, EIES, KOM, NOTEPAD, PARTI, CONFER, and EQUAL [2]; [4]; [5]. These systems were distinguished from message systems in that their primary orientation was toward communications to support group tasks, and their internal design was based upon central data bases of these group communications.

Despite significant design differences among the earlier systems, they had many application successes [4]. Design differences included such fundamental considerations as how to organize and deliver new discussion comments to the individuals in the group. For example, three very different forms of delivery were linear chronological transcripts (e.g. EIES, FORUM, KOM), tree structured transcripts (e.g. PARTI, EQUAL), and inquiry-response structuring (e.g. CONFER). In general, these delivery design choices produced significant differences in the behavior of communicating groups and in the types of applications for which the systems were best suited [4]. Just as there are many different communication structures used in face to face communication, there is also a need for different CMC structures to serve different communication objectives.

THE GOALS OF TEIES

Since the early 80's the evolution of Computer Mediated Communication can be characterized by two trends. One is the proliferation of new systems

Reprinted from *The Proceedings of the 22nd Hawaii International Conference on System Sciences (HICSS)*, 1989, pages 403-411.

to take advantage of changes in the technology. This includes systems which operate on powerful micros and minis and in network environments. As micros become more powerful, bulletin board systems are beginning to evolve into conferencing systems. As message systems become popular, there is a natural tendency to try to extend them to incorporate group support. However, message systems represent one highly specialized structure whose metaphor and resulting internal design does not lend itself to full support of group activities.

Another significant trend is the incorporation of communication functionality into highly specialized or tailored application-oriented systems. There is, for example, a growing number of Hypertext systems, designed for very particular applications [6], [7], [8], which have incorporated structures for contributions of material to the data base by groups of individuals. In fact, a recent hypertext implementation for policy analysis [9] replicates the first computerized conferencing system [3]. The area of Group Decision Support Systems [10], [11], [12] also illustrates specialized tailoring. In summary, traditional systems designed for databases and text processing are adding communication features to support group activities.

As a result, "collaborative systems" are being developed either as systems oriented toward generalized communication, or as highly specialized systems tailored for specific applications. We have always felt that group oriented systems need to be tailored to the nature of the group and its application [2], [13], [14], [15], [16], [17]. However, users cannot deal with numerous systems to match different communication objectives. An approach in which the user must shift to a different system for each communication task is doomed to failure. The challenge for the next generation of collaborative systems is integrated systems that provide tailorability of communication structures directly to the user. The traditional computer facilities of data bases and analysis routines must become subservient to a common communication system rather than to an operating system.

The challenge we have faced with the design of TEIES has been to provide tailorability and an interface that allows the user to take advantage of that tailorability. The detailed goals of our project can be summarized as follows:

General CMC Objectives:

. Service for the frequent user who uses the system as the primary medium of day-to-day communication activities in an organization.
. Honesty in communications, to encourage the establishment of explicit norms and values by groups to govern communications.

. Learning by trial and error so that new capabilities can be acquired by users when they need them.

. Open ended user interface design metaphors that will allow the evolution of facilities to support a wide variety of applications.

Tailorability Objectives:

. Alternative group communication structures and protocols for different group communication needs, based upon the application, size of the group and the nature of the group.

. Alternative methods of organizing, tracking and integrating the resulting database of communications on an individual and group basis.

. Specific software support for alternative human roles that are required for facilitating group communication processes.

. Integration into the communication processes of any required type of computer resource or support.

. Tailorability of the interface to satisfy individual cognitive and collaborative metaphors.

TEIES SYSTEM OBJECTS

TEIES is internally an object-oriented database. The objects are those that have been common to a number of conference systems: members, groups, messages, conferences, comments, and a directory. There are also two new objects that have not been present in earlier systems: notifications and activities. We first present an overview of the principal characteristics of these objects and will return later to some unique properties that provide enhanced tailorability.

DIRECTORY: A database of primary objects

lists:	members, groups, and conferences
indexes:	names, locations, ownership, roles, interest keys for members and groups, topic keys for conferences

MEMBERS: An authorized user of the system

owner of:	conferences and groups
author of:	messages, conference comments
creator of:	activities and notifications
possessing:	private files, indexes, lists of marked and authored items
indexed by:	interest keys, description, addresses, roles and memberships

GROUPS: A set of members that may act as a "super" member for the purposes of collaboration.

owning:	conferences and group mail
having:	membership and special roles for group members
allowing:	shared group files, indexes, and lists
indexed by:	topic keys, description and membership

MAIL & MESSAGES: A central cyclic database of messages sent between and among members and groups.

allowing:	attachment of activities, modification, retrieval, copying

indexed by: keys, authors, receivers,
                  date-time, replies
triggering: notifications

CONFERENCES & COMMENTS: A structured discussion space treated as a database.

owned by: member or group
having: membership and roles, structures
                 and protocols
allowing: activities attached to comments
indexed by: comment keys, authors, date-time,
                 association

ACTIVITIES: Executable programs and forms that may be attached to text items to carry out an open ended variety of collaborative procedures or to serve as interfaces to other computer and information resources.

allowing: voting, documents, memberships,
              conditional actions, programs, etc.
triggering: tailored notifications

NOTIFICATIONS: Short notices delivered to a member's personal file space.

conveying: alerts, closure confirmations,
            reminders, notice of transactions,
            canned messages, etc.
allowing: direct retrieval and manipulation
            of objects
providing: a tracking oriented database

TEIES INTERNAL FEATURES

The ability of TEIES to be tailorable and to be integratable with other computer resources is largely a function of the internal structure. It is the foundation facilities described below which make TEIES representative of a new generation of Computer Mediated Communication Systems.

The degree to which this power can be brought to the user and put under his control depends upon the user interface. The TEIES interface provides a metaphor which minimizes the cognitive differences between the understanding of the system by the user and the way the system actually operates.

TEIES is composed of four virtual machines (i.e. Master, Data Base Server, User & Network). A single TEIES system consists of one Master and any number of other machines. Each machine may reside anywhere on a network of independent computers and workstations. This means complete tailorability, in a system sense, of what is at any processor in the network. The master server only verifies authority to establish communication channels between different machines.

The Master machine contains an index of all objects within a given TEIES implementation so that the overall database may be distributed on a number of different machines. Since no user machine has an access to any database machine until authentication has occurred, there is a high degree of security. The master indexes function by unique id, author or owner of an object, date/time of creation and key words.

The TEIES database contains access and utilization privileges as a form of linkage attribute between users and the objects they are working on. Thus, no application program or interface tailoring has to be concerned with the protection and security of the data involved. The database can internally determine the rights or privileges of any user request regardless of its source. This also means that an application written in any language as an independent application can call on or be interfaced to TEIES.

Privileges in TEIES are also collected into groupings that define human roles in the communication process. The process of defining both privileges and human roles is open ended and may be accomplished by someone with a command of the C programming language.

TEIES incorporates its own forms subsystem which utilizes the proposed Standard Generalized Markup Language [18]. The forms subsystem has extensions that contain all TEIES interfaces as forms. These forms are stored as regular TEIES text items with public privileges. This reduces the design of interfaces to more of an editing task than a programming task. Forms may also be used to call up and execute programs available through the executive system in which TEIES resides. As a result special activities can be created by designing forms to provide the interface to the computer resources they call up.

All system and help messages exist as text within the TEIES system. One may create alternative interfaces and system messages and selectively provide these alternatives to individuals and groups. For example, different users of the same system can use interfaces in different languages.

Activities are designed in forms and may be attached to any text item. Activities can include executable programs or procedures. Users of TEIES can "do" any of these activities as well as "viewing" the text object to which they are attached. Activities, as a general extensible concept, can be used to integrate any application tool from any language or database into a given collaborative system design. Associated with activities is "notifications," which is a general transaction tracking and alerting system that can be linked to any activity.

TEIES provides two-way linkages among data objects. Therefore, if a user wishes to link another user's material into an item, the original author will have references to that linkage in his data. This allows for experimentation with many protocols to handle the sharing of material among groups and is critical to working with collaborative Hypertext applications.

A TEIES user object and group object are equivalent in that they both have the same functionality. As a result groups may share any of the functionality provided to an individual.

Personal TEIES is a workstation-based graphics editor and display system. Graphics are coded in NAPLPS and linked to other objects in TEIES via

GML. The result is that any graphics produced by one individual on the system may be manipulated and edited by another at a macro level as opposed to dealing with bit mapped representation. Icons in PERSONAL TEIES are higher level objects that may link in text and programs. Individuals and groups may create and share icons and what they link to. The result is that any icon may become a window or direct manipulation link to anything in PERSONAL TEIES or TEIES.

All software development work is in C and all systems are designed to isolate and restrict hardware and executive system dependencies to an OSI kernel (Operating System Interface). Programming standards have been imposed to make the code operational across a wide range of C compilers. This makes the system software easily transportable to different hardware and operating systems. The first version of TEIES is being created for the IBM/VM environment. However, it is planned to port it to other environments including broadband LAN configurations. Likewise the first version of Personal TEIES operates on IBM PC's or compatibles.

TYPE OF TAILORING	HUMAN ROLE OR REQUIRED KNOWLEDGE
Creation of:	
System membership & roles	System Monitor
Directory Indexes	System Indexer
User tailorable features:	TEIES Member
Conference creation	
Group creation	
Directory Interest keys	
Private Personal Index	
Marked & Authored lists	
Tickets	
Conferences & Groups:	
Structure Choices	Owner
Directory Topic Keys	Owner
Roles	Owner
Membership	Monitor
Text content	Editor
Collaborative Index	Indexer
Activities utilized	Organizer
Creation of Forms:	Knowledge of
Interface alternatives	SGML
Design of Activities	
Design of Notifications	
Data Collection	
Triggering Programs	
Using TEIES database from:	
Computer Languages	Application
Database Systems	Programming
MIS and DSS	(any language)
Reconfiguring TEIES	System
Networking TEIES	Programming
Defining new:	(C language)
Roles & Privileges	
Database Objects	

Figure I: Tailorability Summary

Figure I summarizes the primary tailorability features of the system based upon the internal features and the characteristics of the basic objects that make up the system. The ability to specify any configuration of conferences, groups, memberships and roles, together with the classifications of private and public access, means that just about any desired organizational structure can be reflected within a given TEIES implementation.

INTERFACE: DIRECT AND INDIRECT METAPHORS

We agree with Carroll and Thomas [19]; [20] that metaphors are not merely a method of facilitating learning, but must also be viewed as a psychological model that underlies user interface design. It is quite natural to utilize the human communication metaphor for a collaborative system; however, we have extended this to utilize the communication metaphor to incorporate the utilization of any computer resource or functionality made available to the group or the individual. The same processes whereby individuals communicate with other humans provide the ability to utilize data bases, models and other computer based resources. Use of the same metaphor cuts through the problem of "system opacity" [21]. The merger of many computer facilities into the Collaborative System means complete tailorability of both communication and information resources into a single integrated interface. For example, within TEIES the metaphor of "activities" provides a single focus for direct integration of any special computer based facility. The operations of "viewing" or "doing" an activity apply uniformly to all types of integrated facilities.

The user of TEIES deals with choices of the type of object, modifiers (which result in a limited subset of the objects, or a "list"), and of a "generic" action (which establishes a "work mode" for the user). The result of the three simultaneous choices is a list of specific objects to process (e.g. VIEW NEW MAIL). The user is then provided a tailored set of alternative process actions that can be applied to any entry on the list or to all entries. The system is designed as a one-level system with respect to the use of commands. Therefore, experienced users may use any commands they aware of at any time, rather than just those provided by the standard action mode menu.

Internally, the user has chosen a user state that produces a list and a set of processing alternatives to act on the list. It is possible for the more knowledgeable user to directly evoke the concept of list processing. Different lists from different user states may be manipulated in a general list processing framework.

The "list processing" metaphor is an underlying capability for which we wish the user to evolve an understanding. In part, this understanding is initiated by providing each user and group with the ability to "mark" items, which results in a stored list that may be called up for later processing. The benefit of this approach is the ultimate ability of users to manipulate and organize both their communications and the results of use of other computer facilities through a single interface structure. Besides commands to operate on lists, there are a large set of MODIFIER terms (e.g. NEW, DONE, PUBLIC, URGENT) that are available to directly manipulate a given list in terms of what is to be included or excluded.

This focus on list processing is based upon the hypothesis that it ultimately provides the user with a more powerful interaction tool than alternatives such as direct manipulation. Once a user has mastered list processing as an abstraction, there is a considerable degree of leverage available for the control and processing of communications.

STRATEGIC CONTROL INTERFACE SCREENS

The primary interface to TEIES is provided by either the HOMEBASE (See Figure II) screen which is the top level list of OBJECTS, MODIFIERS and ACTIONS available to the user, or by a CASUAL user's screen which presents most of the day to day tasks of a user. Both screens provide versions of a "control panel" approach which enables the user to specify a strategy to accomplish a task.

The HOMEBASE menu presents the top level set of choices for the categories of objects, modifiers and actions. Making a specific top level choice always results in the system inferring a specific default choice for the user. Therefore, the new user does not have to know all the options that are available and their meanings. The sub-menus for each top level choice are intended for the more experienced user who wishes a higher degree of tailoring in their interaction. Each of the three menus exhibited on the Homebase screen provides approximately 100 alternative choices if one includes the three possible levels for each. In a sense, the full list of each of these menus presents a hierarchical index to the planned capabilities for TEIES, much like a book index. Therefore, the Homebase screen can be used to explore the system for new features or features one wishes to learn about, in the same way one would use a book index. Help may be obtained on any menu choice and any of the hidden submenus through this index aspect of the menus. These three menus can be tailored for any specific installation of TEIES and provide a way of configuring the system for structuring a very unique version of the system.

The CASUAL screen will provide most of the common options a user needs the majority of the time. However, for the experienced user it provides an ability to structure quickly very detailed and powerful requests through a single control screen. For example saying "yes" to find conferences and placing the word "public" in the modifier option will produce a list of all the public conferences. Therefore a user who knows specific modifier terms can tailor many more strategic choices than appears obvious from the screen itself. In addition, logic about what a user most likely wishes to do is incorporated as a mini-expert system in support of the CASUAL screen.

GENERIC COMMANDS AND ACTION MODES

The user is provided seven generic commands [22] which may be applied to any object or collection of objects. The exact meaning of each command is a function of the state the user is in and the type of objects it is applied to. For each generic command, there are available more specific commands that carry out very specific actions. However, the system always picks the expected default if the user chooses the generic version. This set of generic commands is:

Command	Generic Explanation
VIEW	Display individual objects or lists of objects.
FIND	Provide search options appropriate to the object type.
REVIEW	Provide summary information such as distribution of items and activity.
CREATE	To create new objects.
MODIFY	To modify existing objects.
DO	To trigger an execution of a process.
ORGANIZE	To perform various housekeeping functions provided for objects.

The use of a generic action approach means the user does not have to learn a new functionality to be able to deal with tailored and specialized capabilities.

MODIFIERS

A large number of "modifiers" may be applied directly to a given list or by choosing them from the HOMEBASE menu. They are meant to supply the experienced user a great deal of selectivity on the contents of a list. Some examples of modifiers are:

. PUBLIC will reduce the list to those groups or conferences that can be joined by any member on the system.

. URGENT will reduce the list to those comments or messages that have been designated as "urgent" by the author.

. UNDONE would reduce a list to those activities that had not yet been done by a user.

. MARKED would condense the list to only those items that had been marked.

Using the personal index that each member and group has, it is possible to designate index terms that are classified as categories. These may then be used as personal or group modifiers to match against the keys that are on lists of messages or comments, in much the same way as one uses the above system-wide modifiers. Since a list may be made up of different types of objects it is then possible to collect communications and other information into topic lists that are specialized to the group and what it is working on. It is expected, for example, that various project and task labels would be used by a working group as categories to set up their personal set of modifiers.

INDEXES AND CATEGORIES

An important object for the experienced user is indexes, which may be associated with individuals, groups, conferences, and the directory. Indexes can be set up to allow free entry of keys on a collaborative basis or to restrict use of index terms to a fixed set of keys specified by an individual acting in the role of "indexer" for the group or conference. Indexes may also have multiple levels (e.g. train.education, train.transportation).

The generic commands can be used to operate on an index just as they can be used to operate on any other object type in TEIES. Individuals may choose to use a group index if they are members of the group. The group index provides a powerful way of sharing information since any text item linked into the group reference keys by a member makes that item viewable by the other members of the group.

The directory has a number of index types, including interest keys and topic keys. Any individual may specify interest keys to indicate their interests. Any member of the system may address a message to an interest key and it will be sent to all the members who have associated themselves with that interest. Members may also choose to remove their association with an interest key. Topic keys indicate the topics that groups are interested in and that conferences are concerned with.

There is a system wide index and in it are a large number of category keys that are available for use on messages and comments. Through the modifier sub-menus one may select new, marked, or old items by these categories. These may, of course, be modified for any installation of TEIES. Currently the following system wide categories are planned:

FYI, Inquiry, Request, Problem Proposal, Decision, Assignment, Announcement Respond, Investigate, Do, Take-care-of Consider, Hold, Follow-up, Action Urgent, Business, Formal, Personal

The ability to provide indexing and control of the indexing by the individual members and groups is considered very critical to the utility of these systems for work oriented tasks. Most successful applications of this technology to project management do result in very large conference databases (e.g. thousands of comments) and the need to regularly review what has occurred in the past. This is particularly critical when there are changes in the membership of the project group or unforeseen problems arise. Conferencing systems for organizational use must deal with the classical information retrieval problem for text data files.

NOTIFICATIONS

Notifications are short one or two line messages that serve a wide variety of objectives intended to reduce the amount of effort necessary to communicate about complex tasks. These objectives are to:

Generate automatic alerts based upon transactions that have taken place. For example, a reply to an "urgent" item might notify the readership of that item that a reply exists. Most automatic alerts are optional in nature.

. Provide a direct manipulation handle, since one may point to a notification and retrieve the material it is referring to.

. Provide a data base to the member for tracking the actions associated with a particular task. Each member has a cyclic file of the notifications delivered to him or her.

. Provide the interface function of "closure" on processes that the member or group has triggered. Each activity defined for the system may incorporate its own set of tailored notifications and the conditions under which they are triggered.

. Reduce the need for messages by the use of "canned" notifications. A member may point to an item and trigger a standardized notification expressing any of a large number of common communication tasks such as expressing agreement or disagreement, desirability or undesirability, responsibility for taking care of something, etc. These notifications may be incorporated as attachments to the original message or comment.

. Enhance communication awareness through notifications, such as information about new members added to a private conference or the introduction of new classification categories for use by the group.

Notifications represent a general open-ended concept that provides a great deal of flexibility as to how they may be used in association with groups, conferences and activities. Through extensions to the forms subsystem on TEIES, individual users can create tailored notifications triggered by actions on a text item, such as viewing it, creating attachments such as "delta edits," or by triggering hypertext linkages. The importance of the concept of notifications is that a wide variety of applications for alerting, closure, and tracking is served by one interface metaphor and not by a variety of interfaces for different applications.

ACTIVITIES

Activities may be formulated out of any facilities in the computer system or broadband network in which TEIES operates. Ultimately the types of activities available will depend on the particular installation and the evolution of facilities to support collaborative tasks such as education, project management and composition. The general categories of activities we have already designed include:

. APPENDAGE activities which allow users to append information to existing objects (e.g. delta edits, approval notifications, etc.)

. CONDITIONAL activities which allow the user to receive additional information based upon the

reader's choice (e.g. choosing to read a
document).

. RESPONSE activities which allow the user to
respond to an object (e.g. fill in data, vote,
answer a question, etc.)

. CHOICE activities which allow the user to make
choices (e.g. picking a task to do).

. GENERATION activities which allow the user to
start a process to work for him or her (e.g. an
analysis or a database query).

. FUNCTIONAL activities which are a catch all for
such things as triggering network agents or
establishing a virtual terminal connection to
another system.

The first set of about ten activities we have been
implementing are those tied to support of the Virtual
Classroom [15], [23] and there is a large list planned
for the support of other applications. The activities
planned are based upon our own assessment of what
appears to be desirable from prior work in Computer
Mediated Communications, Group Decision Support
Systems, and Collaborative Systems.

The interface for a specific activity may be designed
in the forms subsystem of TEIES using SGML
(Standardized General Markup Language: ISO/DIS
8879) and may trigger programs written in any
language. We will be introducing, in the future, a
user oriented version of SGML that will allow users
to do some degree of personal activity creation.
However, there should be no difficulty with any
application programmer integrating any existing
computer applications in the organization into
tailored activities that may then be directly
embedded in the TEIES communication process.

PRIVILEGES, ROLES, AND TICKETS

The definition of a role on TEIES is based upon a
combination of the fundamental internal privileges
allowed for the role and the object to which the role
is linked. There are over 25 privileges defined which
are based upon the types of conditional
communication actions individuals can take in day-to-
day situations (e.g. placing material in someone's file
without being able to see what is there). Roles are
defined to be meaningful metaphors at the user level
and are open-ended in that it is quite easy to
introduce new roles and privileges as needed.

Tickets are a mechanism whereby any member may
transfer specific privileges to another member. For
example, a ticket may be issued by an author to allow
the modification of a text item by someone who does
not normally have that editing privilege. A ticket
may be made conditional on such parameters as
number of times it can be used or the time period
during which it is valid. The person issuing the ticket
may also withdraw it at any time.

The associated concepts of privileges, roles and tickets
are completely open-ended and allow for the future
expansion and tailoring of the human communication
protocols.

CONFERENCES

The core of any collaborative system is the shared
group discussion space. Over the years, many specific
computer mediated conferencing structures have
been evolved for specific purposes. A great deal of
the variation among these structures can be
accounted for by such parameters and functionality
as the sizes of allowed root items and replies,
organization and conditions placed upon the entry
and delivery of text items, voting procedures, roles of
humans within the group and conference, indexing
alternatives, and the incorporation of specialized data
structures and hypertext-like linkages among text
items. In TEIES all of these features have degrees of
tailorability which may be selected by the person
creating a conference for a specific application.

There are seven default conference structure choices
that a beginning user may select from when
establishing a conference, which will automatically
set parameters according to system-wide settings.
These are:

. Discussion Conference: Structured to optimize
general purpose discussion by active groups of
up to fifty or more individuals.

. Seminar Conference: Designed to facilitate
learning oriented seminars and the "Virtual
Classroom" [15]. It will include such
special activities as "question branches" where
a member cannot see the answers of others to a
question until he or she has supplied an answer
or opinion.

. Information Exchange: Optimized for very large
groups (hundreds) engaged in unpredictable
information exchange. It allows a high degree
of branching, controlled indexing, and self
selection of what sub-branches to track.

. Project Management: Incorporates various
tracking, selection, and organizing features to
maintain awareness of modifications, milestones,
status, and task assignments that are taking
place.

. Composition Notebook: Allows a high degree of
selective roles in different designated portions
of the conference, and tracks the updates and
changes being made to the generation of a
collaborative document.

. Data Collection Conference: Designed for the
organization of structured data, and the
tracking and validation of data changes for a
group building and utilizing a collaborative
data base.

. Simulation-Game Conference: Structured to allow
a group to carry out a role playing,
event-oriented scenario game. It allows the
game director to control allowed communication
channels and the conditions and timing for
events to occur and actions to be taken.

The above default conference types preset the many structuring options that are available for the design of a conference. More experienced users can choose their own combinations of tailoring options for conferences they own. This provides very detailed tailoring of the fine parameters of a conference structure (e.g. the size of the comment allowed at any response level).

Key to any conferencing activity is the ability of any member of the conference to be able to find out the status of the other members as to what they have read and what they have done. TEIES will enhance this aspect considerably over prior conferencing systems. Summary reviews will be available on both the activity and the resulting structure of the discourse.

SUMMARY

The TEIES effort represents a new generation of CMC software that will allow the design, development and evaluation of tailored collaborative systems. The ability of application programers to integrate other computer resources and systems with TEIES without any concern for the problems of security and access privileges is the principal key element to facilitating this objective. TEIES provides the toolbox to overcome the tremendous programming bottleneck present in the development of collaborative systems. Everything has been done to minimize the human effort needed to create a tailored system. The forms based interface for TEIES and the open ended concepts of privileges, roles, activities, group sharing, and notifications allow the incorporation of tailored facilities without any fundamental change to the interface or to the basic metaphor of the communication process and associated list processing.

Undoubtedly the planned design we have laid down for the development of TEIES will undergo much evolution and change based upon the feedback from its utilization. Based upon our experiences with the evolution of the original EIES system since its inception in 1976, we strongly believe that the use of CMC systems in an organizational setting has to be viewed as an evolutionary process. The CMC, itself, should serve as the vehicle for the users to provide feedback and to allow them to participate in the evolving design of the system. We have attempted to design TEIES as a tool for that process. Furthermore, the ability of TEIES to be a primary interface to other computer based resources would allow the evolutionary approach to be applied to all the information systems within the organization.

```
TEIES HOMEBASE          Screen 1 of 1          Screen code: 000

Objects:                   New:    Modifiers:

1.    Notifications:        #      1.    New      items
2.    Mail/Messages:        #      2.    Marked items:      #
3.    Conferences:          #      3.    Item        categories
4.    Directory                    4.    Reception   categories
5.    Member  information          5.    Distribution categories
6.    Group   information          6.    Types       of items
7.    Control information          7.    Status      of items
8.    Special systems              8.    Parts       of items
                                   9.    Ordering    of lists


OBJECT CHOICES? _____       MODIFIER CHOICES? _____

Actions:

View  Find  Review  Create  Modify  Do  Organize   Help   (?/f1)
1.    2.    3.      4.      5.      6.  7.          Quit (--/quit)
ACTION CHOICE? _____
```

```
TEIES CASUAL           Screen 1 of 1          Screen code: 000.C

                                  number
View: NEW notifications ? y_         #
      NEW mail          ? y_         #
      NEW conferences   ? y_         #
      MARKED items      ? n_         #
      UNDONE activities ? n_

                                  Optional fill in:
Enter: conference       ? n_      Member/Group(s) ? _____
Create: notification    ? n_      Message         ? _____
        message         ? n_      Conference      ? _____
        comment         ? n_        Comment       ? _____
        draft           ? n_      Scratchpad      ? 1__
Modify: any item        ? n_      Index key       ? _____
Find:   members         ? n_      Name/label part ? _____
        groups          ? n_      Modifier        ? _____
        messages        ? n_
        conferences     ? n_

ESC/PA2 = get control menu
Command? _____   Screen PgUp/PgDn (f7/f8)
```

Figure II: HOMEBASE AND CASUAL SCREENS

REFERENCES

[1] Zipf, George Kingsley, <u>Human Behavior and the Principle of Least Effort</u>, Addison Wesley, Reading MA, 1949.

[2] Hiltz, Starr Roxanne and Murray Turoff, <u>The Network Nation: Human Communication via Computer</u>, Addison-Wesley, 1978.

[3] Turoff, Murray, "Delphi Conferencing: Computer Based Conferencing with Anonymity," <u>Journal of Technological Forecasting and Social Change</u>, Volume 3, Number 2, 1972, 159-204.

[4] Kerr, Elaine and Starr Roxanne Hiltz, <u>Computer-Mediated Communication Systems</u>, Academic Press, New York, 1982.

[5] Rice, Ronald and Associates, <u>The New Media</u>, Sage, Beverly Hills CA, 1984.

[6] Garg, Pankaj K. and Walt Sacacchi, "A Hypertext System to Manage Software Life Cycle Documents," <u>21st Hawaii International Conference on Systems</u>, Honolulu, HI, 1987.

[7] Lowe, David, "Cooperative Structuring of Information: The Representation of Reasoning and Debate," <u>Journal of Man-Machine Studies</u>, Volume 23, Number 1, July, 1985, 97-111.

[8] Trigg, Randall H. and Mark Weiser, "TEXTNET: A Network-Based Approach to Text Handling," <u>ACM Transactions on Office Information Systems</u>, Volume 4, Number 1, January 1986, 1-23.

[9] Conklin, Jeff, and Michael Begeman, "gIBIS: A Hypertext Tool for Team Deliberation," <u>Hypertext 1987 Papers</u>, Chapel Hill, NC, November 1987.

[10] Bahgat, Ahmed, <u>A Decision Support System for Zero-Based Capital Budgeting: A Case Study</u>, Ph.D.in Management Thesis, Rutgers Graduate School of Management, Newark, NJ, 1986.

[11] DeSanctis, Gerardine and Brent Gallupe, "A Foundation for the Study of Group Decision Support Systems," <u>Management Science</u>, Volume 33, Number 5, May 1987, 589-609.

[12] Scher, Julian M., "Distributed Decision Support Systems for Management and Organizations," <u>First International Conference on Decision Support Systems</u>, (DSS-1), Execucom Systems Corporation, June 8-10, 1981, 130-140.

[13] Hiltz, Starr Roxanne and Murray Turoff, "The Evolution of User Behavior in a Computerized Conferencing System," <u>Communications of the ACM</u>, Volume 24, Number 11, November, 1981.

[14] Hiltz, Starr Roxanne and Murray Turoff, "Structuring Computer-Mediated Communications to Avoid Information Overload," <u>Communications of the ACM</u>, July 1985.

[15] Hiltz, Starr Roxanne, "The 'Virtual Classroom': Using Computer-Mediated Communication for University Teaching," <u>Journal of Communication</u>, Spring 1986, 95-104.

[16] Turoff, Murray, "Information, Value and the Internal Marketplace," <u>Journal of Technological Forecasting and Social Change</u>, Volume 27, Number 4, July, 1985, 357-374.

[17] Turoff, Murray and Starr Roxanne Hiltz, "Computer Support for Group versus Individual Decisions," <u>IEEE Transactions on Communications</u>, Con-30, Number 1, January, 1982.

[18] Coombs, James H., Allen H. Renear and Steven J. DeRose, "Markup Systems and the Future of Scholarly Text Processing," <u>Communications of the ACM</u>, Volume 30, Number 11, November 1987, 933-947.

[19] Carroll, John M. and John Thomas, "Metaphor and the Cognitive Representation of Computing Systems," <u>IEEE Transactions on Man, Systems and Cybernetics</u>, Volume SMC-12, March-April, 1982, 107-116.

[20] Chandrasekaran, B., "Natural and Social System Metaphors for Distributed Problem Solving: Introduction to the Issue," <u>IEEE Transactions on Systems, Man and Cybernetics</u>, Volume SMC-11, Number 1, January 1981.

[21] Brown, John Seely and Susan E Newman, "Issues in Cognitive and Social Ergonomics: For our House to Bauhaus," <u>Human-Computer Interaction</u>, Volume 1, 359-391, 1985.

[22] Rosenberg, Jarrett K., and Thomas P. Moran, "Generic Commands," <u>Human Computer Interaction - INTERACT 1984</u>, edited by B Shackel, IFIP, 1985.

[23] Hiltz, Starr Roxanne, "Collaborative Learning in a Virtual Classroom," <u>Proceedings of the Conference on Computer Supported Cooperative Work</u>, Portland, September, 1988.

Intensional Concepts

in an

Object Database Model

David Beech

Hewlett-Packard Laboratories
1501, Page Mill Road
Palo Alto, CA 94304

ABSTRACT: There is a requirement for a stronger treatment of intensional concepts and more general inferential ability within database systems. A framework for achieving this will be described in terms of extensions to an object data model.

The type Concept is introduced into the model as a subtype of Action. Intensional concepts may then be defined as filters or generators, depending on the nature of the defining formula. In either case, the dual action should be available—provided automatically by the system or explicitly by the user.

Finally, sets and types are treated as special cases of extensional concepts, leading to a novel structure of the hierarchy of system types.

1. Introduction

One of the main features of database interfaces or sublanguages has been their treatment of large collections of information, with search and retrieval operations applicable to hierarchical structures [Tsichritzis & Lochovsky 76], or DBTG sets [CODASYL 69], or relations [Codd 70], or functional models [Shipman 81]. Apart from notable exceptions such as SETL [Schwartz 73], Smalltalk [Goldberg & Robson 83], and Prolog [Clocksin & Mellish 81] in their various ways, programming languages have generally fought shy of providing more than toolkits for dealing with large collections other than arrays.

However, previous database models (and Smalltalk) have emphasized the extensional definition of collections, requiring them to be populated explicitly with their members rather than implicitly by terms which satisfy, or are generated by, some formula. The motivation for wanting a strong intensional model is that much human information is of this kind, employing intensional concepts rather than relying on memory of large extensions, and that different people in any case use different views of the same information. Rela-

"Intensional Concepts in an Object Database Model" by D. Beech from *Object-Oriented Programming Systems, Languages, and Applications (OOPSLA) Proceedings*, 1988, pp. 164-175. Copyright © 1988 by The Association for Computing Machinery, Inc., reprinted by permission.

tional views provide retrieval capability on intensionally defined collections, but are weak in the necessary flexibility of update semantics because of the absence of general operations in the relational model.

The various object models now current in programming languages may be combined with database ideas to provide the answer, since the essence of an object model is that it comprises both the representation and the manipulation of objects. Moreover, object concepts are deeply ingrained in natural language and human thought generally, and find their formal expression in the terms and classes of mathematical logic and in languages such as Prolog.

This paper modifies and develops some ideas originally introduced as part of a comprehensive object database model [Beech 87]. A Concept type is introduced to define an intensional concept as either a filter or a generator, depending on whether the defining formula tests whether an object (or n-tuple of objects) exemplifies the concept in the filter case, or produces exemplifying objects iteratively in the generator case. Update operations Assert and Retract are defined on this type, and provide the hooks for dealing with view update by specialized actions where necessary.

The treatment of Concepts may be seen to be in the spirit of Prolog functions, except that formulae are not limited to Horn clauses, negation is given its conventional predicate calculus semantics, and generative definitions are provided. The treatment of generative definitions is most like that of Iterators in CLU [Liskov *et al.* 79]. A kind of duality is exhibited between the filter and generator definitions of Concepts, and may be exploited in providing transparent usage of these objects. Collections such as Sets are then treated as a degenerate (purely extensional) case of Concepts, and Types are treated as a specialization of Sets, having additional properties.

Examples will be given in a higher-level language syntax to illustrate how the underlying primitives can be utilized by extending SQL [ANSI 86].

1.1 Motivation

Before developing a proposal for the treatment of intensional concepts in an object database model, we will first try to clarify our terminology, and expand on our view of the requirements.

Consider some *concepts* involved in family relationships. There are those like "person", "parent", "grandfather", or "head of family", which correspond to nouns or noun phrases. A given object may be an example of one or more such concepts. Another way of regarding this is that there are corresponding predicates "is-person", etc., which may be defined to determine whether an object is an example of a given concept. ("It seems suitable to say that a *concept* is a function whose value is always a truth-value." [Frege 93, p.135])

Verbal concepts such as "_ is the grandfather of _", "_ is head of family comprised of _", or "_ loves _", or "_ is child of _ and _", may be regarded as a generalization of the above. They may be exemplified by n-tuples of objects, which satisfy corresponding functions of n arguments (usually called "relations" in logic when n > 1, although we shall refrain from doing so in order to avoid confusion with database parlance).

When we say that a concept has been given an *extensional* definition, we shall mean that its exemplification is solely determined by a succession of explicit assertions that individual objects (or tuples of objects) are or are not examples of the concept. We will show in italics a first approximation to how this might be expressed:

Create concept Person (Object o);

Assert Person(o1), Person(o3),

  Person(o4);

Retract Person(o1);

Assert Person(o9);

Create concept

FatherOf (Person f, Person c);

Assert FatherOf(o3, o4);

An *intensional* definition of a concept employs some formula or algorithm or rule which enables its exemplification to be determined from other information without requiring direct assertions about this concept. For example:

Create concept Father (Person p) as

Exists Person c such that FatherOf(p, c);

Create concept

GrandfatherOf (Person gf, Person gc) as

Exists Person p such that FatherOf(gf, p)

and ParentOf(p, gc);

(Note that the extensional/intensional distinction refers to a particular definition of a concept, not to the concept itself. There may be many ways of defining an interrelated set of concepts with different choices as to what is to be extensional or intensional. Paradoxically, an extensionally defined concept is a rock on which we can build intensional definitions, and at the same time is inherently meaningless. In a way, the choice of something as extensionally defined is a confession of arbitrariness or disinterest or ignorance— we may have to be told explicitly who someone's parents are because we were not present at the birth, and lack other intensional evidence.)

Of course, an intensional definition may use other extensionally defined concepts. It is also often the case in a world of incomplete information that an intensional definition may be indecisive, and yet may be supplemented

by direct extensional information about the same concept. For example:

Assert GrandfatherOf(o1, o9);

We shall say that these are *hybrid* definitions. In this respect, Prolog provides the right structure.

So one major requirement for the kind of database model that we are focussing on is to have a general and convenient means for the representation and manipulation of intensional concepts, well integrated with the treatment of extensional and hybrid ones.

With respect to relational database technology, this calls for major advances in the treatment of "views". First, of course, there must be an object model with a sound entity concept. Then the presence of actions (messages, operations, functions) as a first-class part of an object model makes it possible to define more general views, and especially to specify any desired form of view update. There will also be a shift of emphasis, with the database system depending, like the human mind, much more on knowing how to generate, and iterate over, examples of concepts when it has to, rather than relying on rote memory.

With respect to artifical intelligence, there is a greater emphasis here on *representation* of information, even where we do not at present know how to automate efficient reasoning with all forms of it. The next generation of database systems will need to evolve to satisfy the requirements of much of the next century. As soon as such systems are available, they can begin collecting information which is intelligible to human users. Initially, these systems will sometimes have to ask users to reformulate questions, just as we do in conversation ourselves, but over the next few decades they will become much smarter and more efficient, and the information they have been amassing for years will be more tractable.

Another major requirement is to be able to get there from here. In this introduction so far, we have tried to suggest a change of perspective, and now we want to balance this by stressing the need to pay attention to existing programming languages and database technology. We shall try to make it clear that our proposals offer the hope of real-world evolution rather than requiring the adoption of completely new languages and systems.

2. Object Model

We will summarize here as much of a basic object model as needed to introduce the treatment of intensional concepts.

2.1 Types

Every object is an instance of one or more types. There is the usual notion of a type semi-lattice, i.e. the possibility of multiple inheritance, although we shall not discuss the details of this here. Types may also be added to and removed from objects dynamically, to reflect the need to retain the identity of long-lived objects in a database even while their nature may change considerably. A language interface to this model can look as follows:

```
Create type Person,

        Employee subtype of Person,

        Pilot;

Create Employee instance Smith;

Add type Pilot to Smith;
```

Types are themselves modelled as objects, and like other objects may be alterable and versionable.

2.2 Actions

We intend the term "action" to be a neutral way of referring to the general idea of a procedure, operation, function, or message, without implying any of the more specific conno-

tations which these terms might have—some of them may deserve to be modelled as subtypes of Action. Actions are also objects, defined to take arguments of certain types and return a result (possibly many-valued) of a certain type. Actions are *applied* to their arguments—"apply" is not itself an action, but is a meta-action of the model. Actions may produce truth-values or results of any other type, and may be defined by explicit update or by formulae:

```
Create action name(Person)

                --> String;

Assert name(Smith) = 'Z.Y. Smith';

Assert name(Mendoza) =

                'Carlos Mendoza';


Create action ManagerName

        (Employee e)  --> String

    as Select name(m)

        for each Employee m

        where m = manager(dept(e));
```

Formulae in the model provide recursive computability. Actions may also be defined by algorithms with side-effects, and they may be *foreign actions* written in programming languages provided that their argument and result interfaces are consistent with this model.

2.3 Extensional Collections

We treat extensional collections of objects differently from pure sets, and have previously called them *combinations*. A combination is itself an object, and obeys the usual rules for object identity. Objects must be inserted and removed explicitly, and it is thus possible for two combinations to have the same members without being considered identical. This corresponds to the semantic situation in a time-varying world where the objects being modelled are distinct, although at a given level of abstraction and at a given time they cannot be distinguished by their components. Having emphasized this distinction from mathematical sets, we feel it is probably simpler to proceed by calling our combinations Sets in what follows:

```
Create Set S1, S2;

Insert Hecht, Mendoza into S1;

Remove Hecht from S1;


If Empty(S1) or Smith in S2

  Create Set S3;
```

Finite collections that are ordered and may contain duplicate references to the same object are known as *lists*. Lists also are treated as objects. They have Lisp-like actions defined on them as primitives:

```
Create List L1, L2, L3;

L1 := ⟨ Smith, Hecht, Mendoza ⟩ ;

L2 := tail(L1);

L3 := ⟨ head(L1), L2 ⟩ ;
```

Iteration is possible over the members of a set or of a list:

```
For each Person p

        in {Hecht, Mendoza}

    SomeAction(p);
```

3. Intensional Concepts

This section will show how to satisfy the intensional requirements described in the introduction. The main thrust is to determine how the notion of *concept* used in the introductory examples should be expressed in an object model with types, actions, and extensional sets and lists. We will continue to use the original example, with Person and Father respectively as extensional and intensional concepts of one variable, and FatherOf and GrandfatherOf as concepts of two variables.

3.1 Actions or Types?

Types in an object model seem to play a classificatory role which equips them to correspond to concepts—yet actions have the greater generality in addressing the different kinds of concept definition that we have discussed.

Extensional concepts of two or more variables may be modelled by actions (e.g. predicates) whose values are explicitly set to determine whether the given arguments exemplify the concept (see Figure 1).

Intensional concepts of any number of variables may likewise be modelled by actions defined procedurally or non-procedurally in terms of other information.

#Args	Extensional	Intensional
1	*Person(o)* Action or Type	*Father(p)* Action
>1	*FatherOf(p1,p2)* Action	*GrandfatherOf(p1,p2)* Action

Figure 1. Concepts as Actions or Types

With an extensional concept of one variable, however, there is a choice between using an action or a type:

```
Create action Person(Object)

              ⟶ Boolean;

Create Object instance Smith;

Assert Person(Smith) = True;
```

or:

87

```
Create type Person;
Create Person instance Smith;
```

In the latter case, a corresponding predicate IsPerson may be maintained, but there is more to it than this. A type, in our model at least, can be instantiated, whereas setting a predicate True for given arguments does not create a new object—the semantic power of an action to remember such information is primitive, rather than being modelled in terms of other objects which have some other primitive powers of memory. Moreover, there is another property of types which is very widespread in programming language and data models. This is their use for type checking of parameters and results of actions. The type specified for a parameter or result serves as a constraint, yet is clearly a very partial mechanism, governed usually by the desire for simplicity and as much static checking as possible. Type expressions, and more general constraint expressions, are the subject of important research, but have not yet found their way into general practice. Perhaps we shall see type systems evolve to become richer, or perhaps we shall see the existing limited systems survive as a well-judged engineering trade-off between simplicity and power, to be supplemented by more general constraint systems (not limited to argument and result checking) as these become practicable. In any case, the retention of the existing form of types as one way of modelling extensional concepts of one variable appears justified.

But now it is reasonable to pose the question whether *intensional* concepts of one variable should be expressible, not only as actions, but also as types? It would certainly be possible to introduce intensional types into the model, but it would conflict with the current tendency for types to be instantiable. It may be argued that system types like Integer are already not explicitly instantiable, and that in systems which support unbounded integer computation, it may be philosophically uncomfortable to some (the author included) to postulate an infinite set of instances already instantiated. However, this suggests a solution, that new instances of such types may be implicitly created as required, and thereafter remain in existence just like explicitly created instances of a type. This leads to consideration of the second conflict with current usage of types—that the instantiation of types becomes highly dynamic and difficult to check. Worse than this, determination of the types of objects would have to be defined very precisely as to when and in what order it was carried out, in case any of the actions involved had side-effects (which are hard to exclude in database systems which are largely designed to achieve side-effects). Then much optimization might be inhibited in case it led to different results, not merely of the computation, but even of the type checking itself.

So for the present, it looks advisable to avoid intensional types. This also helps with the requirement to evolve from the present, without requiring a complete change to a new language. Possible approaches such as the embedding of a data language in a programming language (*à la* SQL), and the sharing of type definitions between languages, are facilitated by adopting a conservative treatment of types.

So we are left with a uniform treatment of the four cases considered, in which extensional or intensional concepts, of one or more variables, may all be modelled by actions. Supplementing this, there is the alternative, in the case of extensional concepts of one variable, of being able to define them as types and to instantiate them explicitly and to have conventional type checking carried out.

3.2 Concepts as Actions

The next stage of the inquiry will focus on closer examination of the kinds of actions appropriate for the definition of concepts, and on the relationship between these actions and the collections of objects which exemplify the concepts.

Some actions are essentially filters, whose primary purpose is to determine whether an object exemplifies a certain concept, or whether certain objects are in a specific relationship to each other. In the multi-argument case, they may be defined symmetrically on their arguments to return a truth-value, or they may be rearranged into equivalent forms:

```
Create action nameP

    (Person, String)  ⟶  Boolean;

Create action name ( Person )

                ⟶  String;
```

We shall want to assert and retract specific propositions involving such actions, and to iterate over the tuples of objects that satisfy them.

Other actions, such as to display a circuit on some class of device, may have a similar interface:

```
Create action display

    (Circuit, Device)  ⟶  Integer;
```

The semantics of such an action are essentially directional—given certain input arguments, it will cause certain side-effects, and return a result. In this example, the integer result may serve as a return code to indicate error situations such as -1 for a device malfunction. While a syntactic rearrangement into a form returning a Boolean is possible here too, it does not correspond to any semantic symmetry. It will often be the case that the definer of such a function does not want to give any semantics to assertions and retractions and iterations—e.g., the assertion that display(c2,d9) = -1 will not be allowed to mean that the device d9 must be caused to malfunction when passed c2.

Thus not all actions are used to model concepts in our sense. Concepts are a specialization of actions, and we therefore introduce the type Concept as a subtype of Action. The meta-action "apply", and certain actions (e.g., to retrieve the action definition) are defined on the Action type, and are applicable to all actions. Other actions such as assertion, retraction and iteration, are defined on the Concept type, and are available only if an action also has this type.

So in section 2.2 above, between the creation of the action name and the assertion, we should now have to insert:

```
Add type Concept to name;
```

Better still, if we know in the first place that the action is to be a Concept, we can create it as such, and automatically acquire the supertype Action:

```
Create Concept name(Person)

                ⟶  String;
```

Now for the intensional examples, we shall employ an SQL-like syntax, as in Object SQL [Beech 88], in order to illustrate the evolutionary possibilities, and the analogies with view definition:

```
Create Concept Father(Person p) as

        Select

        exists Person c

        where FatherOf(p,c);


Create Concept GrandfatherOf

    (Person gf, Person gc)  as

        Select

        exists Person p

        where FatherOf(gf,p) and

            ParentOf(p,gc);
```

Beneath this slightly higher-level language, the underlying object model makes it possible to iterate over instances of a type, or (tuples of) objects satisfying a Concept. Query evaluation strategies must choose between the alternatives in combining the each or for each clause with the where clause. To evaluate

```
Select each Person gf,Person gc

    where GrandfatherOf(gf,gc)
```

it would be possible, for example, to iterate over the Person type and simply apply the FatherOf and ParentOf Concepts to each p; or to iterate over the ParentOf Concept and within that to apply the FatherOf Concept. The Iterate primitive in the model passes an Action to be applied to each satisfying tuple, and also an Integer which places an upper bound on the number of iterations if non-negative.

It is also possible to define GrandfatherOf as a hybrid Concept:

```
Create Concept GrandfatherOf

        (Person gf, Person gc)

    with Set S1  as

        Select

        exists Person p

        where FatherOf(gf,p) and

            ParentOf(p,gc);
```

The default semantics of querying such a Concept are that the Set object S1 is searched first for an extensional assertion about the given Persons gf and gc, and only if none is found will the intensional formula be evaluated. Other treatments of semantics, such as checking for conflicts between the extension and the intension, can be explicitly specified if desired.

Explicit specification of semantics becomes a much bigger issue for update of intensional or hybrid concepts. The default for Assert or Retract is to make some minimal unique change, if such can be found, to some other extensional information so that the effect is achieved via the intensional part of the con-cept definition. To override these defaults, the Assert and Retract actions can be defined for specific Concepts:

```
Create Concept GrandfatherOf

        (Person gf, Person gc)

    with Set S1  as

        Select

        exists Person p

        where FatherOf(gf,p) and

            ParentOf(p,gc)

    semantics

      Assert:(GrandfatherOf(gf,gc) :

            /* no-op ---

                already true */,

        ... /* try to change

            FatherOf, etc. */,

        else add ⟨gf,gc⟩ to S1;

        );
```

To summarize this intuitive introduction, we list the primitive set of actions defined on Concepts:

Initialize (Concept; Assertions:List of Sets; Semantics:List of Actions) $\longrightarrow$ Concept

GetAssertions (Concept) $\longrightarrow$ List of Sets

GetSemantics (Concept) $\longrightarrow$ List of Actions

Assert (Concept; Tuple:List; Logical) $\longrightarrow$ Concept

Retract (Concept; Tuple:List; Logical) $\longrightarrow$ Concept

Iterate (Concept; Action; UpperBound: Integer) $\longrightarrow$ Concept

The Assertions parameter on Initialize allows for a List of Sets to be provided, so that they may be referenced within the Action part of the combined Action-Concept object. A single set would often suffice, as in the `GrandfatherOf` example above. However, if the definer of the Concept does not want to make the closed world assumption that what is not asserted to be true is false, a separate set may be used for explicit assertions about people known not to be grandfathers (or for those about whom it is unknown, depending on the likely rarity of each case). So an arbitrary number of sets may be provided in the initialization, to be used as desired in the defining Formula for the Action.

The Logical type used in the definition of Assert and Retract is similarly a generalization of Boolean to allow an Unknown truth value, but further discussion of this is beyond the scope of the present paper.

3.3 Generative Definition

There is another kind of intensional definition of a concept, where the defining action is not a test of given objects to see whether they exemplify the concept, but is a means of generating successive examples.

Filter and generator definitions have a kind of duality, with similar actions available on the concepts but different relative difficulties of performing them. It is straightforward to use a concept defined as a filter to test given objects, but may be difficult to find an efficient means of generating all examples; whereas for a generatively defined concept, the definition provides a direct means of producing examples, but the method of testing may be difficult to derive, or may even be non-terminating.

We illustrate simple creation of a generative definition and bounded iteration using it:

```
Create concept Fibonacci()
    ──→ List of Integer
  generated by sequence (1:) of
  F (Integer n)  ──→ Integer
```

```
( n < 0: error(),
  n = 0: 1,
  n = 1: 2,
  else F(n-1) + F(n-2) );
```

```
For first 10 Fibonacci() f
  print(f);
```

It is also worth noting that a generative definition, unlike a filter definition, provides for iteration over newly-generated as well as pre-existing objects, for example allowing generated objects to be inserted into a collection to materialize the extension of the concept.

4. Collections and Types Revisited

It is now instructive to compare the actions defined on concepts with those defined on collections such as sets:

Test	⟷	IsMember
Assert	⟷	Insert
Retract	⟷	Remove
Iterate	⟷	Iterate

The semantic similarities suggest that corresponding actions be given the same names, and that Collection becomes a subtype of Concept in the type hierarchy—collections are the subset of concepts which are purely extensionally defined. Collections themselves can be classified into a hierarchy according to further constraints and additional actions available, such as the ordering constraint on a list, and an action to reverse the order. We cannot develop this topic fully here, but will indicate the positions of Bag, Set, List and OrderedSet in our hierarchy (cf. the Smalltalk collection hierarchy, which includes other types, and is also somewhat complicated in structure by the absence of multiple inheritance).

This treatment of collections is in the spirit of data abstraction, where the actions on a collection provide the interface to the collection and make it unnecessary to visualize objects existing inside the collection. It may also ease the philosophical worries as to whether collections exist, at least as regards existence in an information model or as mental objects. Thus in *Principia Mathematica* [Whitehead & Russell 10, p.135]: "Classes, so far as we introduce them, are merely symbolic or linguistic conveniences, not genuine objects as their members are if they are individuals. ... an extension (which is the same as a class) is an incomplete symbol, whose use always acquires its meaning through a reference to intension." In our model, we attempt to close the gap by treating extensions as degenerate intensions, whose defining formulae are essentially conjunctions of explicit assertions, of the form

$$\lambda\,(x,y,\dots).\;(x{=}a \wedge y{=}b \wedge \dots) \vee \dots$$

Finally, we return to the question of the relationship between a type and an extensional concept of one variable. The actions available on concepts again correspond to actions on types:

Test	$\longleftrightarrow$	HasType
Assert	$\longleftrightarrow$	AddType
Retract	$\longleftrightarrow$	RemoveType
Iterate	$\longleftrightarrow$	Iterate

Since the instances of a type do not include duplicates or have a guaranteed ordering, types are analogous to concepts defined as sets. However, they are a special case of sets with additional properties, for example being specifiable for argument and result positions in action definitions, so Type may be placed in the hierarchy as a subtype of Set.

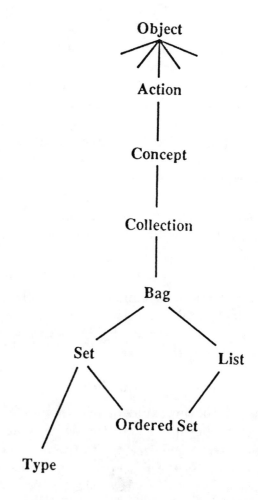

Figure 2. Actions, Concepts, Collections, and Types in the Type Hierarchy

4. Conclusion

A model of intensional concepts for object databases has been presented at two levels— an intuitive higher level in order to illustrate its potential as an evolutionary continuation of existing programming languages and database languages, and a more primitive level defining the essential semantic actions beneath the syntactic sugar. Semantic similarities between actions, concepts, sets and types are captured by defining Action to be a supertype of Concept, which is a supertype of Set, which is a supertype of Type.

Something very close to the foundations of this model has been implemented as part of the Iris system [Fishman *et al.* 87]. The extensions proposed above aim to distinguish updatable from non-updatable functions, to provide comprehensive view update facilities, to introduce an appropriate treatment of collections such as sets, and to provide a base for more inferential power in the database system, including the use of recursive function definitions and queries.

Much future work will be needed to explore pragmatic issues of how far the default semantics can be carried by the system, how unfruitful searches will be terminated by timing out or other measures, and what new forms of query optimization are called for. The hope is for cumulative progress rather than an immediate breakthrough.

Another major question which arises, as always, is the extent to which the language used to define actions for specifying intensional concepts and their update semantics needs to approach a full-fledged programming language. The conclusion section of a paper is no place to begin that discussion, but, as we have indicated earlier, we make a small extension to give us computability of recursive functions, and provide for this to be supplemented by the use of foreign actions written in other languages.

References

[ANSI 86]

American National Standards Institute. Database Language SQL. ANSI X3.135-1986.

[Beech 87]

Beech, D. Groundwork for an Object Database Model. In: Shriver, B. and Wegner, P. (eds.) Research Directions in Object-Oriented Languages. MIT Press, 1987.

[Beech 88]

Beech, D. A Foundation for Evolution from Relational to Object Databases. In: Schmidt, J.W., Ceri, S., and Missikoff, M. (eds.) Advances in Database Technology—EDBT '88. Lecture Notes in Computer Science 303. Springer-Verlag, 1988.

[Clocksin & Mellish 81]

Clocksin, W.F. and Mellish, C.S. Programming in Prolog. Springer-Verlag (1981).

[CODASYL 69]

Data Base Task Group of CODASYL Programming Language Committee. *Report* (1969 October).

[Codd 70]

Codd, E.F. A Relational Model of Data for Large Shared Data Banks. *Comm. ACM* 13:6 (1970 June), 377-387.

[Fishman *et al.* 87]

Fishman, D.H., Beech, D., Cate, H.P., Chow, E.C., Connors, T., Davis, J.W., Derrett, N., Hoch, C.G., Kent, W., Lyngbaek, P., Mahbod, B., Neimat, M.A., Ryan, T.A., and Shan, M.C. Iris: An Object-Oriented Database Management System. *ACM Transactions on Office Information Systems* 5:1 (January 1987), 48-69.

[Frege 93]

Frege, G. Grundgesetze der Arithmetik. 1893. In: Geach, P., and Black, M. Translations from the Philosophical Writings of Gottlob Frege. Blackwell, Oxford. 1952.

[Goldberg & Robson 83]

Goldberg, A. and Robson, D. *Smalltalk-80: The Language and its Implementation.* Addison-Wesley (1983).

[Liskov *et al.* 79]

    Liskov, B., Atkinson R., Bloom, T., Moss, E., Schaffert, E., Scheifler, B., and Snyder, A. CLU Reference Manual. MIT/LCS/TR-225. 1979.

[Schwartz 73]

    Schwartz, J.T. The SETL Language and Examples of its Use. Courant Institute, New York University. 1973.

[Shipman 81]

    Shipman, D.W. The Functional Data Model and the Data Language DAPLEX. *ACM Trans. on Database Syst.* 6:1 (1981 March), 140-173.

[Tsichritzis & Lochovsky 79]

    Tsichritzis D.C., and Lochovsky, F.H. Hierarchical Database Management Systems. *ACM Computing Surveys,* 8:1 (1976 March).

[Whitehead & Russell 10]

    Whitehead, A.N., and Russell, B. Principia Mathematica. Cambridge University Press. 1910.

Reprinted from *IEEE Transactions on Software Engineering*, May 1988, pages 611-629. Copyright © 1988 by The Institute of Electrical and Electronics Engineers, Inc. All rights reserved.

PROBE Spatial Data Modeling and Query Processing in an Image Database Application

JACK A. ORENSTEIN AND FRANK A. MANOLA, MEMBER, IEEE

Abstract—The PROBE research project has produced results in the areas of data modeling, spatial/temporal query processing, recursive query processing, and database system architecture for "nontraditional" application areas, many of which involve spatial data and data with complex structure. PROBE provides the *point set* as a construct for modeling spatial data. This abstraction is compatible with notions of spatial data found in a wide variety of applications. PROBE is extensible and supports a generalization hierarchy, so it is possible to incorporate application-specific implementations of the point set abstraction. PROBE's query processor supports point sets with the *geometry filter*, an optimizer of spatial queries. Spatial queries are processed by decomposing them into 1) a set-at-a-time portion that is evaluated efficiently by the geometry filter and 2) a portion that involves detailed manipulations of individual spatial objects by functions supplied with the application-specific representation. The output from the first step is an approximate answer, which is refined in the second step. The data model and the geometry filter are valid in all dimensions, and they are compatible with a wide variety of representations. PROBE's spatial data model and geometry filter are described, and it is shown how these facilities can be used to support image database applications.

Index Terms—Object-oriented database system, spatial data, spatial query.

I. Introduction

THE numeric and string types available in most programming languages and database systems were designed to support applications that are much simpler than the computer-aided engineering, geographical, and image database applications being contemplated. In traditional business applications, fixed-point types are used. Several languages offer extensive built-in capabilities for describing the range, precision, and format of these numbers. Traditional engineering applications require floating-point numbers, which are well supported in virtually all programming languages, and standards for floating-point representation and precision are under development. Even though there is much specialization within each of these application areas, there seems to be no need for corresponding specializations of the data types mentioned. For example, the floating-point facilities used by mechanical

engineers also serve the purposes of electrical and civil engineers.

The situation is much different in applications that manipulate spatial data. Notions of spatial data differ greatly from one application to another. The most obvious difference is in the dimensionality of the data. Temporal data can be viewed as one-dimensional (1-D) spatial data. Geographic applications and VLSI design involve two-dimensional data. Geological applications require three dimensions, and solid modeling sometimes requires four dimensions (to detect interference between moving 3-D objects). In some applications, spatial objects are continuous, while in others, space is best thought of as being discrete. Finally, spatial operations and representations of spatial objects differ greatly from one application to another. For example, the techniques of solid modeling (parametrically defined curves and surfaces and constructive solid geometry) are not used in geographical applications. For these reasons, it is unlikely that there will be a small collection of spatial data types that will become as widely accepted as the simpler types discussed above.

The term "image database" is a broad one, and again, there is no single view of spatial data that is adequate for all image database applications. For example, image databases often have to support both continuous and discrete representations [7], [23]. In addition to supporting a variety of image representations, an image database system has to be able to store images; provide access to special-purpose functions that process images, e.g., for feature extraction (which would be written in a conventional programming language); provide a query language to retrieve images based on content (once the features have been identified); and provide access mechanisms to evaluate these spatial queries efficiently. Unfortunately, conventional database systems provide no support for spatial data types and provide little support for the invocation of special-purpose functions. This paper is concerned with extending database system functionality to satisfy the requirements of spatial database applications in general, and we show how our approach can be used to support image database applications.

Attempts at supporting spatial applications using existing database systems (e.g., [9], [35]) have not been satisfactory. Common data models such as the relational model are not adequate for handling spatial data. While it is usually easy to develop a schema that will capture all

Manuscript received June 30, 1987; revised September 30, 1987. This work was supported in part by the Defense Advanced Research Projects Agency and in part by the Space and Naval Warfare Systems Command under Contract N00039-85-C-0263.

J. A. Orenstein is with the Computer Corporation of America, Cambridge, MA 02142.

F. A. Manola was with the Computer Corporation of America, Cambridge, MA 02142. He is now with GTE Labs, Waltham, MA 02254.

IEEE Log Number 8819884.

95

the data and relationships in an application, it is extremely difficult to specify even the simplest spatial operations using a query language. Furthermore, the access paths supported in existing database systems are unlikely to offer good performance since they were not designed for spatial data. For example, for containment and nearest-neighbor queries, clustering objects by proximity in space is likely to lead to better performance than clustering by a nonspatial attribute.

Attempts at extending database system capabilities (for spatial and other nontraditional applications) have been extremely application-specific. Extensions for text retrieval [33], [36], geographic information processing [22], image and pictorial databases [8], [15], and VLSI design [16], among others, have been proposed.

Recently, there has been much interest in a new approach to the problem of extending database system functionality. The key idea is to build in *extensibility* rather than a particular set of extensions. *Object-oriented* database systems permit the incorporation of *object classes* that provide a collection of specialized operations. The data model and query language of an object-oriented database system must provide a way to invoke these new operations, and the physical database must provide a way of storing the representations of objects that it does not "understand." These objects can be of variable size and may be arbitrarily large.

PROBE is a research project into object-oriented database systems (OODB's). Other OODB projects include POSTGRES [37], EXODUS [6], and STARBURST [34]. The goal of PROBE is to provide a general-purpose database system for applications involving spatial and temporal data and other kinds of data with complex structure.

In Section II, we provide an overview of PROBE, focusing on the facilities for dealing with spatial and temporal data. In Section III, we show how the PROBE database system and simple application-specific object classes combine to efficiently support PROBE's spatial data model. In Section IV, it is shown how an image database application can be supported using PROBE's data model and spatial query processor. Section V provides a summary and discusses the current status of the PROBE project and future plans.

II. PROBE'S APPROACH TO SPATIAL DATA

In order to meet the needs of the application areas considered, we found it necessary to do research on data modeling, spatial and temporal query processing, recursive query processing, and database system architectures. In this section, the relevant results of this research are surveyed, and we focus on those results necessary for the further discussion of spatial data modeling and query processing.

A. *The PROBE Data Model*

The PROBE data model (PDM) has two basic types of data objects: *entities* and *functions*. An *entity* is a data object that denotes some individual thing. The basic characteristic of an entity that must be preserved in the model is its distinct indentity. Entities with similar characteristics are grouped into collections called *entity types*. For example, an image database might have an entity type **feature**, representing geographic features.

Properties of entities, relationships between entities, and operations on entities, are all uniformly represented in PDM by *functions*. Thus, in order to access properties of an entity or other entities related to an entity, or to perform operations on an entity, one must evaluate a function having the entity as an argument. For example,

- the single-argument function **population (CITY)** → **INTEGER** allows access to the value of the population attribute of a **CITY** entity;
- the function **location (POINT_FEATURE)** → **(LATITUDE, LONGITUDE)** allows access to the value of the location attribute of a point feature (note that a function can return a complex result);
- the multiargument function **altitude (LATITUDE, LONGITUDE, MODEL)** → **HEIGHT** allows access to the altitude values contained in a digital terrain model;
- the function **components (FEATURE)** → **set of FEATURE** allows access to the component features of a group feature (such as a city); and
- the function **overlay (LAYER-1, LAYER-2)** → **LAYER-3** provides access to an overlay operation defined for sets of polygons separated into different coverage layers.

Functions may also be defined that have no input arguments, or that have only boolean (truth-valued) results. For example,

- the zero-argument function **feature ( )** → **set of ENTITY** is implicitly defined for entity type **feature** and returns all entities of that type (such a function is implicitly defined for each entity type in the database) and
- the function **overlaps (POLYGON-1, POLYGON-2)** → **BOOLEAN** defines a predicate that is true if two polygons geometrically overlap. All predicates within PDM are defined as boolean-valued functions.

In PDM, a function is generically defined as a relationship between collections of entities and scalar values. The types of an entity serve to define what functions may be applied with the entity as a parameter value. There are two general classes of functions: *computed functions*, with output values computed by procedures, and *stored functions*, with output values determined by a conventional database search of a stored function *extent*. (Computed functions may involve the use of stored extents, in addition to computation.) References to all functions are treated syntactically as if they were references to computed functions, even when a stored extent exists, rather than treating the various classes of functions differently. However, particularly in the case of stored functions, functions can often be evaluated "in reverse," i.e., with "output" variables bound, to return "input" values (since both are available in a stored extent).

Entity types may be divided into *subtypes*, forming what are known as *generalization hierarchies*. For example, one might define **POINT_FEATURE** as a subtype of **FEATURE** and **ZOO** as a subtype of **POINT_FEATURE**. As another example, the declarations

> **type LAND_DIVISION is ENTITY**
> **description(LAND_DIVISION)** → **STRING**
> **area(LAND_DIVISION)** → **POLYGON**
>
> **type OWNED_PARCEL is LAND_DIVISION**
> **ownership(OWNED_PARCEL)** → **OWNER**

define a **LAND_DIVISION** entity type having two functions and a subtype **OWNED_PARCEL** having an additional function. Because **OWNED_PARCEL** is a subtype of **LAND_DIVISION**, any entity of type **OWNED_PARCEL** is also an entity of the **LAND_DIVISION** supertype and automatically "inherits" the **description** and **area** functions. On the other hand, it is sometimes desirable that specialized versions of what appears to be the "same function" be available for different subtypes. For example, one might wish to provide a general **square_miles** function to compute the number of square miles in any 2-D shape, but have different specialized implementations for various representations of those shapes.

At the top of the generalization hierarchy, both entities and functions are members of the generic type **ENTITY**. In addition, the entity and function type definitions themselves are modeled as a collection of entities and functions, so that information in database definitions can be queried in the same way as database data.

Generic operations on objects (entities and functions), such as selection, function application, set operations, and formation of new derived function extends, have been defined in the form of an algebra [20] similar in some respects to the algebra defined for the relational data model. For the purposes of this paper, we discuss only two of the operations.

- **select(F, P)** works as in the relational algebra, selecting those tuples of **F** that satisfy the predicate **P**.

- **Apply-append(F, G)** is a function having all the arguments of **F** and **G**. **F** and **G** each have input arguments and output arguments. Semantically, the functions are composed by feeding the output of **F** into **G**. The result is similar to the natural join of **F** and **G** (natural join is an operation from the relational algebra).

Examples: The cities whose population exceeds 100 000 can be evaluated by **select(CITY, population > 100 000)**. To obtain the area by each of these cities, apply-append can be used: **apply-append(apply-append(select(CITY, population > 100 000), shape), square_miles)**.

B. PROBE's Architecture

We now describe the architectural ideas behind object-oriented database systems in general and then discuss PROBE's architecture in more detail. The architecture of an OODB has two main components:

- a *database system kernel*, a query processor designed to manipulate objects of arbitrary types, not just the numeric and string types of conventional database systems, and

- a collection of *object classes*, where an object class specifies the representation of objects of a new type and provides operations for manipulating objects of the type.

The data model of an OODB must provide a construct that represents object class functions, and the query language must provide a way for these functions to be invoked. EXODUS can handle this task in an application-specific way since customization of the data model and query language is supported. POSTQUEL generalizes QUEL by allowing, for example, predicates from object classes to be used in place of a fixed set of predicates [38]. In PROBE, (computed) functions are used to represent object class functions. These functions are invoked when referred to in certain PDM algebra operations.

The process of adding an object class to an OODB is not completely trivial. The designers of EXODUS describe their system as a *database generator* and discuss the need for a *database implementer* (DBI), a person who creates a database system for an application by adding object classes to EXODUS [6] (the DBI has other duties also). This is an accurate view of how any OODB would be used, and the PROBE and POSTGRES systems would also benefit from the services of a DBI since this process of customization requires expertise beyond what could reasonably be expected of an application programmer. The other duties of a DBI must depend on the particular OODB being customized.

A more detailed specification of OODB architecture will focus on the database system kernel and its relationship to the object classes. It is therefore necessary to examine the "division of labor" between these components. Given a query involving specialized application objects, what part of the query should take place in the database system kernel, and what should be expected of the object classes? Different answers to this question correspond to different database system architectures.

There is a range of possibilities for splitting up the processing of a query involving specialized types. One extreme position is that the database system kernel should handle the entire query, including the parts dealing with the specialized data types. In spatial applications, this would require specific notions of spatial data to be "hardwired" into the database system. This option sacrifices generality, so we reject it. The other extreme is to pass to the object classes the parts of queries that involve specialized data. The specialized data could be stored in the database system and passed to the object class with the query, or the data could be stored in a storage device "owned" by the object class. The problem with this approach is that the object class must be concerned with database implementation issues relating to the manipulation of large collections of objects. For example, in order to handle queries over a collection of spatial objects, the object class will have to contain an implementation of an efficient spatial data structure appropriate for secondary

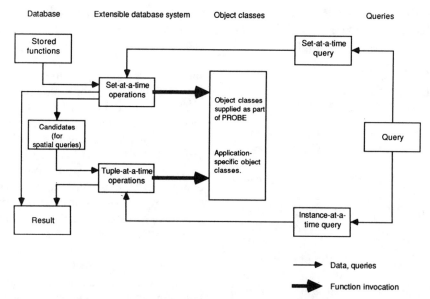

Fig. 1. Architecture of the PROBE database system.

storage, as well as concurrency control and recovery algorithms for the data structure.

We believe that an appropriate division of labor is for the database system to carry out suitably generalized basic database operations (e.g., joins, selection) on sets of generic objects, while each object class is responsible only for working on individual objects of more specialized types. (The operations described above, **select** and **apply-append**, are examples of the generalized database operations.) This division of labor corresponds well with a desirable division of labor among implementers—no implementer will be concerned with both database and application issues. For example, consider a proximity query: find all objects within a given distance of a given object. Instead of requiring an object class capable of processing this entire query, PROBE only requires the object class to provide a function that indicates whether a pair of objects satisfy the selection condition.

The decision to have the database system handle generic types and leave the more specialized types to the object classes raises the question of where the dividing line should be. The PROBE data model supports the notion of generalization. At the root of the hierarchy is the most generic type, ENTITY. Below this are types with more semantics, such as numeric types, string types, and spatial types. Application-specific types can be added. The dividing line was drawn so that PROBE supports only the most generally useful types: ENTITY and POINT-SET. POINT-SET is used to model all kinds of temporal and spatial objects (regardless of dimension and other application-specific concerns). POINT-SETs are described more fully in the following section.

An architecture based on this division of labor is shown in Fig. 1. It is an extensible architecture, and it supports a division of labor in which the database system kernel handles sets of generic objects, while the object classes handle individual objects of specialized types. The appli-

cation program invokes database operations as usual. What is different under this architecture is that the invocation will refer to functions provided by the object classes. For example, an image database application built on top of PROBE might invoke a feature extraction function supplied by an IMAGE object class (see Section V).

C. Spatial and Temporal Data

Our approach to spatial and temporal data is highly compatible with the features of PDM presented above. Both spatial and temporal objects are modeled by mathematical abstractions called point sets. The *point set* of an object is the set of points in space occupied by that object. The discussion here is in terms of spatial data, but it applied equally well to temporal data. We view temporal data as one-dimensional spatial data [10].

A point set is a member of the POINT-SET type. This type is a specialization of the ENTITY type which introduces a collection of spatial operators such as union, intersection, and difference, as well as spatial predicates such as overlap, containment, and proximity. (These operations are discussed below.) Further specializations for POINT-SETs of specific dimensions, and for specific kinds of space (e.g., discrete or continuous), can be included as object classes. Since point sets are entities, functions that relate spatial/temporal and "conventional" entity types can be defined. Functions are also used to specify topological relationships between point sets, e.g., containment and adjacency. The modeling of spatial data has been described more fully in [19], [27].

In addition to dealing with POINT-SET entities as individual objects, there are many situations in which it is necessary to deal with POINT-SETs contained within other POINT-SETs. For example, a map feature might have a POINT-SET describing its shape. The POINT-SET for the containing map would have to contain all the POINT-SETs of features contained within the map. Similarly, POINT-SET entities that represent individual parts within an assembly may be grouped as components of the POINT-SET entity that represents the entire assembly. When we deal with a POINT-SET in its role as a container of other POINT-SETs, we refer to the container POINT-SET as a *space*. Since a POINT-SET contained in one space can itself contain other POINT-SETs, POINT-SETs naturally exhibit a hierarchical structure. We represent the hierarchical structure in the model by a set-valued **contains** function from the space to the spatial entities contained within the space. Multiple decompositions of the same set of points (such as a geographic area) can be defined using multiple POINT-SET entities denoting the same set of points.

Since entities of type POINT-SET are first-class PDM entities, they can be used as arguments of generic PDM functions in the same way as conventional PDM entities. In addition, specialized operations associated specifically with entities of type POINT-SET are defined. The operations provided for operating on generic POINT-SET entities fall into two categories: *point-set operations* and *structural operations*.

The point-set operations include set operations on POINT-SET entities, spatial selection, and overlay. The set operations intersection, union, and difference provide the primary means for combining POINT-SET entities into new POINT-SET entities. These operations are defined for entities $P1$ and $P2$ of type POINT-SET as follows. **POINT-SET_union**$(P1, P2)$ is an entity of type POINT-SET that denotes the set of points belonging to either $P1$ or $P2$ (or both). **POINT-SET_intersect** and **POINT-SET_diff** are defined analogously.

We introduce the following definitions to simplify notation in later sections. If S is the set of spatial objects $\{P_1, P_2, \cdots, P_{n-1}, P_n\}$ and X and Y are spatial objects, then

- $\cup S =$ **POINT-SET_union**$(P_1,$ **POINT-SET_union**$(P_2, \cdots,$ **POINT-SET_union**$(P_{n-1}, P_n) \cdots))$,
- $\cap S =$ **POINT-SET_intersect**$(P_1,$ **POINT-SET_intersect**$(P_2, \cdots,$ **POINT-SET_intersect**(P_{n-1}, P_n) $\cdots))$, and
- $X - Y =$ **POINT-SET_diff**(X, Y).

Also defined as point-set operations are special variants of generic PDM functions that are tailored to operate with POINT-SET entities. Specifically, predicates are added to functions such as selection that test various spatial conditions, such as whether a point set is empty, contains another point set, or intersects another point set. A whole range of other spatial relationships (e.g., "left-of," "above," and "adjacent-to") can be added in the same way.

Given a space containing objects that may overlap with one another, it is often useful to identify maximal subspaces that do not contain any object boundaries. For example, a crucial operation in geographic information systems is "polygon overlay." This operation superimposes two maps of the same area (e.g., land usage and political districts) and creates all the regions due to the intersection

of regions from the input maps. PROBE's spatial data model includes an *overlay* operator to facilitate this kind of processing.

In discussing overlay, it is useful to have the concept of a uniform region. Let obj(p, S) be the set of objects in a space S that contain p, a point in S. Then a *uniform region* is a maximal subspace u in a space S such that, for every point p in u, obj(p, S) is the same. That is, u is a uniform region if, for all $p1$, $p2 \in u$, obj$(p1, S) =$ obj$(p2, S)$, and no subspace properly containing u has this property. To support operations such as polygon overlay, it is useful to be able to turn uniform regions into first-class objects. This is the finest partitioning that can be obtained given a set of objects (using only object boundaries to define partitions). Any coarser partitioning can be obtained by combining uniform regions (using **POINT-SET_union**). From the point of view of the data model, a space containing objects is indistinguishable from a space containing the uniform regions derived from a set of objects. They are both represented by a space containing spatial objects.

Based on this discussion of uniform regions, we can now define *overlay*: **overlay**(S) returns a space containing a spatial object for each uniform region of space S. The **overlay** operation can be used to compute polygon overlay as follows. Each input map is represented by a space containing a POINT-SET for each region of that map. The POINT-SETs from the two maps are placed in a single space by the **OB_union** operation (discussed below). The **overlay** operator is applied to the resulting space.

The point-set operations defined above form an algebra on point sets. As a result, given these operations, POINT-SET entities denoting complex shapes can be constructed by specifying algebraic expressions of point-set operations applied on POINT-SET entities.

The structural operations are concerned with the hierarchical structure of spaces described earlier. In general, these are convenient "macros," as they can be defined in terms of the nonspatial operators of the PDM algebra. The *object set operations* are defined for spaces $S1$ and $S2$ denoting the *same* point set, but having possibly different contained POINT-SETs (i.e., $S1$ and $S2$ register different information about a single point set). The definitions are as follows. **OB_union**$(S1, S2)$ is a space denoting the same point set as $S1$ and $S2$ that contains the set of objects contained in $S1$, $S2$, or both. (The objects in the result may not be spatially distinct, although their identities are retained.) **OB_intersect** and **OB_diff** are defined analogously.

The *expand* and *reduce* operators provide additional control over the CONTAINS relationship in spaces. If S is a space, X is in S's CONTAINS function, and Y is in X's CONTAINS function, **expand**(S) produces a space S' denoting the same point set, having moved Y into S's CONTAINS function without altering X's CONTAINS function. That is, for each immediate child X of S, **expand**(S) effectively copies each child of X so that it is also an immediate child of S. Note that placing an object in a new space (Y in the space of S in the above example) requires computation of the position of the object within the space. If the position is specified as a transformation, then a composition of transformations is necessary (e.g., multiplication of 4×4 matrices). **Reduce** is, in some sense, the inverse of **expand**. **Reduce**(S) produces a new space having no immediate children that are also contained in some other (immediate or indirect) child object of S.

Finally, since the substructure of a particular spatial representation is structured hierarchically, it is possible to use recursive processing techniques to search this hierarchical structure by traversing the **CONTAINS** relationship. PROBE's recursion operators (described in [30], [31]) can be used for this purpose.

III. Supporting the Spatial Data Model

Point-set entities and operations are useful in a wide variety of spatial applications. Point sets generalize spatial constructs found in many application areas, and the operations provided seem to be generally useful. However, in order to use PROBE in a spatial application, it is necessary to add object classes that provide specific representations for individual spatial objects and implement operations on instances of the representations.

Set-at-a-time spatial queries, e.g., selection with a spatial predicate, can be specified in PDM algebra. The processing of such queries is consistent with the division of labor discussed in Section II-B: PROBE processes sets of spatial objects and relies on the instance-at-a-time object class operations to manipulate individual spatial objects (e.g., to decide if a given object satisfies a spatial selection predicate). PROBE can support this approach to spatial data, but still provide good performance through the use of the *geometry filter*, a dimension- and representation-independent optimizer of spatial queries.

This section describes how the geometry filter and the object classes work together efficiently to support the point-set operations of PROBE's spatial data model. The structural operations do not require use of the filter. They can be supported using "ordinary" PDM algebra operations, and it is expected that more traditional query optimization techniques will be applicable. For spatial selection and overlay, the filter provides optimization of the query. For other geometric operations, e.g., the point-set set operations, the filter does not provide any optimization, but permits optimization of later operations. For example, the optimization of spatial selection on **POINT-SET_union**(A, B) is not possible unless the geometry filter's representation of **POINT-SET_union**(A, B) is available.

A similar approach to spatial query processing is taken in the PSQL project [32]. PSQL is an extension of SQL for "pictorial" data. The architecture of PSQL is very similar to PROBE's. Both systems advocate the division of labor discussed above. As a result, PSQL, like PROBE, can support a set of standard spatial operations that can be used with application-specific representations. (Abstract data types in PSQL are similar to object classes in PROBE.) The PSQL spatial query processor is based on the R-tree, a special-purpose spatial file organization [14]. The approach presented here is different. It is highly compatible with existing database system software and does not require the introduction of new file organizations.

A. Principles of the Geometry Filter

Many spatial queries (including the point-set operations of PROBE's spatial data model) can be expressed in terms of iteration over one or more collections of spatial objects and a function that considers each object or group of objects, invoked in the innermost loop. For example, in order to find all pairs of objects in a set S of spatial objects that overlap one another, the following algorithm can be used:

```
for each x in S
    for each y in S
        if overlap(x, y) then
            output(x, y)
```

(It is a simple matter to eliminate symmetric results (x overlaps y iff y overlaps x) and reflexive results (x always overlaps x).) This kind of algorithm is compatible with the proposed architecture since it embodies the desired division of labor. The database system implements the scans of S (this does not require any "understanding" of the objects belonging to S), while the spatial object class indicates whether individual objects overlap. This algorithm can be expressed in PDM algebra as follows:

result := select(cartesian-product(S, S), overlap)

(Here, and throughout this paper, details relating to the handling of argument names are suppressed. In this case, the spatial objects in the first appearance of S must be distinguished from those in the second through the renaming of function arguments.)

The problem with algorithms of this kind is one of performance. The nested loops lead to polynomial-time algorithms (whose degree is equal to the level of nesting). This will not be acceptable in practice, given that much more efficient special-purpose algorithms are often known.

PROBE's geometry filter is also compatible with the proposed architecture (refer again to Fig. 1) and provides much better performance, comparable to some of the best special-purpose algorithms [27]. The purpose of the filter is to optimize the nested loops that characterize brute-force geometric algorithms. The output from the filter is a set of *candidate* objects (or a set of groups of objects—one member of the group comes from each nested loop). Any object or group that is not included in the candidate set is certain not to satisfy the query. An object or group in the candidate set is *likely* to satisfy the query. The set of candidates will be refined to yield the precise answer by applying to each candidate a predicate from the supplied spatial object class (**overlap** in the example above).

The geometry filter contains algorithms that optimize spatial selection and overlay. As an example, consider spatial selection. Given two sets of spatial objects R and S, the *overlap query* returns all pairs of objects (r, s) such that r belongs to R, s belongs to S, and r and s overlap spatially. (This generalizes partial-match and range queries and can also be used to deal with a variety of containment and proximity queries.) This query would be processed by PROBE in two steps. First, a geometry filter algorithm, *spatial join*, would be invoked. This algorithm identifies candidates, pairs of objects (one from R and one from S) that are likely to overlap. Next, ordinary database operations would be used to refine the candidate set. These steps can be expressed in PDM algebra as follows:

```
candidates := spatial-join(R, S)
result := select(candidates, overlap)
```

This approach to spatial selection is consistent with the division of labor discussed in Section II-B. The database system kernel supplies the spatial join algorithm, which processes a collection of spatial objects (whose representation is not understood) to obtain candidate pairs. Each candidate is examined by the application-specific spatial object class. Of course, the spatial join algorithm must have *some* notion of spatial data in order to conclude that certain pairs of objects could not satisfy the query. Specifically, there must be a representation derivable from whatever representation is specified in the application-specific object class. The following subsections explain the principles behind the representation of spatial data used by the geometry filter. The construction of the representation is discussed in Section III-B. Sections III-C–III-E analyze each operation of the spatial data model. For each operation, the geometry filter algorithm is given, the interaction with the application-specific object class is described, and the requirements imposed on the object classes (for the geometry filter and application-specific representations) are described. Table I summarizes these results.

The requirements placed on the application-specific object class are minimal. As long as overlap, containment, union, intersection, and difference can be computed, the object class can be plugged in as a specialization of the POINT-SET object class, and spatial queries involving the object class can be optimized by the geometry filter.

1) Elements: The representation used by the geometry filter is conceptually a grid. A k-dimensional (k-D) point set in a k-D space is *approximated* by superimposing a k-D grid of cells on the space and noting which cells contain part of the point set (see Fig. 2). (In this section, we assume that the space contains a single point set. This assumption is relaxed in Section III-B). This approximation is *conservative* since the object being approximated is contained by the **POINT-SET_union** of the cells overlapping the object. While the presentation is in terms of 2-D data, all the ideas extend to higher dimensions (and to 1-D) without difficulty.

Algorithms for grid representations are often extremely

TABLE I
OBJECT CLASS REQUIREMENTS

Spatial operation	Application-specific object class operations
Creation of geometry filter representation	overlap, containment
Spatial selection	overlap, containment (for refining result)
Point-set set operations	union, intersection, difference
Overlay	union, intersection, difference

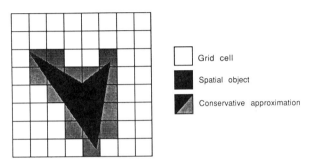

☐ Grid cell

■ Spatial object

▨ Conservative approximation

Fig. 2. Conservative approximation of a spatial object.

simple—the same action is repeated for each cell. However, the space and time requirements are very large for high-resolution grids. For this reason, the geometry filter uses an encoding of the grid. This encoding is obtained by recursively partitioning the space containing the object of interest. Partitioning continues until partitions that do not contain the object's boundary are obtained or until some maximum resolution is reached. (The resolution is that of the grid that is being encoded.)

In a k-D space, a partition is a $(k-1)$-D hyperplane perpendicular to the dimension being "split." The position and orientation of a partition are highly constrained, as described below. As a result of these constraints, the size, shape, and position of a partition can be described very concisely. Furthermore, the constraints impose a simplicity on the structure of the partitioning that can be exploited in geometry filter algorithms. (For example, if p and q are partitions, then p can contain q or q can contain p, but overlap other than containment can never occur.)

We will use the following notation: $<s_1:n_1 \mid s_2:n_2 \mid \cdots \mid s_m:n_m>$ denotes the string

$$\underbrace{s_1 s_1 \cdots s_1}_{n_1} \underbrace{s_2 s_2 \cdots s_2}_{n_2} \cdots \underbrace{s_m s_m \cdots s_m}_{n_m}.$$

If $n_i = 1$, then $s_i:n_i$ may be written as s_i. For example, $<011:2 \mid 01> = 01101101$.

The discussion will be simplified by assuming that the space is a grid of resolution $2^d \times 2^d$. Call the axes x and y. A cell in the grid is specified by providing two coor-

101

dinates of d bits each: $(<x_0|x_1|\cdots|x_{d-1}>,$ $<y_0|y_1|\cdots|y_{d-1}>)$.

A vertical split through the middle of this space amounts to discriminating on the value of x_0. In the left-hand half of the space, $x_0 = 0$; in the right-hand half, $x_0 = 1$. If the next split is horizontal, this corresponds to discrimination on the value of y_0. There are now four regions corresponding to the possible values of x_0 and y_0. Each additional split of a region creates two subregions characterized by the value of a specific bit from x or y. The sequence of splits defining a region can therefore be summarized by a corresponding sequence of these characteristic bits. If the direction of splitting alternates, then the sequence of bits corresponds to the interleaving of x and y bits. This interleaving creates a bit string that uniquely identifies a region. If r is a region obtained by splitting, then the corresponding bit string is the *z value* of r, denoted $z(r)$. (See Fig. 3.)

The z value of a region provides a concise description of the shape, size, and position of the region, as these attributes can be derived from the z value. In general, if the z value contains the first m bits of x and the first n bits of y, then the region described extends from $<x_0|\cdots|x_{m-1}|0:d-m>$ to $<x_0|\cdots|x_{m-1}|1:d-m>$ horizontally and from $<y_0|\cdots|y_{n-1}|0:d-n>$ to $<y_0|\cdots|y_{n-1}|1:d-n>$ vertically.

Partitions obtained by the splitting process described are called *elements*. These are the basic objects manipulated by the geometry filter. In general, a spatial object is represented by a collection of disjoint elements. The process of recursively partitioning a space to obtain elements is called *decomposition*. The decomposition algorithm appears below. Fig. 4 shows the elements generated in the decomposition of a spatial object.

```
function decompose(e: element, p: point-set,
                       result: list of element):
                       list of element;
begin
if contains(p, e) then
    Report-Element(e, result)
else if overlap(p, e) then
    if minimal(e) then
          Report-Element(e, result)
    else
          begin
          decompose(left(e), p, result);
          decompose(right(e), p, result);
          end;
(* else no overlap - nothing to do *)
return result;
end;
```

The algorithm is invoked with e bound to the single element representing the entire space. p is the object being decomposed, and *result* accumulates the elements generated. The **minimal** function returns true iff the input element is the smallest possible, i.e., if the resolution of the grid has been reached.

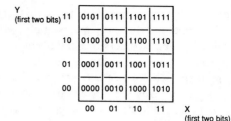

Fig. 3. The interleaving of bits from X and Y yields a bit string that characterizes regions obtained by recursive splitting.

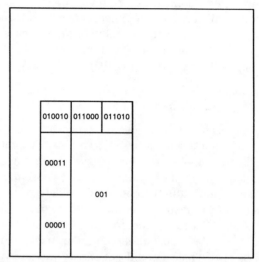

Fig. 4. Decomposition of a spatial object into elements. Each element is labeled with its z value. The z value is obtained by recording the relationship of the element to each split. If the element is to the left-hand side of or below a split, a 0 is generated; otherwise, a 1 is generated.

Recursive partitioning yields one-cell (i.e., minimal) elements if carried far enough. (The recursive calls of **decompose** may stop before minimal elements are reached. This occurs when a nonminimal element is contained in the object being decomposed.) The z values of the individual cells inside any element are consecutive. Furthermore, the lower left-hand and upper right-hand cells have the lowest and highest z values (respectively) inside the region. These z values are denoted $zlo(e)$ and $zhi(e)$ (see Fig. 5).

While the discussion so far has assumed that the direction of splitting alternates between x and y (corresponding to an $xyxy\cdots$ interleaving pattern), other patterns can be used. This issue is discussed in [27]. In the rest of this paper, we assume the $xyxy\cdots$ splitting pattern.

2) Z Order: Z values can be compared lexicographically, i.e., the bit strings are left-justified and then compared one bit at a time. Therefore, a collection of elements can be ordered by sorting lexicographically on their z values. Precedence in z order is denoted as $<_z$.

The spatial interpretation of this ordering is interesting. If each cell of a 2-D grid is treated as an element, then the z values of the elements trace out the path shown in Fig. 6. This ordering has been discovered many times [1], [5], [12], [17], [24], [28]. The oldest reference that we are aware of is to Peano in 1908 [29]. In [24], [25], we called it z ordering and we use that name here. The curve is recursive in that it consists of the same N shape (cov-

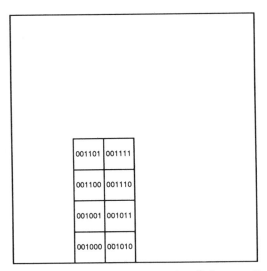

Fig. 5. The element whose z value is 001 contains all elements whose prefix is 001. The *zlo* and *zhi* values are in the low left-hand and upper right-hand corners, respectively.

Fig. 6. Traversal of cells in z order. Compute the z value of each cell by interleaving the bits of the coordinates. For example, $(3, 5) = (011_2, 101_2) \rightarrow 011011_2$. Interpret the z values as integers and then "connect the dots."

ering four points) repeated throughout the space. Groups of four N's are connected in an N pattern, groups of four of these groups of four are connected in the same pattern, etc. (It is called z order because our first drawing of it had Z's instead of N's.)

Z order can be viewed as a mapping from multidimensional space to 1-D space which preserves proximity. That is, if two points are close in space, then they are likely to be close in z order. A practical benefit of preserving proximity is that elements are clustered for efficient access on secondary storage. Elements that are close in space are likely to be stored on the same disk page. (See [27] for more information on the preservation of proximity.) A curve related to z order can be obtained by a simple transformation of z values [11]. This alternative curve is compatible with the use of all algorithms to be described and improves on the preservation of proximity obtained with z order.

B. Creation of the Geometry Filter Representation

So far, we have seen how individual spatial objects (point-set entities) can be decomposed into z-ordered se-

quences of elements. However, PROBE's spatial data model allows spaces to contain multiple point sets. This section discusses the geometry filter representation of such a space and points out that this representation suggests algorithms based on familiar nonspatial data structures.

The geometry filter representation of a space is a z-ordered sequence of the elements from the decompositions of all the objects contained in the space. All that has to be done to obtain this representation is to decompose each object and merge the resulting z-ordered sequences into a single sequence. A *label* associated with each element identifies the object from which the element was obtained. In terms of PDM algebra, this construction can be achieved using the **apply-append** operation. For example, if the spatial objects representing geographical regions are provided by **shape(REGION)** $\rightarrow$ **POLYGON** and M is a map (a set of regions), then the geometry filter representation of M is obtained by **apply-append(apply-append(M, shape), decompose)**. By asking for an index to be constructed on the result, the required sorting (and indexing) will be performed.

During the decomposition of an object, the **decompose** function checks the relationship (overlap, containment, or disjointness) between elements and the object being decomposed. The **overlap** and **contains** functions invoked *directly* by **decompose** are generic. Each application-specific spatial object class provides implementations of these operations that are written specifically for that object class. PROBE senses the type of the object being decomposed and invokes the appropriate implementation. (For this reason, the geometry filter is general enough to deal with multiple representations within the same query.) Since the type-specific **overlap** and **contains** predicates expect two arguments of the same type, the boxes corresponding to elements (or conservative approximations thereof) must be describable in the same representation as that of the object being decomposed. The derivations appear to be simple in practice. The code to derive the application-specific representation is not part of the geometry filter, as this would limit the generality of the filter.

With the ideas presented so far, it is possible to sketch the spatial join algorithm. Recall that the inputs to spatial join are two functions R and S storing spatial objects. Internally, stored functions would be represented using a B-tree (or other conventional file organization) keyed by z value. Besides the z value, each record carries a label identifying the spatial object from which the z value was obtained. A merge of the two z-ordered sequences can be performed to locate cases in which a z value from R contains, or is contained by, a z value from S. This indicates that the corresponding spatial objects are likely to overlap spatially, so a candidate pair has been identified. (See Fig. 7.)

The time required for the merge is proportional to the number of elements representing the objects in the two spaces. The number of elements arising from the decomposition of an object can be controlled in a number of

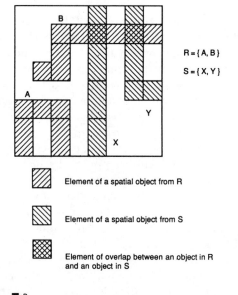

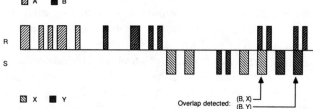

Fig. 7. The overlap query can be processed by merging z-ordered sequences of elements. Overlap is detected where an element from R contains an elements from S or vice versa.

ways (e.g., by selecting the resolution of the space), so the time is actually linear in the number of objects (and the constant can be tuned to optimize the tradeoff between precision and time for the testing of candidates). This is clearly superior to the nested loops algorithm presented in Section III-A. Furthermore, it will be seen in the following section that *sublinear* performance can be obtained.

C. Spatial Join

As discussed in the previous section, spatial join can be implemented by a merge of z-ordered sequences of elements. In this section, we discuss the implementation and optimization of this merge. Before getting into the details, it will be useful to summarize the results. First, with the optimization, sublinear performance is obtained. A special case of the overlap query is the range query (useful in traditional database applications). The spatial interpretation of the range query is to find all the data points in a given box. It is shown in [27] that, for the range query, the performance obtainable with the geometry filter is comparable to that of the best special-purpose data structures, such as the k-D tree [4]. Second, the data structure requirements are minimal: *any data structure that supports random and sequential accessing can be used by all the geometry filter algorithms.* This is important since it allows the use of existing file organizations such as B-trees (for secondary storage), and binary or AVL trees (for main memory), which are in common use in current

database systems and elsewhere. There is no need to develop new special-purpose file organizations for spatial indexing. Other requirements are also compatible with existing database system software: z values can be represented by integers. Therefore, existing sort utilities can be used to create z-ordered sequences of elements. Also, the LRU buffering strategy is exactly what is called for in the implementation of the merge.

The following discussion refines the ideas presented in [24]–[27].

The merge logic of **spatial-join** is somewhat unconventional because elements represent intervals and because the elements within a sequence may exhibit containment. (When containment occurs, the elements involved are from different objects in the space.) Fig. 8 demonstrates some of the difficulties. In the example, the spatial join would report the candidate pairs (A, D), (A, E), (A, F), (B, E), (B, F), (C, H), and (C, I). The interaction between sets of nested elements ($\{A, B\}$ and $\{E, F\}$ in the example) is especially tricky to handle correctly.

The spatial join algorithm depends heavily on the mathematical properties of elements. First, the only possible relationships between elements are precedence in z order and containment. Overlap (other than containment) cannot occur. Second, in a sequence of elements ordered by zlo, nested elements are consecutive, with the larger elements appearing before the smaller elements. This is because of the relationship between containment and z values. If x and y are elements, then x contains y iff $z(x)$ is a prefix of $z(y)$. The only way an element could appear between x and y in the lexicographic ordering would be for it also to be part of the nesting, between x and y.

In order to keep track of a set of nested elements from a sequence, a stack is associated with each sequence. This stack is called a *nest*. The nest is updated as the input sequence is scanned. At any point in the merge, the top of a nest stores the "current" element from the corresponding sequence, and containing elements (from the same sequence) are stored deeper in the stack. The order of elements in the stack reflects the nesting of the elements. Previously examined elements that do not contain the current element are not present in the nest (see Fig. 9).

The state of each input sequence is defined by the sequence itself (including a cursor to indicate the next input element) and by the nest. The **state-of-input** data type is used to encapsulate this information. In each iteration of the merge, the state of one sequence is updated by advancing the cursor (by at least one position) and updating the nest.

Even though there are only two input sequences, the merge is conceptually four-way. As a sequence of elements is scanned during the merge, elements are "entered" and "exited." Element e is entered at $zlo(e)$ and exited at $zhi(e)$. Therefore, there are four kinds of events that occur (the input sequences are X and Y):

1) entering an element from sequence X,
2) exiting an element from sequence X,

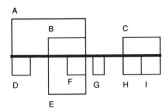

Fig. 8. In order to compute spatial join, the overlap between *A* and *D*, *A* and *E*, *A* and *F*, *B* and *E*, *B* and *F*, *C* and *H*, and *C* and *I* must be detected during the merge.

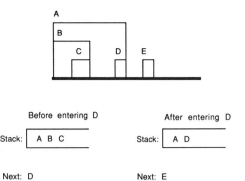

Fig. 9. State of the input sequence before and after entering an element.

3) entering an element from sequency *Y*, and
4) exiting an element from sequence *Y*.

Each kind of event constitutes an input to the merge, and hence the merge is four-way. An entering element comes from a sequence (at the position indicated by the cursor), while an exiting element comes from a nest. When an element is entered, it is placed on the nest. Eventually, the element will be exited, and (for a set of nested elements) the order of exiting is opposite to the order of entering. Because of this last-in first-out behavior, it is appropriate to use stacks to represent nests.

The details of the algorithm are as follows:

```
function spatial-join(left-sequence, right-sequence: list of labeled-element): list of candidate;
var
     result: list of candidate;
     L, R: state-of-input;
     event: element;
begin
L := initial-state-of-input (left-sequence);
R := initial-state-of-input (right-sequence);

while not(eof(L.sequence) and empty(L.nest) and
          eof(R.sequence) and empty(R.nest))
     begin
     event := min(zlo(current(L)), zhi(top(L.nest)),
                     zlo(current(R)), zhi(top(R.nest)))
     if event = zlo(current(L)) then
             enter-element(L, R, result)
     else if event = zhi(top(L.nest)) then
             exit-element(L, R, result)
     else if event = zlo(current(R)) then
             enter-element(R, L, result)
     else (* event = zhi(top(R.nest)) *)
             exit-element(R, L, result);
     end;
   return result;
end;

procedure enter-element(X, Y: state-of-input; result: list of candidate);
begin
while not contains(top(X.nest), current(X))
     pop(X.nest);
push(X.nest, current(X));
advance(X, Y);
end;

procedure exit-element(X, Y: state-of-input; result: list of candidate);
begin
report-pairs(top(X.nest), Y.nest, result);
pop(X.nest);
end;
```

105

Spatial-join begins by setting up an initial **state-of-input** for each sequence. This is done by setting the cursor of each sequence to the beginning of the sequence and by pushing an element representing the entire space onto an empty nest. Although it is not strictly necessary to push this element, it will simplify the algorithm later. The loop of **spatial-join** implements the merge logic. In each step, the four inputs to the merge are checked for the next "event." The *zlo* and *zhi* extract the start and end points of an element, respectively. The four-way "if" statement detects which event has occurred. The event is either an entry or an exit for an element from the left or the right sequence. The procedures invoked (**enter-element** and **exit-element**) take care of "advancing" the input.

In **enter-element,** X represents the sequence that contributed the element being entered (either L or R). Y represents the other sequence. First, $X.nest$, the stack associated with sequence X, is updated. In order to maintain the property that stack elements are nested, it may be necessary to pop some elements. For example, in Fig. 9, it is necessary to pop the stack twice before the current element, **current**(X), can be pushed. This loop is guaranteed to terminate before the nest is empty because of the element representing the entire space, placed at the bottom of the stack. The last step is to advance the input sequence of X. The procedure for doing this is discussed below.

In **exit-element**, X represents the sequence that contributed the element being exited (either L or R). Y represents the other sequence. **Report-pairs**(**top**$(X.nest)$, $Y.nest$, $result$) appends to the list of results pairs of the form (u, v) where $u =$ **top**$(X.nest)$ and v is an element in $Y.nest$, for all elements of $Y.nest$ (except the bottom element, which represents the whole space—that element was inserted "artificially"). Popping $X.nest$ represents the advancing of the input sequence (recall that the nests provide "input" of exiting elements).

The advancing of the input sequence (in **enter-element**, using **advance**) must be handled carefully. A correct implementation is simply to advance to the next element of the sequence. This would mean that the spatial join requires every element of every sequence to be examined. This is normal for a merge, whose running time is proportional to the sum of the lengths of the input sequences. However, it is possible to do better. Spatial queries are often localized in one region of the space, and it should not be necessary to examine every element. Ideally, it would be possible to ignore parts of the space that are "obviously" not going to be fruitful. This can be done by advancing the input sequence by more than one element at a time.

In order to do this, we will require sequences to be stored in data structures that support both random and sequential accessing. This is a very modest requirement since, as noted above, many data structures have this property. We will assume the following operations:

• **randac**(**s, k**): random access to sequence s, using search key k; if the search fails, then the record with the smallest key greater than k is located; and

• **seqac**(**s**): sequential access on sequence s.

Advance(X, Y) finds the first labeled element of sequence X past **current**(X) that could possibly be relevant (i.e., overlap with an element from Y). The procedure begins by advancing to the next element in X following **current**(X). (The current and next elements are denoted by $Xcurrent$ and $Xnext$, respectively.) The procedure ends here, not advancing further, if $Xnext$ is contained by an element from Y that has already been examined. Such an element can be found in $Y.nest$. (See Fig. 10(a) and (b).) It would be incorrect to advance further because the overlap between $Xnext$ and the relevant Y objects would be missed.

On the other hand, if $Xnext$ is not covered by any Y element, then it is not relevant. The only thing that is certain at this point is that the next relevant X element ends past the beginning of $Ycurrent$, the current element of Y [see Fig. 10(c)]. *Xnext, and all subsequent elements until the next relevant X element, can be skipped.* Due to the fact that elements may exhibit containment, but never overlap, there are now two possibilities: 1) that a random access in $X.sequence$ using $Ycurrent$ will locate the first X element contained by $Ycurrent$ [as in Fig. 10(c)] and 2) that the random access will locate the first X element that begins after the end of $Ycurrent$ [as in Fig. 10(d)]. Remember that the position of an element within a sequence is based on the beginning of the interval zlo, not the end, so in the second case, the random access may actually miss a relevant element of X. If this occurs, the correct element can be located by stepping back one position in the X sequence.

Now, either an element containing or contained by $Ycurrent$ has been found, or such an element does not exist. In the former case, it is still possible that there are larger containing elements [as in Fig. 10(d)]. The largest such element (that begins after $Xcurrent$ begins) must be located (there are a variety of methods for doing this). In the latter case (in which $Ycurrent$ does not interact with any X element), the X element located by the random access is the proper place to resume the X sequence [see Fig. 10(e)].

D. Point-Set Set Operations

Set operations are commonly implemented by merging, and this is how the point-set set operations are implemented in the filter. Many of the peculiarities of the merge used for **spatial-join** are applicable here, and for the same reason: sequences of elements are being merged. The merge logic is, in fact, identical. The merge is four-way, and the events detected are entry to and exit from elements. All that differs are the actions taken for each event. Therefore, it is possible to describe the implementation of **POINT-SET_union** and **POINT-SET_intersect** by specifying the **enter-element** and **exit-element** algorithms, using the spatial join algorithm without modifi-

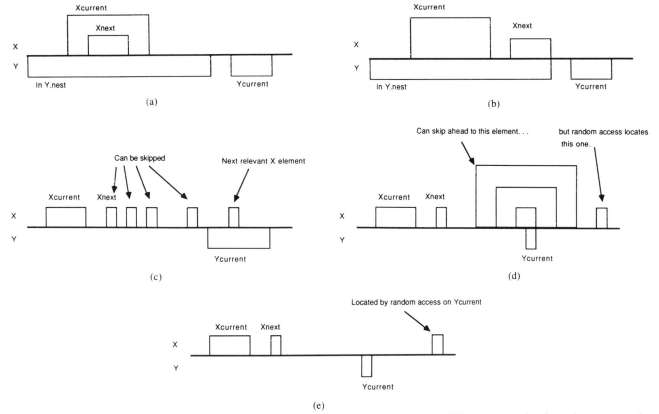

Fig. 10. (a) *Xnext* is contained by an element in *Y.nest*. (b) *Xnext* is contained by an element in *Y.nest*. This is the same situation as in (a), except the *Xnext* is after *Xcurrent*, not inside it. (c) Random access in *X.sequence* using *Ycurrent* locates next relevant element in *X*. (d) Random access misses elements that cover *Ycurrent* but begin before *Ycurrent*. Stepping back by one position in *X* locates an element containing *Ycurrent*, if there is one. (e) If there is no element containing or contained by *Ycurrent*, advance to the element located by the random access.

cation. **POINT-SET_diff** can be implemented on top of **POINT-SET_intersect**.

For the set operations, each input sequence contains elements comprising a *single* point set. For this reason, elements within one input sequence exhibit the precedence relationship only. Containment arises only between elements from different point sets. This allows some simplification of the algorithms. In particular, because containment within a sequence cannot occur, a stack is no longer needed to keep track of nested elements. However, for ease of presentation, we describe the algorithms as derivatives of **spatial-join**.

These algorithms show how set operations can be computed directly from geometry filter representations. An alternative is to first carry out the set operation on the application-specific representation and then to decompose the result. Performance considerations will dictate which approach is preferable.

1) POINT-SET_union: The problem in computing **POINT-SET_union** is to combine adjacent elements from opposite sequences into maximal intervals. A global variable *I* is used to keep track of the endpoints of the interval under construction. When an element from either sequence is entered, either the element is adjacent to *I* or it is not. In the former case, *I* is extended. In the latter case, *I* is maximal, so the elements of its decomposition are added to the result, and a new interval is started. The end-

points of the new interval are those of the current element. Following the update of *I*, the next relevant element in *each* input sequence is the one starting after the end of *I*. These can be located using random access.

It is simplest to detect adjacent and maximal intervals in the **enter-element** algorithm. The code appears below. Nothing needs to be done by **exit-element**.

```
procedure enter-element(X, Y: state-of-input,
        result: list of element);
var
    X, Y: state-of-input;
    result: list of element;
begin
(* I is an interval with components lo and hi *)

if adjacent(I, current(X)) then
    I.hi := zhi(current(X))
else
    begin
    report-elements(decompose(I), result);
    I.lo := zlo(current(X));
    I.hi := zhi(current(X));
    end;
randac(X.sequence, I.hi + 1);
randac(Y.sequence, I.hi + 1);
end;
```

2) POINT-SET_intersect: This algorithm is very similar to spatial join. As with spatial join, and unlike **POINT-SET_union**, the only cases of interest are those in which an element from one sequence contains an element from the other sequence. However, instead of reporting the pair of elements, only their intersection is of interest, i.e., the smaller of the two (since overlap other than containment cannot occur). Because of the resemblance to **spatial-join**, the call to **advance** is preserved. Since the modifications are so minor, the algorithms for **enter-element** and **exit-element** are omitted.

3) POINT-SET_diff: There is a subtlety involved in the computing of **POINT-SET_diff** relating to the correctness of the result. In order to retain the precision of a filter (i.e., that positive results are not lost), each operation must return a conservative approximation of the exact result. To preserve this property through a **POINT-SET-_diff**, some care must be taken with the boundary elements, those elements containing the boundary of the decomposed spatial object.

If P and Q are point sets, P' is the **POINT-SET_union** of the elements of **decompose**(P), and Q' is the **POINT-SET_union** of the elements of **decompose**(Q), then P' is a conservative approximation of P and Q' is a conservative approximation of Q. Furthermore, **POINT-SET_union**(P', Q') and **POINT-SET_intersect**(P', Q') are conservative approximations of **POINT-SET_union**(P, Q) and **POINT-SET_intersect**(P, Q), respectively (see Fig. 11). This means that sequences of operations consisting of invocations of **POINT-SET_union** and **POINT-SET_intersect**, carried out on both the application-specific and the geometry filter representations, will yield a geometry filter representation that retains the filtering property. However, **POINT-SET_diff**(P', Q') is not, in general, a conservative approximation of **POINT-SET_diff**(P, Q). The difficulty is that **POINT-SET_diff**(P, Q) = **POINT-SET_intersect**$(P,$ **complement**$(Q))$ (where the complement is with respect to the containing space) and that **complement**(Q') is not a conservative approximation of **complement**(Q) (see Fig. 12). Further analysis shows that the problem is due to boundary elements. The decomposition of Q and the decomposition of **complement**(Q) have some common boundary elements, yet the complement of the decomposition of Q' does not include these elements. Stated more concisely, decomposition (followed by the **POINT-SET_union** of the elements) and **complement** do not commute: **POINT-SET_union**(**decompose**(**complement** $(x))) \neq$ **complement**(**POINT-SET_union**(**decompose**$(x)))$.

To compute the conservative approximation of **POINT-SET_diff**(P, Q), compute **POINT-SET_intersect**$(P',$ **complement***$(Q'))$ where **complement***(Q') is **complement**(Q') plus sufficient elements to guarantee that the boundary of Q is contained in the result. (See Fig. 12.)

To compute **complement***(Q'), first compute **complement**(Q'). Then, for each element of **complement**(Q'),

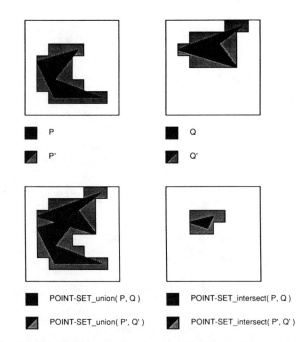

P P'

Q Q'

POINT-SET_union(P, Q) POINT-SET_intersect(P, Q)

POINT-SET_union(P', Q') POINT-SET_intersect(P', Q')

Fig. 11. P' and Q' are conservative approximations of P and Q, respectively. **POINT-SET_union**(P', Q') is a conservative approximation of **POINT-SET_union**(P, Q), and **POINT-SET_intersect**(P', Q') is a conservative approximation of **POINT-SET_intersect**(P, Q).

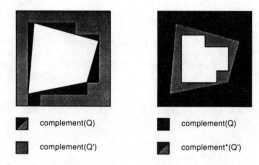

complement(Q) complement(Q)

complement(Q') complement*(Q')

Fig. 12. **Complement**(Q') is not a conservative approximation for **complement**(Q), but **complement***(Q') is.

generate the decomposition of the point-set obtained by expanding the element in all directions by one cell. Sort this collection of elements by the z value and then, in one pass, discard duplicates and merge smaller elements into larger ones (this is analogous to what is done in **POINT-SET_union**). It is unfortunate that this implementation is superlinear (due to the sort), but we know of no other solution.

Expansion by one cell is correct, but is likely to generate a large number of elements in the following decomposition. For performance reasons, a greater expansion can be used (e.g., using two or four cells), but as usual, there is a tradeoff with precision. This expansion is expensive (requiring a sorting step), and it may be cheaper to decompose the complement of the application-specific representation.

E. Overlay

A space of n objects can have as many as 2^n uniform regions, one for every member of the power set of the n

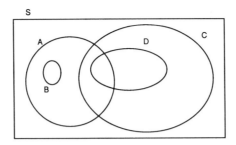

Fig. 13. Overlay of a space. The candidate sets found by the geometry filter are $\{A, B\}$ and $\{A, C, D\}$.

objects. (Uniform regions were defined in Section II-C.) An obvious brute-force algorithm is to enumerate the power set of the objects in the space and to compute the mutual intersection of each combination of objects. In geographical applications, overlays involving hundreds and even thousands of 2-D objects are computed routinely, so it is clearly the case that, in practice, the vast majority of the combinations yield regions that are empty or not uniform (and therefore not of interest) and are not even considered. (Otherwise, the algorithm would still be running.)

Compared to spatial join, support for overlay is more complicated, but conceptually there is nothing different: the filter returns candidate sets of objects. The set of candidates is a subset of the power set of the space. The objects within a candidate set are likely to interact with one another to produce (nonempty) uniform regions. If no candidate set contains a given set of objects G, then the objects in G do not interact to produce nonempty uniform regions.

Computationally, it is (almost always) far more efficient to enumerate the power set of each candidate than it would be to enumerate the power set of the entire space. This is not the most useful comparison since enumeration of the power set of the space is not feasible anyway. A performance comparison of our overlay algorithm with algorithms in use has not yet been attempted. One clear advantage of our algorithm is its generality. It is valid for all dimensions and for all representations. The application-specific spatial object class only has to supply a function that computes the overlay of two objects. This is simple once the point-set set operations have been supplied: the overlay of A and B comprises the three objects $A \cap B$, $A - B$, and $B - A$.

The geometry filter's overlay algorithm has two steps.

1) Identify candidate sets, groups of objects that are likely to overlap spatially.
2) Compute the uniform regions due to the overlap of objects within each candidate.

The following two subsections discuss these steps in detail. Overlay takes as input a set of objects within a single space. The geometry filter representation of this space is a z-ordered sequence containing all the labeled elements from the decompositions of all the objects in the space. The first step can then be accomplished in a single

pass over the z-ordered sequence as described in Section III-E1. The output is a collection of candidate sets. In Fig. 13, B and C do not appear together in any candidate, indicating that B and C do not overlap anywhere in the space. Certain candidates are subsumed by others and so do not have to be considered explicitly. For example, $\{A, C\}$ does not have to be considered because all interactions between A and C will be examined when candidate $\{A, C, D\}$ is considered. The second step, described in Section III-E2, discusses the generation of uniform regions from the candidate set.

1) Finding Candidate Sets: The **overlay** algorithm takes as input a space S and returns a set of candidates. A candidate is a subset of objects in S that is likely to generate nonempty uniform regions.

S is represented by a z-ordered sequence of labeled elements. To simplify termination of the algorithm, assume that S is terminated by an element whose z value is larger than any other in S. As with spatial join, it will be useful to record the status of the scan of S using the **state-of-input** type. During the scan, the *nest* field of **state-of-input** stores elements that have been entered but not exited. The spatial objects corresponding to these elements (which can be located via the labels) are likely to overlap. Therefore, the candidates are located by sampling the stack at "appropriate" times.

One possibility is to sample the stack upon entering each element. However, this is more frequenct than is necessary. Suppose that the stack has the labeled elements $[A, B, C]$ (these are the labels). When the next element, with label D, is entered, there are two possibilities. If C's element contains D's element, then the stack becomes $[A, B, C, D]$. Since $[A, B, C, D]$ subsumes $[A, B, C]$ (as discussed above), it is not necessary to report $[A, B, C]$. If, on the other hand, D's element is not contained by C's element, then it is necessary to pop the stack at least once before pushing D. The result is $[A, B, D]$ (assuming that B's element contains D's). In this case, the candidate $[A, B, C]$ is relevant since C is missing from the updated stack.

The **overlay** algorithm operates by sampling the stack when its size reaches a "local maximum," i.e., just before it is popped to accommodate a new element. At this moment, the top of the stack corresponds to some region of the space that is maximal in terms of occupancy. If the new element can be accommodated without popping the stack, it must be true that the current stack has not reached a local maximum; i.e., "moving" into the new element does not result in the leaving of any objects already represented in the stack.

The complete algorithm is as follows:

```
function overlay(S: state-of-input):
set of candidate;
begin
     result: set of candidate;
     e:   labeled-element;

   reset(S.sequence);   (*Start at the beginning*)
                        (*of the sequence*)
   clear(S.nest);   (*Start with an empty nest*)
   e := next(S.sequence);   (*Get next*)
                            (*element and*)
                            (*advance the*)
                            (*sequence*)
   push(S.nest, e);

   while not end-of-file(S.sequence) do
       begin
       e := next(S.sequence);
       if not(top(S.nest) contains e) then
           (*At a local maximum*)
           begin
           add(result, nest(S));
           while not(top(S.nest) contains e) do
                   pop(S.nest);
           end;
       push(S.nest, e);
       end;

   return result;
   end;
```

2) Generating the Uniform Regions: The generation of uniform regions from candidates is implemented jointly by the geometry filter and the application-specific spatial object class. The geometry filter provides control and management of intermediate results, as will be described. The object class provides the intersection and difference operations (which are also required to support the set operations). Suppose, in the example of Fig. 13, that candidate $\{A, C, D\}$ is processed first. The geometry filter uses the object class to compute $A \cap C$, $A - C$, and $C - A$. Next, each of these is combined with D to obtain $A \cap C \cap D$, $(A \cap C) - D$, $(A \cap D) - C$ (which is empty and therefore discarded), $A - (C \cup D)$, $(C \cap D) - A$, and $C - (A \cup D)$.

When candidate $\{A, B\}$ is processed, the uniform regions B and $A - (B \cup C \cup D)$ will be computed. The overlay algorithm (running in the kernel) understands that $A - B$ is not uniform because pieces of A have already been "removed" to contribute to other uniform regions. Therefore, it is appropriate to substitute $A - (C \cup D)$ for A in $A - B$, yielding the correct result.

In general, a uniform region can always be described by an expression of the form $\cap X - \cup Y$ where X and Y have no objects in common. The resulting uniform region is characterized by X. In a given space S, the uniform region corresponding to X is $UR(X) = \cap X - \cup$OB_diff(S, X). Other expressions may produce equivalent results. For example, in Fig. 13, $UR(A)$ is described by $\cap \{A\} - \cup \{B, C, D\}$, but also by $\cap \{A\} - \cup \{B, C\}$. (Note that the characteristic part $\{A\}$ is the same in both cases.)

Unfortunately, it is not always possible to compute a uniform region by processing a single candidate. In Fig. 13, $UR(A)$ requires the processing of both candidates. We therefore take the following approach. *$UR(X)$ is obtained by computing a series of approximations, the last of which is exact:* $UR_o(X)$, $UR_1(X)$, $\cdots$, $UR_n(X) = UR(X)$. Each new approximation reflects the processing of a candidate, and $UR_i(X) \supseteq UR_{i+1}(X)$, $0 \le i < n$. It is not necessary to keep track of each approximation; only the most recent approximation of each uniform region is needed. For this reason, we introduce a set of variables: $UR^*(X)$ is the most recent approximation of $UR(X)$.

The complete algorithm appears below. It is consistent with PROBE's architecture—the object class never has to deal with more than a fixed number of objects at a time (two in this case).

```
function uniform-regions(candidates:
set of set of point-set): set of point-set;
var
   c, u: set of point-set;
   include, exclude: point-set;
   UR*: table of point-set;   (*indexed by*)
                              (*set of point-set*)
   result: set of point-set;
begin

clear(UR*);

for each c ∈ candidates
   for each u ∈ power-set(c)
     begin

       if UR*[u] is undefined then
       (*This combination of objects has not*)
       (*been encountered in the processing*)
       (*of previous candidates. *)
       (*Form the initial approximation.*)
       UR*[u] := ∩ u;

       include := UR*[u];

       if not empty(include)
         begin
         exclude := ∪ OB_diff(c, u);
         UR*[u] := include - exclude;
         end;
     end;

   result := {};
```

```
for each u ∈ UR*
    if not empty(u)
        insert(result, u);

    return result;
end;
```

The evaluations of ∩ and ∪ can be optimized by storing intermediate and final results, reusing them whenever possible. For example, if ∩ {A, B, C} is computed as **POINT-SET_intersect** (**POINT-SET_intersect** (A, B), C), then ∩ {A, B, D} can be optimized by reusing ∩ {A, B}.

The size of an input space occurring in practice is such that it is reasonable to represent c and u, using bit strings. This simplifies and optimizes many aspects of the algorithm: iteration through the power set of c is particularly simple, the computation of **OB_diff** (c, u) just requires pairwise bit operations on the bit string, and finally, the bit string is amenable for use as an index into the UR* table.

IV. Example of an Image Database Application

The PROBE data model, the spatial operations supported, and the spatial query processor provide general support for applications involving spatial data. This section shows how these tools can be used to support an image database application. This example has not been implemented, but a geographic application has been implemented on top of a ''breadboard'' implementation of PROBE [13].

The schema for this example describes images and features derived from those images. The extraction of features is accomplished automatically or semiautomatically by an IMAGE object class. Regardless of how this is accomplished, the set of features in an image can be accessed by a function of the schema. Once the features are extracted and classified, queries involving these features can be evaluated.

```
type IMAGE is ENTITY
    pixels(IMAGE, X, Y) → PIXEL
    place(IMAGE) → BOX(*Bounding box*)
                      (*giving*)
                      (*bounding latitudes*)
                      (*and longitudes.*)
    time(IMAGE) → TIME(*When the image*)
                      (*was taken*)
    frequency(IMAGE) → FLOAT (*spectral*)
                      (*band*)
    feature (IMAGE) → set of FEATURE
                      (*Set of notable*)
                      (*features,*)
                      (*extracted*)
                      (*by an image*)
                      (*interpreter*)
    .
    .
    .
```

```
type FEATURE is ENTITY
    entity-type(FEATURE) → FEATURE-TYPE
    location(FEATURE) → (LATITUDE,*)
                      (*LONGITUDE*)
                      (*Real-world coordinates*)
    occurrences(FEATURE) → set of
    (IMAGE, X, Y)
                      (*Describes occurrence of*)
                      (*a feature in each image*)
                      (*containing the feature,*)
                      (*and gives the position *)
                      (*of the feature within *)
                      (*the image.*)
    near(FEATURE) → set of FEATURE
                      (*A set of nearby features*)
    .
    .

type ROAD is FEATURE
    name(ROAD) → STRING
    crosses(ROAD) → set of ROAD
    length(ROAD) → REAL
    .
    .

type BUS-STOP is FEATURE
    buses(BUS-STOP) → BUS-LINE
    .
    .
```

The database stores images in whatever representation is specified by the IMAGE object class, presumably an array of pixels. The individual pixels can be accessed via the database system (as is done in [19]); however, it is expected that most of the processing of images would be carried out by IMAGE object class functions. Using **apply-append**, a fully or partially automated image interpreter is invoked through the **features** function. Alternatively, **features** could be a stored function that is populated when images are brought into the database system. The image interpreter analyzes an image and returns a set of FEATURE entities. Classification of features (e.g., placing a ROAD feature in the extent of the **road** function) is also performed by **features**. Other PDM algebra operations permit comparisons of the features found to features already in the database. Features not seen before will get new surrogates. For all features, old or new, the association between the image and the feature is noted in the **occurrences** function of the FEATURE object class.

A database described by this schema could be used to answer a query such as the following: What bus lines have stops within 100 yds. of Massachusetts Avenue and Tremont Street? One strategy for evaluating this query is the following.

• Using the **occurrences** function, the set of images containing Massachusetts Avenue and the set of images containing Tremont Street are located. Pick one of the images containing both of these roads (e.g., the most recent).

- Using **POINT-SET_intersect**, find the position of the intersection of the two roads. A 100 yd "buffer" around the intersection is then constructed.
- Find an image that (spatially) contains the buffer, and in which bus stops are visible. This can be done using spatial join and spatial selection. The selection predicate has both spatial and nonspatial parts.
- Spatial join and spatial selection can now be used to locate the bus stops that fall within the buffer.

V. Summary and Future Plans

PROBE is an object-oriented database system. Its capabilities can be extended through the addition of object classes. The PROBE data model offers two constructs, entities and functions (stored and computed), and an algebraic query language. Object class instances can be stored in the database. An object class function is modeled by a (computed) function and invoked by referring to the function in a PDM algebra operation.

PROBE supports a spatial data model in which the basic spatial objects are point sets. Point sets have a well-defined set of operations that are useful in many applications. Further specialization of the model, as determined by the application, is accomplished by the addition of spatial object classes.

Efficient evaluation of spatial queries is achieved through a geometry filter. An application-specific spatial object class to be included in PROBE must support only the most basic unary and binary operations. Set-at-a-time processing of spatial objects is the responsibility of the geometry filter. The geometry filter also relies on the extensibility feature to incorporate its own dimension-independent representation of spatial objects.

A "breadboard" implementation of PROBE has been completed. It includes most of the PDM algebra, parts of the geometry filter (enough to include spatial join), object classes to support a geographic application, and application code. The system has a graphical interface, which was also incorporated as an object class.

Future PROBE plans include testing the data model and query processor in a real application and research on extensible query optimization. Much work remains to be done on the geometry filter. Experience with the implementation of spatial join in the breadboard has shown that even the simplest spatial query can be solved in a variety of ways. There is a choice as to what spatial objects should be decomposed (e.g., polygons or polygon edges), what dimension to work in (most k-D problems can also be solved by a simple transformation to $2k$ dimensions), how precise the decomposition process should be, etc. Even less is known about the performances of overlay and the set operations.

Acknowledgment

The authors gratefully acknowledge the contribution of A. Buchmann, U. Chakravarthy, U. Dayal, M. DeWitt, D. Goldhirsch, S. Heiler, and A. Rosenthal to the ideas described here. M. DeWitt also helped to improve the presentation by contributing several extraordinarily thorough reviews of earlier versions of this paper.

References

[1] D. J. Abel and J. L. Smith, "A data structure and algorithm based on a linear key for a rectangle retrieval problem," *Comput. Vision, Graphics, Image Processing*, vol. 27, no. 1, pp. 19–31, 1983.

[2] D. S. Batory and A. P. Buchmann, "Molecular objects, abstract data types and data models: A framework," in *Proc. 10th Int. Conf. Very Large Databases*, 1984.

[3] D. S. Batory and W. Kim, "Modeling concepts for VLSI CAD objects," *ACM Trans. Database Syst.*, vol. 10, no. 3, 1985.

[4] J. L. Bentley, "Multidimensional binary search trees used for associative searching," *Commun. ACM*, vol. 18, no. 9, pp. 509–517, 1975.

[5] W. A. Burkhard, "Interpolation-based index maintenance," in *Proc. 2nd ACM SIGACT-SIGMOD Symp. Principles Database Syst.*, pp. 76–89, 1983.

[6] M. J. Carey et al., "The architecture of the EXODUS extensible DBMS," in *Proc. Int. Workshop Object-Oriented Database Syst.*, pp. 52–65, 1986.

[7] S.-K. Chang et al., "A relational database system for pictures," in *Proc. IEEE Workshop Picture Data Description Management*, 1977.

[8] S.-K. Chang, Ed., *IEEE Comput.*, Special Issue on Pictorial Information Systems, vol. 14, no. 11, 1981.

[9] M. Chock et al., "Database structure and manipulation capabilities of a picture database management system (PICDBMS)," *IEEE Trans. Pattern Anal. Mach. Intell.*, vol. PAMI-6, no. 4, 1984.

[10] U. Dayal et al., "PROBE—A research project in knowledge-oriented database systems: Preliminary analysis," Computer Corporation of America, Tech. Rep. CCA-85-03, 1985.

[11] C. Faloutsos, "Multiattribute hashing using gray codes," in *Proc. ACM SIGMOD*, 1986.

[12] I. Gargantini, "An effective way to represent quadtrees," *Commun. ACM*, vol. 25, no. 12, pp. 905–910, 1982.

[13] D. Goldhirsch and J. A. Orenstein, "Extensibility in PROBE," *Database Eng.*, June 1987.

[14] A. Guttman, "R-trees: A dynamic index structure for spatial searching," in *Proc. ACM SIGMOD*, 1984.

[15] *Proceedings of the IEEE Workshop on Picture Data Description and Management*, 1977.

[16] R. H. Katz, *Information Management for Engineering Design*. New York: Springer-Verlag, 1985.

[17] R. Laurini, "Graphics databases built on Peano space-filling curves," in *Proc. EUROGRAPHICS Conf.*, pp. 327–338, 1985.

[18] R. A. Lorie and A. Meier, "Using a relational DBMS for geographical databases," IBM Res. Rep. RJ 3848 (43915) 4/6/83, 1983.

[19] F. Manola and J. Orenstein, "Toward a general spatial data model for an object-oriented DBMS," in *Proc. 12th Int. Conf. Very Large Databases*, 1986.

[20] F. Manola and U. Dayal, "PDM: An object-oriented data model," in *Proc. Int. Workshop Object-Oriented Database Syst.*, 1986.

[21] F. Manola, "PDM: An object-oriented data model for PROBE," Computer Corporation of America, Tech. Rep., to appear.

[22] S. Morehouse, "ARC/INFO: A geo-relational model for spatial information," in *Proc. Seventh Int. Symp. Comput. Assisted Cartography*, American Congress on Surveying and Mapping, 1985.

[23] G. Nagy and S. Wagle, "Geographic data processing," *ACM Comput. Surv.*, vol. 11, no. 2, pp. 139–181, 1979.

[24] J. A. Orenstein, "Algorithms and data structures for the implementation of a relational database system," School Comput. Sci., McGill Univ., Montreal, P.Q., Canada, Tech. Rep. SOCS-82-17, 1983.

[25] J. A. Orenstein and T. H. Merrett, "A class of data structures for associative searching," in *Proc. 3rd ACM SIGACT-SIGMOD Symp. Principles Database Syst.*, pp. 181–190, 1984.

[26] J. A. Orenstein, "Spatial query processing in an object-oriented database system," in *Proc. ACM SIGMOD*, 1986.

[27] J. A. Orenstein and F. A. Manola, "Spatial data modeling and query processing in PROBE," Computer Corporation of America, Tech. Rep. CCA-86-05, 1986.

[28] M. Ouksel and P. Scheuermann, "Storage mappings for multidimensional linear dynamic hashing," in *Proc. 2nd ACM SIGACT-SIGMOD Symp. Principles Database Syst.*, pp. 90–105, 1983.

[29] G. Peano, "La curva di Peano nel 'formulario mathematico,'" in *Selected Works of G. Peano*, H. C. Kennedy, Ed. (transl.). Allen and Unwin.

[30] A. Rosenthal, S. Heiler, U. Dayal, and F. Manola, "Traversal recursion: A practical approach to supporting recursive applications," in *Proc. ACM SIGMOD*, 1986.

[31] —, "Traversal recursion: A practical approach to supporting recursive applications," Computer Corporation of America, Tech. Rep. CCA-86-06, 1986.

[32] N. Roussopoulos and D. Leifker, "Direct spatial search on pictorial databases using packed *R*-trees," in *Proc. ACM SIGMOD*, 1985.

[33] H.-J. Schek and P. Pistor, "Data structures for an integrated data base management and information retrieval system," in *Proc. VLDB 8*, pp. 197–207, 1982.

[34] P. Schwarz *et al.*, "Extensibility in the Starburst database system," in *Proc. Int. Workshop Object-Oriented Database Syst.*, pp. 85–93, 1986.

[35] J. D. Smith, "The application of data base management systems to spatial data handling," Dep. Landscape Architecture Regional Planning, Univ. Massachusetts, Amherst, MA, Project Rep., 1984.

[36] M. Stonebraker *et al.*, "Document processing in a relational data base system," *ACM TOOIS*, vol. 1, no. 2, pp. 143–158, 1983.

[37] M. Stonebraker, "Object management in POSTGRES using procedures," in *Proc. Int. Workshop Object-Oriented Database Syst.*, 1986, pp. 66–72.

[38] M. Stonebraker and L. A. Rowe, "The design of POSTGRES," in *Proc. ACM-SIGMOD*, 1986, pp. 340–355.

Jack A. Orenstein received the Ph.D. degree in computer science from McGill University, Montreal, P.Q., Canada, in 1983.

He is a Computer Scientist at the Computer Corporation of America. Before that he was an Assistant Professor in the Department of Computer and Information Science at the University of Massachusetts, Amherst. His research interests include the modeling and processing of spatial data and object-oriented database systems.

Frank A. Manola (S'67–M'71) received the B.S. degree in civil engineering from Duke University, Durham, NC, in 1966 and the M.S.E. degree in computer science from the University of Pennsylvania, Philadelphia, in 1971.

In 1971 he joined the Naval Research Laboratory, Washington, DC. From 1978 to 1987 he was a Senior Computer Scientist at the Computer Corporation of America. He is currently a Principal Member of the Technical Staff in the Department of Intelligent Database Systems, GTE Laboratories, Inc., Waltham, MA. His research interests include object-oriented database technology, multimedia database applications, and data security.

Mr. Manola is a member of the Association for Computing Machinery and the IEEE Computer Society.

Reprinted from *IEEE Transactions on Software Engineering*, May 1988, pages 675-681. Copyright © 1988 by The Institute of Electrical and Electronics Engineers, Inc. All rights reserved.

An Object-Oriented Knowledge Representation for Spatial Information

L. MOHAN AND R. L. KASHYAP

Abstract—This paper suggests an abstract formalism for the representation of spatial knowledge. It focuses on developing a comprehensive representation scheme for pictorial information where the knowledge model of the given world has a high degree of perceptual map with a typical user's view of the same world.

The model that has been developed uses the object-oriented method of knowledge representation. This kind of knowledge modeling vastly enhances data structuring flexibility and allows for the representation of a large amount of semantic information. Further, the object model is enhanced by 1) the use of predicate logic for the representation of abstract information and 2) an inference engine based on pattern matching for automatic inferencing. The intention is that, with this model, any user of the system should be equipped to easily depict pictorial information. Also, he should be able to portray spatial as well as conceptual abstractions, generalizations, and rules at various levels.

Index Terms—Multiple inheritance, object-oriented, pictorial information, spatial knowledge, spatial resolution.

I. INTRODUCTION

Necessity has been felt for the development of systems for simplifying the management of spatial or pictorial information. Various types of picture database models, along with corresponding information retrieval mechanisms, have been proposed in the past [1]-[3], some of them with special reference to the management of spatial information contained in geographic maps [4]-[7].

Of the many proposed models, the relational data model [8]-[10] has been the most popular method for encapsulating spatial information. The relational model has also been specifically used in the past for representing image data in systems such as IMAID [3], [11].

Although the relational model is simple and easy to implement, it is not properly suited for handling image data. The relational model is ideally suited for single dimensional data (or "linear" data) which can be put in tabular form. Pictorial information, which is two-dimensional (or "spatial") does not fit naturally into this framework. Whenever the relational model has been used to depict pictorial information, the two-dimensional data has been converted such that it fits into tabular format. Moreover, the relational model has other severe drawbacks [12], some of which are discussed below.

Firstly, there is a limitation on data-structuring flexibility. Hierarchically structured data cannot be easily represented using a relational model. It is of course possible to set up tabular formats at different levels of the hierarchy, but the hierarchical nature of the data itself is not easy to capture in a direct manner. Consider any spatial object such as a picture or an image. This image can be viewed at the top level as one composite object. At a higher level of spatial resolution, it may be perceived as an aggregate of many regions. Each of these regions could be further divided into subregions and each level of fragmentation corresponds directly to adding an extra level of spatial resolution. If we were to represent specific information about each sub-region using a relational data model, we would be left with no option but to have individual tables for each subregion, along with having many more tables to establish the hierarchical links.

Manuscript received June 30, 1987; revised September 30, 1987. This work was supported in part by the National Science Foundation under Grants CDR-85-00022 and IST-84-05052.

The authors are with the School of Electrical Engineering, Purdue University, West Lafayette, IN 47907.

IEEE Log Number 8819890.

Secondly, whenever the table format is used, there is a lack of ability to *explicitly specify* semantic informaton about relationships. The exact nature of the relationship between the attributes in a relational table is implicit. Whereas information inside each relation is made explicit, the information which is obtained from combining different relations has to be guessed by the user. Consequently, the system becomes difficult to handle, especially by a naive user, since he does not know how to navigate through the relational tables.

The relational model has another major shortcoming. In almost all the query languages used for getting information out of a relational database, the user is expected to have a fairly good understanding of the precise tabular structure of the database. Also, in languages such as SQL [13], the user is expected to be able to make the query in a specific format. Very often slight variations that inadvertently creep into a query formulated by even an experienced user could lead to answers that are semantically way off the mark. A similar problem is seen in the relational query language QUEL, which is used in the INGRES system [14], where it is not necessary to specify the relations from which the information is to be retrieved. If there are multiple relationships between the same set of attributes, the path that the system uses to link these attributes is not unique, and consequently there is a possibility of semantically inaccurate information retrieval.

Several query languages for pictorial information retrieval have been proposed in the past. GEO-QUEL [6] is one such language based on the relational query langauge QUEL. Here too, for the user to benefit from using this language, the original information has to be made available in a table format. Another pictorial query language is the QPE [3], [11], which is based on the language QBE [15] developed for querying a relational database by specifying examples. It is important to note here that in QPE one does not specify a picture example by using a picture format (or a graphics interface). The QPE example that is entered by the user is a tabular example, and it is implicit that the user has precise knowledge as to how the spatial information has been converted to tabular format.

For any knowledge representation scheme to be successful, it is vitally important that its *structure* be consistent with the knowledge of the given world. The guiding principle behind the development of an object representation for the two-dimensional spatial world is that the representation should adequately represent the relevant complex relationships between the various entities in the real world. By using an object-oriented knowledge model for the pictorial information, rather than having the same information stored in relational tables, various types of relevant information about the picture (both spatial and relational) can be directly represented, as will be demonstrated in the examples to follow.

As contrasted with the relational model, the object-oriented approach provides a more elegant paradigm for knowledge representation [16], [17]. An object-oriented approach allows direct representation of hierarchical information. Also, it provides the necessary framework for representing pictorial information in its most natural form—which is storing data explicitly at various levels of abstractions. The various features of an object-oriented representation and the advantages of such a representation over a relational model are discussed in Section II of this paper.

Although an object-oriented database by itself does capture the inherent structure of the pictorial data, it still comes up short when trying to represent semantic generalizations and relationships existing in the information base. In earlier object databases, augmenting the database with predicate logic assertions together with an inference mechanism or deductive reasoning has been proposed as a method for overcoming this problem [18], [19]. Our scheme for the representation of pictorial information follows this approach where an object based representation is coupled with predicate logic and automatic inferencing. The idea is to get maximum advantage out of both explicit and implicit information representation. While the object model does a good job of capturing much of the structural information, the predicate logic assertions and rules serve to encapsulate semantic abstractions in the knowledge base. Section III shows how predicate logic and automatic inferencing help capture meaningful relationships between various entities or objects. Also discussed in this section is how the use of predicate logic is beneficial for designing a simple and elegant query language for retrieving information from the object-oriented database.

Later on in Section IV a discussion of how to use both explicit representation and deductive representation simultaneously, and where to strike an optimal balance between the two, is presented. Section V is a summary of some conclusions drawn about such a representation.

II. Object Representation of Spatial Information

Any object-based system has at its core the primary entity called the object. An object is an entity that combines the properties of both procedures and data. Apart from saving the local state of the information it can also perform computations [20]. All operations made inside an object-oriented system are in the form of message-passing between various objects. The fundamental aggregate unit in such object representations is the "class" [16]. A class is an intentional description of data, and the various instances of a class form the extensional data. Individual procedures (called "methods") may be defined specific to a class of objects.

This form of knowledge representation has some inherent advantages [21]–[23]. First, object-oriented system support the concept of data abstraction at various levels. By data abstraction, we mean that various procedures specific to a particular data-type or "class" can be tied together, and this increases the modularity of the database. In a relational database, this type of abstraction is not possible. This is primarily due the fact that only *atomic* data can be stored in a relational database and any one-to-many correspondences such as a common feature of a particular set of data elements cannot be directly represented. New tables would have to be created for each and every abstraction, and searching such a database would become an elaborate task.

Second, an object representation allows specializations, which also is not available with a relational model. For instance, a certain class of objects may be made a specialization of another class of objects, wherein it not only inherits the properties of the original class, but also has additional class descriptors of its own. The new class is then a subclass of the original class, and hence, hierarchical information is easily modeled in such a representation. Apart from hierarchical subclassing, which results in a *tree* structure, it is possible for us to model *lattice* structures. Such structures are discussed in detail later on in this section.

Another advantage of having an object-oriented data representation is the ability to easily capture integrity constraints in the data. This facility comes from the structure of an object class. Special functions can be tagged on to a class of objects to keep a data-integrity check on the object instances of that class. In a relational data model, integrity constraints can be specified only at a very elementary level. Conceptual constraints on the information in the knowledge base cannot be depicted in a relational model, whereas it is easily possible with an object representation.

An object representation for spatial information exploits the fact that any spatial entity which has a defined shape can be represented as an individual object. Image data, in general, has certain overall characteristics. There is, inherent in most maps, the concept of spatial hierarchy. Subregions in an image which are adjacent and nonoverlapping can be spatially aggregated into larger composite regions. This same unit–subunit relationship manifests itself at various levels in any spatial information base.

It is easy to see that an object representation can naturally capture the inherent structure of the image data. Objects can be created at various levels of spatial resolution and the information about the hierarchical links between objects can be stored along with the objects themselves. Consider an image "O", made up of three regions O_1, O_2, and O_3. Let each of these regions be made up of subregions as shown in Fig. 1.

Each of the O's is represented as an individual object. We abstract the two-dimensional spatial information into its most natural semantic equivalent by creating a set of generic classes C_1, C_2, $\cdots$, C_n, wherein there is one generic class for each level of spatial resolution. Thus O_1, O_2, and O_3 are instances of class C_2, O_{11}, O_{12}, $\cdots$, O_{32} are instances of class C_3, and so on. The information about specific hierarchical links is captured in the manner described below. In the object representation for each spatial object we have slots of the attributes "component-of" and "comprised-of."

Consequently, the representation for the object O_2 would look like the following:

Object Subclass C_2
Name: O_2

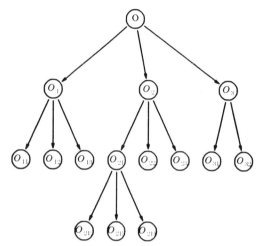

Fig. 1. A spatial object hierarchy.

Component-of: O
Comprised-of: O_{21}, O_{22}, O_{23}
——

——

Similarly, the representation for the object O_{21} would be:

Object Subclass C_3
Name: O_{21}
Component-of: O_2
Comprised-of: O_{211}, O_{212}, O_{213}
——

——

Thus any spatial tree structure can be represented by the above formalism.

At the same time, the modular nature of the independent entities in the image data can be captured in full. The object data model has the important feature of "entity identity" [12] wherein any entity (or object) can be directly referenced as a single unit. By using the object representation, special features of any region in a picture can be easily made part of the object description of that particular region.

Although the image data may be stored individually as a set of independent objects, there are a lot of spatial and conceptual relationships between various component entities. An object based representation provides a clean method for any form of conceptual abstraction. This is achieved by utilizing the availability of aggregate or "class" objects. Suppose that a group of various spatial objects had a feature or a conceptual property in common. With an object model it is easy to create a new subclass which has that specific group of objects as its instances, and this new class object would then represent that particular abstract property.

Suppose that in our example, the objects O_{13}, O_{21}, O_{22}, O_{23} shared a common spatial property P_1. We can create a subclass C_{p1}, having these five objects as its instances. C_{p1} will then be a subclass of the generic class C_3. This is shown in Fig. 2.

Because of the availability of the inheritance feature in the object model, further specializations can be directly represented. In the above case, suppose that out of the five objects that shared property P_1, two of these, say O_{22} and O_{23}, had an additional conceptual property P_2. This can be incorporated with the creation of subclass C_{p2} as shown in Fig. 2.

Apart from being able to represent *mutually exclusive* objects as a class, an object-oriented model also allows us to directly represent conceptually *overlapping* objects. For instance, consider two classes, both of which are aggregations of smaller objects, having some overlapping regions. Such overlaps automatically lead to a *lattice* type of structure. In any general lattice, any node can have more than one parent node, as opposed to a tree structure which is

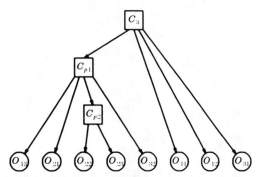

Fig. 2. Conceptual abstraction by subclassing.

more restrictive where a node can have only one parent. In terms of objects and classes, this means that an object can belong to more than one class. In object-oriented environments, this feature which allows arbitrary intersection of class boundaries is known as *multiple inheritance* [16]. Consequently we have a situation wherein some objects are instances of two or more classes while other objects are instances of one of the classes.

Consider the situation where the objects O_{11}, O_{12}, O_{21}, and O_{23} share the property P_A, and the objects O_{21}, O_{23}, and O_{31} have the property P_B. Here we have a conceptual overlap of regions (since O_{21} and O_{23} are part of both concept groups). If we were to represent this information in the form of a lattice, it would result in the structure shown in Fig. 3.

In the remaining part of this section we apply this object-oriented knowledge representation formalism to a very specific case. We have chosen for our spatial data the pictorial information contained in the geographical map of the U.S. The object descriptions used here are similar to the way they would be described in the Smalltalk-80 object-oriented programming environment. We note that the class "Object" is the root of a class hierarchy, and that it has no superclass.

In this representation, all those objects that fall at the same horizontal level in the spatial hierarchy are grouped together in the same class, as is shown in Fig. 4. Consequently we have four primitive classes "country," "state," "county", and "city." All the 50 states are instances of the class "state" and any county belonging to any state is an instance of the general class "county." So also, all the cities, regardless of which county they belong to, become object instances of the general class "city."

The information about which "county" belongs to which "state" has been included as part of the attributes of each individual object. Each instance of "county" has associated with it the instance variable "In-state" where the appropriate state to which that county belongs, is recorded. Also, every "state" object has a slot where the full list of its counties is stored explicitly. A similar mechanism is used at the city level to establish city-county "belonging-to" relationships.

Object subclass: Country
Instance Variables:

NAME	(string)
SIZE	(integer)
BOUNDARY	(set of ordered pairs of real numbers)
___	

Object subclass: State
Instance Variables:

NAME	(string)
HAS-COUNTIES	(set of strings)
BOUNDARY	(set of ordered pairs of real numbers)
POPULATION	(integer)
CENTER-OF-GRAVITY	(ordered pair of real numbers)

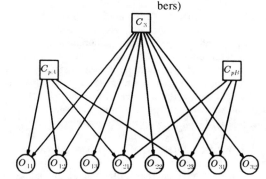

Fig. 3. Concept overlap by multiple inheritance.

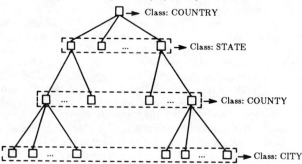

Fig. 4. Grouping by levels of spatial resolution.

___

___

Object subclass: County
Instance Variables:

NAME	(string)
IN-STATE	(string)
HAS-CITIES	(set of string)
BOUNDARY	(set of ordered pairs of real numbers)
POPULATION	(integer)
CENTER-OF-GRAVITY	(ordered pair of real numbers)
___	
___	

Object subclass: City
Instance Variables:

NAME	(string)
IN-COUNTY	(string)
LOCATION	(ordered pair of real numbers)
POPULATION	(integer)
___	
___	

It is now very easily possible to represent various pieces of relational information. For instance, if we wanted to group together all those states through which the river Mississippi flows, we could use the feature of multiple inheritance. (It may be noted here that Smalltalk-80 allows only *subclassing*, which is a more restrictive form of multiple inheritance). Therefore, all we need to do is create a new class object called ''Mississippi-river-states'' and have as its instances only those states through which the river passes. The object instances would be grouped similar to the example shown in Fig. 3.

Alternately consider the formation of ''electorates.'' Any set of counties may be directly grouped together to form an electorate. The advantage of representing geographical (spatial) entities at each level of the spatial hierarchy as individual objects makes it easy for depicting such aggregate concepts. The key point here is that an object can be an instance of any number of classes, and in each case, the object is perceived from a certain viewpoint. As an example, a particular county may be an instance of a class ''county'' where it portrays itself as a part of a particular state, and it may also be an instance of another class which depicts an electorate, and simultaneously it may also be an instance of another class which represents a group of counties which have a low crime-rate.

Thus we see that it is possible to depict not only one-to-many relationships (which result in tree structures), but also to capture many-to-many relationships (which result in lattice and network structures) by using an object-oriented model. This freedom of regrouping and the ability to visualize the same entity from different aspects is not available in a traditional relational data model. If this geographic information were to be represented as a relational data base, new relations would have to be created to represent each of the concepts mentioned above.

III. The Use of Predicate Logic

It is generally accepted that it is not practical or feasible to explicitly represent all the relations that exist in any knowledge base [24]. It takes up too much space and effort, and also will slow down the system tremendously while retrieving information. A large amount of ''inherent'' knowledge about the spatial data may have to be stored in a nonexplicit manner. For this we require a mechanism by which facts (or information) can be deduced from the system. Consequently this leads to the formulation of deductive databases [25]–[27]. In a deductive database the data model is augmented by predicate logic. Also built into the system is an automatic inferencing mechanism, with the help of which new information can be deduced from existing information. In effect, by making the knowledge base deductive, we add declarative semantics to the system.

Our knowledge model provides a logic predicate based method for representing nonexplicit information. Moreover, the formalism that has been developed integrates the predicate representation with the object representation. This, coupled with the automatic inference mechanism based on symbolic pattern matching over the predicates, allows for efficient storage and retrieval of deduced information. Thus, various shared properties of different objects can be easily represented as will be demonstrated by the examples to follow.

The first order predicate language used in describing the properties of this kind of a knowledge base makes use of two types of predicates. The first and more commonly used type of logic predicate is the *descriptive* logic predicate. These predicates are used to serve as descriptions of particular attributes of objects, and act as symbols over which pattern matching can be performed. Any n-ary descriptive predicate is of the form:

$$p(x_1, x_2, \cdots, x_n)$$

where p is the predicate symbol and all the x_i's are the arguments of the predicate. In our formalism, all the arguments have to be objects. (We note here that character strings as well as numbers are also objects).

Assertions about the knowledge can be made in terms of rules and facts. For our purpose let us abbreviate

$$p(x_1, x_2, \cdots, x_n) \quad \text{by} \quad p(\ ).$$

Any rule can then be represented by a predicate logic statement such as

$$p_0 < = p_1(\ ) \wedge p_2(\ ) \wedge \cdots \wedge p_n(\ ).$$

where the $<=$ symbol represents logical implication and the $\wedge$ symbol stands for logical conjunction. If the number of predicates to the right of the implication symbol is zero, then it represents a fact, as shown in the illustration below.

$$q_1(\ ) < =.$$

The second and more powerful type of logic predicate is the *procedural* predicate. A procedural predicate is actually a little procedure (or method) associated with a particular object [28]. These predicates automatically invoke procedures to act on their arguments. After the procedure is executed, pattern matching can be performed over the predicate. The syntax of the procedural predicate is exactly the same as that of a descriptive predicate and any such predicate can be represented as

$$p(x_1, x_2, \cdots, x_n).$$

Only, here the predicate symbol p is not just a symbol but is also a call to a procedure by the same name.

With the availability of these predicates, it is possible to represent conceptual information in the form of generalization rules. Consider the following illustration. Supposing we wish to obtain the value of any attribute of an object, we could have a procedural predicate

$$\text{Value}(Y, A, X)$$

which will have Y as the value of the attribute A associated with the object X. Using such a predicate, it is possible to specify generalization rules. Consider a general property P of a composite spatial object S which is also shared by its component objects. This fact can be stated in the form of the following rule:

$$\text{Value}(p\text{-value}, P, X) < = \text{Value}(X, \text{Belongs-to}, S)$$
$$\wedge \text{Value}(p\text{-value}, P, S)$$

which states that for any X that is a component object of S, the attribute P has the same value as the attribute value of the composite object S. Similarly, many other generalizations can be performed, using a variety of procedural predicates.

Right away it can be seen that we now have an alternate mechanism for depicting property inheritance among groups of objects. Also, because each logic rule can be explicitly specified, the knowledge base can have selective-inheritance (where only certain properties are inherited by subclasses). This feature makes the representation very powerful.

Using predicate logic for asserting deductive knowledge also presents the knowledge base users with a whole new method of *querying* the knowledge base. As in any logic programming language, there is only a subtle difference between an assertion of a deductive fact or rule and a logic query. Both deductive rules (or generalizations and knowledge base queries take the same form:

$$p_0 < = p_1(\ ) \wedge p_2(\ ) \wedge \cdots \wedge p_n(\ ).$$

The only difference would be that while using these logic constructs as queries, we include *variables* in the argument positions of those objects whose values we wish to deduce from the query.

In the remaining part of this section, we present a wide selection of example queries formulated using these predicate logic constructs. In all of the following examples, the spatial knowledge base is the same that was used in Section II, namely the information contained in the geographic map of the U.S.

117

Consider the following assertion of the fact depicting the intersection of two expressways at a particular point on the map. For instance, I-94 and I-65 intersect at a point in northern Indiana having the spatial coordinates $(370, 55)$. {Assume that the top left corner of the screen is the origin with spatial coordinates $(0, 0)$}. This fact can be asserted as follows:

$$\text{Exp-way}(65) \land \text{Exp-way}(94)$$
$$\land \text{Intersect}(65, 94, \text{Point}(370, 55)).$$

The ground instance (where all the variables are instantiated to constants) as in the above statement represents a fact. Whereas, if we wished to find out from the knowledge base where the expressways I-65 and I-94 intersect, the query would take the exact same format as the assertion above, except that we would use variables in place of the constants for the coordinates of the intersection point.

The query is shown below:

$$?\ \text{Exp-way}(65) \land \text{Exp-way}(94) \land \text{Intersect}(65, 94, \text{Point}(X, Y)).$$

The automatic inference mechanism would come up with the instantiations $X = 370$ and $Y = 55$, as an answer to the query.

Let us suppose that we wish to know which counties in the state of Wisconsin are hilly. Assume that we already have a property (attribute) called "Terrain" and this attribute can take either of two values, "hilly" or "flat," associated with our class description of the class "county." Then our query would take the form:

$$?\ \text{Value}(\text{'Hilly'}, \text{terrain}, X) \land \text{Value}(\text{Wisconsin}, \text{In-state}, X).$$

The resulting instantiations of the variable X would give the list of all the hilly counties in Wisconsin.

Many special relationships are captured deductively. In case we require to know what distance a river (or an expressway) traverses inside a particular state or county, we can adopt the following methodology. Consider each river as an individual object—represented as a series of line-segments. (A similar representation may be made for expressways also.) The answer to the query "For how many miles does river X flow in State Y?" may be obtained procedurally from the method predicate

$$?\ \text{Riv-segment}(X, Y, R) \land \text{Length}(R, D)$$

where the predicate Riv-segment(X, Y, R) computes R as the spatial intersection of a line X and a bounded polygon Y, and the predicate Length(R, D) computes the distance D of the segment R. Thus predicate logic serves as a powerful tool for representing derived information.

High levels of abstract information can be derived through the use of predicate logic queries. Suppose we wish to come up with a *route plan* between two cities. Firstly, we include the list of all the interstate expressways that pass through any state (along with the information on interchanges) inside the object description of that state. A quick method of arriving at a way of finding a short path would be to first locate the state of the route's origin and the route's destination state. Next, locate a state that is adjacent to the origination state which is closer to the destination state, and check for common expressways between the adjacent states. (If no common expressways are found, we look for interchanges.) This process is *recursively* applied till the goal state is reached. This algorithm does not necessarily come up with an optimum path, but yields a practical near-optimal path.

Route$(X, Y, R) <=$ Adjacent$(X, Y) \land$ Path(X, Y, R)

Route$(X, Y, R) <=\ \tilde{}$Adjacent$(X, Y) \land$ Adjacent(X, Z)
$$\land \text{ Closer-to}(Z, Y, X) \land \text{Route}(X, Z, P1)$$
$$\land \text{ Route}(Z, Y, P2) \land \text{Append}(P1, P2, R)$$

In the above example the predicate Adjacent(X, Y) is computed to be true if X is spatially adjacent to Y. We might note here that the predicate ~Adjacent (X, Y) is true when X and Y are not adjacent to each other. The predicate Closer-to(B, C, A) returns true if B is closer to C than A is. (This can be easily accomplished since

the Center-of-Gravity of each object is stored along with the object.) Append$(P1, P2, R)$ does the actual collating of the individual path segments into a final list R.

Implicit in such a predicate calculus representation is the concept of *recursive evaluation*. The terminating condition for the recursion is found in the first rule where the route between X and Y is given by the value of R in Path(X, Y, R), and is applicable only when X and Y are adjacent to each other. When X and Y are not adjacent, the second rule is applicable. An intermediate state Z, which is adjacent to X and also closer to Y (than X is to Y) is located, and the path between X and Z is obtained, and the entire procedure is now applied recursively to find a route between Z and Y. This way the whole route is generated as a set of piecewise Paths.

Thus we have a simple and yet powerful query language to obtain information from such an object-oriented knowledge base. We also note that with such a query language, there is no requirement for the special "spatial operators" that are necessary when using a relational-model-based query language such as QPE. Practically any sort of query may be formulated in the predicate calculus language.

IV. DEDUCTIVE KNOWLEDGE VERSUS EXPLICIT REPRESENTATION

A recurring question in the design of such knowledge bases is what knowledge should be stored explicitly and what should be stored implicitly. For instance the feature of adjacency can be represented in either of two ways. Each object could have a variable associated with it which contains a list of all its adjacent objects. This way the additional list variable associated with the instance of Indiana State would be:

ADJACENT-TO [Michigan, Illinois, Kentucky, Ohio]

Alternately, the adjacency information could be obtained deductively. Suppose each object had associated with it a list of line-segments which represented the borderlines enclosing the object (where each line-segment could be a set of two points in coordinate space). Adjacency of two objects could be inferred if they had a common borderline segment. The deductive representation would be as follows:

$$\text{Adjacent}(X, Y) <= \text{Value}(L1, \text{Borderlines}, X)$$
$$\land \text{ Value}(L2, \text{Borderlines}, Y)$$
$$\land \text{ Member-of}(L1, LS1)$$
$$\land \text{ Member-of}(L2, LS2)$$
$$\land \text{ Equals}(LS1, LS2)$$

The attribute "Borderlines" associated with an object would contain a list of ordered quadruplets, such as $(x1, y1, x2, y2)$, which would denote single line segments which make up the object's boundary. The predicate Member_of$(L1, LS1)$ would instantiate $LS1$ to any single quadruplet in the list $L1$. (Note that the predicate Value$(L1, \text{Borderline}, X)$ has already instantiated the variable $L1$ to the entire list of quadruplets which form the boundary of object X.) Only when a particular line segment corresponding to the object X is numerically equal to a line segment corresponding to the object Y, can we say that the two objects X and Y are adjacent.

A representation that makes a compromise between computational overheads and redundant storage in the above case would be to store the adjacency information explicitly at the "state" level, and employ the deductive approach while computing adjacency at the "county" and lower levels.

Also important is the related concept of aggregation. Since the geographical data consists of various types of entities where certain entities are aggregates of other smaller entities, proper representation of aggregate quantities such as "population" or "area" is necessary.

If deductively represented, the population of a state can be computed by aggregating the population of each of the counties that belong to that state. The same could be said of the "area" of an aggregate object such as a state. Or alternatively the same information can be explicitly stored along with the aggregate object itself.

Here again, a utilitarian approach would be to store explicitly at the upper levels "static" information, that is data which are not likely to vary over time, such as "area," whereas, dynamically varying information—such as "population"—can be stored at the lowest levels (and updating is done at the lowest levels), and whenever the population of an aggregate object such as the country itself is required, it can be procedurally inferred from the object knowledge base by using a predicate logic statement.

The implementation of such an object-oriented knowledge base requires a combination of two facilities. First, we need an object-oriented data representation formalism. Next, we require an inference engine which will reason over both descriptive as well as procedural logic predicates. Currently, an object-oriented system such as Smalltalk-80 satisfies only the former requirement. This Smalltalk environment could be augmented with a pattern matching mechanism, much like what is available in Prolog, by which automatic inferencing can be made available. Moreover, even though multiple inheritance is indirectly available in Smalltalk, it would be extremely useful to be able to have direct multiple inheritance properties, wherein an individual instance can be made to belong to more than one class at the same horizontal level in the class hierarchy. Such an enhanced version of Smalltalk would be ideal for implementing an object-oriented pictorial knowledge base.

V. Conclusion

Representing the entities in our domain as objects provides us with a natural way of viewing our information at different levels of abstraction. We thereby reduce the number of components we wish to deal with, and consequently reduce computational complexity. Implicitly, this hierarchical object representation facilitates logical zooming in and out of the knowledge base, which is a semantic equivalent of the visual zooming one would perform on a pictorial (image) database. This ability to make abstractions to various levels, coupled with the ability to make generalizations and rules at various levels (which is available due to the deductive power of predicate logic), allows the system to capture practically any type of information that we wish to represent about our given pictorial world.

References

[1] R. B. Abhyankar and R. L. Kashyap, "Picture data description and retrieval with relational query languages," in *Proc. IEEE Comput. Soc. Workshop Picture Data Description and Management*, Aug. 1980.

[2] S. K. Chang and T. L. Kunii, "Pictorial data base systems," *Computer*, vol. 25, no. 11, pp. 13–21, Nov. 1981.

[3] N. S. Chang and K. S. Fu, "Picture query languages for pictorial data-base systems," *Computer*, vol. 25, no. 11, pp. 23–33, Nov. 1981.

[4] G. C. Roman, "Formal specification of geographic data processing requirements," in *Proc. Int. Conf. Data Engineering*, IEEE, 1986, pp. 434–446.

[5] G. Nagy and S. Wagle, "Geographic data processing," *Comput. Surveys*, vol. 11, no. 2, pp. 139–181, June 1979.

[6] R. R. Berman and M. Stonebraker, "Geo-quel: A system for the manipulation and display of geographic data," in *Proc. Conf. Very Large Data Bases*, 1977, pp. 186–191.

[7] M. Chock, A. F. Cardenas, and A. Klinger, "Manipulating data structures in pictorial information systems," *Computer*, vol. 25, no. 11, pp. 43–50, Nov. 1981.

[8] J. D. Ullman, *Principles of Database Systems*. Rockville, MD Computer Science Press, 1983.

[9] E. F. Codd, "A relational mode of data for large shared data banks," *Commun. ACM*, vol. 13, no. 6, pp. 377–387, June 1970.

[10] —, "Extending the database relational model to capture more meaning," *ACM Trans. Database Syst.*, vol. 4, no. 4, pp. 397–434, Dec. 1979.

[11] N. S. Chang and K. S. Fu, "Query by pictorial example," *IEEE Trans. Software Eng.*, vol. SE-6, no. 6, pp. 519–524, Nov. 1980.

[12] G. Copeland and D. Maier, "Making Smalltalk a database system," *ACM SIGMOD Rec.*, vol. 14, no. 2, pp. 316–325, June 1984.

[13] D. D. Chamberlin and R. F. Boyce, "Sequel: A structured english query language," in *Proc. ACM SIGDIFET Workshop*, Ann Arbor, MI, 1974.

[14] M. R. Stonebraker, E. Wong, G. D. Held, and P. Kreps, "The design and implementation of INGRES," *ACM Trans. Database Syst.*, vol. 1, no. 3.

[15] M. M. Zloof, "Query by example," in *Proc. Nat. Comput. Conf.*, May 1975, pp. 431–438.

[16] A. Goldberg, *Smalltalk-80: The Language and its Implementation*. Reading, MA: Addison-Wesley, 1983.

[17] M. Minsky, "A framework for representing knowledge," in *The Psychology of Compuer Vision*, P. Winston, Ed. New York: McGraw-Hill, 1975, pp. 211–277.

[18] R. Fikes and T. Kehler, "The role of frame-based representation in reasoning," *Commun. ACM*, vol. 28, no. 9, pp. 904–920, Sept. 1985.

[19] P.C.-Y. Sheu and R. L. Kashyap, "Object-based process planning in automated manufacturing environments," in *Proc. IEEE Int. Conf. Robotics and Automation*, 1987.

[20] M. Stefik and D. G. Bobrow, "Object-oriented programming: Themes and variations," *AI Mag.*, vol. 6, no. 4, pp. 40–62, 1986.

[21] R. W. Peterson, "Object-oriented data base design," *AI Expert*, pp. 26–31, Mar. 1987.

[22] R. King, "A database management system based on an object-oriented model," in *Expert Database Systems*, L. Kershberg, Ed. California: Benjamin/Cummings, 1986.

[23] E. P. Stabler, Jr., "Object-oriented programming in PROLOG," *AI Expert*, pp. 46–57, Oct. 1986.

[24] J. Minker, "An experimental relational data base system based on logic," in *Logic and Databases*, H. Gallaire and J. Minker, Eds. New York: Plenum, 1978, pp. 107–147.

[25] J. Grant, *Logical Introduction to Databases*. New York: Harcourt Brace Jovanovich, 1987.

[26] R. Reiter, "Deductive question-answering on relational data bases," in *Logic and Databases*, H. Gallaire and J. Minker, Eds. New York: Plenum, 1978, pp. 149–177.

[27] C. L. Chang, "Deduce: A deductive query language for relational data bases," in *Pattern Recognition and Artificial Intelligence*, C. H. Chen, Ed. New York: Academic, 1976, pp. 108–134.

[28] C. V. Ramamoorthy and P.C-Y. Sheu, "Logic object-oriented bases," in *Proc. IEEE 3rd Int. Conf. Data Engineering*, Los Angeles, CA, Feb. 1987, pp. 218–225.

SECTION 4:
IMPLEMENTATIONS AND APPROACHES TO IMPLEMENTATION ISSUES

Abstract Types and Storage Types in an OO-DBMS

Craig Damon and Gordon Landis

Ontologic, Inc.

47 Manning Road

Billerica, Mass. 01821

Abstract

The Vbase object-oriented database management system (OO-DBMS) extends the basic paradigm offered by other object-oriented systems, by allowing the creation of "storage classes", in the same way other systems allow the creation of abstract classes. Storage classes control object storage, including dereferencing, object faulting, clustering, sharing and persistence.

This facility is based upon the notion of a storage manager. Storage managers are types, which are organized into a hierarchy, similar to but orthogonal to the hierarchy of abstract types. The storage manager type hierarchy is user-extensible by subtyping, just as the abstract type hierarchy is. The implementation of the storage manager abstraction relies upon generalizations to operation dispatching and reference resolution.

1. Introduction

Section 1 of this paper provides an introduction to the concepts of object-oriented programming, including a definition of an Object-Oriented DBMS, and a brief outline of the Vbase data model. Section 2 describes what a storage manager is and how it is used in Vbase. Section 3 describes some features of our implementation. Finally, Section 4 offers some conclusions based on our experiences.

1.1. What is an OO-DBMS ?

Even within object-oriented circles, there is not a clear consensus on what an object-oriented database is, but we will start with the guidelines given in [Wegner87]. He defines an object-oriented language as possessing three characteristics: objects, classes, and inheritance. An *object* is a combination of state and a set of operations defined on that state. A *class* (or *type*) is a definition of the state and operations that are valid for all objects that are members of the class. *Inheritance* is the ability to make subtypes by "inheriting" all of the operations defined by a super-type.

To define an object-oriented database, we add three additional criteria: persistence, sharing and transactions. *Persistence* simply means that objects may live longer than the process that created them. *Sharing* means that objects are accessible to multiple processes (which might run concurrently or sequentially). A *transaction* lumps one or more actions into a single atomic action, which is both indivisible, in that either all of it happens or none of it happens, and non-interfering, in that it does not see the effects of another concurrent transaction [Weihl82]. Note that there are other features commonly associated with a database, such as query capabilities, but these are less fundamental to the notion of a database, and we do not take them to be definitional.

1.2. Introduction to Vbase

Vbase incorporates these basic concepts, adding to them the notions of data abstraction and static type checking, both heavily influenced by the CLU programming language [Liskov81]. In a system supporting *data abstraction*, an object's state and implementation are accessible only through operations defined by the type. *Static type checking* requires that all validation of type compatibility can happen at compile time.

In Vbase, an object's abstract behavior is defined by an abstract typing mechanism. This behavior may have been defined by the object's abstract type, or directly inherited from its supertype, or inherited from the supertype with a refinement by the type. In a *refinement*, the subtype adds some additional behavior to the behavior defined by the supertype. A type must provide the implementation for all behavior that it defines and for the additional behavior that it has added through refinements.

When an operation is invoked, Vbase uses a mechanism called *dispatching* to determine which

Reprinted from *Digest of Papers, COMPCON*, 1988, pages 172-176. Copyright © 1989 by The Institute of Electrical and Electronics Engineers, Inc. All rights reserved.

subtype's implementation to execute, based on the abstract type of the supplied argument.

At the top of the abstract type hierarchy is the type Entity. All objects in the Vbase system are instances of Entity. Subtypes of Entity (including user-defined types) define additional state and operations to model application-specific behaviors.

To model state, an abstract type defines properties for its instances. Unlike the notions of state in many traditional data models, Vbase properties do not give the user direct access to the object's internal implementation. Instead, the user accesses the state through a collection of abstract operations. A typical property consists of three operations: Get, Set and Init.

The state of an object is stored in one or more representation pieces defined by the abstract type of the object. Each piece of representation is itself an object. The representation of a primitive Vbase type is Space, which is in turn its own representation.

Typically, each type defines a single representation piece, containing all of the state needed for the behavior defined by the type. The actual storage used to represent the object is allocated and managed by a type called a *storage manager*.

2. Vbase Storage Managers

2.1. Overview

Every Vbase object is an instance of some abstract type, and derives all of its visible behavior from that type (and, via the inheritance mechanism, from the supertypes of that type). The behaviors associated with the object's storage, however, are implemented not by the object's abstract type, but by its storage manager. These behaviors include the object's persistence, location, its clustering with other objects, its paging (or "object-faulting") behavior, etc.

These behaviors are not directly visible at the abstract level, but are used internally by the type to manipulate its instances. Most types, however, will choose to export the higher level features of the storage manager, by allowing the user to specify, when an object is created, which storage manager to use, and how to cluster the object (thus determining the object's persistence, paging behaviors, etc.)

For example, when a user creates an instance of type Document, or CircuitDesign, or, say, Cat, the type might allow specification of whether the cat should be stored in persistent storage, or in tempo-

rary storage. Many types, however, will limit the set of allowable storage managers, either for semantic or performance reasons. If the set is limited to only one allowable storage manager, then the type most likely will not allow user specification of the storage manager at all.

Storage managers are much like other types, in that they define a set of behaviors, can have subtypes, etc. They differ, though, in that they do not have instances in the same sense as abstract types do. Instead, their operations apply to pieces of storage, which might be used to store instances of other types.

There is a strong analogy between the way an application makes calls on the operations defined by abstract types, and the way an abstract type makes calls on a storage manager. For example, an application could invoke an operation on a Cat, like Get-HairColor (defined, say, on type Mammal), and it would dispatch to the appropriate subtype of Cat, based on the actual abstract type of the argument (Fig. 1)

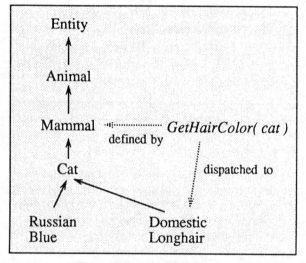

Fig 1. Dispatching an Abstract Operation

Internally, the type Cat processes the GetHair-Color operation by accessing the instance's storage, by invoking the StorageManager$Wire operation. This operation will dispatch the appropriate subtype of StorageManager, based on the actual storage manager of the argument (Fig. 2).

Note that if the cat in question is of the type RussianBlue, then the original GetHairColor operation will dispatch to this type. In this case, the question can be answered without looking at any storage at all: the operation can simply return the value

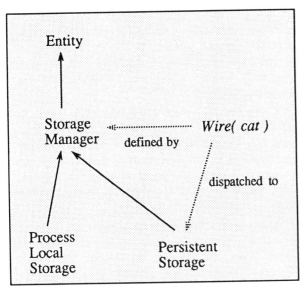

Fig 2. Dispatching a Storage Manager Operation

Blue, because all instances of RussianBlue cats are blue.

2.2. Operational Interface.

Vbase supports a hierarchy of storage managers, which support a variety of object lifetimes, clustering capabilities, and levels of inter-process sharing.

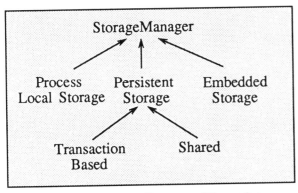

Fig 3. Storage Manager Hierarchy

The type StorageManager defines operations for allocating, deallocating, and accessing storage. There are nine operations altogether for managing storage, which are defined by type StorageManager, and refined by its subtypes.

```
Allocate(  storagemanagerindex: integer,
           size: integer,
           where: entity,
           hownear: cluster )
    returns( space );

Deallocate( e: space );

Wire( e: space )
    returns( pointer );

Unwire( e: space,
        modified:boolean );

Resize( e: space,
        delta: integer );

Getsize( e: space )
    returns( integer );

BeginTransaction(
        timestamp: time );

CommitTransaction(
        timestamp: time );

AbortTransaction( );
```

Allocate: The arguments to the Allocate operation are a "StorageManagerIndex", indicating which storage manager to use (described in the section on Implementation); the size of the storage piece to allocate (in bytes); an entity with which to cluster the new storage; and a cluster-specification, indicating how closely to cluster it. (These last two arguments are optional and are described in the section on Clustering.) Allocate returns a reference to a piece of storage, which is used by the abstract type (which made the call) to store an instance. The type of the return from the Allocate operation is Space. Space is the type used as the representation for the primitive system types (out of which, in turn, the non-primitive types build *their* representation).

Deallocate: The Deallocate operation takes only a single argument, the piece of storage to be deleted.

Wire: The Wire operation brings a piece of storage into memory, and returns a Pointer to it. A Pointer is the abstract equivalent of a virtual memory address. Once this Pointer is returned by the storage manager, it is guaranteed that the storage piece will remain fixed ("wired") in virtual memory until a corresponding Unwire operation is called.

Unwire: The Unwire operation releases a wired object from its virtual memory address. This operation takes two arguments: a piece of storage (which must be currently wired) and a boolean, indicating whether the storage was modified. If the storage was modified, the storage manager will take appropriate measures to ensure that the changes are preserved. If the storage manager supports persistent object storage, then this will mean writing the object out to stable storage at the end of the transaction. If the storage manager supports only transient (process-local) object storage, then the Modified flag might well be ignored.

Resize: The Resize operation changes the size of a previously allocated piece of storage. It takes two arguments: a piece of storage, and a delta, indicating the number of bytes to add or remove.

Getsize: The Getsize operation simply returns the current size in bytes of a piece of storage. It takes one argument, a piece of storage, and returns an integer.

BeginTransaction: This storage manager operation is called by the user-visible operation, Transaction$Begin. Not all storage managers support the transaction protocol. In fact, one Vbase storage manager, SharedStorage, is specifically designed for implementing objects that are used for inter-transaction communication. If these objects obeyed the normal transaction protocol of non-interference (that is, the effects of one transaction are not visible to another concurrent transaction), then inter-transaction communication would be impossible.

For those storage managers that do support the transaction protocol, BeginTransaction starts a transaction scope. The timestamp argument controls the resolution of future Wire calls: the storage manager will ensure that this transaction will not see the changes made by other transactions whose commit time is later than this transaction's start time.

CommitTransaction: This operation has the effect of making the current transaction's changes visible to subsequent transactions (probably by writing the changes out to stable storage). If the storage manager does not support a transaction protocol, this operation might be a no-op.

AbortTransaction: This operation throws away all of the current transaction's changes. Again, if the storage manager does not support the transaction protocol, this might be a no-op.

2.3. Clustering

Raising the storage problem to being a semantically visible portion of the system has advantages for clustering. *Clustering* is the ability to store logically related objects close together.

The storage managers all support a series of hierarchical clustering levels. The normal arrangement is to support chunks (contiguous storage), segments (a clustering of chunks) and areas (a clustering of segments). Any storage manager, however, is free to support more levels of clustering or ignore some or all of these standard levels. For the default persistent storage type, a segment is the unit of transfer to and from disk, and an area maps to a disk partition or file. As alternatives, process local objects have only two levels of clustering: chunks and segments, where segments are built along operating system paging boundaries in a virtual memory system; while a distributed storage manager might add another higher level of clustering: a node.

The user can cluster an object's storage explicitly by making use of the clustering arguments to the abstract type's create operation, but types also generally provide a default clustering. The user's preferences, or the type's defaults if no preferences are given, are passed on to the Allocate operation via the *where* and *hownear* arguments. These specify an object to cluster with and how tight (area, segment or chunk) the clustering should be.

Since all storage managers support the same basic model of clustering, it becomes a much simpler problem to export a strong clustering pragma language to the type implementor. In Vbase, objects may be clustered at any clustering level, along semantic relationships. Typically, all of the storage pieces required to implement an object are clustered within the same chunk. This chunk is then clustered within the same segment as the chunk(s) implementing another related object. For example, in a CAD application, all of the subpieces of an assembly might be clustered within the same segment, thus requiring only a single disk transfer when accessing the assembly.

In some cases, it is even desirable to state what you do *not* want clustered together. For example, if an object has a raster image as part of its representation, it is likely that having the image clustered in the same paging unit as the rest of the object would severely degrade the access time to other parts of the object's state, due to the disk-read cost associated with bringing a large image into memory.

3. Implementation

3.1. Reference Resolution

When a piece of storage is allocated, the storage manager returns a reference to the storage. This reference is only interpretable by the storage manager. It may or may not map directly to a physical address. (This allows the storage manager to shuffle the storage under its control to facilitate its management functions.)

This reference serves as the only handle that the type manager has on the underlying piece of storage. The type manager then (typically) passes this reference on to the user, as the user's only handle on the abstract object being created. The reference is a surrogate for the object, and as far as the user is concerned, it *is* the object.

The user accesses or updates the object by passing the reference to an operation of the abstract type. The type in turn calls the storage manager to dereference the storage, map it into memory, and return a pointer to it. Upon completing its access, the abstract type relinquishes the storage piece, thus allowing the storage manager to move the object within memory, or page it out to disk.

3.2. Dispatching

Just as with the abstract operations, storage manager operations must be dispatched to the appropriate implementation. But this dispatching is based on the storage manager of the object, rather than its abstract type.

When dispatching an abstract operation, it is necessary to determine (at runtime, in general) the abstract type of the entity being operated on. This is typically done by examining the object's storage, which contains a reference to the object's type. When dispatching a storage manager operation, however, it is not possible to examine the object's storage to determine what storage manager to dispatch to, as this would result in a recursion problem. This means that the storage manager must be directly inferred from the reference.

To accomplish this, one field of the reference, called the StorageManagerIndex, is reserved for indicating the storage manager of the object. The remainder of the reference is considered the storage address of the object, and its use is defined by the particular storage manager.

The actual dispatch occurs by using the form as an index into a table of dispatch tables. Each operation (together with its refinements) is assigned a unique index into the dispatch table. The corresponding entry in the dispatch table is a list of pointers to the method or methods that implement the given operation. Since this table is brought into memory when the database is opened, storage manager dispatching is very fast.

4. Experiences

In contrast with most object systems, which provide only a single storage type for all instances [Goldberg83], or perhaps a single storage type for all instances of a single abstract type [Stroustrup86], Vbase provides a set of storage managers. These can be employed on an object-by-object basis to store the instances of any type. Vbase has storage managers that implement temporary, process local objects, and both shared and non-shared permanent, database resident objects. Depending upon the lifetime and other features of the object in question, any one of the available storage managers might be the most appropriate.

An important goal of the design of the storage manager facility in Vbase was to make the storage class of an object independent of its abstract class. Just as the use of inheritance in traditional object-oriented systems makes it possible for a user to define a new type, and immediately begin to make use of that type in existing code, a user of Vbase can add new storage managers, and immediately begin to make use of these storage managers in existing abstract types.

When we started this project, we had only a single storage manager (for persistent database-resident objects). We have since added two others (for process-local storage, and shared storage). Because existing types interfaced with the storage subsystem only through the interface defined by type StorageManager, the integration of these new storage managers was straightforward. We could immediately begin creating instances stored in the new storage managers, and the users of the abstract types involved were unaffected by the change.

We are now engaged in work to add a stronger clustering model and a richer transaction interface at the abstract level. We also expect to add versioning and distribution support to our storage managers.

References

[Goldberg83] Goldberg A., Robson D., Smalltalk-80 The Language and Its Implementation, Addison-Wesley 1983.

[Liskov81] Liskov B., Atkinson R., Bloom T., Moss E., Schaffert C., Scheifler R., Snyder A., CLU Reference Manual, Springer-Verlag 1981.

[Stroustrup86] Stroustrup B., The C++ Programming Language, Addison-Wesley 1986.

[Wegner87] Wegner P., Dimensions of Object-Based Language Design, OOPSLA 87.

[Weihl82] Weihl W., Liskov B., Specification and Implementation of Resilient, Atomic Data Types, MIT Technical Memo 1982.

Oonix: An Object-Oriented Unix Shell*

Edward C. Bueché   Maurice T. Franklin [†]   Edward R. Holley   Henry F. Korth

Gene C. Sheppard[‡]

Department of Computer Sciences
University of Texas at Austin
Austin, Texas 78712-1188

Abstract

There are several "shells" available as user interfaces to the Unix operating system. Oonix is intended to be an alternative to these shells that offers the user an iconic, object-oriented environment. As an alternative shell, Oonix interacts with the Unix file system and co-exists with other shells. Furthermore, Oonix interacts with the window system on the host machine.

This paper describes a preliminary version of Oonix running on a Sun-3 workstation and interfacing with Sun-Windows. It discusses issues in the user interface, the Unix interface, and the internal structure of Oonix itself. We consider performance questions and describe techniques built into Oonix for efficiency's sake as well as improvements that are either planned or in development. Finally, we compare the object-orientation as a paradigm for operating systems interfaces with alternative paradigms.

1 Introduction

There has been considerable interest in object-oriented systems in both the programming language community and the database community. Applications of object-oriented systems include office information systems, computer-aided design, hypertext, and others. In this paper, we consider the use of an object-oriented approach to the user interface of an operating system. Several products, most notably the Apple Macintosh,[1] have taken an object-oriented approach to both the design of the user interface and its implementation.

The system we discuss here, Oonix, is an object-oriented interface to the Unix[2] operating system. The interface is designed primarily to meet the needs of the less technically oriented Unix user. The interface represents files and subdirectories as icons in a directory window. Most commands are selected from pop-up menus associated with each icon. Others are selected by clicking on an object and "dragging" it over another icon. For more sophisticated users, Oonix includes a shell-like programming language called the OSL. This language allows the user to define new classes, modify instance variables and edit methods.

Developing an interface to Unix presents a greater challenge than developing an interface to a new operating system. The

---

*Research partially supported by NSF grant DCR-8507224 and a grant from the IBM Corporation
[†]Current address: Randolph AFB, Texas
[‡]Current address: School of Business, UCLA
[1]Macintosh is a trademark of Apple Computer Corporation
[2]Unix is a trademark of AT&T

main difficulty arises from the fact that there are already several existing shells providing alternatives to the Oonix interface. These include the Cshell(csh), the Bourne Shell(sh), and the Korn Shell(ksh). It is essential that Oonix allow these existing interfaces to co-exist with it at least as well as the existing interfaces co-exist with each other. In order to achieve this co-existence, it is essential that each Oonix operation affect not only the internal data structures of Oonix but also the underlying Unix file system.

2 The Object Paradigm

In this section we provide a brief introduction to object-oriented systems. For a more detailed presentation see, e.g. [Stefik and Bobrow 1986]. The object-oriented programming paradigm is based on the encapsulation of data and the code to manipulate that data in an *object*. Data is represented by a collection of *instance variables*. Code is represented by a collection of *methods*. Methods are procedures that are invoked as a result of the receipt of a specific *message* by an object. A method can manipulate instance variables of the object to which it belongs. It can also send messages to other objects causing them to execute methods. Note that a method cannot access data in instance variables of other objects directly. To access such data, a message must be sent to the object requesting that it return the value of a specified instance variable. This is possible only if the object has a method that responds to such a message. Thus, each object has full control over its own instance variables. Messages represent the only interface among objects. It is this encapsulation of data and code in a single module (object) that provides the elegance of the object-oriented approach.

It is usually the case that many similar objects exist. By "similar," we mean that they have the same set of instance variable types and methods, though they have possibly distinct values for the instance variables. Such objects are grouped into *classes*. Objects belonging to a class are said to be *instances* of the class. Classes, themselves, are objects.

Object-oriented systems represent specialization and generalization relationships among classes using a *class hierarchy*. We say that a class C_1 is a *subclass* of a class C_2 if every member of C_1 is also a member of C_2. In this case, we also say that C_2 is a *superclass* of C_1. If C_1 is a *subclass* of C_2 then C_1 has all of the instance variables and methods of C_2. This is referred to as *inheritance*. In addition, C_1 may have other instance variables and methods.

Reprinted from *The Proceedings of the 22nd Hawaii International Conference on System Sciences (HICSS)*, 1989, pages 928-935.

Several object oriented systems allow subclasses to redefine instance variables and methods inherited from superclasses. It is also possible in some systems to have multiple immediate superclasses for a class, thus allowing a directed acyclic graph of classes. One system with these features is MCC's Orion system [Banergee, Chou, et al. 1987]. When multiple immediate superclasses are allowed, inheritance is complicated by the fact that conflicts can occur when the same instance variable or method is defined in more than one superclass.

The complexity of multiple inheritance is useful in general purpose object-oriented languages and object-oriented database systems. However, we did not feel that this degree of complexity was justified in an operating system interface.

3 Internal Structure of Oonix

The design of Oonix was influenced heavily by the Smalltalk implementation described in [Goldberg and Robson 1983]. Oonix is structured internally in three levels as shown in Figure 1 and listed below:

- Capability-Based Memory Manager (CBMM): This level creates a controlled-access object memory for Oonix.

- Object Manager (OM): This level provides an interface between objects and their internal state. The internal state of objects is stored in the CBMM, but the CBMM does not attach any semantics to its data. It is the OM that attaches object semantics to data in the CBMM.

- Virtual Machine (VM): This level is the interpreter of methods in Oonix. Oonix methods are, in general, coded in the Oonix Shell Language (OSL). Certain primitive methods, however, are coded directly in C.

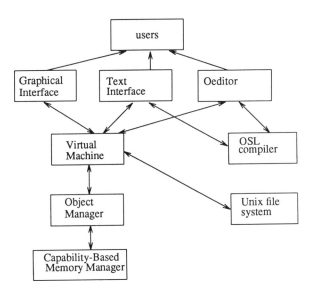

Figure 1: Internal structure of Oonix

The separation of low-level memory management into a single module and the definition of a higher-level object management module was used also in the GemStone system [Maier, et al. 1986]. GemStone's architecture is more complex than that of Oonix due to GemStone's support of the full set of features of a database system. We discuss each of the levels of the internal structure of Oonix in this section.

3.1 The Capability-Based Memory Manager

The capability-based memory manager (CBMM) is based on [Amsterdam 1986]. It provides safe memory management by protecting against dereferencing of dangling pointers. Every time a block of memory is allocated, a capability is returned. Access to a block is allowed only by the use of a capability.

This level of protection is needed in an object-oriented system because the value of an instance variable may itself be an object. Thus, the deletion of an object may turn the value of several instance variables into dangling references. Since a capability refers to a unique block of memory, it is guaranteed to be unique. Thus, we may use the capability for the block of memory storing an object's data as the unique name of the object.

3.2 The Object Manager

The object manager (OM) interfaces with the CBMM to obtain storage for newly-created objects and to free storage for deleted objects. The CBMM views an object as an uninterpreted byte string. It is the OM that imposes the C record structure on the byte string. The separation of memory management functions (in the CBMM) from the object functions (in the OM), makes it possible for almost all methods to be coded in OSL. However, for reasons of efficiency as well as practical considerations during system development, the basic object functions of the OM were written in C.

Each object has two types of data: explicit and implicit. Implicit data are used by the OM for internal purposes only. Explicit data is accessible outside the OM.

Because Oonix is designed to serve as a shell, it was important to build in direct support for variable length strings and lists. Also, the object structure had to be rich enough to support both classes and instances.

Every object has at least three fields.

- Type: This field contains the object's type (class or instance).

- Parent-Capability: This field contains a capability to the class of the object if the object is an instance, and a capability to the superclass if the object is a class.

- Data-Capability: This field contains a capability to an array that contains the capabilities to the values of the explicit data items of an object. The definition of data-capability as a pointer to an array allows support of variable length datatypes while allowing each explicit data item to be accessed directly using an offset that can be computed without first retrieving the entire structure from the CBMM.

Class objects have several fields in addition to the three listed above.

- Instance-Methods: This field contains a capability to a list of messages to which instances of this class will respond. This list includes only those messages not appearing in the instance-method list of a superclass.

- Method-Dictionary: This field contains a capability to the *method dictionary* of (message, method) pairs. The list of (message, method) pairs in the method dictionary includes all methods to which an instance of the class will respond, except for those appearing in the method dictionary of a superclass. The method dictionary provides the mapping from messages to executable code.

- Instances: This field contains a capability to a list of all instances of this class.

- Instance-Template: This field contains a capability to a template used to create a new instance. The template is an array of capabilities to a structure consisting of a field name and an offset. The field name distinguishes a particular field and the offset is used to reference the correct field in an object's data field array. Each template holds only the information that distinguishes it from the templates of superclasses.

- Sub-Classes: This field contains a capability to a list of all subclasses (if any) of the class.

- Class-Methods: This field contains a capability to a list of those messages to which the class itself will respond, except for those messages to which a superclass will respond.

- Class-Template: This field contains a capability to a template for the class itself.

Earlier, we said that classes themselves are objects. However, we see here that a class object has a much richer structure than a generic object. These two types of objects could have been unified by defining a class *Class* and making all class objects instances of this class. Our structure trades elegance of design for the simplicity of a single hierarchical structure.

We note also that by storing the (message, method) pairs in a method dictionary it is possible to modify methods while Oonix is running. Dynamic modification of methods is essential since Oonix users who write OSL methods need to be able to modify and test them without having to exit from the Oonix environment. A similar "instance-variable dictionary" is not needed. The reason for this is that while methods are stored in one place (the class), instance variables are stored in each instance, and can be modified directly.

We do not allow dynamic creation of new instance variables. This limitation is imposed for performance reasons: The creation of a new instance variable would require the modification of all existing instances of a class. The overhead of performing such a large-scale change is unacceptable in an interactive operating system interface. An alternative approach is to leave existing instances unchanged initially. When an instance is accessed, it is compared with the current class definition and any changes to the set of instance variables are applied [Banergee, Kim, et al. 1987]. While we may consider this approach at a later time, we decided for now that even this reduced amount of overhead would have too severe an affect on interactive performance. We expect to revisit this decision when we augment Oonix to include a run-time type-checking capability.

```
1   method display_contents;
2   locals
3       count,item,x,y,flag;
4   count <- contents;
5   self update_label;
6   loop
7       if not count then
8           break;
9       endif;
10      item,x,y <- self get_display_item:count;
11      flag <- item display:self X:x Y:y;
12      if flag
13      then
14          self store_coords:item X:x Y:y;
15      endif;
16      decrement count;
17  endloop;
```

Figure 2: A sample OSL method.

3.3 The Virtual Machine

The Oonix virtual machine (VM) is the basis of all object actions. All user input results in VM commands which perform the requisite accesses to the Oonix data structures (through the OM) and to Unix. The VM is a simple stack machine, consisting of a small set of instructions including stack manipulation, test and branch, and method invocation.

The design of the VM is based on the Smalltalk virtual machine [Goldberg and Robson 1983]. Internally, VM instructions are represented in the form of low-level codes. Methods for the VM can be written directly in the VM instruction set, but typically code is written is the Oshell language (OSL) and compiled into VM instructions. The OSL is a procedural programming language. It relieves the programmer of VM stack management issues and uses names in place of the low-level VM operation codes and storage addresses. Figure 2 shows an example of an OSL method that causes a directory to display as icons all files in the directory. (The line numbers in the figure are for reference only and not part of the program itself.) Below, we give a line-by-line description of the example:

- Line 1: This line declares the selector for this method to be 'display contents'.

- Lines 2,3: This declares local variables referred to as count, item,x,y and flag.

- Line 4: The value of the variable contents is placed into the variable count.

- Line 5: The object sends the message 'update label' to itself.

- Line 6: Beginning of a loop.

- Lines 7-9: If the value of count is zero, then the loop is exited.

- Line 10: The object sends itself the message 'get display item:' with argument count. This message has 3 return values, which are placed into the variables item,x, and y.

- Line 11: The object represented by the value of item is sent the message display:X:Y: and the return value is placed in variable flag.

- Lines 12-15: If the value of flag is non-zero, the object sends the message 'store coords:X:Y:' to itself.

- Line 16: The value in variable count is decremented by one.

- Line 17: The end of the loop started at line 6.

Not all methods are coded in OSL. We allow methods to be written directly in C. Such methods, called *primitive* methods are used within Oonix to implement a basic set of methods for built-in classes. Besides providing the foundation for Oonix methods, primitive methods allow us to exploit the efficiency of compiled C code for the most frequently used methods.

We shall not describe the entire VM instruction set in this paper. Instead, we shall consider here only the instructions that implement method invocation. The *send* instruction has two arguments: a capability for the object that is to receive the message, and a method selector string, which represents the message. If the method turns out to be a primitive method, the corresponding C function is called. If the method is coded in VM instructions (presumably, though not necessarily, compiled from OSL), the VM saves its state on the stack and executes the method. The *enter* instruction performs this saving of state and the *ret* instruction restores the state after the execution of the method.

For the sake of efficiency, one might want to represent primitive methods in C as pointers to functions. There is a major problem with this, however, since data in object memory (the CBMM) needs to be retained even if we should find it necessary to modify and recompile parts of the Oshell. Thus, variables of type pointer-to-function may be become invalid. In order to achieve efficient invocation of primitive methods without exposing the system to incorrect pointer references, the OM stores unique identifiers for primitive methods in the *instance method* array (see Section 3.2). An initialization routine run when the Oshell is started to associate with each unique identifier the memory location of the function. The result is safe and relatively efficient access to primitive methods.

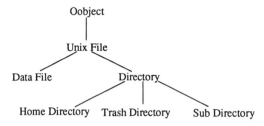

Figure 3: Currently-implemented class hierarchy.

4 Oonix - Unix Interface

Our initial work on the Unix interface has involved the manipulation of directories and files. In this section, we describe the class structure used to store directories, the primitive methods used to manipulate directories, and the issues of starting Oonix and shutting it down.

4.1 Oonix Class Structure

The root class of the Oonix class hierarchy is a class called *Oobject*. The various elements of the Unix environment appear as subclasses of *Oobject*. These include *UnixFile*, which is the class of all files, and *Process*, which is the class of all processes. At the current time, we have considered only the class *UnixFile* for which we have defined two subclasses: *DataFile* and *Directory*. The class *Directory* has received the most attention at this stage of the implementation and, as such, has the richest collection of methods. The *Directory* class is divided into subclasses *HomeDirectory*, *SubDirectory*, and *TrashDirectory*. Home directories are a special subclass because of the special role they play in several Unix applications. A trash directory holds all deleted files so as to permit undeletion. All other directories are of class *SubDirectory*. Figure 3 shows the currently-implemented class hierarchy. Figure 4 shows a richer class hierarchy representing the planned complete set of built-in Oonix classes.

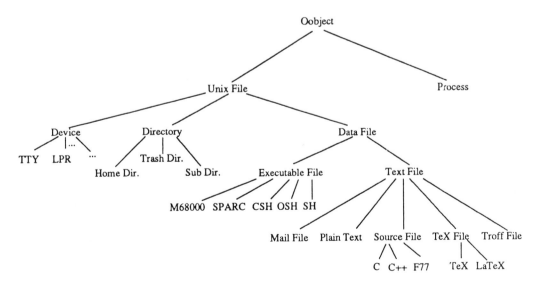

Figure 4: Oonix hierarchy of built-in classes.

The complete hierarchy will simplify the user interface by allowing a relatively compact set of messages to apply to a wide variety of file types. For example, a *print* message would be interpreted as:

- "tbl *file-name* | eqn | troff" by an instance of subclass *Troff-File*

- "tex *file-name*.tex; implaser -Plw *file-name*.dvi" by an instance of subclass *TeXFile*

- "lpr *file-name*" for an instance of subclasses *SourceFile*, *MailText*, *PlainText*, *csh*, etc.

- *error* by an instance of *68000ObjectCode*

The attraction of Oonix as a user interface is that much of the knowledge about Unix commands can be encoded in the methods of the class hierarchy. The casual user need not be aware of the details of these commands, which have inconsistent syntax whose details are not easily remembered.

4.2 System Calls

All interaction with Unix is made through Unix system calls. Although it is possible to implement all required operations using the *fork* and *execve* calls, this would impose the overhead of process creation on every interaction with Unix. Instead, we used system calls that directly implement primitive methods for frequently used commands to manipulate Unix files.

We have adopted a default philosophy of considering only the visible names, that is, those names not beginning with a dot. This avoids any potential conflict with the *.trash* directory and *.oonix* file (discussed below), but does create difficulties for sophisticated users. We anticipate relaxing this restriction in a future version of Oonix.

Using primitive methods, all system software installed in the Unix environment is accessible. The files containing the code for these programs are, by default, not part of the user's Oonix environment, which includes only files within the home-directory subtree. When it is desired to include system files within the Oonix environment, a link may be created within the home-directory subtree. This default is imposed in order to limit the size of the Oonix data structure. As we shall see in the next section, representation of all system files as a default would generate substantial additional overhead both in terms of space as well as the time it takes to start Oonix.

We are now adding a special object to Oonix with methods to access system files directly without the need to establish links.

4.3 Startup and Shutdown

When Oonix (the Oshell) is invoked, it looks for the file *.oonix* in the user's home directory. This file is the *image* representing the state of the Oonix environment at the time of the previous shutdown. In the event that no *.oonix* file exists, it is assumed that Oonix is being invoked for the first time, and a default image is used. In either case, the class object *HomeDirectory* is sent the message *create(home directory name)*.

The *create* causes the class *HomeDirectory* to check to see if an instance exists whose name is the name of the home directory. If not, it creates such an instance. In either case, it sends the home directory instance the message *initialize*. Home directory instances respond to the *initialize* message by checking the current contents of the home directory in the Unix file system against the contents as indicated by the image file. It accomplishes this by sending a *verify* message to each member of the directory. Subdirectories, upon receipt of a *verify* message verify their contents, etc. Thus the entire user directory structure is verified and the image modified to match the current state.

Upon shutdown, the home directory is sent a *save* message. This causes it to save in object memory such data as the directory's display list, window parameters, etc. that will be needed for restart. Directories that receive a *save* message also send this message to their subdirectories.

The verification of the home-directory subtree is a result of our desire to allow access to the user's Unix environment through existing shells as well as through Oonix. Thus, when Oonix is invoked, it may be the case that the home-directory subtree has been modified from the state when Oonix was last shut down. We believe that the overhead resulting from verification is justified, due to the importance of compatibility with existing shells.

5 Oonix - User Interface

The user interface of Oonix includes three interfaces:

- A graphical interface that allows the manipulation of directories and file objects using the mouse.

- A editor/browser, called the *Oeditor* which allows the user to modify the value of instance variables, create or modify methods, and browse the class hierarchy.

- Direct support for OSL commands using a textual interface

The textual interface is relatively simple. OSL programs are compiled by the OSL compiler and executed by the VM. This interface is of use primary as a debugging aid in implementation. We shall focus here on the graphical interface and the Oeditor.

5.1 Graphical Interface

The Oonix graphical interface has as its primary objective the support of casual Unix users, those who currently invoke Unix commands, but do not write shell scripts. The user-interface paradigm is similar to that of the Xerox Star or Apple Macintosh. Objects are represented by icons which may be grouped into a window. The mouse is used to move and manipulate icons, and thus, objects.

We chose to implement the graphical interface within the Sun-View environment, and to adopt Sun conventions regarding the semantics of mouse clicks, menu formats, etc. A major advantage of conforming to Sun conventions is that Oonix windows can co-exist with Cshell windows and other Sun applications, and the SunWindows interface can be used to transfer data between these environments.

Figure 5 shows a sample graphical interface screen. Icons are used to represent files, directories, and subdirectories. The trash icon represents the directory ~/.trash, regardless of where the icon appears. This directory holds deleted files for possible undeletion. Clicking with the left mouse button on a directory icon creates a window for that directory, with icons representing the contents of the directory. The right mouse button brings up a menu of messages to which the object in question responds.

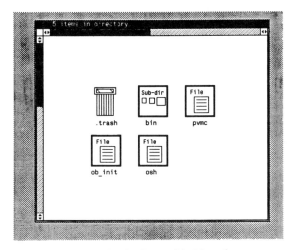

Figure 5: The Oonix graphical interface

Icons may be "dragged" by clicking and holding the middle mouse button. An icon being dragged tracks the mouse. When the mouse button is released the icon is placed at the current cursor location.

The response time for interactive use of the graphical interface is comparable to typical Sun applications provided there are few concurrent user processes. We discuss performance in more detail in Section 6.

5.2 The Oeditor

The Oeditor provides the programming interface of Oonix, and, as such, can be compared with the shell script feature of typical Unix shells. Changes to instance variables, methods, etc. are made dynamically. This allows the programmer to edit, compile, and test interactively.

The Oeditor interface is a mix of text and graphics. Text is used for editable fields such as variable values and method source code. Icons are not used, primarily to save space on the screen. Information is presented to the user through a collection of windows. Figure 6 illustrates the interface. The types of windows presented by the Oeditor include:

- *class windows:* These windows display data pertaining to a class: name, superclass, class variables, class methods, subclasses, instance variables, instance methods, and instances. Associated with each class window is a background menu which is accessed using the right mouse button. This menu includes commands to create new class variables, class methods, etc.

- *variable modification windows:* These windows display the name and value of all of the variables of an object, and provide an interface for the modification of variable values.

- *method windows:* These windows are Sun TextEdit windows that display the OSL source code for a method. The background menu for method windows is similar to that of TextEdit, but it also includes a command to compile methods using the OSL compiler. If the compiler detects an error, it uses an error window to report the error. If the compile succeeds, the new method is installed immediately and is available for execution.

- *error windows:* These windows pop up to display error messages.

The Oeditor is designed to handle only OSL methods. Changes to primitive methods must be made by editing the C code and recompiling the appropriate modules of Oonix. Thus, unlike OSL methods, primitive methods cannot be installed dynamically while Oonix is running.

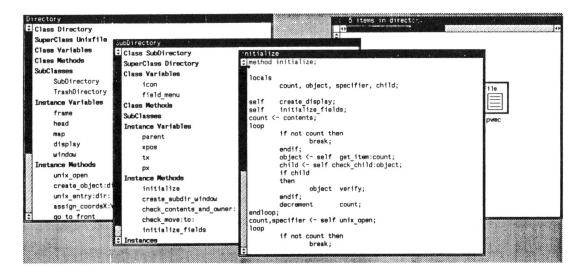

Figure 6: The Oeditor Interface.

6 Performance

Despite our efforts to build an efficient system, the startup procedure is unacceptably slow for all but the smallest home directories. This slowness is due to our decision to verify the entire home directory and, recursively, all its subdirectories. As a first step towards providing more acceptable performance we are considering two options:

- Verify only the top level of the home directory. Verify subdirectories only when they are displayed.

- Initially verify only the top level of the home directory. Spawn a low-priority process to verify subdirectories concurrent with the user's work.

The second of the approaches listed above offers the promise of being able to manage Oonix access to shared directories. In the current implementation, if two users share the same directory, a change by one user will not be seen by the other until a shutdown/restart is performed. A low-priority verifier could reverify shared directories at an acceptably frequent interval. Of course, the ideal solution would be for Oonix to be notified of all changes to directories so that it can update object memory. However, to achieve that, we would have to integrate Oonix with the Unix system itself. This is an option which may eventually be chosen, but we hope to keep the Oonix-Unix interface at the Unix system call level.

For moderate sized directories, Oonix response time, though slower than the popular shells (csh, sh, ksh), is acceptable. Since Oonix is in only its first version, we anticipate that minor tuning may be able to improve performance considerably. There are several design changes that we could make to improve performance:

- Implement a memory management facility in the CBMM that reorganizes object memory to achieve greater locality of reference. This could be accomplished by ensuring that related files have their object data stored close together, etc. The result would be less paging.

- Redesign the VM to allow multiprogramming. In order to implement background verification (as suggested above), it must be possible to run multiple OSL programs at the same time. The current implementation of the VM places unnecessarily severe restrictions on the degree of concurrency achievable.

Overall, we feel that with minor tuning, Oonix is sufficiently efficient to be an acceptable interface and that the overhead it imposes is justified by the enhanced user interface.

Many of the performance issues faced in designing an efficient interface based on object orientation are similar to those faced by designers of database systems for such applications as computer-aided design. Maier[1987] discusses the performance of object-oriented databases and presents an agenda of performance-related research issues.

7 Comparison and Evaluation

Although most operating system interfaces are textual in nature, there are several interfaces based on alternative paradigms. In this section we compare some of these with Oonix as it now stands and with Oonix as we envision it in the future.

7.1 The Macintosh Interface

A natural comparison to make is between Oonix and the Macintosh user interface. Both systems represent directories (folders, in Macintosh terminology) as windows, and files as icons. Opening a Macintosh icon causes the object to invoke its application program automatically. Each application has a collection of messages grouped into categories that appear in pull-down menus. Oonix is more complicated, since each icon can respond to a vast variety of messages (see, e.g., the class hierarchy of Figure 3). It is essential that Oonix integrate into its environment applications that do not follow the object-oriented paradigm. Apple has, for the most part, been able to convince developers of new applications to work within the standard Macintosh interface. Given the long history of Unix, we cannot ever hope to have that luxury with Oonix. Thus, Oonix is an attempt to solve a much different problem than the Macintosh interface. Nevertheless, the Macintosh has been highly influential in the design of the Oonix interface.

7.2 The ROSI Relational Operating System Interface

A system that attempts to solve the exact same problem with which Oonix is designed to deal is the ROSI system [Korth and Silberschatz 1985]. ROSI represents all aspects of the operating system interface as relations in a relational database. Roughly speaking, what Oonix represents as an object, ROSI represents as a tuple in a relation. Hierarchical structures are represented by nested relations [Korth and Roth 1987, Korth 1986], as are repeating fields such as the "to" list of a mail message, or the membership list of a access-permissions group.

The power of the ROSI concept lies in the ability to use a relational query language to perform simply operations that would be complex and tedious in a standard operating system interface. Simple interactions with the operating system are expressed by clicking and moving tuples. This latter feature is similar in spirit to the clicking and moving of icons in Oonix. Whether icons or tuples are a more friendly interface is a matter of taste. Casual users are likely to prefer icons. However, tuples provide the advantage of displaying the contents of fields directly, while a Oonix user must take special action to display instance variables. Clearly an iconic interface could be built on top of ROSI to assist casual users.

Complex interactions such as "print all mail messages from 'Smith' on the subject of 'computers' " are expressed in ROSI using a relational query language. Using a relational language, files can be groups based on any selection criterion on their properties. This relational retrieval capability is more powerful than Unix's regular-expression-based retrieval (e.g. *grep*). Oonix does not have a general-purpose query language. We discuss the inclusion of such a feature in the next section.

Where Oonix has its principal advantages over ROSI is in the enforced modularity of the object-oriented paradigm and in system performance. ROSI uses a relational database system as its memory. Since this database is disk-resident, the overhead of memory access is much higher. Conceivably, ROSI could compete with Oonix in performance by moving to a main-memory database system.

The ROSI experience taught us several lessons that helped us design Oonix for better performance. ROSI made extensive use of Unix processes for access to the database and the invocation of Unix commands. We found this to be impractical, at least until lightweight processes become available to us under Unix. Thus, in Oonix, we incorporated the entire system in one Unix process.

We do not believe that the object-oriented paradigm necessarily leads to better performance than the relational paradigm. Indeed, the opposite is more likely to be true. This is suggested by current work in the use of nested relational databases as a basis for the construction of object-oriented database systems [Korth 1988]. Using a relational implementation allows for algebraic optimization of queries. Optimization of object-oriented programs in general is a more difficult problem due to the coding of methods in general-purpose programming languages. Instead, we believe Oonix's superior performance to ROSI is based on the lessons learned from ROSI.

7.3   Other Interfaces

In effect, any database system interface can serve as an operating system interface. However, most database interfaces are bad operating system interfaces since database languages are often too cumbersome for simple user interactions with the system. However, several recently proposed graphical database languages offer viable alternatives to the Oonix interface. See [Kim 1986] for a survey of these languages. Although the interface concepts of graphical database languages may be useful in an operating system interface, the database systems themselves are not likely to perform adequately in this application for reasons we discussed above.

8   Conclusion and Future Plans

The primary contribution of the Oonix project is an evaluation of whether Unix can be provided with a friendly iconic interface similar to those offered by some personal-computer file systems. We have applied a fairly standard object-oriented paradigm in building Oonix and taken care to design the implementation to provide both safety from dangling references and acceptable performance.

We have directed our initial attention at the system internals rather than in the provision of the rich class hierarchy needed before we can release Oonix to a broad user community. We made this choice so that we could establish the practicality of Oonix before devoting effort to the "sugar coating." The most recently completed system feature is the Oeditor. The Oeditor allows us to define new classes and methods without having to hard-code them into the system. This will allow us quickly to extend the class hierarchy to include those file types used by most casual users.

We noted above that grouping of objects (files) is not currently supported in Oonix. We would like to include a *group* class in Oonix that would allow the grouping of an arbitrary collection of objects. A message to a group would be forwarded to all members of the group. Such a feature would allow Oonix to handle more easily the aggregate operations supported by ROSI.

Ultimately, we would like to revise the OSL so that it becomes a graphical rather than textual programming language.

9   References:

Amsterdam, J. "Safe Storage Allocation," *Byte,* October 1986, 122-132.

Banerjee, J., H. Chou, J. Garza, W. Kim, D. Woelk, N. Ballou, and H. J. Kim [1987], "Data Model Issues in Object-Oriented Applications," *ACM Transactions on Office Information Systems,* March 1987.

Banerjee, J., W. Kim, H.-J. Kim, and H. F. Korth [1987], "Semantics and Implementation of Schema Evolution in Object-oriented Databases," *Proc. ACM SIGMOD'87 Conference on the Management of Data.*

Goldberg, A., and D. Robson [1983], *Smalltalk-80: The Language and Its Implementation,* Addison-Wesley, 1983.

Kim, H. J. [1986], "Graphical Interfaces for Database Systems: A Survey," *Proc. Mountain Regional ACM Conference,* Santa Fe, NM, April 1986.

Korth, H. F., [1986], "Extending the Scope of Relational Languages," *IEEE Software,* 3:1, 19–28.

Korth, H. F. [1988], "Query Processing in Nested Relational Databases," manuscript in preparation.

Korth, H. F. and M. A. Roth [1987], "Query Languages for Nested Relational Databases," TR-87-45, Department of Computer Sciences, University of Texas at Austin.

Korth, H. F. and A. Silberschatz [1985], "A User-Friendly Operating System Interface Based on the Relational Data Model," *Proc. International Symposium on New Directions in Computing.*

Maier, D. [1987], "Making Database Systems Fast Enough for CAD Applications," Technical Report CS/E-87-016, Oregon Graduate Center, December 1987.

Maier, D., J. Stein, A. Otis, and A. Purdy [1986], "Development of an Object-Oriented DBMS," *Proc. Conference on Object-Oriented Programming: Systems, Languages and Applications,* ACM SigPlan Notices, **21**:11, pp. 341-346, November 1986.

Stefik, M. and D. G. Bobrow [1986], "Object-Oriented Programming: Themes and Variations," *The AI Magazine,* 40–62.

Uniform Support for Collections of Objects in a Persistent Environment

J. Leslie Keedy and John Rosenberg

Department of Computer Science
University of Newcastle
N.S.W. 2308
Australia

Abstract

Ideally a language to support persistence should provide a uniform set of mechanisms for declaring and manipulating objects (and collections of objects) regardless of such attributes as their sizes and their lifetimes. However, the practical requirement of efficiency encourages the use of different mechanisms to support, say, a large permanent database (e.g. a B-tree) or a small temporary collection (e.g. an array or linked list).

The LEIBNIZ programming language, developed as part of the MONADS project at the University of Newcastle, N.S.W., supports implementation-independent high-level constructs, based on sets and sequences, for manipulating collections of objects in such a way that the compiler can be guided to select a suitably efficient implementation mechanism. This paper describes the relevant LEIBNIZ constructs and discusses how the structure of the compiler allows new implementations, written in LEIBNIZ, to be added.

1. Introduction

In early computer systems there was a clear distinction between (a) the computational memory, which typically had a relatively small capacity and was usually volatile, but provided fast access to information and (b) the file store, which typically had a substantially larger capacity and was persistent, but provided very much slower access to information. The programming languages designed to operate in such systems reflected this distinction by providing data structuring facilities such as arrays and pointers for use in the computational memory and providing some form of interface to a file system which managed the file store. Although the invention of virtual memory somewhat blurred the physical distinction between computational memory and file store, it had little influence on the programming language distinction between compiler-supported features such as arrays and pointers and the file system-supported language features.

Such a distinction is clearly out of place in a persistent programming environment, not least because it simply reflects old technology rather than being based on appropriate kinds of abstractions. Indeed, one of the main advantages which persistent systems should be expected to offer is the provision of a uniform method of accessing data structures, irrespective of their sizes and their lifetimes. Thus it should be possible for a programming language designed to work in a persistent environment to support, in a uniform manner, both the temporary structures used in the execution of computations and the persistent structures used to store enduring information which might be accessed and modified over many computations.

However, the provision of a uniform access mechanism to implement a range of data structures of such diversity is not a trivial matter. There are two levels at which the problem can be tackled. The first has the aim of improving memory technology to provide a single uniform persistent (virtual) memory, thus enabling all kinds of data structures to be implemented in a common way at the architectural level. The present authors have worked extensively on this problem and have produced a new computer architecture, known as the MONADS architecture [1], the very large virtual addresses of which provide the basis for a persistent virtual memory which eliminates the need for a separate filestore. Two implementations of this architecture have been undertaken: a workstation known as the MONADS-PC [2] (of which two working prototypes exist) and the MONADS-MM, which is designed to support a massive main memory (of the order of 32 gigabytes) and the first prototype for which is currently under construction [3].

The second level at which the problem can be tackled is to develop a programming language which provides uniform access to data structures. A successful solution for this problem requires at least two ingredients: a set of programming language constructs well suited for expressing such a wide range of data structures, and an implementation mechanism which ensures that efficiency can be maintained over the entire range of applications.

In a persistent memory environment such as that provided by the MONADS architecture the special constructs for supporting file access, with all their attendant limitations (such as the restricted access to data via buffers, and the often cumbersome synchronisation facilities), are clearly redundant. What is needed are constructs which allow all data structures to be accessed in the more direct manner characteristic of the techniques normally associated with access to temporary computational structures.

However, it is not self-evident that the constructs typically provided to support access to temporary computational structures are entirely adequate for accessing persistent data. Certainly, some persistent structures can reasonably be implemented as arrays, and all can be implemented as structures linked by pointers. But pointers, unfortunately, are a low-level mechanism corresponding to memory addresses, so that programming with pointers is both time-consuming and error prone. In this respect pointers are comparable to *goto* statements, and are best avoided if at all possible.

Reprinted from *The Proceedings of the 22nd Hawaii International Conference on System Sciences (HICSS)*, 1989, pages 26-35.

Indeed, the commercial programmer accustomed to accessing persistent data via file access mechanisms can hardly be expected to embrace persistent programming based on pointers. The sophisticated file access mechanisms usually available to him, ranging from indexed, hashed and B-tree files to relational database software, already relieve him of a low-level view of data organisation, and he is scarcely likely to see the idea of developing all his data structures from scratch using pointers as an attractive alternative.

It seems then that a persistent programming language designed to operate in a persistent memory system should offer a higher view of data structuring constructs than pointers, constructs which can ideally offer the power of relational database facilities and the efficiency of file systems. Yet such constructs should be suitable for access not only to persistent structures, but also for organising temporary computational structures. This paper describes how these issues are resolved in the programming language LEIBNIZ. The following section, which is kept deliberately brief, since more detailed descriptions have been published elsewhere [4], outlines the data structuring constructs of LEIBNIZ, while later sections explain how the language can be efficiently implemented.

2. An Overview of Data Structuring in LEIBNIZ

LEIBNIZ offers the programmer the opportunity to write pointer-less programs in the form of its facilities for collecting objects into *sequences* and *sets*. In the following two subsections we briefly describe the kinds of objects supported by LEIBNIZ and then the constructs available to collect them into sequences and sets.

2.1. Objects in LEIBNIZ

All LEIBNIZ objects are defined in terms of the information-hiding principle [5] and the object model [6], as separate modules with associated operations. However, three *levels* of objects can be recognised: scalars (including enumerated types and subranges, with which the programmer may associate operations), structured items (including abstract data types, known as *elements*, and tuples), and separately compiled modules. The differences between the three levels of objects allow the language to provide natural semantics for the different kinds of uses to which collections of objects are put. For example, mathematicians, handling sets of integers, have different requirements from database specialists, handling sets of tuples, and software engineers and operating system designers, handling sets of separately compiled modules, have yet different needs. Furthermore, these different semantics allow efficient implementations for supporting collections of such objects. Put simply, sequences and sets of scalars are collections of values, sequences and sets of structured items are actually collections of *names* for objects (i.e. using pointer semantics), and sequences and sets of separately compiled modules are represented as collections of *capabilities*.

In this paper we shall describe only the facilities associated with *tuples*, since these are representative of all structured items, and this is the level of most practical interest for implementing persistent databases.

Tuples in LEIBNIZ correspond loosely to records in Pascal or in file and database systems. However, a tuple is actually a form of data abstraction with which operations can be associated. The externally visible fieldnames of a tuple may be defined either

as constants (in which case they may not be changed after they have been initialised) or as variables[*]. A *new* procedure associated with a tuple type has a special status, being the only procedure normally allowed to create a new tuple object and the only procedure permitted to assign values to the **const** fields.

The declaration of a tuple variable is viewed as the declaration of a *name* for a tuple, with the tuple only coming into existence when the appropriate *new* procedure is invoked. However, a tuple declaration can also be initialised by assigning another tuple of the same type to it, using the *name assignment* operator (the left arrow **<-**, equivalent to denotation in Simula 67 [8] and *shallowcopy* in Smalltalk [9]). This causes the tuple name on the left side of the assignment to be a synonym of that named on the right side. Following a name assignment, any changes to the tuple made using either name will be visible using the other name. The identity operators **is** and **isnt** (cf. Simula's == and =/= and Smalltalk's == and ~~ operators) return a boolean result which allows the programmer to check whether two tuple names are synonyms for the same actual tuple.

Tuples can also be initialised using the copy assignment operator **:=** . This causes the tuple name on the left side of the assignment to refer to a new tuple which is a copy of that named on the right side.

Other operators on tuples can be implemented by providing additional routines in the tuple definition, and these can, as appropriate, be used to redefine the standard operator symbols, including for example the relational operators. (The default routines for comparing equality = and inequality ~= compare all the fields of tuples.) If the = and the < operators are defined for a tuple type, all the relational operators are considered to have been defined in the obvious way.

The following illustrates a simple tuple definition in LEIBNIZ and will be used in examples in the following section:

```
tuple bank_account
    const   account_number: int
            date_opened: date
    var     customer: person_name
            cust_address: address
            ...
            current_balance: currency
    proc new (acc_num: int
            opening_date: date
            cust_name: person_name
            starting_balance)
    body    account_number := acc_num
            date_opened:= opening_date
            customer := cust_name
            current_balance := starting_balance
    end new
end bank_account
```

---

[*] LEIBNIZ formally regards tuples as information hiding modules with an entirely procedural interface, such that the fieldnames are syntactic sugar for *get_fieldname* (for constants and variables) and *put_fieldname* (variables only) operations. Similarly the usual dot notation for fieldnames is shorthand for calls on these operations (see [7]).

2.2. Collections in LEIBNIZ

Collections in LEIBNIZ consist of sequences or sets of objects (including sequences and sets). In this discussion we shall primarily consider sequences, since sets are simply unordered sequences not containing duplicate elements.

Sequences always have a defined ordering of elements, specified at the time of the declaration. An *insertion order* sequence, which is ordered explicitly by the programmer as its elements are inserted, is declared as follows:

account_file: **seq of** bank_account

A *key order* sequence, on the other hand, is explicitly ordered according to the values of one or more nominated fields of its tuples, by increasing and/or decreasing values. These effectively serve as key fields, where the first expression is equivalent to a primary key, the second to a secondary key, etc. A key order sequence is declared as follows:

named_account_file: **kseq of** bank_account
on incr customer, **decr** date_opened

Name assignment (using the left arrow <-) can be used to provide synonyms for sequences, and the identity operators **is** and **isnt** check whether the sequence names supplied refer to the same sequence. Copy assignment (using :=) copies entire sequences (including the members). A further form of assignment, known as *collection assignment* and using the symbol :@, allows a new sequence (on the left side) to be initialised, such that its members are, in the sense of name assignment, the members of the sequence expression appearing on the right side. These three forms of assignment reflect the three kinds of object relationships described in [10].

The relational operators =, <, <=, etc. compare the *values* of elements in the specified sequences. A sequence is defined to be less than another sequence of the same type if a left to right comparison of values of the member tuples shows that a lower value is first detected in the left sequence or the members of the left sequence are exhausted first[*]. The remaining relational operators are defined in a similar way.

For sequences, the relational operators @= and @~= can be used to compare the *names* of members in the specified sequences, thus testing whether the sequences are sequences of synonyms for the same members[**].

The membership test operator @in returns a boolean result based on the identity relationship, indicating whether there exists a member in the collection which **is** the object supplied as the first operand, while the **in** operator performs a similar test based on value equality. There is also a unary operator #, which returns a count of the number of elements in a collection.

A member of a set or sequence can be selected by enclosing a boolean expression in round brackets after the name of the collection. The fieldnames of tuples may be used in the boolean expression, e.g.

account_file (customer = "J. Smith").current_balance := 20000

---

[*] If the type of the sequence members has no defined < operator, the less than operation on sequences is not defined.

[**] For sets, the full range of relational operators can be compounded with @, i.e. @=, @<, @<=, etc., to test for subsets, etc., of the *names* of elements in the specified sets.

In the case of a set any member which satisfies the boolean expression is (nondeterministically) selected; for a sequence the first member which satisfies the boolean expression is selected. For sequences, the predeclared identifier **pos** may also be used to select a member at a particular position in the sequence, as if it were an additional fieldname of a tuple automatically updated to represent the current position of a member in a sequence, e.g.

working_ac <- named_account_file (pos = 3)

The predeclared identifiers **first** and **last** can be also used to select the first or last member of a sequence.

Member selectors can appear on both sides of assignment statements. They can also conveniently be combined with the **with** statement (similar to that of Pascal) as follows:

with s2.last
do   if current_balance < 30000
         then ...
endwith

In the case of key order sequences a shorter form of member selection may be used, resembling selection from arrays in other languages. In this case the selector consists of a list of expressions separated by commas, with each expression being of the type of the corresponding key defined in the sequence declaration. If this form of selection is used there must be exactly one expression for each key field, e.g.

named_account_file (123456)

which is equivalent to

named_account_file (account_number = 123456)

The operations **insert** and **remove** cause the named object to be inserted into or deleted from the specified collection. An object inserted into a key order sequence is placed in the position appropriate to its key value(s). An object inserted into an insertion order sequence using *insert* is placed at the head of the sequence. The operations **before** and **after** insert a new member into an insertion order sequence either immediately before or immediately after a named member, e.g.

account_file.after(account_file(123455), working_ac)

They cannot be used with sets or key order sequences.

For sets, the operator "+" returns a union of the two sets (based on the identity relation), while for insertion order sequences it returns a concatenation of the two sequences (starting with the first named sequence) and for key order sequences it returns a merge of the two sequences in key order. For sets and sequences of tuples, the collection which is returned is a collection of names for the tuples.

For sets, the operator "−" is the usual set difference operator, while for sequences it returns a new sequence containing the name of each member of the left named sequence except when that name is duplicated in both named sequences. The resulting sequence is in the order of the left named sequence. (If the same name appears five times in the left sequence and twice in the right sequence, it will appear three times in the resulting sequence.)

For sets, the operator "*" is the usual intersection operator. For sequences, it produces a new sequence of names (in the order of the left named sequence) with a name appearing only for each name which appears in both the original sequences. (If the same name appears five times in the left sequence and twice in the right sequence, it will appear twice in the resulting sequence.)

A new collection can be formed from some other collection in the same way that a single member can be selected, except that in the case of a subset the boolean expression is enclosed by curly brackets, and in the case of sequences it is enclosed by the brackets <: ... :>, e.g.

short_account_list :@ account_file <: pos > 3 and pos < 10 :>

Such expressions may not appear on the left side of assignments. For tuples the returned collection is a set of names.

There is a **for** statement which iterates through all the members of a set (nondeterministically) or of a sequence (in the order defined for the sequence), e.g.

    for x **in** named_account_file <: account_number < 200000
        and current_balance > 0 :>
        do ...
        otherwise ... [executed if the sequence is empty]
    endfor

The control variable, which is not explicitly declared, is local to the **for** statement. There is also an implicit **with** statement associated with the control variable.

Finally, there is a special **with one** statement, which selects one element (nondeterministically for sets, the first for sequences) from the defined collection. If the defined collection is empty, the **otherwise** clause is executed, as in the **for** statement.

For a fuller discussion of sequences and sets in LEIBNIZ, including "complete sequences", "multisequences" and the rules for type compatibility, the reader is referred to [4].

3. Efficient Implementations of LEIBNIZ Data Structures

The expressive power of LEIBNIZ sequences and sets can be used in an infinite variety of ways, ranging from simple computational structures such as stacks and queues through to advanced persistent structures appropriate to large data bases. Throughout this range of applications the programmer is able to develop small, elegant and natural programs to manage these structures, at the data base level — we have argued elsewhere [4] — with an ease surpassing that of relational algebra or calculus.

Given the range of techniques which have been developed to manage data structures efficiently both in computations (e.g. arrays, linked lists, hash tables) and in data bases (e.g. indexed sequential, hashed random and B-tree structures), it would be foolish to expect that a single compiler-supplied implementation mechanism provided for a persistent environment could compete effectively with the conventional techniques.

Similarly, even if the compiler had at its disposal a range of implementation techniques competitive with those found in conventional systems, it would not be a trivial matter for it to make sensible decisions about which implementation technique to use for which data structures. The problem here is that a static program text does not reveal the key dynamic features of a structure (such as its maximum size, the volatility of the data, the frequency of keyed seeks for data using particular keys, etc.), and it is these dynamic features which generally determine the most appropriate implementation technique for particular cases.

Furthermore, a limited range of implementation techniques built into a compiler could only provide the programmer with an extremely restrictive environment compared with conventional

methods, where for computational data structures the basic features of a language (e.g. arrays and pointers) can be used to develop new implementation techniques, and for persistent file structures it is often possible, for system programmers at least, to write their own file managers. The option of developing a new compiler scarcely seems as attractive.

The designers of SETL [11], a language based on sets (but with a very different flavour from LEIBNIZ), tackled the efficiency issue by means of a "representation sublanguage" via which the programmer could provide refinements to his original abstract program to transform it into a more efficient one [12]. But this again places the onus on the programmer to modify his algorithms to achieve efficiency.

Our aim in the design of LEIBNIZ has been to separate completely the high level problem solutions (based on sequences and sets) and the efficient implementation of these solutions. In database environments the application programmer is not expected to refine his algorithms to provide more efficient access to data, but can usually choose between different existing mechanisms. The more advanced (systems) programmer can add new mechanisms to this collection without being concerned about individual application programs. We have aimed to provide similar flexibility in LEIBNIZ, such that the separate concerns of application development and efficient implementation can be treated separately, allowing the application programmer to nominate an existing implementation technique, and allowing the implementation specialist to add new techniques, quite independently of each other.

The strategy which we have adopted is to build into the compiler a few straightforward implementations for sets and sequences, together with a mechanism which allows the compiler to incorporate independently defined *implementation modules*, some of which will typically be in a system-supplied library, while others may have been developed separately by systems or applications programmers.

For any given sequence or set in a program there is always a default implementation which the compiler uses in the absence of further directives. This may, depending on the nature of the declaration, be one of the built-in compiler implementations or it may be a separately defined implementation. However, at the time of compiling his program, the programmer may direct the compiler, via a *pragma*, to use some other implementation, which may also be selected from the built-in or from the separately defined implementations.

In straightforward cases the default implementation may suffice, or the application programmer might make a reasonable decision about which implementation module to use. However, the selection of a suitable implementation can in some cases be a crucial decision, in which case the choice of implementation might be handed over to an implementation specialist, who will then have the responsibility of defining the pragma which selects the implementation module. Another possibility which might be employed is automatic selection of appropriate data structures using techniques such as are described in [13] in relation to the programming language SAIL [14, 15] and its associated LEAP data language [16], a language which also supports sets, again adopting a very different approach to LEIBNIZ. Indeed more recent literature has suggested the use of expert system techniques for selecting appropriate implementations [17]. However, the subject of this paper is not the problem of selecting the best technique from an existing library of techniques, but the more fundamental problem of how to develop such implementation modules, how to integrate them with the compiler and what implementations to build directly into the compiler.

3.1. The Built-In Implementations

In accordance with the aim of keeping the compiler as simple as possible, only two implementations are provided directly by the code of the compiler: bit lists and arrays.

The implementation of bit lists needs little comment for anyone familiar with Pascal sets. The maximum length of a bit list is compiler-dependent. As in Pascal, the presence or absence of a value in the set is indicated by the boolean value at the corresponding position in the bit list. Bit lists serve as the default implementation for sets of scalars with a limited domain. They may also be used, as a result of a pragma directive, to implement a complete sequence of tuples with a single boolean **var** field (corresponding to an array of booleans).

Arrays, which serve as the default implementation for key order sequences and complete sequences with restricted key values, have the obvious implementation: there is a dimension for each specified key field. The base type of the array is constituted from the non-key fields. The maximum ranges of the keys which may be used in an array implementation are compiler-dependent.

3.2. Implementation Modules

Although a LEIBNIZ environment typically provides a library of implementation modules, these have no special status: any programmer can, if he is prepared to make the effort, provide an implementation module. This has two important implications for implementation modules. First, there must be standard interfaces for the implementation modules to support sets, insertion order sequences, key order sequences, etc. Second, it must be possible to develop implementation modules in LEIBNIZ. We consider these points in turn.

3.2.1. The Classes of Implementation Modules

Clearly it is necessary, in order to standardise the interactions between compiler and implementation modules, that all such modules present a common interface to the compiler. This interface must be couched in terms of the information-hiding principle [5], since the objective of the exercise is to allow different implementation modules to provide different data structures and algorithms for sequences and sets. Hence, the visibility of data structures on the interface would be self-contradictory.

The interface definitions for information-hiding modules in LEIBNIZ are known as *class* interfaces [7]. Of the various class interfaces to support LEIBNIZ collections, we discuss, by way of example, the insertion sequence class, a definition of which appears in Appendix A.

The insertion sequence class provides operations to support

- initialisation (**new, create_empty_seq**),

- assignments (**copy, copy_structure**),

- seeking for particular items in the sequence (**seek_item, seek_position, seek_first, seek_last**),

- insertion of new items into the sequence (**insert_item, insert_item_before, insert_item_after**),

- removal of existing items (**remove_item**),

- sequential access operations (**get_current_item, step_next_item, at_end_of_seq**),

- testing for membership (**at_in_seq, in_seq**),

- comparison of sequences (**at_equal, equal**),

- a function which returns the length of a sequence (**elem_count**), and

- operations to produce the concatenation (**concat_seqs, concat_seqs_left, concat_seqs_right**), the intersection (**intersect_seqs, intersect_seqs_left, intersect_seqs_right**) and the difference (**difference_seqs, difference_seqs_left, difference_seqs_right**) of two sequences.

The purpose of most of these operations will be obvious to readers. One or two comments are nevertheless required.

First, although the class sequence superficially resembles an abstract data type for a sequence, it is in fact rather more than this, since it supports the concept of a current position in the sequence. In fact, it is more appropriate to consider it as an abstraction of a current position in a sequence. Different instances of the module provide different current positions (which may be used and updated by the interface routines, but which are otherwise invisible outside the module), but several such instances may refer to different current positions within a single sequence. This simplifies the compilation of nested loops (in which each loop variable may be at a different position in a single sequence) and of concurrent processing (where different processes may be independently accessing the same sequence[*]).

From the viewpoint of implementation modules, particular sequences are characterised via the hidden class *header*, which is defined within the module (so that each implementation can provide its own representation). Although the definition is internal to the module, a "handle" for a header can be passed outside the module (allowing the compiler to maintain pointers to particular sequences). The procedure **create_empty_seq** creates a new (empty) sequence and returns a handle for it. The procedure **new** creates a new instance of a current position, initialised to the invalid position, and associates this with an existing sequence, passed in as a parameter. The various seek routines modify the value of the current position, and are typically used in preparation for insertion, removal or **get_current_item** operations. The **step_next_item** procedure also moves the current position along the sequence for use in **for** loops.

The concatenation, intersection and difference operators are each provided in three forms, allowing the implementor to produce more efficient code in the cases where the variable on the left side of an assignment also occurs either on the left or right of the operator in the expression on the right side of the assignment.

3.2.2. Writing Implementation Modules in LEIBNIZ

The purpose of implementation modules is to provide the compiler with a framework which it can use to translate the

---

[*] Synchronisation of access is not the responsibility of the writer of the implementation module.

powerful language of sequences and sets into lower level operations which can easily be implemented using linked lists, B-trees or any other suitable technique. Consequently, the writer of implementation modules must be able to program such structures in a straightforward manner. This means that he must be in a position to use pointers.

Although pointers do not appear visibly in LEIBNIZ, the semantics of tuple declarations (which declare *names* for tuples, with the creation of actual tuples being effected by the associated **new** procedure), the availability of synonyms and the semantics of the *name assignment* operator <-, together make it a straightforward matter to develop data structures in a pointer-like manner. Appendix B provides an implementation of some of the routines of the class insertion sequence, showing a trivial implementation as a singly-linked list.

Thus implementation modules can in practice be written in LEIBNIZ.

3.3. Compilation of Sequences and Sets

As indicated above, the compiler has built-in implementations for those sequences and sets which can trivially be implemented as bit lists or arrays. All other implementations are provided in the form of implementation modules, which can, in Pascal terminology, take advantage of pointers, arrays and sets (bit lists).

For each set or sequence in a LEIBNIZ program there is a default implementation, which may, depending on the nature of the declaration, be either built-in or provided in the basic library of implementation modules. This default implementation may be overridden by directing the compiler (via a *pragma*) to use a different implementation (which also may be either built-in or an implementation module).

The compilation of built-in implementations, whether by default or by pragma, requires no discussion. However, some comments on the compilation of sequences and sets using implementation modules will not be out of place.

3.3.1. The LEIBNIZ Compiler for the MONADS System

The compilation process described in this section is that used to compile LEIBNIZ programs for execution on the MONADS-PC system [2]. The latter has an unusual architecture [1], in that it supports a large persistent virtual memory with 60 bit virtual addresses, with microcoded support for addressing data structures held both in process stacks and as linked lists in heaps. Consequently LEIBNIZ sets and sequences are implemented directly in the virtual memory without the need for underlying file system mechanisms.

The LEIBNIZ compiler translates programs written in LEIBNIZ into MONADS Pascal. The latter is standard Pascal supplemented by a few additional features which make it useful in the MONADS-PC environment, most notably by its support for information-hiding modules. The first advantage of compiling to Pascal is that a Pascal compiler already exists. The second relates to the use of implementation modules for compiling sets and sequences.

As indicated earlier, the form of LEIBNIZ available to the writer of implementation modules effectively supports Pascal-like pointers (through the use of name semantics for tuples), arrays (through key order and complete sequences with restricted key

domains) and bit lists (through sets of scalar subranges and enumerated classes). Consequently, the translation of LEIBNIZ implementation modules into Pascal code is a relatively straightforward procedure. The remaining non-standard features of MONADS Pascal are also "compatible with" the ideas of LEIBNIZ, so that the entire translation process is relatively straightforward. Thus the choice of MONADS Pascal as the target language for the LEIBNIZ compiler has given us a rapid path for developing a prototype LEIBNIZ compiler.

3.3.2. Translation Using the Implementation Modules

An implementation module is defined as an *element*, which is a data abstraction that can be separately specified (via a class interface) and for which one or more implementations can be independently developed, as has been illustrated in Appendices A and B. However, all elements are "compiled into" the module(s) in which they are used[*]. Most of the activity of compiling the implementation modules for sets and sequences into other modules is identical with that for compiling in an implementation for an element, and it will be useful for us to summarise this, before going on to consider the special activities associated with sequence/set implementation modules.

The implementation for an element typically includes a **uses** section which either defines or names[**] the classes (cf. Pascal types) used within the module. These class definitions are transformed into Pascal type definitions and procedure definitions. Generic classes which appear in the **uses** section must be compiled-in classes (e.g. elements or tuples) and consequently the actual type required can be determined at compile time.

The instance data of an element's implementation follows the **uses** section. The constants and variables in this section are transformed into a Pascal record type definition, which can be used later to declare individual instances of the element type.

Next appear the internal routines of the element, if any, followed by the interface routines. These are translated into Pascal procedures[†].

This standard procedure for compiling elements into the modules which use them is used to integrate the implementation modules for sequences and sets into the modules which use them. However, the additional step is necessary of translating sequence and set declarations and the statements which use them into calls on the interface procedures of the implementation module. This is, of course, a genuine translation process, from the higher level language of sets and sequences to the lower level of Pascal via calls on the routines of the implementation modules. Although the compiler accomplishes this in a single step, it is most simply

---

[*] There are also facilities in LEIBNIZ for independently compiled modules, but these are not relevant to the present topic.

[**] The name of a class allows the compiler access to its definition, held in a library.

[†] Optionally these routines, and any routines associated with embedded elements, tuples, etc., can be translated into in-line code, if indicated via a pragma.

understood as a two step operation, whereby the original program is translated into a form of LEIBNIZ without sets or sequences, which is then transformed into Pascal.

To illustrate this notional process we consider the simple case of loop iteration through an insertion order sequence, showing how the following fragments of LEIBNIZ are transformed, using the code of the implementation module in Appendix B, into Pascal.

```
uses  tuple t
        var   i, j: int
        end t
        ...
var   s: seq of t
        total: int
...
body ...
        total := 0
        for x in s do total := $ + i endfor
        ...
end
```

The intermediate LEIBNIZ form (which never appears, but represents the compiler's view of the text) is as follows:

```
uses  tuple t
        var   i, j: int
        end t
        element simple_link
        — as defined in Appendix B —
var   s: simple_link_header
        total: int
        x_1: t
        b_1: bool
        simple_link_1: simple_link
...
body ...
        total := 0
        simple_link_1.new(s)
        % for x in s do total := $ + i endfor
        simple_link_1.seek_first (b_1)
        until at_end
        do    if not b_1 then at_end endif
              simple_link_1.get_current_item (x_1)
              total:= $ + x_1.i
              simple_link_1.step_next_item
              b_1 := not simple_link_1.at_end_of_seq
        enduntil
        ...
end
```

This in turn is straightforwardly transformed into Pascal:

```
type  record t
        begin i, j: int
        end;
        — expansion of required components of element simple_link
        — into Pascal types and procedures, as used below
var   s: ^simple_link_header
        total: int;
        x_1: ^t;
        b_1: bool;
        % below is is the record representing instance data
        simple_link_1: ^simple_link_instance
...
```

```
begin ...
        total := 0;
        simple_link_new(simple_link_1,s);
        % for x in s do total := $ + i endfor
        simple_link_seek_first (simple_link_1, b_1);
        while b_1 do
        begin simple_link_get_current_item (simple_link_1, x_1);
              total:= total + x_i;
              simple_link_step_next_item (simple_link_1);
              b_1 := not simple_link_at_end_of_seq (simple_link_1);
        end;
        ...
end.
```

4. Concluding Remarks

One of the main benefits which persistent systems can offer is a uniform set of programming constructs for managing data structures, removing the traditional technology-based distinction between computational memory structures and file store structures which appears in conventional programming languages. Clearly the conventional file system approach would not create a suitable basis for achieving this. On the other hand widely used computational constructs, such as arrays and pointers, require programmers to invest substantial effort in order to achieve efficient structures, and furthermore programming with pointers can be a very error prone activity. An alternative which we have considered in this paper is the use of very high level data structuring constructs based on sets and sequences. However, this raises the question whether such constructs can be efficiently implemented.

In this paper we have described how it is possible to produce efficient versions of programs which use such data structures by developing implementation modules, which are independent of the application programs but which can be used by the compiler to produce an appropriate implementation. The use of pragmas to guide this process means that an application program does not need to be modified in order to produce an alternative implementation of its data structures. This means, *inter alia*, that rapid prototyping becomes a relatively straightforward process.

At present a Pascal compiler exists for the MONADS-PC and a LEIBNIZ compiler (translating into Pascal) is currently under development. We have formulated the rules necessary to produce the transformations from LEIBNIZ to Pascal, using implementation modules, and these have recently been incorporated into the compiler. The resulting Pascal code was then tested and found to be correct. This has given us confidence that we shall soon have a working compiler which will automate the necessary transformation rules.

ACKNOWLEDGEMENTS

The authors wish to thank Dr. Mark Evered of the Technical University, Darmstadt, whose doctoral work on an earlier version of the LEIBNIZ language provided an inspiration and starting point for the present work [18]. We also wish to acknowledge the contributions of Carolyn Guest and Linda Schembri. Finally, we thank the Commonwealth Scientific and Industrial Research Organisation (Collaborative Program in Information Technology) and the Australian Research Grants Committee (Grant Number 8525141) for their support of the LEIBNIZ project.

REFERENCES

1. Rosenberg, J. and Keedy, J.L. "Object Management and Addressing in the MONADS Architecture", *Proc. Workshop on Persistent Object Systems,* Appin, Scotland, 1987.

2. Rosenberg, J. and Abramson, D.A. "MONADS-PC - A Capability-Based Workstation to Support Software Engineering", *Proceedings 18th Annual Hawaii International Conference on System Sciences,* January, 1985, pp 222-230.

3. Rosenberg, J, Koch, D.M. and Keedy, J.L. "A Massive Memory Supercomputer", *Proceedings 22nd Annual Hawaii International Conference on System Sciences,* January, 1989.

4. Keedy, J.L. and Rosenberg, J. "Data Engineering with Sets and Sequences", *Proceedings of 3rd. Australian Software Engineering Conference,* Canberra, May 1988, pp. 79-100.

5. Parnas, D.L. "On the Criteria to be Used in Decomposing Systems into Modules", *Comm. ACM,* 15, 12, pp 1053-1058.

6. Jones, A.K. "The Object Model, a Conceptual Tool for Structuring Software", in Bayer et al, "Operating Systems, An Advanced Course", Lecture Notes in Computer Science, 60, Springer Verlag, Berlin, 1978, pp 7-16.

7. Keedy, J.L. and Evered, M.P. "Modularity in the Language LEIBNIZ", *Proceedings of the First Australian Software Engineering Conference,* Canberra, May 1986, pp. 7-13.

8. Birtwistle, G. et al "DECSYSTEM-10 SIMULA Language Handbook", Rep. C8399, Swedish Nat. Defense Res. Inst., Stockholm, Sweden, 1974.

9. Goldberg, A. and Robson, D. "SMALLTALK-80 — The Language and its Implementation", Addison-Wesley, 1983.

10. Khoshafian, S.N. and Copeland, G.P. "Object Identity", *Proceedings of OOPSLA-86,* in Special Issue of SIGPLAN Notices, 21, 11, November 1986, pp. 406-416.

11. Kennedy, K. and Schwartz, J. "An Introduction to the Set Theoretical Language SETL", *Comp. and Maths with Appls,* Vol. 1, 1975, pp. 97-119.

12. Dewar, R.B., Grand, A., Ssu-Cheng, L., Schonberg, E. and Schwartz, J.T. "Programming by Refinement, as Exemplified by the SETL Representation Sublanguage", *ACM Transactions on Programming Languages and Systems,* 1, 1, 1979, pp. 27-49.

13. Low, J.R. "Automatic Data Structure Selection: An Example and Overview", *Comm. ACM,* 21, 5, May, 1978, pp. 376-385.

14. Feldman, J., et al "Recent Developments in SAIL — an ALGOL-based Language for Artificial Intelligence ", *Proc. AFIPS 1972 FJCC,* AFIPS Press, Montvale, N.J., pp. 1193-1202.

15. Reiser, J. "SAIL USER MANUAL", Tech. Rep. STAN-CS-76-574, Comp. Sci. Dept., Stanford University, Stanford, Calif., Aug. 1976.

16. Feldman, J. and Rovner, P. "An Algol-based Associative Language", *Comm. ACM, 12, 8, Aug. 1969, pp. 439-449.*

17. Ford, R. and Norton, J. "An Expert System for Selection of Module Implementations", *Proc. 1985 Conf. on Intelligent Systems and Machines,* Rochester, Minnesota, April, 1985.

18. Evered, M. "LEIBNIZ — A Language to Support Software Engineering", Dr.Ing. Thesis, Faculty of Informatics, Technical University of Darmstadt, 1985.

APPENDIX A

Class Definition for Insertion Sequences

```
% This is the class definition for implementation modules for an
% insertion sequence

class insert_sequence is element

uses  generic elem_type
      internal header

interface

proc new (new_header: header)
% creates a new current position set to nil, and associates it with a
% header

proc create_empty_seq (out newseq: header)
% creates an empty sequence, as the current header, and invalidates
% current position

proc copy (in oldseq: header  out newseq: header)
% s1 := s2, copies an existing sequence by value; newseq becomes the
% current header, current position is invalidated

proc copy_structure (in oldseq: header  out newseq: header)
% s1 :@ s2, copies an existing sequence by structure; newseq becomes
% the current header, current position is invalidated

proc seek_item (in elem: elem_type  out success: bool)
% seeks the provided item by name in the current sequence; current
% position is set to elem or nil if not found)

proc seek_position(in posn: int  out success: bool)
% seeks a defined position in the current sequence; current position is
% set to this position (or nil if not found)

proc seek_first (out success: bool)
% seeks first item in the current sequence; current position is set to
% this position (or nil if not found)

proc seek_last (out success: bool)
% seeks last item in the current sequence; current position is set to this
% position (or nil if not found)

proc insert_item (in elem: elem_type)
% inserts an element at the head of the current sequence; current
% position is set to inserted item

proc insert_item_before (in elem: elem_type)
      raises invalid_position
% inserts elem in a sequence before current position; but causes
% exception if current position is nil; current position is set to inserted
% item

proc insert_item_after (in elem: elem_type)
      raises invalid_position
% inserts elem in a sequence after current position; but causes exception
% if current position is nil; current position is set to inserted item

proc remove_item
      raises argument_not_in_seq
% removes the current element from the current sequence; current
% position is set to item following removed item (or nil if item
% nonexistent)
```

```
proc get_current_item (out elem: elem_type)
      raises end_of_seq
% gets item at current position

proc step_next_item
      raises invalid_current_item
% moves current position to next item

enq at_end_of_seq (out result: bool)
% indicates whether the current position is at the end of the sequence

enq at_in_seq (in elem: elem_type   out result: bool)
% tests whether an element is in a sequence (by name)

enq in_seq (in elem: elem_type   out result: bool)
% tests whether an element is in a sequence (by value)

enq at_equal (in seq1,seq2: header   out result: bool)
% compares 2 sequences by structure to implement @= and @~=

enq equal (in seq1,seq2: header   out result: bool)
% compares 2 sequences by value to implement = and ~=

enq elem_count (out result: int)
% returns the number of elements in the current sequence

proc concat_seqs (in seq1,seq2: header   out newseq: header)
% s :@ s1 + s2,  current position is set to first element in newseq

proc concat_seqs_left (in seq1: header   inout seq2: header)
% s2 :@ s1 + s2,  current position is set to first element in seq2

proc concat_seqs_right (in seq1: header   inout seq2: header)
% s2 :@ s2 + s1,  current position is set to first element in seq2

proc intersect_seqs (in seq1,seq2: header   out newseq: header)
% s :@ s1 * s2,  current position is set to first element in newseq;
% the order of s is that of s1

proc intersect_seqs_left (in seq1: header   inout seq2: header)
% s2 :@ s2 * s1,  s2 contains the intersection in the order in which
% elements appear in s2; current position is set to first element in
% seq2

proc intersect_seqs_right (in seq1: header   inout seq2: header)
% s2 :@ s1 * s2,  s2 contains the intersection in the order in which
% elements appear in s1; current position is set to first element in
% seq2

proc difference_seqs (in seq1,seq2: header   out newseq: header)
% s :@ s1 - s2,  current position is set to first element in newseq;
% the order of s is that of s1

proc difference_seqs_left (in seq1: header   inout seq2: header)
% s2 :@ s2 - s1,  s2 contains the difference in the order in which
% elements appear in s2; current position is set to first element in
% seq2

proc difference_seqs_right (in seq1: header   inout seq2: header)
% s2 :@ s1 - s2,  s2 contains the difference in the order in which
% elements appear in s1; current position is set to first element in
% seq2

end insert_sequence
```

APPENDIX B

Sample Implementation Module for Insertion Sequences

```
% This module defines a singly linked implementation of a sequence

element simple_link is insert_sequence

uses  generic elem_type

      tuple header
          var       element_count: int
              forward_link: link
          interface
            proc new
            body element_count:= 0
                forward_link <- nil
            end new
      end header

      tuple link
          var       forward_link: link
              elem: elem_type
          interface
            proc new
            body forward_link <- nil
            end new
      end link
var   current_header: header
      current_pos: link

% INTERNAL ROUTINES

proc find_previous (out temp_link: link)
% sets temp_link to link before current_pos
% if current_pos is nil or is first link then temp_link is set to nil
body if current_pos is nil or current_pos is current_header.forward_link
      then  temp_link <- nil
      else  temp_link <- current_header.forward_link
          until found
          do    if temp_link.forward_link is current_pos
                        then found endif
                      temp_link <- $.forward_link
          enduntil
      endif
end find_previous

…

% INTERFACE ROUTINES

interface

proc new (new_header: header)
body current_header <- new_header
      current_pos <- nil
end new

proc create_empty_seq (out newseq: header)
% creates an empty sequence
% current_header names newseq
% current_pos is invalidated
body newseq.new
      current_header <- newseq
      current_pos <- nil
end create_empty_seq
```

```
proc seek_first (out success: bool)
% seeks first item in the current sequence
% current_pos is set to this position (or nil if not found)
body if current_header.element_count > 0
     then  success:= true
           current_pos <- current_header.forward_link
     else  success:= false
           current_pos <- nil
     endif
end seek_first


proc insert_item (in elem: elem_type)
% inserts an element at the head of the current sequence
% current_pos is set to inserted item
var   link
body link.new
     link.elem <- elem
     link.forward_link <- current_header.forward_link
     current_header.forward_link <- link
     current_header.element_count := $ + 1
     current_pos <- link
end insert_item


proc insert_item_after (in elem: elem_type)
        raises invalid_position
% inserts elem in a sequence after current_pos
...
end insert_item_after


proc remove_item
        raises argument_not_in_seq
% removes the current element from the current sequence
% current_pos is set to item following removed item
% (or nil if item nonexistent)

var   previous_pos: link
body if current_pos is nil then raise argument_not_in_seq endif
     if current_pos is current_header.forward_link
     then  current_header.forward_link <- $.forward_link
           current_pos <- current_header.forward_link
     else  find_previous (previous_pos)
           previous_pos.forward_link <- current_pos.forward_link
           current_pos <- previous_pos.forward_link
     endif
     current_header.element_count := $ - 1
end remove_item


proc get_current_item (out elem: elem_type)
        raises end_of_seq
% gets item at current_pos
body if current_pos isnt nil
     then elem <- current_pos.elem
     else raise end_of_seq endif
end get_this_item


proc step_next_item
        raises invalid_current_item
% moves current_pos to next item
body if current_pos is nil
     then  raise invalid_current_item
     else  current_pos <- $.forward_link
     endif
end step_next_item


enq at_end_of_seq (out result: bool)
% indicates whether the current position is at the end of the sequence
body result:= current_pos is nil
end at_end_of_seq
```

```
enq elem_count (out resuit: int)
% returns the number of elements in the current sequence
body   result:= current_header.element_count
end elem_count


end simple_link
```

Object eXchange Service for
an Object-Oriented Database System

Girish Pathak, John Joseph, and Steve Ford

Texas Instruments Incorporated

1 Abstract

This article describes an Object eXchange Service (**OXS**)
and an EXTernal Object Representation (**EXTOR**) in the
context of a distributed object-oriented database. EXTOR
is the common representation which facilitates the sharing of information among a network of machines. This
work is guided by the desire to represent complex structured information in an efficient external form and to provide maximal sharing of information among computing sessions. OXS is a service which, together with the concepts
of object boundary, global objects, and object closure, provides the exchange of information via EXTOR. The article
also contains a brief description of the distributed object-
oriented system which utilizes this service, the performance
results of OXS, and the future directions for the design of
generalized object exchange services in heterogeneous computing environments. The work described here is part of
Zeitgeist[1], a Distributed Object-Oriented Database system which is being developed at the Computer Science Center of Texas Instruments, Dallas.

2 Introduction

A major goal of the Zeitgeist project[8] is to provide a programming environment where a programmer can manipulate persistent and transient data in the same manner. Furthermore, transactions can be implemented on persistent
objects to support cooperative design applications. This
goal is achieved by providing a seamless integration of an
object-oriented database with an object-oriented programming environment, namely Common Lisp with Flavors on
a network of Texas Instruments Explorer^{TM} workstations.
A key component of our system (as shown in Figure 2.1) is
the translation of an object into a representation which can
be easily stored onto and retrieved from disk. The repre-

---

[1] The name *Zeitgeist* is a German word meaning "spirit of the age,"
and is intended to reflect the leading edge characteristic of the project,
as well as the elements of time included in the project architecture.

sentation of an object on disk is referred to as an EXTOR.
The EXTOR of any object is an array of 16 bit elements,
which is essentially a linearized representation of the object
in virtual memory with encoding of type information. An
EXTOR can embed references to other EXTORs by means
of **long pointers**. The embedded references are necessary
to preserve the correct semantics of shared objects. A long
pointer is a system-wide unique identifier in time as well as
in space; the long pointer mechanism expands the address
space of the machine virtually without limits. An object
management system, with the help of the Object eXchange
Service (OXS), transparently resolves the long pointer references. The loading of objects from disk, on demand, to
resolve such references is called **Object Faulting**.

Common Lisp systems on conventional machines provide
two ways of making objects persistent. One can make objects persistent by saving the entire Lisp environment to a
disk band. This is a *memory dump* and the user has no
control over which objects are saved; also there is no way
in which objects made persistent under two separate save
operations can interact. There are cases where this is the
right facility, namely when we are creating an operating environment mostly consisting of programs. A second way of
making objects persistent is to use the *fast dump* facility[7];
in this case, individual objects can be made persistent and
retrieved by recreating the data when disk representations
are loaded into memory. The main drawback of this facility
is the inability to provide inter-object references for sharing purposes. Our external representation is designed to
preserve the structure of the object's memory image form.
One of the design goals for external representation is to
provide isomorphism between in-memory and external representations of objects for the reason of preserving the type
information of objects. Due to this memory image form,
there is little performance penalty involved in recreating an
object from its EXTOR. The design of EXTOR combines
the reference flexibility of memory dumps and the object
selectivity of fast dump. In addition, it supports the object
faulting mechanism for demand loading and address space
expansion.

The work described in this article is guided by the desire

146

Reprinted from *IEEE 5th International Conference on Data
Engineering*, 1989, pages 27-34. Copyright © 1989 by The
Institute of Electrical and Electronics Engineers, Inc. All rights
reserved.

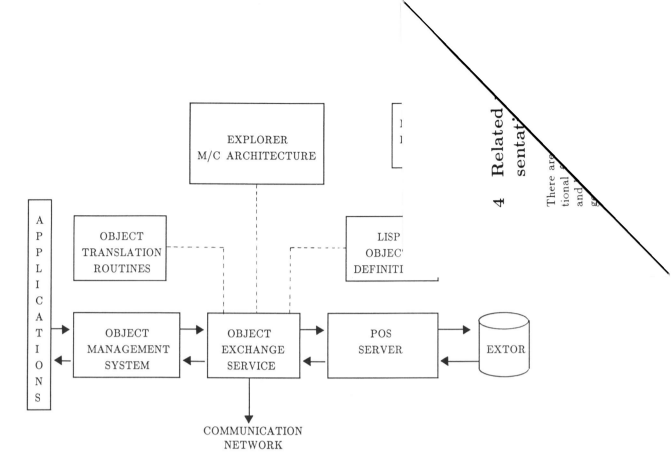

FIG. 2.1 - DISTRIBUTED OBJECT-ORIENTED DATABASE SYSTEM
(ZEITGEIST)

to represent complex structured information in an efficient external form and to provide maximal sharing of information among computing sessions. We discuss EXTOR and OXS and briefly touch on the Object Management System (OMS) which makes use of all the features of OXS in building a distributed OODB. A detailed report on the Zeitgeist project appears in [8].

Section 3 of the article introduces the problems associated with external representation. Section 4 briefly describes related work done in the area of external representation. Section 5 describes EXTOR with the help of an example. OXS and its design concepts are presented in section 6 and 7. Section 8 briefly describes the implementation of OXS and provides early performance results. Finally, section 9 discusses directions for further research.

3   Problems associated with external representation

There are several problems associated with the creation of the external representations of objects. One of the most obvious is that of object boundary. In Lisp systems (like in many other systems), the objects in memory are highly interconnected with the system's run-time environment. Simple tree traversal based translation of an object graph in memory could lead to visiting all the objects in memory.

The concept of object boundary, which is discussed in section 6 of this paper, solves this problem.

The second problem is caused by the desire to share objects among various users of a distributed system. Since the objects are being shared across machine boundaries, a mechanism for identifying shared objects and primitives for referencing these objects becomes necessary. Section 6 of this article discusses an object boundary mechanism which addresses the identification of shared objects and Section 5 discusses a long pointer mechanism which provides referencing primitives for these objects.

The third problem in creating external representations relates to the global objects of the run-time environment. Objects like NIL and T are universally available in all Lisp systems. Translation of these objects is unnecessary and the concepts introduced above are insufficient to deal with objects of this kind. In Section 6, the concept of global objects is introduced to address this issue.

Finally there is the critical issue of performance in creating external representations. The creation of external representations for large numbers of small objects and the transportation of them across machine boundaries creates a performance bottleneck. The concept of object closure, introduced in section 6, provides a step towards solving this problem.

ork in external representation

several approaches to translating the computational form of an object into a form that can be saved and later translated back into the computational form. A generic approach is to translate the object into structured text. This is the approach taken, for example, in the Electronic Data Interchange Format standard[6]. This approach has the advantage of genericity, but it suffers from performance problems and excess storage due to object size expansion. The appearance of portability is misleading; even though the external form is readable on any machine, a different filter is needed for each machine to translate the data back to its computational form.

XDR from Sun Microsystems[14] addresses the performance problem to a large extent. The XDR standard provides library routines for deriving the external representation of primitive data types. More complex data are built using the primitive data types and user written read and write routines. Portability is achieved using various filters. XDR facilitates the transmission of data between machines having different word types and different representations for primitive types like numbers. XDR's approach of linearizing data structures is similar to our approach. However, inter-object referencing and object faulting are critical to our design, and XDR leaves it up to the user to provide these capabilities. XDR's emphasis on providing primitive data types, and our primary goal of providing a persistent world (with demand-driven incremental object retrieve/save) which effectively parallels the programmer's workspace of complex objects, contributes to the divergence of the designs.

University efforts, such as the Mach/Matchmaker system at Carnegie-Mellon University[10] and the Saguaro project at the University of Arizona at Tucson[1] are driven by the need to integrate the heterogeneous environments of languages and computers. These efforts are directed towards designing an object specification language and an external representation. However, their external representations can handle only the primitive data types of the programming languages and lack the ability to handle composite structures with pointers and abstract data types. In the general programming community, there has been interesting research aimed at eliminating the impedance mismatch between programming languages and databases[2], [5], [11]. Researchers have also pursued the ideas of uniform memory abstraction[12] and extended address space[4], [9]. The Orion object-oriented database project at MCC[3] and Statice at Symbolics[13] have addressed issues similar to the ones discussed here.

Existing approaches delegate responsibility for representing complex structures to the user; they provide no mechanisms for specifying object boundaries and inter-object references. We believe that the EXTOR adequately addresses issues of complex object representation, object boundaries and inter-object references. Zeitgeist provides a seamless integration of programming language and database using EXTOR and OXS.

5 The EXTernal Object Representation

This section describes the EXTOR with the help of an example. The external representation scheme, EXTOR, defines a collection of primitive data types, a collection of composite data types, and a set of object referencing primitives.

In object-oriented programming, the descriptions of data and operations are encapsulated in an entity called an **object**. In control-oriented programming, such encapsulation is not present. In both cases, we can think of the data in an object as a piece of typed information. The type information may be present directly in the object at run-time or may be derivable from the system's compile-time environment.

The EXTOR of an object consists of a set of data types and values. Some of the data types are primitive data types whose values are atomic and others are composite data types. Composite data types help build a complex object from primitive data types and constructors.

Primitive data types of the EXTOR include numbers and characters. Composite data types may consist of complex structures such as lists, symbols, arrays, records, functions, and abstract data types (object instances and object handlers[7]).

In addition to these two classes of data types, EXTOR supports relative references and named references, which allow sharing within an object and among different objects. A system with 64-bit long pointers is currently employed by Zeitgeist. Encoding the long pointer, rather than using a character string, provides a compact representation which reduces storage requirements.

Let us consider the external representation of an array object in further detail. Figure 5.1 shows an example of an array object which contains information about the city of Dallas. It has three elements: the first is a character (a primitive data type), the second is a list of two elements (a composite data type of city name, DAL, and, state name, TX), and the third is an object of user-defined type (airport object). The external representation of this array object is shown in Figure 5.2. The 0th word of the EXTOR defines the header. The total size of the EXTOR is 14 words. The 1st word contains the header information of the array object and word 2 to 4 contain objects (or their relative references) pointed to by the array object. The character object is in the 2nd word. The list object in the 3rd word and airport object at 4th word contain relative references. The two elements of the list are represented in the 5th and 6th words, which have relative references in them for the real string objects in the 7th and 9th words. In this example, the user-defined airport object forms the boundary (a concept described in the following section) for the array object. In the 11th word, where the airport object should be represented, a long pointer identifying the airport object has been placed in the EXTOR.

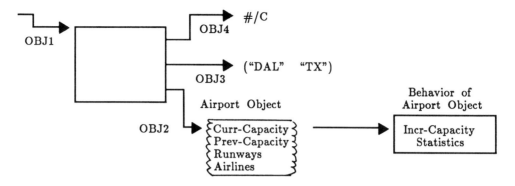

FIG. 5.1 - AN ARRAY OBJECT

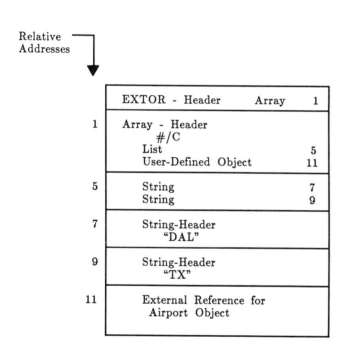

FIG. 5.2 - EXTOR for Object in Fig. 5.1

6 Design Concepts of Object Exchange Service

This section describes three concepts, Global Objects, Object Boundary, and Object Closure, which form the kernel of the Object Exchange Service (OXS).

6.1 Global Object

Global Objects are those objects which are always present in the environment, or can be created on demand by the Object Management System (OMS). Examples of global objects are the primitive objects *nil* and *t* and various font map encodings. It is not necessary to save global objects to the disk. In some cases, e.g. the display screen, saving and retrieving a global object may create consistency problems. Applications, in consultation with OMS, decide which objects are global. OMS manages a catalogue of global objects and is responsible for generating and resolving externally referenced data for OXS. For global objects, OXS encodes an external reference of type Global Object. A transient object referenced from a persistent object but whose value is uninteresting may be encoded as the global object *nil*. When translating from an external representation, OXS resolves global object references by asking OMS to return the corresponding object from its catalogue. If OMS cannot find or create the object, it may consult the user or generate an error.

The concept of global objects helps in isolating the content of an object from its environment. The contention is that the environment, or a large portion of it, will exist because of the presence of the application or of the software platform on which the application runs. Our experience with Computer Aided Design applications bears this out and indicates that the conscious use of global objects can significantly reduce OXS overhead.

149

6.2 Object Boundary

The **Object Boundary** determines the granularity of the objects which are individually handled for system facilities like object transport, object locking, and clustering. It is quite conceivable that the system may provide differing levels of granularity for some of these facilities. For example, transporting an automobile object in a design environment conceptually moves everything in the closure of the automobile object, but, in order to reduce access-time to the root object, or to permit sharing of components (e.g. engines) between designs, some sub-objects may be defined as separate referenced by long pointers. OXS does not allow accessing a partial disk object or locking a partial disk object; therefore, object boundary determines the lowest level of granularity addressable in the system.

Virtual memory objects reference other objects by pointers. In saving an object to disk, we need to save all the objects which are also referenced by the object, namely the transitive closure. The transitive closure may consist of global objects, shared objects (objects which are also in the transitive closure of another object) and other objects. The global objects and the shared objects should be handled as external references for semantic reasons. Other objects in the transitive closure may also be handled via external reference. The object boundary consists of all objects in the transitive closure which are referenced by an external reference in the EXTOR. It determines where an object ends and where another object begins. All objects within the boundary of an object are separately persistent and can be transported, locked, and accessed independent of other objects. However, OMS does not guarantee that these objects have handles which are available to users. In EXTOR, a reference to an object within the boundary of an object is a relative reference and a reference which crosses the object boundary is an external reference. As shown in Figure 5.1, although OBJ2 is in the transitive closure of OBJ1, it is not within OBJ1. OBJ1 contains OBJ3 and OBJ4. These objects are represented in EXTOR as they are; whereas for OBJ2 only the corresponding external reference is placed.

In OXS, we write large objects as separately persistent objects basically for network performance reasons. Also, all Lisp symbols are made separately persistent, based on the knowledge that they are often shared.

6.3 Object Closure

Object Closure is important in deciding how much should be restored when the user requests an object.

Is it better to restore just the referenced object (i.e. the 1st level closure), or should the objects it references in the transitive closure be restored as well? To answer this question, the object closure level, an integer passed to OXS, is used. An object closure level of zero implies that all the objects in the transitive closure shall be restored at once.

The default policy is to use first level closure. The referenced objects are brought in on demand by object faulting.

The closure level specification is a performance tuning parameter and basically provides the system control over the amount of pre-loading of data. When an EXTOR is developed, the layering of the object into different levels results from embedding long pointers at strategic points. Users can control this layering by giving directives to the Object Management System. The default layering we have implemented in Zeitgeist's OMS attempts to guarantee proper semantics for shared objects and increased efficiency at the storage level.

7 Object eXchange Service

Figure 2.1 shows the various components of Zietgeist. Applications interact with the objects through the Object Management System (OMS). The Object Exchange Service (OXS) has little knowledge of the application environment which exists in the programmers' workspace. OXS queries OMS to decide which objects are shared objects and which objects are global objects; boundaries of objects are also determined by OMS. OMS makes these decisions based on a set of rules. By default, OMS has a list of global objects and a set of rules to determine sharing. Applications add or remove rules to this default set to customize the application environment. In the case of abstract data types, this may be done by inheriting a shared-object attribute flag. Particular instances of the abstract data type may be marked as shared by turning on the flag. More typically, all instances of the type may be marked as shared by defaulting this flag to be on when an instance is created. The list of global objects is also modified by the application; individual objects or collection of objects (e.g. Common Lisp Packages) may be declared as global. For space and time efficiency, it is ideal to determine the minimal set of shared objects and the maximal set of global objects for an application. This is not practical in most cases. We believe that the decision to delegate these determinations to OMS and ultimately to the user is the right approach.

When translating an object into external form, OXS first determines the boundary of the object. An object is bounded by the global objects and the shared objects it references. The boundary determines which references are external references and which references are relative references. With the help of an object definition dictionary and a machine representation dictionary, objects are encoded into EXTOR by translation routines in OXS. The object definition dictionary is a collection of the type definitions of the objects. The machine representation dictionary defines the virtual machine for the hardware on which objects have been implemented. External references are encoded as **long pointers** and relative references are encoded as byte offsets. External reference may be of two types, Global Objects and Non-Global Objects. OXS, via OMS, interacts with a multi-level name server to generate and manage the **long pointers** used by EXTOR. Header words are added to indicates properties of the external representation, (i.e. an identifier for the routine to be used to restore the ob-

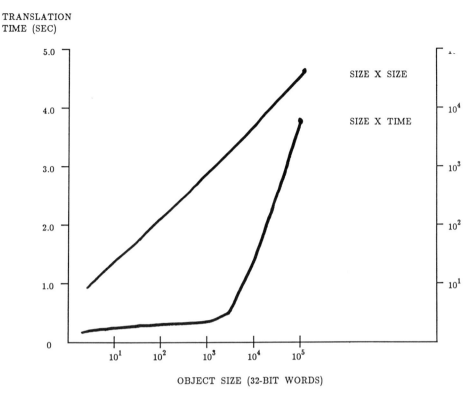

TRANSLATION TIME (SEC)

OBJECT SIZE (32-BIT WORDS)

FIG. 7.1 - PERFORMANCE OF OXS

ject), and characteristics of the object itself (i.e. read-only status). The OXS approach closely resembles Bishop's[4] object copying algorithm for area-wide garbage collection in virtual memories, except that in OXS the object boundary concept with global objects provides a stopping point for the transitive traversal of an object. Furthermore, in our scheme, storage devices and/or distributed systems appear to be extensions of the virtual memory of a computing system.

When an object is brought back from persistent storage, OXS translates the EXTOR into an internal representation, possibly using some information stored in the header words. During this translation, relative references are replaced by virtual memory pointers. When an external reference (long pointer) is encountered, OXS determines, based on type, whether the long pointer references a global object. In this case, the long pointer is replaced by a virtual memory pointer to the referenced global object. Other external references are replaced by encapsulations. Encapsulations are OMS data structures which are surrogates for the actual objects on disk. The surrogates implement an indirection; when an application reference resolves to a surrogate, the actual object is brought from disk and returned to the application in a transparent fashion (object faulting). Alternately, users can request that objects are fetched in an eager fashion to avoid run time faulting in; the surrogates are still set up so that the sharing semantics can be derived

when the objects are written back to the disk. It is also possible to specify that eager fetching take place up to a certain level beyond which objects are faulted in. Object characteristics contained in the header words of the EXTOR (e.g. read only status) are passed to OMS.

8 Implementation and performance results

OXS is built around a dictionary of translation routines for the various types of objects in the Lisp environment. A depth-first search algorithm is used to traverse the nodes of the object graph in memory. Depending on the type of a node, a specific routine is invoked to linearize the node into EXTOR form. Each node is examined to determine whether or not it should be within the boundary of the object being translated. If outside, then a long pointer corresponding to the object is found or created. Global objects are handled in a similar manner. When retrieving an object from disk, the reverse process is executed. Each long pointer is converted to a physical pointer if the object corresponding to the long pointer is already in memory, otherwise the object fault mechanism is set up to bring the object from disk when it is referenced.

We have not yet optimized EXTOR and OXS for perfor-

151

mance; however the following is a brief summary of our preliminary observations. In general, OXS translation time is proportional to the size of the Common Lisp object and its transitive closure being translated. The size of an EXTOR is about the same as the Common Lisp object it represents. Figure 7.1 graphs object size versus translation time and EXTOR size for a representative set of Common Lisp objects. All measurements were taken on a Texas Instruments Explorer^{TM} II. Notice that there is currently about a 0.15 second overhead per top-level translation, which makes small objects more expensive to translate.

For flat or immediate objects, restoration times are comparable to save times, but for objects with sub-objects that have been made separately persistent, significant reductions in access time can be realized by avoiding restoration of the sub-objects before they are needed. For example, OXS translation time for an array of 100 *1Kx1K* bitmaps is 109.391 seconds, 3.405 seconds for the 100 element array, and 1.060 seconds for each of its bitmaps. Restoration of this array takes 0.18 seconds of OXS translation time because only the 100 element array is restored; the bitmaps are not. The object faulting mechanism takes care of restoring the bitmaps if and when needed. The execution of the standard Common Lisp array accessor causes the first bitmap to be restored and returns it as a value. The OXS translation of the bitmap adds 0.95 seconds to the normal execution time of the array reference, but only the first time. Subsequent accesses of the same element have no overhead. If two slots point to the same persistent element, then the first slot referenced will cause the object to be restored, and the second will incur a very small overhead to resolve the reference. Furthermore, subsequent saves of the object also benefit. If the array were to be saved again, bitmaps that had not yet been faulted in would not be saved.

We plan to speed up translation, improve the heuristics for the OMS, and add sparse data compression protocols to the EXTOR to reduce space in the persistent store and improve speed on restoration.

9   Conclusions and directions for future research work

EXTOR provides ability to reference the elements of an object via relative pointers and to reference other objects using embedded long pointers. Relative references allow structured information to be conveniently represented in the external form. This can be used to build a composite object from primitive objects. Long pointers provide correct semantics for shared objects and also expand the address space of a machine limitlessly. EXTOR, being very close to native representation, is compact and efficient for translating from/to native form. We have designed the external representation to be open ended; new types or classes can be easily added if the language is enhanced. This feature will be utilized in making our system cognizant of CLOS[2].

EXTOR can also be used for the distribution of processes among the computing elements of a distributed/parallel computing environment. Further research is required, however, to comprehend the abstraction of processes as data structures. Once this is done, EXTOR can be used in parallel/distributed systems to transfer processes or save processes for continuing computation later.

EXTOR and OXS are used extensively in a distributed OODB for VLSI design application at Texas Instruments. VLSI designs are so data intensive that most designs will not fit all at one time in the virtual memory of a work station. The ability of EXTOR to handle complex structures and to provide support for the fetching of objects on demand make our system a natural fit for handling large designs. Design libraries are implemented using the notion of read-only objects. Database support, in the form of concurrency control, recovery, and transaction management are provided by other components of Zeitgeist.

Finally, it is our intention that OXS evolve into a truly generic object exchange service, providing language and hardware independent support to a variety of clients for the exchange, storage and retrieval of structured information and unstructured data. At present, we are examining current work, especially in the fields of distributed and parallel computing, as we put together a design that is flexible and expressive enough to support at least Common Lisp, C++, and Ada implementations on different hardware and software platforms, and is efficient enough to minimize storage space, communication time, and translation overheads. In many respects, these goals are conflicting. Our current design favors efficiency in Common Lisp on Lisp machines over flexibility, because our customers wouldn't use a low-performance system, no matter how elegant. If we can provide an efficient common external object representation for a representative set of programming languages, then we can avoid providing a multitude of translation routines from one language-specific representation to another. This would be a combinatorially explosive task as new languages are added, and one which depends for success on minimal object movement between heterogeneous environments, a situation we expect will not be the norm, especially in the CAD environment we work in. It is our objective, therefore, to design and implement a truly heterogeneous object exchange service centered around a generic external object representation.

---

[2]The Common Lisp Object System, an object-oriented extension to Common Lisp, has been adopted by the X3J13 committee, which is defining ANSI Standard Common Lisp.

References

[1] G. R. Andrews, R. D. Schlichting, R. Hayes, and D. M. Purdin. "The design of the Saguaro Distributed Operating System," *IEEE Transaction on Software Engineering*, vol. SE-13, no. 1, pp. 104–119, January 1987.

[2] M. P. Atkinson, P. J. Bailey, K. J. Chisholm, P. W. Cockshott, and R. Morrison, "An approach to persistent programming," *The Computer Journal*, vol. 26, no. 4, pp. 360–365, December 1983.

[3] Banerjee et.al. "Data Model Issues for Object-Oriented Applications," *ACM Transactions on Office Information Systems*, vol. 5, no. 4, pp. 3–26, January 1987.

[4] P. B. Bishop. "Computer systems with very large address space and garbage collection," Technical Report Number TR-178, MIT Laboratory for Computer Science, Cambridge, MA, May 1977.

[5] M. H. Butler. "An approach to persistent LISP objects," In the proceedings of the *COMPCON*, pp. 324–329, IEEE, San Fransisco, CA, March 1986.

[6] Electronic Design Interchange Format Steering Committee "EDIF Electronic Design Interchange Format."

[7] Texas Instruments Incorporated. "Explorer^{TM} Lisp Reference Manual," June 1985.

[8] S. Ford, J. Joseph, D. Langworthy, D. Lively, G. Pathak, E. Perez, R. Peterson, D. Sparacin, S. Thatte, D. Wells, and S. Agarwal. "ZEITGEIST: Database support for object-oriented programming," In the proceedings of the *Second International Workshop on Object-Oriented Database Systems*, Published by Springer-Verlag, pp. 23–42, September 1988.

[9] R. Greenblatt. "MOBY address space," Lisp Machine Inc., Los Angeles, CA, August 1985, Seminar report on research in progress.

[10] M. B. Jones, R. F. Rashid, and M. Thompson. "Matchmaker: An interprocess specification language," In *ACM conference on principles of programming languages*, January 1985.

[11] N. Mishkin, "Managing permanent objects," Technical Report YALEU/DCS/RR-338, Department of Computer Science, Yale University, New Haven, CT, November 1984.

[12] S. M. Thatte. "Persistent memory: A Storage Architecture for Object-Oriented Database Systems," *1986 International Workshop On Object Oriented Database Systems*, pp. 148–159, September 23-26, 1986.

[13] Daniel Weinreb, Neal Feinberg, Dan Gerson, and Charles Lamb, "An Object-Oriented Database System to Support an Integrated Programming Environment," Preliminary Draft Version, February 1988.

[14] Sun Microsystems Incorporated. "External Data Representation (XDR)," Reference Manual, Part Number 800-1177-01, Mountain View CA, January 1985.

FEATURES OF THE ORION
OBJECT–ORIENTED DATABASE SYSTEM

Won Kim, Nat Ballou, Jay Banerjee,
Hong–Tai Chou, Jorge F. Garza, Darrell Woelk

MCC
3500 West Balcones Center Drive
Austin, Texas 78759

ABSTRACT

In this paper we describe major features of ORION, a prototype object–oriented database system built in the Advanced Computer Architecture Program at MCC. These include dynamic schema evolution, version control, composite objects, associative queries, transaction management, and multimedia information management. ORION has been implemented in Common LISP, and runs on the Symbolics 3600 LISP machines and the SUN workstation under UNIX. As a substantial partial validation of the system, we have successfully interfaced ORION with the PROTEUS expert system shell, also prototyped in the Advanced Computer Architecture Program.

1. INTRODUCTION

In the Advanced Computer Architecture Program at MCC, we have built a prototype object-oriented database system, called ORION. Presently, it is being used in supporting the data management needs of PROTEUS, an expert system shell prototyped in the Advanced Computer Architecture Program at MCC. In ORION we have directly implemented the object-oriented paradigm [GOLD81, GOLD83, BOBR83, SYMB84, BOBR85], added persistence and sharability to objects through transaction support, and provided various advanced functions that applications from the CAD/CAM, AI, and OIS domains require. Advanced functions supported in ORION include versions and change notification [CHOU86, CHOU87], composite objects [KIM87b], dynamic schema evolution [BANE87a, BANE87b], and multimedia data management [WOEL86, WOEL87].

ORION is a single-user, multi-task database system which runs in a workstation environment, and is intended for applications from the AI [STEF86], multimedia documents [AHLS84, IEEE85, WOEL86], and computer-aided design domains [AFSA86], implemented in the object-oriented programming paradigm. ORION has been implemented in Common LISP [STEE84] on a Symbolics 3600 LISP machine [SYMB85], and has also been ported to the SUN workstation under the UNIX operating system. The Symbolics version of ORION will directly support data management needs of a number of data-intensive application systems under development at MCC.

In Section 2 we present a high-level overview of the architecture of ORION. Sections 3 through 8 highlight six of the major features of ORION, namely, dynamic schema evolution, version control and change notification, composite objects, associative queries, transaction management, and multimedia information management, respectively. Section 9 summarizes the paper.

2. OVERVIEW OF THE ORION ARCHITECTURE

Figure 1 shows a high level block diagram of the ORION architecture. The message handler receives all messages sent to the ORION system. The messages include messages for user-defined methods, access messages, and system-defined functions. A *user-defined method* is a method that the user defines and stores in ORION. An *access message* is one that retrieves or updates the value of an attribute of a class. System-defined functions include all

ORION functions for schema definition, creation and deletion of instances, transaction management, and so on.

The object subsystem of ORION provides high-level functions, such as schema evolution, version control, query optimization, and multimedia information management.

The storage subsystem provides access to objects on disk. It manages the allocation and deallocation of segments of pages on disk, finds and places objects on the pages, and moves pages to and from the disk. It also manages indexes on attributes of a class to speed up the evaluation of associative queries.

The transaction subsystem provides a concurrency control and recovery mechanism to protect database integrity while allowing the interleaved execution of multiple concurrent transactions. Concurrency control uses a locking protocol, and a logging mechanim is used for recovery from system crashes and user-initiated aborts.

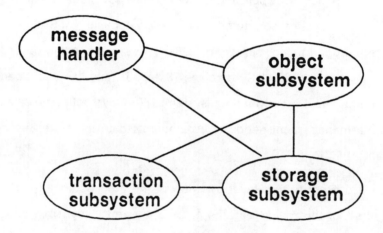

Figure 1.   ORION-1 Architecture

3. SCHEMA EVOLUTION

ORION applications require considerable flexibility in dynamically defining and modifying the database schema, that is, the class definitions and the inheritance structure of the class lattice [WOEL86]. Existing object-oriented systems support only a few types of changes to the schema, without requiring system shutdown. This is the consequence of the fact that existing object-oriented systems are programming language systems. Even existing conventional database systems allow only a few types of schema changes: for example, SQL/DS only allows a dynamic creation and deletion of relations (classes) and addition of new columns (instance variables) in a relation [IBM81]. This is because the applications they support (conventional record-oriented business applications) do not require more than a few types of schema changes, and also the data models they support are not as rich as object-oriented data models.

We have developed a taxonomy of schema change operations which are useful and which can be supported in a database system without causing either system shutdown or database reorganization. We have also developed a framework for understanding and enforcing the semantics of each schema change operation. Our formal framework consists of a set of properties of the schema called *invariants*, and a set of *rules* for preserving the invariants. The invariants hold at every quiescent state of the schema, that is, before and after a schema change operation. They provide a basis for the definition of the semantics of every meaningful schema change, by ensuring that the change does not leave the schema in an inconsistent state (one that violates any invariant). However, for some schema changes, the schema invariants can be preserved in more than one way. The rules guide the selection of one most meaningful way.

In this section, we provide a taxonomy of schema changes which we support in ORION, and summarize the set of invariants and rules. We refer the reader to [BANE87b] for a detailed discussion of schema evolution in ORION.

3.1 SCHEMA EVOLUTION TAXONOMY

ORION supports two types of schema changes to the contents and structure of a class lattice: changes to the definitions of a class (contents of a node) on a class lattice, and changes to the structure (edges and nodes) of a class lattice. Changes to the class definitions include adding and deleting attributes and methods. Changes to the class lattice structure include creation and deletion of a class, and alteration of the IS-A relationship between classes. The taxonomy of schema changes given below is an abbreviated version of that given in [BANE87b].

(1) Changes to the contents of a node (a class)

    (1.1) Changes to an attribute
        (1.1.1) Add a new attribute to a class
        (1.1.2) Drop an existing attribute from a class
        (1.1.3) Change the name of an attribute of a class
        (1.1.4) Change the domain of an attribute of a class
        (1.1.5) Change the inheritance (parent) of an attribute
                (inherit another attribute with the same name)

(1.2) Changes to a method

    (1.2.1) Add a new method to a class

    (1.2.2) Drop an existing method from a class

    (1.2.3) Change the name of a method of a class

    (1.2.4) Change the code of a method in a class

    (1.2.5) Change the inheritance (parent) of a method

         (inherit another method with the same name)

(2) Changes to an edge

    (2.1) Make a class S a superclass of a class C

    (2.2) Remove a class S from the superclass list of a class C

(3) Changes to a node

    (3.1) Add a new class

    (3.2) Drop an existing class

    (3.3) Change the name of a class

We review the semantics of four of the schema change operations: Operations 1.1.2, 2.1, 2.2, and 3.2.

(1.1.2) Drop an instance variable V from a class C

If V is dropped from C, it must also be dropped recursively from the subclasses that inherited it. If C or any of its subclasses has other superclasses that have instance variables of the same name as that of V, it inherits one of those instance variables. In case V must be dropped from C or any of its subclasses without a replacement, existing instances of these classes lose their values for V.

(2.1) Make a class S a superclass of a class C

The addition of a new edge from S to C must not introduce a cycle in the class lattice. C and its subclasses inherit instance variables and methods from S, provided that no name conflicts arise. Instances of C and its subclasses receive the null value for the newly inherited instance variables. Operations 1.1.1 and 1.2.1 are applied, respectively, to add instance variables and methods of S to C.

(2.2) Remove a class S from the superclass list of a class C

The deletion of an edge from S to C must not cause the class lattice to become disconnected. In case S is the only superclass of C, the immediate superclasses of S now become the immediate superclasses of C as well, while the ordering of these superclasses with respect to S remains the same for C. Thus, C does not lose any instance variables or methods that were inherited from the superclasses of S. C only loses those instance variables

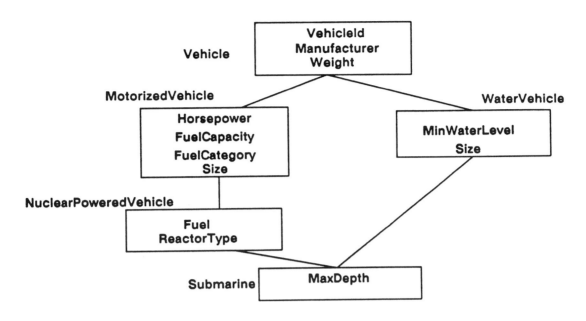

Figure 2. Resolution of Name Conflicts

and methods that were defined in S. If the deletion of the edge from S to C does not leave the disconnected, C is left with one fewer superclasses, and it must drop the instances variables and methods it had inherited from S. The operations for dropping an instance variable (Operation 1.1.2) and a method (Operation 1.2.2) are applied, respectively, for each instance variable and method to be dropped from C.

(3.2) Drop an existing class C

All edges from C to its subclasses are dropped, using operation 2.2. Next, all edges from the superclasses of C into C are removed. Finally, the definition of C is dropped, and C is removed from the lattice. The subclasses of C continue to exist. If the class C was the domain of an instance variable V1 of another class C1, V1 is assigned a new domain, namely the first superclass of the dropped class C.

3.2 INVARIANTS OF SCHEMA EVOLUTION

We have identified five invariants of the object–oriented schema from the ORION data model. They are summarized below.

class lattice invariant

The class lattice is a *rooted* and *connected directed acyclic graph* with named nodes and labeled edges. The DAG has only one root, a system–defined class called OBJECT. The DAG is connected, that is, there are no isolated nodes. Every node is reachable from the root.

Nodes are named, and each node in the DAG has a unique name. Edges are labeled such that all edges directed to any given node have distinct labels.

distinct name invariant

All instance variables of a class, whether defined or inherited, have distinct names. Similarly, all methods of a class, whether defined or inherited, must have distinct names.

distinct identity (origin) invariant

All instance variables, and methods, of a class have distinct identity (origin). For example, in Figure 2, the class Submarine can inherit the instance variable Weight from either the class WaterVehicle or NuclearPoweredVehicle. However, in both these superclasses, Weight has the same origin, namely, the instance variable Weight of the class Vehicle, where Weight was originally defined. Therefore, the class Submarine must have only one occurrence of the instance variable Weight.

full inheritance invariant

A class inherits all instance variables and methods from each of its superclasses, except when full inheritance causes a violation of the distinct name and distinct identity invariants. In other words, if two instance variables have distinct origin but the same name in two different superclasses, at least one of them must be inherited. If two instance variables have the same origin in two different superclasses, only one of them must be inherited. For example, in Figure 2, Submarine must inherit Size, whether it is from NuclearPoweredVehicle or from WaterVehicle, or even from both (by assigning new names, in order to maintain the distinct name invariant). Further, Submarine must inherit Weight only once, from either NuclearPoweredVehicle or WaterVehicle.

domain compatibility invariant

If an instance variable V2 of a class C is inherited from an instance variable V1 of a superclass of C, then the domain of V2 is either the same as that of V1, or a subclass of V1. For example, if the domain of the instance variable Manufacturer in the Vehicle class is the Company class, then the domain of Manufacturer in the MotorizedVehicle class, a subclass of Vehicle, can be Company or a subclass of Company, say, MotorizedVehicleCompany.

Another aspect of the domain compatibility invariant is that the shared value or default value of an instance variable must be an instance of the class that is the domain of that instance variable.

160

3.3 RULES OF SCHEMA EVOLUTION

A class lattice in a quiescent state must preserve all the invariants. For some of the schema changes, however, there is more than one way to preserve the invariants. For example, if there is a name conflict among instance variables to be inherited from superclasses, the full inheritance invariant requires that at least one of the instance variables be inherited; but it does not say which. In order to guide the selection of one option among many in an algorithmic and meaningful way, we have established twelve essential rules, including some which we have adopted from existing object-oriented systems. These rules are discussed in [BANE87b], and will not be presented here.

The rules fall into four categories: default conflict resolution rules, property propagation rules, DAG manipulation rules, and composite object rules. The *default conflict resolution rules* permit the selection of a single inheritance option whenever there is a name or identity conflict. They ensure that the distinct name and distinct identity invariants are satisfied in a deterministic way. The ORION user may, however, override these rules by explicit requests to resolve conflicts differently.

The properties of an instance variable, once defined or inherited into a class, can be modified in a number of ways. In particular, its name, domain, default value, shared value, or the composite link property may be changed. Also, an instance variable that is not shared-valued can be made shared-valued, or vice versa. Further, the properties of a method belonging to a class may be modified by changing its name or code. The *property propagation rules* provide guidelines for supporting all changes to the properties of instance variables and methods.

The *DAG manipulation rules* govern the addition and deletion of nodes and edges from the class lattice. These rules ensure that drastic changes are avoided when an edge or a node is added to or removed from a class lattice.

The composite object rules are used to enforce the semantics of composite objects, as we will show in Section 5.

4. VERSIONS AND CHANGE NOTIFICATION

There is a general consensus that version control is one of the most important functions in various data-intensive application domains, such as integrated CAD/CAM systems [KATZ84, KATZ86, CHOU86] and Office Information Systems dealing with compound documents

[WOEL86]. Users in such environments often need to generate and experiment with multiple versions of an object, before selecting one that satisfies their requirements.

An object in general recursively references other 'lower level' objects. An object may be referenced (shared) by any number of objects, and may in turn reference any number of other objects. When an object is updated or deleted, or a new version of the object is created, some or all of the objects that have referenced it may become invalid, and thus need to be notified of the change [NEUM82].

This section provides a summary of ORION support for versions and change notification. We refer the interested reader to [CHOU86, CHOU87] for additional details.

4.1 VERSIONS

We distinguish two types of versions on the basis of the types of operations that are allowed on them. They are transient and working versions.

A *transient version* has the following properties.

1. It can be updated by the user who created it.

2. It can be deleted by the user who created it.

3. A new transient version may be derived from an existing transient version. The existing transient version then is 'promoted' to a working version.

A *working version* has the following properties.

1. It is considered stable and cannot be updated.

2. It can be deleted by its owner.

3. A transient version can be derived from a working version.

4. A transient version can be 'promoted' to a working version. Promotion may be explicit (user-specified) or implicit (system-determined).

The reason we impose the update restriction on working versions is that it is considered stable and thus transient versions can be derived from it. If a working version is to be directly updated, after one or more transient versions have been derived from it, we need a set of careful update algorithms (for insert, delete, and update) which will ensure that the derived versions will not see the updates in the working version.

There are two ways to *bind* an object with another versioned object: static and dynamic. In *static binding*, the reference to an object includes the full name of the object, the object identifier and the version number. In *dynamic binding* [KATZ84, ATWO85], the reference needs to specify only the object identifier, and may leave the version number unspecified. The system selects the default version number. Clearly, dynamic binding is useful, since transient or working versions that are referenced may be deleted, and new versions created.

Implementation

Because of the performance and storage overhead in supporting versions, we require the application to indicate whether a class is *versionable*. When an instance of a versionable class is created, a *generic object* for that instance is created, along with the first version of that instance. A generic object is essentially a data structure for the version-derivation hierarchy of an instance of a versionable class. It is deleted when the version-derivation hierarchy for its instance contains no versioned object. A generic object consists of the following system-defined instance variables:

1. default version number,
2. a next-version number,
3. a version count, and
4. a set of version descriptors, one for each existing version on the version-derivation hierarchy of the object.

The default version number determines which existing version on the version-derivation hierarchy should be chosen when a partially specified reference is dynamically bound. The next-version number is the version number to be assigned to the next version of the object that will be created. It is incremented after being assigned to the new version.

A version descriptor contains control information for each version on a version-derivation hierarchy. It includes

1. the version number of the version,
2. the identifier of the versioned object
3. a list of references to the descriptors of child versions,

Further, each version instance of a versionable object contains three system-defined attributes, in addition to all user-defined attributes. We allow the application to read, but not to update, any of these attributes.

1. version number
2. version type
3. object identifier of its generic object

The version number is needed simply to distinguish a version instance of a versionable object from other version instances of the same versionable object. The version type indicates whether the version instance is a transient version or working version. This information is maintained, so that the system may easily reject an attempt to update a working version. The generic object identifier is required, so that, given a version instance, any other version instances of the versionable object may be found efficiently.

messages

A versioned object is created initially by the *create* command, which creates the generic-object data structure for the object. The *derive* command is used to derive a new transient version and allocate a new version number for it. If the parent was a transient version, it is automatically promoted to a working version. The *replace* operation causes the contents of a transient version to be replaced by a workspace copy the user specifies. A transient version is explicitly promoted to a working version, making the version non-updatable, through the *promote* command. The user may delete a version or an entire version-derivation hierarchy using the *delete* command. If the delete is against a generic object, all versions of the instance for which the generic object was created are deleted. If a working version is deleted from which other versions have been derived, the version is deleted, but the fact that the version existed is not deleted from the generic object. The user uses the *set_default* command to specify the default version on a version-derivation hierarchy of an object. A specific version number or the keyword 'most-recent' may be specified as the default.

4.2 CHANGE NOTIFICATION

In a distributed environment, change notification involves both sending mail messages from the server to the workstations, and recording timestamps in data structures associated with the objects. In ORION, only the version timestamping technique has been implemented. Each object that participates in change notification has two distinct timestamps. One timestamp, called the *change-notification timestamp*, indicates the time the object was created or the last time it was updated. The other, called *change-approval timestamp*, indicates the last time at which the owner of the object approved all changes to the objects it references.

Let V.CA and V.CN denote the change-approval and change-notification timestamps of an object V. Let R be the set of objects that are referenced by object V. If no object in R has a change-notification timestamp that exceeds the change-approval timestamp of V (i.e, for all X in R, X.CN <= V.CA), then V is *reference-consistent*. V is *reference-inconsistent* if there are one or more objects in R that have been updated, but the effects of these updates on V have not been determined.

To make V reference-consistent, the effects of the updated objects in R must be determined, and, if necessary, V must be updated. If the updates to objects in R have no effect on V, only V.CA needs to be changed to the current time. Otherwise, V.CN (and possibly V.CA if the changes are approved) will need to be set to the current time.

Implementation

ORION supports change notification as an option on user-specified attributes of a class. The user may specify attributes to be *notification-sensitive*; if a change occurs on the value of any of these attributes of an instance of the class, the instance is notified of the change.

ORION provides three system-defined attributes for a class for which the notify option is on.

1. change-notification timestamp

2. change-approval timestamp

3. a set of change-notification events

The change-notification timestamp associated with an object indicates the last time at which a change has been made to the object. The change-approval timestamp indicates the last time the user approved changes to all objects referenced through all notification-sensitive attributes. Changes are notified either on an update or on a delete operation, or both. 'Delete' is the default, and 'update' subsumes 'delete'.

If the class D is the domain of a notification sensitive attribute of a class C, then each instance of D, as well as D's subclasses, contains a change-notification timestamp. Whenever a new instance d of D (or a subclass of D) is created, or an existing instance is changed, its change-notification timestamp captures the time of that event. At a later time, when an instance c of C makes a reference to the instance d through a notification-sensitive attribute, the user or application can compare the change-approval timestamp of c with the change-notification timestamp of d, and decide whether the change to d needs approval. When an instance d of the class D is deleted, an instance c of C will have a dangling reference. The dangling reference is itself an indication of reference-inconsistency, if the reference is made through a notification-sensitive attribute. The system maintains the information necessary to determine if an instance is reference-consistent. However, it is the user's or application's responsibility to determine reference-consistency, and then take measures to make the instance reference-consistent, if necessary.

5. COMPOSITE OBJECTS

The notions of instance variables, domains, and object identifier, although powerful, cannot represent the IS-PART-OF relationship between objects. The IS-PART-OF relationship captures the notion that an object *is a part of* another object; and, along with the IS-A relationship, is one of the fundamental data modeling concepts. A composite object is that part of a conventional nested object on which we impose the IS-PART-OF relationship.

Many applications require the ability to define and manipulate a set of objects as a single logical entity for the purposes of semantic integrity, and efficient storage and retrieval [LORI83, IEEE85, KIM87a]. We define a *composite object* as an object with a hierarchy of exclusive component objects, and refer to the hierarchy of classes to which the objects belong as a *composite object hierarchy*. A non-root class on a composite object hierarchy is called a *component class*. Each non-leaf class on a composite object hierarchy has one or more instance variables whose domains are the component classes. We call such instance variables *composite instance variables*. A constituent object of a composite object references an instance of its component class through a composite instance variable. We call such a reference a *composite reference* or *composite link* between an object and its dependent object (or between a class and its component class).

In this section, we summarize the semantics of composite objects, and two ways in which we make use of them to enhance performance of retrieving composite objects. The interested reader will find more details in [KIM87b].

5.1 SEMANTICS

dependent objects

Composite objects augment the semantic integrity of an object-oriented data model through the notion of dependent objects. A *dependent object* is one whose existence depends on the existence of another object, and is owned by exactly one object. For example, we show the schema for a class Vehicle in Figure 3. The body of a vehicle is owned by one specific vehicle, and cannot exist without the vehicle that contains it. As such, a dependent object cannot be created if its owner does not already exist. This means that a constituent object (except the root) of a composite object cannot be created, unless its parent exists. Further, when a constituent object of a composite object is deleted, all its dependent objects must also be deleted.

In a composite object, no dependent object can be referenced more than once. Thus, a composite object is a hierarchy of objects (and not a general digraph). However, any object within a composite object can be referenced by objects that do not belong to the composite object through a non-composite link. These references can have the complete generality of a digraph, including cycles. For example, an instance of the class Vehicle can have a composite link to an instance of the class AutoBody through the instance variable Body. No other instance of Vehicle can reference this instance of AutoBody through the instance variable Body. Further, if an instance of some other class, say Inventory, has a reference to this instance of AutoBody, the reference must be through a non-composite instance variable.

Further, a class may be the domain of more than one composite instance variable. However, again only one object may have a composite reference to any instance of the class as a dependent object. For example, two classes Car and Truck may both have a composite instance variable Body whose domain is the class Autobody. However, no instance of AutoBody can simultaneously be a part of a Car and a Truck.

schema evolution on a composite object hierarchy

The composite link property of an instance variable of a class is inherited by all subclasses of that class. For example, if the class Automobile is a subclass of Vehicle, it inherits the

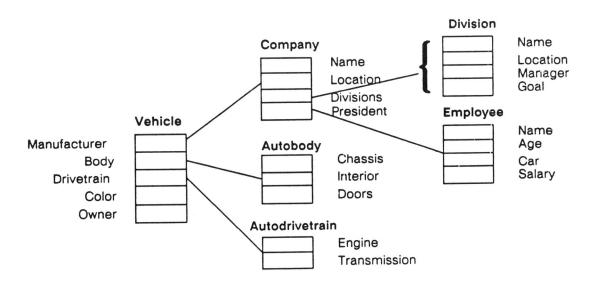

Figure 3.   Schema for Class Vehicle

instance variable Body from Vehicle. Further, because Body is a composite instance variable in the Vehicle class, it will also be a composite instance variable in the Automobile class.

A composite instance variable may be changed to a non-composite instance variable, that is, it may lose the composite link property. However, we do not allow a non-composite instance variable to later acquire the composite link property. The reason is that an object may be referenced by any number of instances of a class through a non-composite instance variable, but a dependent object of a composite object may be referenced by only one instance of a class through a composite instance variable. To change a non-composite instance variable to a composite instance variable, it is necessary to verify that existing instances are not referenced by more than one instance through the instance variable. This in turn makes it necessary to maintain a list of reference counts with each object, one reference count for each instance variable through which the object may be referenced. We avoid this complexity in ORION by not permitting a non-composite instance variable to be changed to a composite instance variable.

The integrity of a composite object lies in the fact that all dependent objects owe their existence to their parents. In particular, if a parent object is deleted, all its dependent objects are deleted; and if a parent object loses a composite instance variable, the dependent object referenced is deleted. However, we allow objects to *disown* their dependents, if their composite instance variables are changed to non-composite. Disowned objects are not deleted when their previous parents are deleted, since they are no longer dependent on the existence of their previous parents.

The composite link property impacts the semantics of only the Operations (1.1.2, 1.1.5, 2.1, 2.2, 2.3, and 3.2). Its impact on Operation 1.1.2 is as follows. The instance variable must of course be dropped from all subclasses of the class. All instances of these classes are affected as well. They lose their values for the dropped instance variable. Further, to preserve integrity, all objects that are recursively dependent on the dropped instances must also be dropped. For example, when the instance variable Body is dropped from the class Vehicle, all objects dependent on instances of Vehicle and its subclasses through the instance variable Body will have to be deleted from the database. Many instances of AutoBody may thus be deleted. However, not all instances of AutoBody need be deleted. Those that are not a part of composite objects rooted at instances of Vehicle or its subclasses will continue to exist.

168

5.2 PERFORMANCE ENHANCEMENT USING COMPOSITE OBJECTS

We now discuss two important ways in which we use the semantics of composite objects in ORION to improve the performance of the system. One is to use the composite object as a unit of clustering in the database, so that a large collection of related objects may be retrieved efficiently from the database. Another is to use it as the unit of locking, so that the number of locks that must be set may be minimized in retrieving a composite object from the database.

5.2.1 Clustering Composite Objects

The notion of a composite object also offers an opportunity to improve the performance of a database system. A composite object may be used as a unit for clustering related objects in the database. This is because, when an application accesses the root object, it is often likely to access all (or most) dependent objects as well. Thus, it is advantageous to store all constituents of a composite object as close to one another as possible on secondary storage.

In ORION all instances of the same class are placed in the same storage segment on disk. Thus, a class is associated with a single segment, and all its instances reside in that segment. The user does not have to be aware of segments; ORION automatically allocates a separate segment for each class. For clustering composite objects, however, it is often advantageous to store instances of multiple classes in the same segment. User assistance is required to determine which classes should share the same segment.

The user may issue a Cluster message as a hint for ORION to cluster instances of a class with instances of other classes. A Cluster message specifies a list of class names. Instances of classes listed in the list are to be placed in a single segment. The user may sometimes need to cluster a new class C with some existing classes which have already been allocated a segment. In that case, the user needs to issue a Cluster message, in which the list of class names is a pair, namely, the class C and any one of the existing classes with which C should share a segment. Instances of C will then share the same segment with the existing classes.

5.2.2 Locking Composite Objects

The fundamental motivation of the *granularity locking protocol* in today's commercial database systems is to minimize the number of locks to be set in accessing the database [GRAY78]. For example, when most of the instances of a class are to be accessed, it makes sense to set one lock for the entire class, rather than one lock for each instance. A lock on a class will imply a lock on each instance of the class. However, when only a few instances of a class need to be accessed, it is better to lock the instances individually, so that other concurrent transactions may access any other instances. The shortcoming of the granularity locking protocol is that it does not recognize a composite object as a single lockable granule, like a class or an instance of a class. To lock a composite object using the granularity locking protocol will mean either locking all component classes on a composite object hierarchy, or locking all constituent objects within a composite object. Neither option is satisfactory: the first option will result in the locking of all composite objects that belong to the composite object hierarchy; and the second option can result in a large number of locks.

In an environment where multiple applications may concurrently access a shared database, a composite object may be used as a unit of locking to reduce the system overhead associated with concurrency control; that is, a composite object should be locked as a unit, rather than requiring a lock for each component of a composite object. The locking protocol is given in [KIM87b], and will not be repeated here.

6. QUERIES AND QUERY OPTIMIZATION

In this section, we provide the model of queries which has been implemented in ORION, and indicate a broad strategy for processing a given query. Further details are found in [BANE88].

6.1 QUERY MODEL

The object–oriented data model, in its conventional form, allows one to represent an arbitrarily complex object as a recursively nested object. An object may be defined with a set of attributes. A class may be specified as the *domain* of an attribute; and the domain class, unless it is a *primitive class* (such as the string, integer, or boolean class), in turn consists of a set of attributes, and so on. The internal state of an object consists of the values of all its attributes. The value of an attribute is an instance of its domain, if the domain is a primitive class; and a reference to (*object identifier* of) an instance of the domain, otherwise. If the domain of an attribute is a set of a class, the value of that attribute for any instance will be a set of object identifiers. If an attribute of a class may take on a single instance of the domain, we will call it a *scalar attribute*; otherwise, we will call it a *set attribute*.

For example, in Figure 3, we show the schema of a Vehicle class in terms of the attributes Manufacturer, Body, Drivetrain, Color, and Owner. The domain of the Color attribute is the primitive String class. The domain of the Manufacturer attribute is the class Company, the attribute Body has Autobody as its domain, and the domain of Drivetrain is the AutoDrivetrain class. The classes Company, AutoBody, and AutoDrivetrain each consist of their own set of attributes, which in turn have associated domains. The domain of the President attribute of the class Company is the class Employee. The attribute Divisions of the class Company is a set attribute whose domain is the class Division. (This is represented by the brace in Figure 3.)

The nesting of an object through the domains of its attributes immediately suggests that to fully fetch an instance, the instance and all objects it references through its attributes must be recursively fetched. This means that to fetch one or more instances of a class, the class and all classes specified as non-primitive domains of the attributes of the class must be recursively traversed. For example, to fetch instances of the class Vehicle in Figure 3, the classes which need to be traversed include not only Vehicle, but also the domains of non-primitive attributes of Vehicle, namely, Company, AutoBody, AutoDrivetrain, as well as the domains of non-primitive attributes of these classes.

A query may be formulated against an object-oriented schema, which will fetch instances of a class which satisfy certain search criteria. A query may restrict the instances of a class to be fetched by specifying predicates against any attributes of the class. In [BANE88] we show that the predicates on the attributes, and attributes themselves, may be expressed using a message-based syntax. An attribute may be one of two types: simple and complex. A *simple attribute* is one whose domain is a primitive class. A *complex attribute* is one whose domain is a class with one or more attributes, including other complex attributes. A predicate (a relational operator message, such as >, <, =, etc.) on a simple attribute is called a *simple predicate*; while one on a complex attribute is called a *complex predicate*. Further, a query that involves only simple predicates is called a *simple query*; and one that involves one or more complex predicates is called a *complex query*.

We may represent a class and the domains of all its complex attributes involved in a query in the form of a directed graph, which we will call a *query graph*. Each node on a query graph represents a class, and an edge from a node A to a node B means that the class B is the domain of a complex attribute of a class A. A query graph has only one root, the class whose instances are to be fetched. Each leaf node of a query graph has only simple attributes. A query graph may contain cycles.

6.2 QUERY PROCESSING

A query with one complex predicate on a class requires the traversal of two classes; the class on which the predicate is applied, and the class that is the domain of the complex instance variable. A complex query, as it involves a number of classes, brings out many of the same issues that complicate joins of relations in relational databases [SELI79]. It is important to consider all meaningful permutations of classes in the query graph representation of a query in object-oriented databases. However, the semantics of queries in object-oriented databases make it possible to eliminate many of the permutations of classes which may not be eliminated in evaluating relational queries [BANE88].

Given any permutation of n classes, there are two fundamental ways of traversing the classes in the permutation: forward and reverse traversal. In the *forward traversal*, the classes on a query graph are traversed in a depth-first order starting from the root of the query graph, and following through the successive domains of each complex instance variable. In the *reverse traversal*, the leaf classes of a query graph are visited first, and then their parents, working toward the root class. The following illustrates the two traversal techniques.

(1)   *Forward traversal*: As an example, let us consider the following query based on the schema of Figure 3. (As the semantics of the query is relatively clear from the syntax, we will not explain it here.)

Q1.   (select 'Vehicle '(equal Manufacturer Name "Ford")

A forward traversal for the query will start with the set of all instances of the class Vehicle. For each of these instances, the value of its attribute Manufacturer is traversed next. That value is an instance of the class Company, and has an attribute Name. The value of the attribute Name is traversed next. It has a simple value (an instance of the primitive class String). If the value is the string "Ford", the Company instance qualifies. In turn, the Vehicle instance which has that Company instance as its manufacturer also qualifies.

A query containing Boolean operators may also be evaluated via forward traversal. Consider the following query:

Q2.   (select 'Vehicle '(and   (equal Manufacturer Name "Ford")

                                             (< Owner Age 20)))

A forward traversal will again start with the set of all instances of Vehicle. Each instance of Vehicle qualifies if the forward traversal is successful along both the logical paths (Manufacturer Name) and (Owner Age).

(2)   *Reverse traversal*: Consider once again the query Q1. Instead of starting with the set of all instances of Vehicle, reverse traversal starts the Name attribute of the class Company (and its subclasses). All instances of Company are identified which have the name

"Ford". The identifiers of these instances are now looked up in the Manufacturer attribute of the instances of the class Vehicle.

Reverse traversal is usually mixed with forward traversal when Boolean operators are present. As an example, consider the query Q2. After reverse traversal is performed along the path (Manufacturer Name), the result is a set of Vehicle instances. Instances of this set are now traversed forward along the path (Owner Age), and only those instances are retained whose owner's age is less than 20.

7. TRANSACTION MANAGEMENT

ORION satisfies the concurrency control requirements of the rich object-oriented data model it supports, in particular, operations on a class lattice and composite objects. ORION incorporates important enhancements to the performance of transactions, including the concepts of sessions and hypothetical transactions. A session is a sequence of transactions, and the active transaction of a session may exist simultaneously in multiple windows on a workstation to alleviate the problem of long-duration waits in long-duration transactions in interactive application environments. A hypothetical transaction is a transaction which always aborts, and is important in application environments in which the users often experiment with 'what-if' changes to the database. A hypothetical transaction allows the database system to avoid much of the overhead involved in concurrency control and recovery of normal transactions.

In this section, we summarize our implementation of the sessions and hypothetical transactions, and summarize our approach to concurrency control and recovery. [GARZ87] describes transaction management in ORION in greater detail.

7.1 SESSIONS

A *session* encapsulates a sequence of transactions. Since the transactions within a session are strictly serial, that is, one transaction ends before the next one starts, there is only one active transaction per session. Hence, the same workspace can be serially used to keep track of properties of all transactions within the session. Thus, the concept of session is useful for improved system performance.

A user can use ORION by first creating a session or using the default session the system provides. A *default session* is created immediately upon the initialization or restart of ORION. The user may open and close any number of session, and multiple windows (or multiple UNIX shells) for the same session (including the default session). All windows of the session run the same transaction, the currently active transaction of the session. Any active transaction of a session will compete for resources (via locking) with those of all other sessions (including the default session).

ORION allows a session to have multiple windows primarily as a short-term solution to the problem of long-duration wait problem that arises in long-duration interactive transactions [HASK82, KIM84, KATZ84]. In a future version of ORION, we plan to implement the long-transaction model which we have proposed earlier [BANC85, KORT87]. When multiple sessions are concurrently active, the active transaction of a particular session S may be blocked if it cannot obtain a lock. In such an event, no more requests will be processed from the blocked window until either (1) a certain installation-determined time-out period expires, or (2) the requested lock is obtained. If the user wishes to continue with session S even while waiting for the lock, the user may do so by creating another window for S. Since all windows of a session run the same transaction, they share the same locks; thus a user may create two windows with the same session name, update an object in one window, and examine (or even update) the same object in another window.

The user may close the windows of a session one at a time. If the closed window happens to be the only window of the session, the session itself is closed. If the presently active transaction of that session has not been committed or aborted, ORION automatically aborts that transaction, and then closes the session. Once a window is closed, the most recently deactivated session of that window is reactivated. In other words, on a single window, sessions are activated and deactivated in a stack-like fashion. The user cannot close the default session; it remains open until an ORION shutdown.

ORION supports two types of transactions: normal and hypothetical. A session may contain any sequence of normal and hypothetical transactions. When a normal transaction commits, all its updates are permanently recorded in the database; and when it aborts, all its changes are undone, and irretrievably lost. A *hypothetical transaction*, in contrast, is a transaction that always aborts. No matter how such a transaction is ended, its changes are never reflected in the database. Thus, hypothetical transactions provide a mechanism for experimenting with the effects of 'what-if' changes to the database. Since the changes are never recorded permanently, the user has the freedom of examining the impact of complex changes to the database, and yet does not have to worry that the database will become corrupted or unavailable due to conflicting concurrent transactions. The concept of a hypothetical transaction is related to that of a hypothetical database proposed in [STON80, STON81].

Of course, the conventional transaction mechanism, with its abort option, can be used to provide the desired effect of a hypothetical transaction. However, the conventional transaction mechanism incurs significant overhead to make it possible for a transaction to be recoverable and to shield a transaction from the effects of other concurrently executing transactions. Within a hypothetical transaction, the first time an object is updated, a copy of the object is made for all subsequent updates within the transaction. The initial object is never updated. We call the initial object the *shadow copy*, and the new copy that gets updated the *current copy*. The current copy is discarded when the transaction terminates, regardless of whether the transaction commits or aborts. Further, each hypothetical transaction has its own current copy of an object for updates, so that multiple hypothetical transactions may concurrently update the same object.

Since a hypothetical transaction makes updates only to the current copy of an object, and each hypothetical transaction has its own current copy of the object, only a Share (S) lock needs to be set on the single shadow copy of an object, both for read and update. An S lock is needed, to prevent some concurrently executing non-hypothetical transaction from directly updating the shadow copy of the object, thereby causing the hypothetical transaction to read *dirty data,* data that is subject to a backout by the non-hypothetical transaction.

7.2 CONCURRENCY CONTROL

The ORION transaction subsystem provides a concurrency control mechanism to protect the database integrity while allowing the interleaved execution of multiple concurrent transactions. We have chosen the locking technique for our concurrency control mechanism. One reason is that locking is a well-understood technique, having been used in most commercial database systems. Another reason is that the current theory of locking provides a sound basis for the incorporation of the sophisticated concurrency control requirements.

Transactions in ORION are *serializable transactions*, which means that ORION completely isolates a transaction from the effects of all other concurrently executing transactions. A serializable transaction acquires a read lock before reading an object, and a write lock before updating an object [GRAY78]. This corresponds to the notion of level-3 consistency in

SQL/DS, and protects a transaction from such consistency anomalies as lost updates, dirty read, and un-repeatable read [IBM81].

Object-oriented databases require three types of hierarchy locking. One is the conventional granularity-hierarchy locking, to minimize the number of locks to be set. To support granularity locking, a database is modeled as a hierarchy (in general, a directed acyclic graph) of successively smaller entities (commonly called *locking granules*), and an explicit lock on any given node of the hierarchy implies locking of all its descendant nodes. As shown in Figure 4, a database may consist of a number classes (relations) and indexes on the classes; a class consists of instances, and an index on a class has pointers to instances of the class. For example, when a write (W) lock is set on a class, all instances of the class are implicitly locked in W mode.

[GRAY78] presents the locking protocol used in SQL/DS for granularity locking. Briefly, to set an R or W lock on a node of the lock-granularity hierarchy, all ancestors of the node are first locked in *intention mode*, either intention read (IR) or intention write (IW), respectively, in a root-to-leaf order. When an explicit lock on a node is released, the intention-mode locks on the ancestors of the node are released in a leaf-to-root order when a transaction terminates.

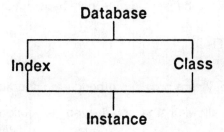

Figure 4.   Hierarchy of Lock Granules

The other two types of locking requirements for ORION applications necessitate significant extensions to the current theory of locking. One is the class lattice. In object-oriented systems, a class inherits attributes and methods from its superclasses, which in turn inherit these properties from their superclasses. Therefore, while a class and its instances are being accessed, ORION must ensure that the definitions of the class's superclasses (and their superclasses) will not be modified.

A second extension to the current theory of locking concerns the composite objects. A composite object is a collection of logically related objects, for example, an assembly of parts, which ORION will treat as a unit of physical clustering, integrity, and locking. Ideally, we should set one lock for the entire composite object, rather than one on each of the component objects.

We have developed and implemented lock modes and locking protocols which satisfy all three types of locking requirements. Further details are given in [GARZ87, KIM87b]. The current commercial database systems only support one of the three requirements, namely the granularity locking.

7.3 RECOVERY

Transaction recovery means preservation of the atomicity property of a transaction. This means that, ideally, despite all possible failures of the computer system all updates of a committed transaction will be reflected in the database, and all updates of an aborted transaction will be purged from the database. Of course, no database system can support transaction recovery against all possible failures of the computer system, which may include simultaneous failures of the processor, main memory, secondary memory, and communication medium between processors.

Most commercial database systems support database recovery from soft crashes (which leave the contents of disk intact) and hard crashes (which destroy the contents of disk). ORION supports transaction recovery only from soft crashes and user-initiated transaction abort. In other words, ORION does not support archival dumping of the database to recover from disk head crashes. The need to support multiple concurrent transactions led us to select the logging scheme over the shadow-page scheme [GRAY81]. There are three options in a log-based transaction recovery scheme: maintain only the UNDO log, only the REDO log, or both the UNDO and REDO logs. We have implemented the UNDO logging option, after weighing the advantages and disadvantages of each option.

UNDO logging means that only the before values of the attributes of an object will be recorded in the log. If a transaction aborts, the log is read backward to back out all updates. When a transaction commits, the log is first forced to disk, and then all pages updated by the transaction are forced to disk, consistent with the Write Ahead Log protocol [GRAY78]. Note that the pages containing updated objects are forced to disk: this is necessary because if the updates only remain in the database buffer and the system crashes, there is no way to re-do

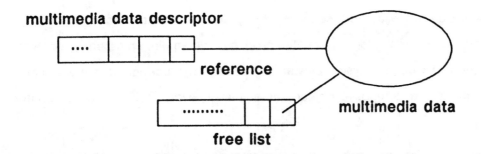

Figure 5. Logging of Multimedia Data

them using the UNDO log. This is one drawback of UNDO logging. The other two logging options require only the log pages to be forced to disk.

multimedia data logging

[HASK82] pointed out that a naive use of the logging techniques can cause some serious problems for the long, multimedia data that ORION must support. A strict log-based recovery will keep UNDO and/or REDO logs of very long data. As shown in Figure 5, we distinguish a multimedia data from its descriptor. The descriptor references, via an object identifier, the multimedia data. The storage subsystem maintains a free list of storage blocks which may be allocated for storing multimedia data. The long data manager in the object subsystem logs the changes in the descriptors and the free list, but not the multimedia data. In this way, if a transaction that created a multimedia data aborts, the descriptor will be returned to referencing nil, and the entry in the free list which points to the storage block allocated to the multimedia data will be reset as available for allocation. Similarly, if a transaction that deleted a multimedia data aborts, the reference in the descriptor will be returned to its initial value and the free-list entry will be deleted. This technique, proposed in [HASK82], achieves the shadowing effect, without the complexity associated with the conventional shadowing mechanism [LORI77, GRAY81].

8. MULTIMEDIA INFORMATION MANAGEMENT

In ORION we have attempted to satisfy three major design objectives for supporting the capture, storage, and presentation of many types of multimedia information: extensibility, flexibility and efficiency. The requirement for extensibility (generalizability and modifiability) is the ability for the system developers and end users to extend the system, by adding new types of devices and protocols for the capture, storage, and presentation of multimedia information.

Flexibility refers to fine control over the capture and presentation of multimedia objects. It is important to be able to store and retrieve both one and two-dimensional multimedia objects, and to transfer multimedia objects into the application workspace or the presentation devices. Further, it is useful to allow control (such as pause, resume, rewind, etc.) of both the capture and presentation of multimedia objects.

Efficiency is important both in storage utilization and data transfer performance. Multimedia objects are in general very large, and keeping multiple copies of large objects such as images and audio can lead to a serious waste of secondary storage media. Multimedia applications require the transfer of large amounts of data between capture devices, storage devices, and presentation devices. In some cases, this information will be transferred from a storage device to a presentation device without ever being written to the system memory. In many cases, however, the digitized multimedia object will be buffered in the system memory.

In this section, we further elaborate on these requirements and summarize the approach we have used in ORION to satisfy them. The interested reader will find details in [WOEL87].

8.1 EXTENSIBILITY

Extensibility is required to support new multimedia devices and new functions on multimedia information. For example, a color display device may be added to a system with relative ease, if at a high level of abstraction the color display can be viewed as a more specialized presentation device for spatial multimedia objects than a more general display device which is already supported in the system. The color display device may be further specialized by adding windowing software, and the windows can in turn be specialized to create new display and input functionality. It is also important to be able to add new multimedia storage devices, or to change the operating characteristics of storage devices. For example, read-only CD ROM [CDRO86] disks and write-once digital optical disks [CHRI86] are both storage devices having desirable characteristics for the storage of certain types of multimedia information.

We have implemented the multimedia information manager (MIM) component of ORION as an extensible framework explicitly using the object-oriented concepts. The framework consists of definitions of class hierarchies and a message passing protocol for not only the multimedia capture, storage, and presentation devices, but also the captured and stored multimedia objects. Both the class hierarchies and the protocol may be easily extended and/or modified by system developers and end users as they see fit.

Class Lattices

Multimedia information is captured, stored, and presented in ORION using lattices of classes which represent capture devices, storage devices, captured objects, and presentation devices. However, each instance of one of the device classes represents more than just the identity of a physical device as we will describe in the following paragraphs. The class lattices for the presentation and storage of multimedia information are described in this section. The class lattice for capture device classes is not described here due to space limitations. The capture device class lattice is described in [WOEL87].

The class lattice for the presentation of multimedia information is described below. The pre-defined presentation-device instances can be stored in the database and used for presenting the same multimedia object using different presentation formats. Methods associated with a class are used to initialize parameters of a presentation device and initiate the presentation process. The class lattice for the presentation devices is shown in Figure 6. The shaded classes are provided with ORION. Other classes in the lattice are shown to indicate potential specializations for other media types by specific installations.

Every multimedia object stored in ORION is represented by an instance of the class captured-object or one of its subclasses. Figure 7 illustrates the class lattice for captured objects. The captured-object class defines an attribute named storage-object which has as its domain the class storage-device. The class lattice for storage devices and for disk streams are also shown in Figure 7. Transfer of data to and from storage-device instances is controlled

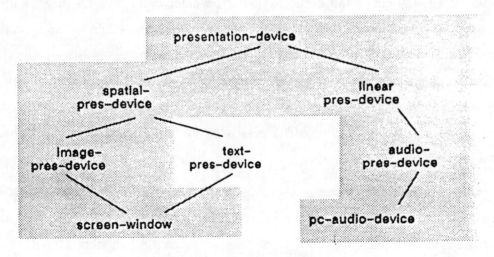

Figure 6.   Presentation Device
Class Lattice

180

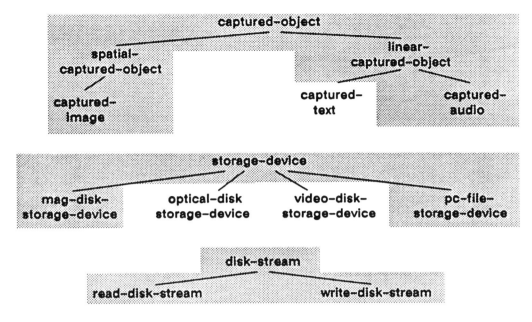

Figure 7.   Captured-Object, Storage-Device, and Disk Stream Class Lattices

through disk-stream instances. An instance of the read-disk-stream class is created whenever a multimedia object is read from disk. The read-disk-stream instance has a storage-object attribute which references the mag-disk-storage-device instance for the multimedia object. It also has a read-block-list attribute which maintains a cursor indicating the next block of the multimedia object to be read from disk. Similarly, an instance of the write-disk-stream class is created whenever data is written to a multimedia object. The shaded classes in Figure 7 are provided with ORION. Other classes in the lattice indicate potential specializations.

Message Passing Protocol

ORION supports presentation of multimedia information using a message-passing protocol between instances of the presentation device, storage device, and stored object classes. The protocol is fully described in [WOEL87]. In this section we outline the protocol for the presentation of multimedia information. The protocol will be discussed by using the example of a bit-mapped image; however, the protocol is similar for many types of multimedia information.

Figure 8 shows an instance of the vehicle class which has been defined by an application program. It also shows instances of the image-pres-device, captured-image, read-disk-stream, and mag-disk-storage-device classes described earlier. The arrows

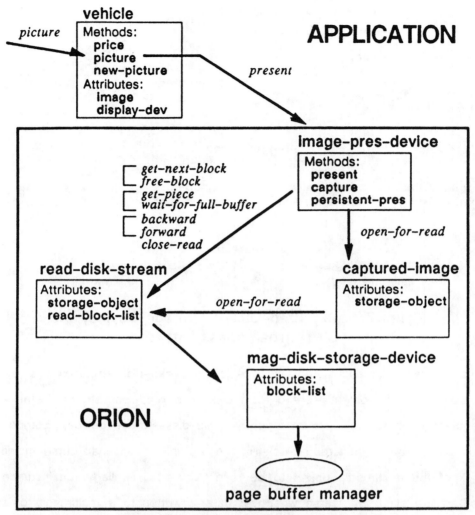

Figure 8.   Message Passing Protocol for Presentation of Multimedia Information

represent messages sent from one instance to another instance. The vehicle instance has the image attribute that specifies the identity of a captured-image instance that represents a picture of the vehicle. It also has the display-dev attribute that specifies the identity of an image-pres-device instance. This image-pres-device instance has attributes pre-defined by the user that specify where the image is to be displayed on the screen and what part of the image should be displayed. When the vehicle instance receives the picture message, the picture method defined for the class vehicle will send a present message to the specified image-pres-device instance.

The present method of the image-pres-device class transfers image data from the captured-image instance and displays the image on a display device. The image-pres-device instance has attributes which specify the rectangular portion of the image to be displayed. It translates these rectangular coordinates into linear coordinates to be used for reading the image data from disk. It then initiates the reading of data by sending the open-for-read message to the captured-image instance.

The captured-image instance then creates a read-disk-stream instance and returns its identity to the image-pres-device instance. The image-pres-device will then send a get-next-block message to the read-disk-stream.

The read-disk-stream instance calls the ORION page buffer manager to retrieve a block of data from disk. The address of the ORION page buffer containing the block is returned. The image-pres-device instance will transfer the data from the page buffer to a physical presentation device, and then send a free-block message to the read-disk-stream, to free the page buffer.

A cursor will also be automatically incremented so that the next get-next-block message will read the next block of the multimedia object. When the data transfer is complete, the image-pres-device sends a **close-read** message to the read-disk-stream instance.

8.2 FLEXIBILITY

For the purposes of capture, storage and presentation, the MIM supports both one- and two-dimensional multimedia objects. One-dimensional multimedia objects are those with a sequential internal format, such as text or audio. A specific audio passage can be presented by specifying an offset and a length in logical units, such as seconds. Two-dimensional multimedia objects are those with a two-dimensional internal format, for example, a bit-mapped image. The application may identify a specific rectangular portion of an image for presentation by specifying the upper-left corner, height, and width of a rectangle. The MIM translates these values into physical offsets in the disk storage. Some multimedia objects, such as an animated bit-mapped image, can be categorized as both spatial and linear.

The MIM supports two types of transfer of multimedia objects from the database: persistent and non-persistent, depending on whether or not the multimedia object remains in the system memory for manipulation by an application after its transfer. An example of non-persistent presentation is the playing of audio data; the audio data is transferred from the database directly to the audio hardware. The MIM handles the buffering and movement of data. An example of persistent presentation is the display of a bit-mapped image in a window on the screen of the workstation. When the application requests that a selected image be displayed in a specific window, the image is transferred from the database to a specific area in the memory space of the application. Following any modifications made to this area of memory during a transaction, the application can transfer the object back to the database.

Once the transfer of data has begun, the MIM allows the application to control the presentation or capture of multimedia data in a variety of ways. For example, during the playback of audio, the application should be able to cause the playback to pause, continue, fast-forward, fast-backward, play faster, play slower, rewind, and stop.

To allow the application to identify a portion of a multimedia object in logical units (such as seconds), we have defined the captured-object class with attributes which describe the general translation from the storage representation to the presentation representation. They include logical-measure and physical-to-logical-ratio. The logical-measure attribute contains the definition of the logical unit of measurement (such as seconds, frames, etc.). The physical-to-logical-ratio attribute indicates the ratio of the physical length to the logical length (such as bytes of digitized audio per second).

The persistent presentation option on a presentation device is set by sending a message. After an image has been displayed and modifications made to the image, the image-pres-device instance can be sent a **capture** message to write the copy of the image to a captured-image instance.

To provide explicit control over the direction of presentation of multimedia information, our implementation has the presentation-device instance explicitly control the cursor that is maintained by the read-disk-stream.

8.3 EFFICIENCY

In ORION, a multimedia object is stored in a number of physical storage blocks, such that versions of the multimedia object will share those storage blocks that contain common information, and new storage blocks are allocated only for those portions of the multimedia object that hold different information. As versions of the multimedia object are updated or deleted, storage blocks that are no longer needed are automatically returned to free space for re-allocation to other multimedia objects.

We have optimized data transfer efficiency in ORION by eliminating unnecessary copying of multimedia data as it is transferred between magnetic disk storage and presentation devices in the system. We accomplish this by giving presentation-device instances and capture-device instances the capability to directly manipulate data in the ORION page buffers, thus eliminating the need to copy the data from the page buffers. Further, rather than logging the before or after image of a multimedia object (which is potentially very large), we log only the mag–disk–storage–device instance which has an attribute describing the disk blocks containing the multimedia object. All disk blocks allocated by a mag–disk–storage–device instance during a transaction are automatically deallocated if the transaction aborts. All disk blocks deallocated by a mag–disk–storage–device instance during a transaction are not actually deallocated until the transaction commits.

9. CONCLUDING REMARKS

In this paper, we provided a high–level description of some of the most prominent features of ORION. ORION is a workstation–based prototype object–oriented database system which we have designed and implemented. ORION will of course be a concrete vehicle for evaluating the performance consequences of directly implementing object–oriented concepts in a database system. We expect that ORION will also be a useful vehicle for experimenting and evaluating various concepts we have developed.

REFERENCES

[AFSA86] Afsarmanesh, H., Knapp, D., McLeod, D., and Parker, A. "An Object–Oriented Approach to VLSI/CAD," in *Proc. Intl Conf. on Very Large Data Bases*, August 1985, Stockholm, Sweden.

[AHLS84] Ahlsen M., A. Bjornerstedt, S. Britts, C. Hulten, and L. Soderlund. "An Architecture for Object Management in OIS," *ACM Trans. on Office Information Systems*, vol. 2, no. 3, July 1984, pp. 173–196.

[ATWO85] Atwood, T. "An Object–Oriented DBMS for Design Support Applications," in *Proc. IEEE COMPINT 85*, pp. 299–307, Sept. 1985, Montreal, Canada.

[BANC85] Bancilhon, F., W. Kim, and H. Korth. "A Model of CAD Transactions," in *Proc. Intl Conf. on Very Large Data Bases*, August 1985, Stockholm, Sweden.

[BANE87a] Banerjee, J., et al. "Data Model Issues for Object–Oriented Applications," *ACM Trans. on Office Information Systems*, January 1987.

[BANE87b] Banerjee, J., W. Kim, H.J. Kim, and H.F. Korth. "Semantics and Implementation of Schema Evolution in Object–Oriented Databases," in *Proc. ACM SIGMOD Conference*, 1987.

[BANE88] Banerjee, J., W. Kim, and K.C. Kim. "Queries in Object–Oriented Databases," to appear in *Proc. 4th Intl. Conf. on Data Engineering*, Los Angeles, Calif. Feb. 1988.

[BOBR83] Bobrow, D.G.. and M. Stefik. *The LOOPS Manual*, Xerox PARC, Palo Alto, CA., 1983.

[BOBR85] Bobrow, D.G. et al. *CommonLoops: Merging Common Lisp and Object–Oriented Programming*, Intelligent Systems Laboratory Series ISL–85–8, Xerox PARC, Palo Alto, CA., 1985.

[CDRO86]   *CD ROM, The New Papyrus,* edited by S. Lambert and S. Ropiequet, Microsoft Press, Redmond, WA., 1986.

[CHOU86]   Chou, H.T., and W. Kim. "A Unifying Framework for Versions in a CAD Environment," in *Proc. Intl Conf. on Very Large Data Bases*, August 1986, Kyoto, Japan.

[CHOU87]   Chou, H.T., and W. Kim. "Versions and Change Notification in an Object-Oriented Database System," to be submitted for publication, 1987.

[CHRI86]   Christodoulakis, S., and C. Faloutsos. "Design and Performance Considerations for an Optical Disk-Bases, Multimedia Object Server," *IEEE Computer*, December 1986, pp. 45-56.

[GARZ87]   Garza, J.F., and W. Kim. "Transaction Management in an Object-Oriented Database System," to be submitted for publication, 1987.

[GOLD81]   Goldberg, A. "Introducing the Smalltalk-80 System," *Byte*, vol. 6, no. 8, August 1981, pp. 14-26.

[GOLD83]   Goldberg, A. and D. Robson. *Smalltalk-80: The Language and its Implementation*, Addison-Wesley, Reading, MA 1983.

[GRAY78]   Gray, J.N. *Notes on Data Base Operating Systems*, IBM Research Report: RJ2188, IBM Research, San Jose, Calif. 1978.

[GRAY81]   J.N. Gray, et al. "The Recovery Manager of a Data Management System," *ACM Computing Surveys, vol. 13, no. 2*, June 1981, pp. 223-242.

[HASK82]   Haskin, R. and R. Lorie. "On Extending the Functions of a Relational Database System," in *Proc. ACM SIGMOD Conf.*, June 1982, pp. 207-212.

[IBM81]   SQL/Data System: Concepts and Facilities. GH24-5013-0, File No. S370-50, IBM Corporation, Jan. 1981.

[IEEE85]   *Database Engineering*, IEEE Computer Society, vol. 8, no. 4, December 1985 special issue on Object-Oriented Systems (edited by F. Lochovsky).

[KATZ84]   Katz, R. and T. Lehman. "Database Support for Versions and Alternatives of Large Design Files," *IEEE Trans. on Software Engineering*, vol. SE-10, no. 2, March 1984, pp. 191-200.

[KATZ86]   Katz R., E. Chang, and R. Bhateja. "Version Modeling Concepts for Computer-Aided Design Databases," in *Proc. ACM SIGMOD Intl. Conf. on Management of Data*, Washington, D.C., May 1986.

[KIM84]   Kim, W., D. McNabb, R. Lorie, and W. Plouffe. "A Transaction Mechanism for Engineering Design Databases," in *Proc. Intl. Conf. on Very Large Databases*, 1984, Singapore.

[KIM87a]   Kim, W., H.T. Chou, and J. Banerjee. "Operations and Implementation of Complex Objects," in *Proc. Data Engineering Conference*, Feb. 1987, Los Angeles, Calif.

[KIM87b]   Kim, W., et al. "Composite Object Support in an Object-Oriented Database System," to appear in *Proc. 2nd Intl. Conf. on Object-Oriented Programming Systems, Languages, and Applications*, Orlando, Florida, Oct. 1987.

[KORT87]   Korth, H., W. Kim, and F. Bancilhon. "On Long-Duration CAD Transactions," to appear in *Information Science* in 1987.

[LORI77]   Lorie, R. "Physical Integrity in a Large Segmented Database," *ACM Trans. on Database Systems*, vol. 2, no. 1, pp. 91–104, March 1977

[LORI83]   Lorie, R. and W. Plouffe. "Complex Objects and Their Use in Design Transactions," *in Proc. Databases for Engineering Applications*, Database Week 1983 (ACM), May 1983, pp. 115–121.

[NEUM82]   Neumann, T., and C. Hornung. "Consistency and Transactions in CAD Databases," in *Proc. Intl Conf. on Very Large Data Bases*, Sept. 82, Mexico City, Mexico.

[SELI79]   Selinger, P.G. et. al. "Access Path Selection in a Relational Database Management System," in *Proc. ACM SIGMOD Conf.*, Boston, Mass. pp 23–34, 1979.

[STEE84]   Guy L. Steele Jr., Scott E. Fahlman, Richard P. Gabriel, David A. Moon, and Daniel L. Weinreb, "Common Lisp", *Digital Press*, 1984.

[STEF86]   Stefik, M., and D.G. Bobrow. "Object-Oriented Programming: Themes and Variations," *The AI Magazine*, January 1986, pp. 40–62.

[STON80]   Stonebraker, M., and K. Keller. "Embedding Expert Knowledge and Hypothetical Data Bases into a Data Base System," in *Proc. ACM SIGMOD Conf. on Management of Data*, pp. 58–66, Santa Monica, Calif. 1980.

[STON81]   Stonebraker, M. "Hypothetical Data Bases as Views," in *Proc. ACM SIGMOD Conf. on Management of Data*, pp. 224–229, 1981.

[SYMB84]   *FLAV Objects, Message Passing, and Flavors,* Symbolics, Inc., Cambridge, MA, 1984.

[SYMB85]   Symbolics Inc., "User's Guide to Symbolics Computers," *Symbolics Manual #* 996015, March 1985.

[WOEL86]   Woelk, D., W. Kim, and W. Luther. "An Object-Oriented Approach to Multimedia Databases," in *Proc. ACM SIGMOD Conf. on the Management of Data*, Washington D.C., May 1986.

[WOEL87]   Woelk, D., and W. Kim. "Multimedia Information Management in an Object-Oriented Database System," to appear in *Proc. Intl. Conf. on Very Large Data Bases*, Brighton, England, Sept. 1987.

SECTION 5:
EVALUATION AND VALIDATION OF OBJECT-ORIENTED DATABASES

Object Oriented Performance
for Electronic Design Automation Tools

Denise J. Ecklund, Roy A. Smith

Advanced Products Division
Mentor Graphics Corporation
8500 SW Creekside Place
Beaverton, Oregon 97005

Abstract

A general discussion of the considerations and possible approaches for achieving high performance interaction using objected-oriented data management for Electronic Design Automation Tools is presented. The basic focus is on an *integrated EDA system* and assumes that performance is not simply the point performance of an individual tool upon a design view but more broadly the performance of an integrated set of tools employed to accomplish System Design.

1. Introduction

The process of designing an electronic system is a continuum spanning concept to manufacture. The design process is also *inherently object-oriented*; that is, it is natural for a designer to think of components (design objects) maniplated by a design tool to achieve a design [1]. Furthermore, the design process spawns a number of distinct but related views of a design which are created and manipulated by different tools. The aggregation and refinement of these views over time yields a complete, manufacturable design. Hence, the tools in the context of the system design process are also objects (tool objects) in that the requirements and parameters of the system drive their usage (figure 1.1).

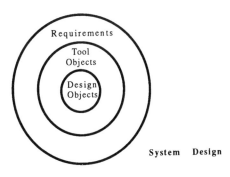

Figure 1.1

1.1 EDA System Performance

Today's EDA tools tend to segment the design process into relatively disjoint activities with respect to both design synthesis steps and design view creation and management at each step. As the size and complexity of the design increases, performance measurements of these disjoint activities are less and less indicative of the performance of the design process because the transitions (which tend to be manual) between design steps begin to dominate the overall measurement. Increasing design size and complexity is a given; therfore, EDA performance must be defined and measured with respect to the total design process which includes the efficiency of the transitions between activities as well as the performance of the individual tools. Another factor which indirectly affects the efficacy of an integrated EDA system is the requirement of the system to support design teams as opposed to just individual designers.

1.2 Managing the Performance Problem

In considering the broader performance problem which is rapidly emerging in EDA, it is obvious that a major part of the bottleneck is poor integration, or more specifically, ineffective sharing of design information across tools. Given the arbitrary nature of design data, an object-oriented paradigm seems to be an obvious approach to managing the problem and is in fact a requirement for EIS (Engineering Information Systems) of the VHSIC program [2]. What is not obvious is where and how to make the trade-offs between information sharing and information localization to get the best possible overall EDA system performance and integration.

We believe that the key to maximizing EDA system performance lies in designing extendable mechanisms for associating design tasks (tool objects) together into logical design tool suites. Once a suite has been established, it drives both a logical and physical clustering of engineering design data and provides opportunites to intelligently partition local and shared information.

2. Clustering in Today's EDA Tool Suites

Physical design data clustering is employed to some degree in most current EDA systems. This section describes the current general strategy which optimizes for local tool performance as a basis for discussion of a synergistic clustering strategy (section 3) which optimizes information sharing.

Reprinted from *Digest of Papers*, COMPCON, 1989, pages 421-424.

2.1 Data Sharing among existing EDA tools

The tool sets currently offered by EDA vendors are not well integrated. This lack of integration is evidenced by two facts; first, users must enact discrete transitions from one tool to another, and second, data sharing among tools is generally restricted to the producer-consumer model of sharing. Figure 2.1 illustrates this situation. Each large triangle represents a tool. The tool triangle is divided into four sections representing the possible states of the data operated on by that tool. Local data is private to the tool; shared data is exchanged or shared among tools at runtime, based on a prearranged and often times special case sharing protocol; swap space data is uncommitted data that is paged by the operating system during tool execution; and committed data is the data that persists after tool execution has completed. Each individual tool manages the representation and manipulation of design data as it transitions through each of these data states. This has resulted in redundant effort and divergent approaches to data representation and data management.

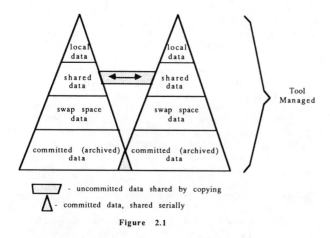

Figure 2.1

Tools in a current EDA system may share data in two restricted ways. First, committed data may be shared in a producer-consumer manner; as one tool commits modified data, that data may be used as the input to another tool. Often, the output format of the first tool must be translated to an acceptable input format for the second tool. Not only does this waste time, but typically the user is responsible for ensuring that the translation is performed. This form of sharing is said to take place between tool executions. Concurrently executing tools may attempt to share data by conforming to a prearranged protocol for exchanging data. To achieve this form of sharing among existing tools requires some rearchitecture and reimplementation. The extent and cost of such modifications severely limits interactive data sharing among existing tools.

2.2 Data Clustering to enhance performance

Figure 2.2 shows where data clustering is utilized in the architecture of a current EDA tool set. Committed data is clustered to improve pre-fetch retrieval performance for an individual tool. Individual tool performance is enhanced under the assumption that each cluster of data objects is managed by exactly one tool. In current systems, where data sharing is highly restricted, this assumption holds true.

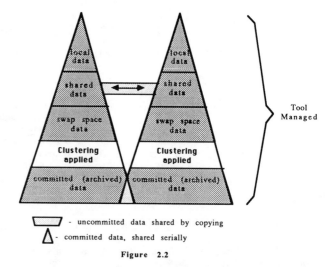

Figure 2.2

3. Future EDA systems

Architecting an *integrated* EDA system is not a simple matter of "pasting together" a large set of existing tools. The result of this approach is a mammoth system whose per tool performance is significantly degraded by the overhead of an excessive number of data sharing paths among the integrated tools. The architecture of a *high performance integrated* EDA system lies in the middle ground, where tools that service closely related design tasks are grouped into small to medium sized tool suites. Each tool suite integrates a set of tools that share data and support the user in accomplishing a set of logically connected design tasks. For example, given the task of analyzing a schematic design, a user wants to utilize a suite of tools that provide the capabilities of schematic editing, real-time analysis of design properties, and design simulation. By grouping a manageable number of logically connected tools, a tool suite provides a context for achieving intelligent data sharing and good individual tool performance.

The tools within a suite are highly integrated via tightly-coupled interfaces for data sharing. A tightly-coupled interface provides a high cost, high performance mechanism for sharing data. Tools architected as members of distinct tool suites can share data when required, but such sharing is accomplished via loosely-coupled interfaces. A loosely-coupled interface provides a low cost, low performance mechanism for sharing data.

The key to good tool suite design is identifying the appropriate granularity of user task to be supported by a suite. Future EDA systems will consist of a set of integrated tool suites that work together to manage design data throughout the lifetime of the design process.

3.1 An Architecture for Data Sharing within a Tool Suite

The general architecture for any integrated tool suite must emphasize support for interactive sharing and serialized sharing of design data. Furthermore, the architecture must avoid the creation of a plethora of sharing mechanisms, customized for each instance of data sharing within the suite. This architectural goal can be achieved by the introduction of an environment manager that controls access to all shared, swapped, and committed data that is operated on by any tool in the suite.

Figure 3.1 illustrates the partitioning of data categories under a general tool suite architecture. Each triangle labeled "local data" represents a single concurrently executing tool (within the suite) and the design data that is accessed only by that tool. Shared data is the set of design data operated on concurrently by more than one tool. Any combination of the tools in the suite may share data interactively at runtime. Similarly, tools (within a suite or across suites) may share committed data according to the producer-consumer model. The environment manager serializes access to committed data that must be accessed serially and facilitates the interactive sharing of data that may be shared at runtime. This architecture achieves the integration goal only if the environment manager can provide high performance management of shared, swapped, and committed data.

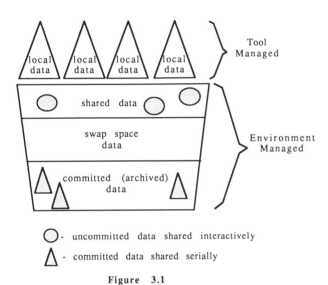

Figure   3.1

3.2 Logical and Physical Clustering
to Enhance Performance

Clustering is the only viable mechanism an environment manager can employ to achieve high performance management of shared data. Traditionally, the same physical clustering of related design objects was used on stable storage and in memory to support efficient access for a single tool. To support efficient access for multiple tools, the environment manager must employ multiple physical clusterings of a set of related design objects or multiple logical clusterings over a single physical clustering of related design objects.

Figure 3.2 illustrates an approach that uses multiple physical clusterings for committed design objects that are shared serially, and multiple logical clusterings over one physical clustering for design objects that are shared interactively. The serial sharing of committed design objects takes place between tool executions. For this reason it is feasible for the environment manager to store multiple consistent copies of the shared objects, each copy clustered optimally for one (or more) of the tools. Under this architecture, the problem of object format translation does not disappear, but the solution can be encapsulated in the environment manager, alleviating the user of the burden of performing translations. (The environment manager can support multiple object formats by performing translations when building the additional cluster copies or by performing translations as part of a logical clustering mechanism applied to memory resident clusters.)

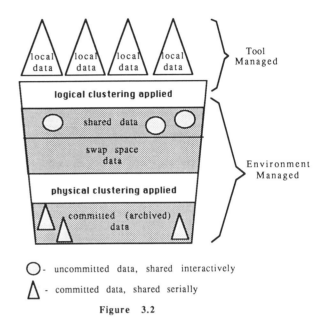

Figure   3.2

When a tool suite is invoked the physical clusters containing the design objects to be operated on will be retrieved from stable storage. (If multiple persistent physical clustering exist, the clustering most appropriate to the invoking tool suite will be retrieved.) Only a subset of the design objects in any given physical cluster will be shared interactively by tools in the suite. The environment manager can support interactive sharing of a subset of the design objects by providing logical views on a single physical clustering or by creating multiple physical clusterings of the shared objects and maintaining consistency among those copies. We believe that any algorithm for maintaining runtime consistency among the multiple copies will result in unacceptable performance from the interacting tools. Thus the environment manager should support logical views over a physical clustering.

A logical view of a physical clustering is a set of filters that make objects appear to be physically juxtaposed when they are not, that make some objects visible and others invisible, and make some objects visible in a format other than the one physically represented. Each tool that interactively shares an overlapping subset of the design objects may require its own unique logical cluster filter. For this reason, management of a logical cluster is shared between the tool suite and the environment manager. The environment manager provides mechanisms for remapping object contiguity, managing object visibility, and translating object representations. The tools define the set of views that must be layered over a single physical clustering. If the logical clustering mechanisms are implemented efficiently and the logical views defined by the interacting tools have reasonable overlap with the physical clustering, then logical clustering can support high performance interactive sharing of design objects.

4. Summary

In this paper we have asserted that efficacy of an integrated *EDA System* is the summation of individual tool performance and the performance of information sharing between serial and concurrent design tools. We also claimed that in existing EDA tools the information sharing portion of the performance total becomes dominant as the size and complexity of a design increases. Having established this context for performance, we examined the general strategy employed in most existing EDA tools for information sharing and came to a (not too surprising) conclusion that today's tools are oriented toward managing the design information local to the tool. We also concluded that because of the local focus, tools tended to use a simple producer-consumer model of information sharing which is, in general, extremely inefficient. We then postulated that since the architecture of an integrated set of tools (tool suite) must emphasize the support for interactive sharing as well as serialized sharing of design data, there must be an extendable mechanism which associates tools into tool suites supported by a mechanism which logically clusters design data for the suite from the physical data. We suggested that the key to achieving maximum overall EDA system performance is the intelligent partitioning of the design tasks (into suites) as opposed to the popular idea that all design tasks be "integrated" with all other design tasks. We concluded that once a tool aggregation was established a logical data clustering mechanism supported by traditional physical data clustering would provide ample opportunity to optimize total system performance.

5. References

[1]   S. Heiler, U. Dayal, J. Orenstein, S. Radke-Sproull, "An Object-Oriented Approach to Data Management: Why Design Databases Need It," in *Proceedings of the Twenty-Fourth ACM/IEEE Design Automation Conference* (June 1987), pp. 335-340.

[2]   J.L. Linn, R.I. Winner, "The Department of Defense Requirements for Engineering Information Systems, DRAFT," Institute for Defense Analysis, Alexandria, VA, (July 1986).

Automatic Validation of Object-Oriented Database Structures

Lois M. L. Delcambre

Karen C. Davis

The Center for Advanced Computer Studies
University of Southwestern Louisiana
P.O. Box 44330
Lafayette, LA 70504
(318) 231-5697
lmd@usl.usl.edu

Abstract

Object-oriented database systems offer rich structuring capabilities that are particularly useful for complex applications. However, the resulting schemas can be difficult to design and validate. In this paper, the philosophy of explicitly representing simple range classes for properties and explicitly specifying range and/or cardinality restrictions on inherited properties is adopted so that the membership of an object in classes is *characterized* by the object's property values. The motivation for this approach is twofold: first, it is in keeping with the database philosophy of emphasizing the *representation* of an application (rather than some intrinsic meaning), and second, it provides a framework for algorithmically verifying the structural aspects of the schema. The contribution of this paper is an automatic classifier for the structural validation of object-oriented schemas based on sound and complete rules of inference. If the Classifier discovers new structural relationships and/or inconsistencies, the designer can refine the schema to reflect the semantics of the application. Thus the Classifier serves as an interactive design tool that can be used at any stage during the design process.

1. Introduction

One well-accepted method for describing the complex structures associated with an object-oriented database [MD86, MSOP86, BCKG87, Fish87, Banc88, CDV88] relies on generalization and aggregation abstraction [SS77]. A problem with this approach is that the resulting schemas can be both large and unwieldy. In this paper, the complexity of object-oriented schemas is addressed by a process that validates the structural aspects of a schema by relying on an automatic classifier. A classifier is a tool that originated in knowledge representation research as a preprocessor for organizing class descriptions prior to reasoning over taxonomic information [Lipk82, SI83, SL83, BFL83]. A classifier can also provide feedback interactively to the designer regarding the development of such a taxonomy [FS84].

The classifiers developed for knowledge representation provide the inspiration for this research. However, both the object-oriented model and the Classifier presented here are simpler than models like KL-ONE [Lipk82, SI83, SL83] because the emphasis is on representation rather than real-world semantics. The contribution of this paper is the application of classifier technology to the problem of developing and managing object-oriented schemas. The Classifier presented here can also be used to support schema evolution, schema integration, and even as the basis for query processing. In this paper, the sound and complete rules of inference for the object-oriented model are presented and the Classifier algorithm is shown to correctly implement the inference rules. The entire Classifier System is presented and its role in the interactive development of object-oriented schemas is discussed.

The model used for this research is presented in Section 2 along with an example. The Classifier algorithm is presented in detail in Section 3. The formal foundation for this research is reviewed in Section 4. Finally, Section 5 offers conclusions and future research directions.

2. Motivation

The object-oriented data model used for this research is presented in this section. The structural aspects of the model are quite expressive and the emphasis is placed on the representational aspects of the schema. The structural assumptions for this model are presented in Section 2.1. This is followed by an example in Section 2.2. The example serves to demonstrate both the data model and the Classifier used to validate schemas.

2.1. Representational Assumptions

The data model used in this research is briefly presented here along with the assumptions that provide the foundation for the Classifier. The model supports generalization and aggregation abstraction through the isa relationship and the specification of properties. Classes that model objects of interest to the application are *abstract* classes. The abstract classes are divided into three types. Classes at the top of the isa hierarchy are *base* classes. The remaining classes are either *defined* or *constrained* subclasses. As an example, a Manager class (a subclass of Employee) could be *constrained* by the Sex property having a range class of {female}. This implies that in order to be a manager the employee must be female, but the

Reprinted from *IEEE 5th International Conference on Data Engineering*, 1989, pages 2-9. Copyright © 1989 by The Institute of Electrical and Electronics Engineers, Inc. All rights reserved.

converse is not necessarily true. There could very well be females who are not managers. On the other hand, Teenager would be *defined* by restricting an Age property to the range of {13..19}. The simple atomic values that provide printable property values must be explicitly defined as *simple* classes. A simple class is analogous to a relational domain. This model is synthesized from semantic or object-oriented models and was heavily influenced by SDM [HM81] and TAXIS [MBW80]. The only additional structural relationship supported is that classes can be declared to be disjoint from each other.

The assumptions concerning the schemas expressed in this model are presented here.

1) Simple classes must be explicitly defined and all structural relationships among simple classes must be provided by the schema designer. As an example, if {0..18} is a simple class named Age-values and {0..1000} is a simple class named Check-amount-values, the schema designer would obviously *not* indicate an isa relationship between these two classes. As another example, if Prime-Number and Number are simple classes, it is outside the scope of the model to infer an isa relationship between them; this information, which reflects the semantics of the chosen representation, must be provided by the designer. The designer is essentially providing the semantics of the underlying representational structure for the schema (much like functional dependencies and foreign keys provide the semantics of a relational database).

2) The range class and/or cardinality constraints of any inherited property can be restricted at any defined or constrained subclass, as in [MBW80, HM81]. This allows the schema designer to indicate precisely how the representation

of objects in the subclass differs from that of the objects in the superclass and thus exploits the strength of the object-oriented approach for creating new types by specializing existing types [Zdon86]. Note that property restrictions constrain the membership of objects in a user-controllable subclass.

3) By relying on Boolean properties at the superclass level to represent arbitrary or user-controllable [HM81] membership in a subclass, then *all* abstract subclasses can be viewed as *defined* subclasses [HM81]. As described above, a defined subclass is one where the property restrictions are definitional. As an example of how a Boolean property can be added to represent membership in a constrained subclass, consider an Employee class with a subclass called Successful-employee where membership in the subclass is determined by some arbitrary, unspecified criteria. A Boolean property, Successful?, can be added to the Employee class to indicate when an employee has been deemed successful. Then the Successful-employee subclass can be viewed as a *defined* subclass where the Successful? property is restricted to the range of {yes}. Such defined classes need not be explicitly represented in the database extension unless they have original properties, in addition to their inherited properties. With an appropriate user interface, the user need not be aware of these schema transformations.

The foundation for the Classifier is established through the semantics of simple classes and the fact that all subclasses are uniformly represented as defined subclasses. The Classifier derives structural relationships primarily by examining properties, as originally specified and as restricted by the various subclasses.

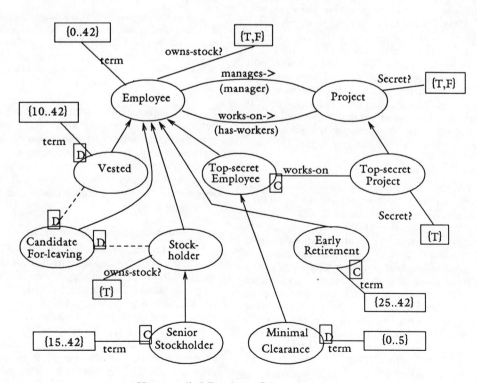

User-supplied Employee Schema
Figure 1

196

2.2. An Example

The representational conventions discussed above are briefly introduced in the Employee example presented in Figure 1. The example also serves to motivate the automatic classifier described in this paper. Figure 1 provides the schema "before validation" and Figure 2 provides the "after validation" version. In both figures, directed arcs indicate isa links, undirected (named) arcs represent properties, and undirected dotted arcs represent disjoint relationships. The *defined* subclasses, as specified by the designer, are indicated by the boxed D symbol. The defining property and/or defining disjoints, along with the isa links for the subclass, constitute the membership definition for the class. The remaining subclasses have arbitrary membership constrained only by the isa and disjoint links and optionally by restrictions placed on inherited properties. Such property constraints at a subclass are indicated by the boxed C symbol.

The abstract base classes for this example are Employee and Project and the simple classes are the range classes for the Term property, the Owns-stock? property, and the Secret? property. Each simple class is indicated by a rectangle with the values specified within set brackets. Although they are not shown in either figure, the appropriate isa relationships between the various range classes for the properties are specified in the schema. The remaining classes are abstract subclasses. The Vested employee subclass is a defined subclass where Term is restricted to ten years or more. In other words, an employee automatically becomes vested when his/her term reaches ten years. The Top-secret Project class is a subclass of Project while the Top-secret Employee class is constrained to include employees who work only on top

secret projects. The Minimal Clearance class is defined as top secret employees with a term of five years or less. The Stockholder class is a subclass of Employee while the Senior Stockholder is constrained to include stockholders with a term of at least fifteen years. Early Retirement is constrained to include employees with a term of at least 25 years. Finally, Candidate For-leaving is defined as all employees who are not vested and not stockholders.

The classified schema in Figure 2 shows the new structural information that has been deduced. The new isas are shown as double directed arcs and the new disjoints are shown as double dotted lines. Although this is a small example, it illustrates the role of the Classifier in the iterative process of database design. If the designer has not modeled the application correctly, structural flaws (redundant classes, for example) can be identified automatically. The designer can modify the schema to correctly reflect the intended semantics and then apply the Classifier again. The analysis can be repeated until a satisfactory schema design is obtained. The strength of the Classifier is that *all* structural relationships and hence *all* structural inconsistencies are automatically discovered within the context of the schema as specified by the user.

3. The Classifier Algorithm

This section presents the algorithm for processing a schema, as shown in Figure 3. The user-supplied schema in a textual format is parsed by the Canonizer, which produces a schema in canonical form. The canonical form simplifies the schema for the purposes of the Classifier. In the second phase, the heart of the processing, the Classifier infers all isa and disjoint relationships between abstract classes in the

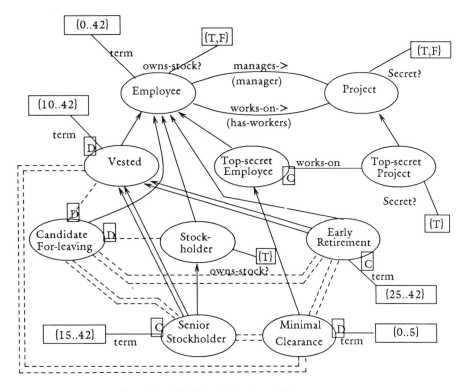

Complete, Validated Employee Schema
Figure 2

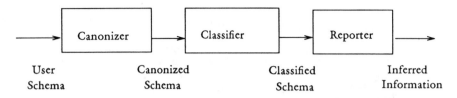

Phases of Schema Processing
Figure 3

schema. The final phase, the Reporter, relates inferred isa and disjoint relationships as well as information regarding redundant and inconsistent classes to the designer. Each of these three phases, the Canonizer, the Classifier, and the Reporter, are discussed in the following sections.

3.1. The Canonizer

The first phase of schema processing involves translating the user-defined schema into a canonical form. Although convenient for classification, the canonical form is not as user-friendly nor high-level as the DDL. An automatic translation mechanism for converting a user schema into canonical form is embodied in the Canonizer. The canonization process generates intermediate classes that represent each feature of the original class's definition. The original class is defined as a subclass of the generated classes and thus inherits all of the appropriate properties. Additionally, a class may have any number of original properties and may inherit properties from superclasses. Figure 4.a illustrates a user schema that is not in canonical form; the additional subclasses in Figure 4.b are generated by the canonizer to enforce the constraint that there is only one locally restricted property at each class.

The Canonizer sets the stage for processing by the Classifier.

3.2. The Classifier

The Classifier deduces isa and disjoint relationships that are implicit in the initial schema. The classification process is divided into several steps, as shown in Figure 5; each step corresponds to a particular set of inference rules that are applied to the schema. These inference rules are stated formally in Section 4.

The steps of the classification phase are discussed in the following subsections.

3.2.1. Initial Isa and Disjoint Information

Based solely on the user-specified isas and disjoints in the original schema, some structural information can be inferred immediately. The information made explicit in this step includes transitive isa, inherited disjoint, and symmetric disjoint information. *Transitive isa* discovers that A isa C when A isa B and B isa C. *Inherited disjoint* deduces that A is disjoint from B when C is disjoint from B and A isa C. *Symmetric disjoint* infers that A is disjoint from B when it is known that B is disjoint from A.

The next step in the Classifier determines disjoint relationships between classes based on properties.

3.2.2. Disjoints Based on Properties

Two classes that restrict the same property can be determined to be disjoint if the ranges or cardinality constraints on the properties imply that the classes are disjoint. The processing proceeds as follows:

(1) A list of classes with locally restricted properties is built; it contains domain name, property name, cardinality constraints, and range name for each class.

(2) Properties that occur only once in the list can be eliminated from consideration, since no disjoint relationship can arise between classes if the property is only restricted by one class.

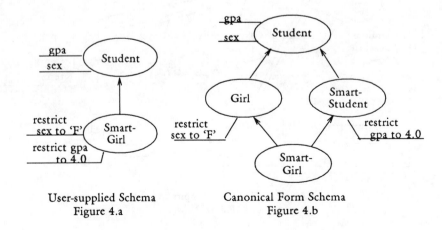

User-supplied Schema
Figure 4.a

Canonical Form Schema
Figure 4.b

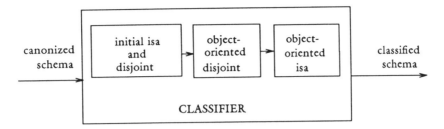

The Steps in Classification
Figure 5

(3) Disjoint relationships between classes with non-overlapping cardinality constraints for the same property can be determined immediately upon inspection.

(4) Disjoints that result from disjoint range classes can be found by starting with simple range classes in the restricted properties list. If the simple classes are disjoint then this information is provided by the user. Thus classes with simple classes as ranges can be determined to be disjoint if the ranges are disjoint. Then classes defined by restricting properties with these ranges can be determined to be disjoint. The processing continues in this fashion until all classes in the restricted property list have been examined and compared with other classes restricting the range of the same property.

Note that symmetric disjoints are recorded whenever a new disjoint is found, rather than analyzing property specifications twice. Also, inherited disjoints are propagated downward through the generalization hierarchy whenever they are discovered.

In order to understand cardinality constraints on properties, consider the following example. Suppose that Employee has a Spouse property. A Single subclass of Employee can be defined by restricting the cardinality of the Spouse property to zero. Married or Polygamous subclasses of Employee could be defined by restricting the cardinality of the Spouse property to one or greater than one, respectively. Obviously, Step 3 above would discover that Single, Married, and Polygamous are all mutually disjoint.

As an example of a disjoint relationship discovered due to property restrictions, consider the Term property of the employee example of Figures 1 and 2. The classes that restrict the range of the Term property (Minimal Clearance, Senior Stockholder, Early Retirement, and Vested) are placed in the list of classes to be examined. Consider the classes Minimal Clearance and Senior Stockholder. Since their simple range classes are {0..5} and {15..42}, respectively, a disjoint relationship exists between them. Thus, a disjoint relationship can be inferred between Minimal Clearance and Senior Stockholder. In turn, if Minimal Clearance and Senior Stockholder were ranges of a restricted property, the classes with that restricted property could be examined to see if they were disjoint.

The next subsection describes the inference of isa relationships based on properties.

3.2.3. Isa Relationships Based on Properties

In this final step of the classification phase, classes are placed in their most specific places in the isa hierarchy based on their properties. The process of inferring isa relationships depends on the type of class. A class is one of the following types:

(1) **simple:** These classes contain atomic objects and their contents are explicitly defined by the user.

(2) **base:** These abstract classes have no superclasses and their only properties are original ones.

(3) **set-based:** These abstract subclasses are defined in terms of set operations (either intersection or set difference), not property restrictions, which translate directly to isa and disjoint relationships.

(4) **restricted:** These abstract subclasses either have a restricted local property or inherit a restricted property from a superclass (or both).

Simple, base, and set-based classes are trivially classified; all information about them is explicit. The interesting processing, where new isa relationships may be deduced, is concerned with restricted classes. The algorithm proceeds as follows:

(1) A list is built containing class names and range class names for properties that are restricted.

(2) A class can be processed only when all of its properties have range classes that have been classified. At first, this means any class with properties whose range classes are combinations of simple, base, and set-based classes can be classified. As restricted classes are gradually classified, classes with classified classes as ranges can be classified. Eventually, all classes in the list will be classified unless they are defined in terms of each other. Classes whose membership is described by mutually referential definitions form *class definition cycles*. If classes participate in a class definition cycle, then they will appear as both range and domain classes in the list, unable to be processed since they are each waiting for the other to be processed. All classes appearing in the cycle are ill-formed and thus need not be classified any further.

In the example of Section 2, an isa relationship between the Senior Stockholder and the Vested classes is inferred. The isa is deduced because the only property of Vested, namely Term, is at least as restrictive at Senior Stockholder as it is at Vested, i.e., the range {10..42} subsumes the range {15..42}, and all of the classes disjoint from Vested (Candidate For-leaving, Minimal Clearance) are also disjoint from Senior Stockholder. Vested is *defined* by the restriction on the Term property; it has all of the employees whose Term falls in the range {10..42}. Even though the Senior Stockholder class contains an arbitrary subset of Employee, because of the restriction on the Term property to the range {15..42}, Senior Stockholder is guaranteed to be a subset of Vested.

Since all types of classes will be classified, all isas will be correctly identified. After the classification phase, feedback is given to the user by the Reporter.

3.3. The Reporter

The classifier finds all isa and disjoint relationships, so any new isas and disjoints are reported to the user. Additionally, the Reporter identifies three types of structural problems within the schema. The problems detected by the Reporter, along with an explanation of how they are identified, are presented below.

(1) Redundant classes are evident through cycles in the isa hierarchy (a class will be a superclass of itself).

(2) Inconsistent classes, those that are necessarily empty, are identified as classes that are disjoint from themselves. For example, a class defined as the intersection of two disjoint classes will be inconsistent. The complex interaction of the inference rules has already been carried out by the Classifier, so the Reporter determines inconsistency simply by inspecting a class's disjoint information.

(3) Class definition cycles are identified by looking in the list described in the previous subsection.

The Reporter provides information based on the classified, canonical schema but the designer expects to see the original schema. The Reporter can easily "uncanonize" the classified schema by ignoring the extra classes. Only the originally specified classes are reported on; the structural relationships are correct because of the inheritance mechanism.

The Reporter provides the basis for interactive schema development. Each new isa and disjoint can be presented to the designer for confirmation. Any disputed isas, disjoints, or ill-defined classes can be remedied by the designer.

The next section provides the formal framework for the classification process.

4. The Formal Foundation

The Classifier algorithm correctly infers all isa and disjoint relationships in an object-oriented schema and allows structural problems to be identified. As described in Section 2, simple classes are explicitly specified and all isa and disjoint relationships between simple classes are assumed to be supplied by the designer. No inferencing is required for simple classes. Only structural relationships of abstract classes containing complex objects are deduced by the Classifier. Thus, classification is complete *with respect to* information given by the designer regarding simple classes. Also as discussed in Section 2, because of the support for restricted properties and because all subclasses are modeled as *defined* subclasses, restricted properties are considered to be definitional. That is to say, when an object has all of the inherited properties at a class, within the constraints on the inherited properties at that class, then the object must be in the class. This enables isas based on property constraints to be inferred.

A discussion of the sound and complete inference rules that are implemented in the Classifier algorithm follows in Section 4.1. The formal foundation concludes in Section 4.2 with a brief discussion of the correctness of the algorithm developed for the Classifier.

4.1. Rules of Inference

The formal framework for the Classifier is provided by rules of inference for structural properties of the model. This section gives an overview of the rules of inference and presents two of the rules that consider properties along with sketches of the proofs of their soundness.

Isa Rules of Inference	
given isa	$(\forall c1)(\forall c2)$name$(c2) \in$ superclasses$(c1) \rightarrow$ isa$(c1, c2)$
given isa	$(\forall c1)(\forall c2)$name$(c1) \in$ subclasses$(c2) \rightarrow$ isa$(c1, c2)$
transitive isa	$(\forall c1)(\forall c2)(\forall c3)isa(c1, c2)$ & isa$(c2, c3) \rightarrow$ isa$(c1, c3)$
object-oriented isa	$(\forall c1)(\forall c2)(\exists p)$hasproperty$(c2, p)$ & hasproperty$(c1, p)$ & $[(\forall p)$hasproperty$(c2, p)$ & hasproperty$(c1, p)$ $\rightarrow$ isa$($range$(p, c1),$ range$(p, c2))$ & cardcontain$($cardconstraint$(p, c1),$ cardconstraint$(p, c2))]$ & $[(\forall c3)($disjoint$(c2, c3) \rightarrow$ disjoint$(c1, c3))]$ $\rightarrow$ isa$(c1, c2)$
Disjoint Rules of Inference	
given disjoint	$(\forall c1)(\forall c2)$name$(c2) \in$ disjointclasses$(c1) \rightarrow$ disjoint$(c1, c2)$
symmetric disjoint	$(\forall c1)(\forall c2)$disjoint$(c1, c2) \rightarrow$ disjoint$(c2, c1)$
inherited disjoint	$(\forall c1)(\forall c2)(\forall c3)isa(c1, c2)$ & disjoint$(c2, c3) \rightarrow$ disjoint$(c1, c3)$
object-oriented disjoint based on ranges	$(\forall c1)(\forall c2)(\exists p)$hasproperty$(c1, p)$ & hasproperty$(c2, p)$ & required$(p, c1)$ & disjoint$($range$(p, c1),$ range$(p, c2))$ $\rightarrow$ disjoint$(c1, c2)$
object-oriented disjoint based on cardinalities	$(\forall c1)(\forall c2)(\exists p)$hasproperty$(c1, p)$ & hasproperty$(c2, p)$ & cardintersect$($cardconstraint$(p, c1),$ cardconstraint$(p, c2)) = \emptyset$ $\rightarrow$ disjoint$(c1, c2)$

Rules of Inference
Figure 6

200

Earlier research [AP86] presented inference rules and proofs for a simple data model based on set theory only, with no support for complex objects. The research reported here extends the rules presented in [AP86] for a semantically richer model. The model used here supports property definition, inheritance, and restriction; it is capable of expressing the structural side of an object-oriented data model.

The rules of inference are presented in detail and proven to be sound and complete in [Davis87]. The rules of inference are summarized in Figure 6 and a few rules are selected for discussion below.

The object-oriented isa inference rule which considers properties can be expressed informally as follows:

> If the properties that a class B and a class A have in common are at least as restrictive at A as they are at B, and all of the classes that are disjoint from B are also disjoint from A, then infer that A isa B.

The soundness of the above rule results from the fact that the two classes in question have a common superclass, the notion of the "at least as restrictive" constraint on the common properties, and the fact that any class disjoint from the potential superclass is disjoint from the subclass. In other words, any object in the class A is not in any class disjoint from the potential superclass B, and for every property that they have in common, the property is at least as restrictive at A as the property is at B. Based on the fact that restricted properties are definitional, when an object meets all property restrictions (for all properties that they have in common) and all disjoint relationships, the object is necessarily in the class. Thus, every object in the class A is necessarily in B.

The disjoint inference rules which consider properties use either disjoint cardinality constraints or disjoint range classes to decide whether two classes with a common property are disjoint from one another. The following rule considers disjoint range classes:

> If two classes A and B have a property in common, which is required for at least one of them, and the range classes of the property at the classes are disjoint, then infer that A is disjoint from B.

When the range of a property is restricted at a class, then an object belongs in the class only when the object's entire image for that property is contained in the restricted range. Thus two distinct subclasses with restrictions on a common property with disjoint ranges imply that no object (with an image under that property) could possibly be contained in both subclasses. Since the property in question is required at one of the subclasses, the two classes must be disjoint.

The correctness of the implementation of the inference rules is discussed next.

4.2. Correctness of the Classifier Algorithm

The correctness of the classifier algorithm is demonstrated by showing that the following three conditions hold:

(1) only valid isa and disjoint relationships are inferred,

(2) all isa and disjoint relationships are inferred, and

(3) the algorithm terminates.

Points (1) and (3) above require only brief comment. Since the algorithm implements inference rules that are sound, the algorithm finds only valid relationships. The algorithm will terminate when all classes have been processed, since a finite set of classes is examined at each step. Showing that the algorithm finds all structural relationships is discussed in detail in the following paragraphs.

The rules are proven to be complete in [Davis87], but since a processing order is imposed on them by the algorithm, care must be taken that no applicable rules are overlooked at a certain step. The first step of the Classifier algorithm uses the transitive isa and inherited and symmetric disjoint rules. This processing is carried out in a top-down fashion through all of the connected isa components. Thus, all classes will be examined, and if any of the rules implemented in this step apply, the appropriate information will be inferred.

The second step of the Classifier algorithm infers disjoint relationships based on properties. Classes that restrict the same property are examined in a pairwise fashion until all disjoints are found. A disjoint relationship based on the range classes of a common property is discovered for classes that actually restrict (i.e. change) the property. Any isa relationships that may be discovered in the next step would only result in inherited disjoints, not the disjoints discovered by examining property ranges. Regardless of the method used to discover a disjoint relationship, the symmetric and inherited disjoints are propagated immediately. Such disjoints have no impact on the disjoints (or isas) based on properties.

The third step of the Classifier infers isa relationships based on properties. At this point, all possible disjoint information is explicit for every class. This results because a disjoint is either based on user-supplied information or is based on the examination of properties. Any isas that can be inferred by this step *cannot* introduce any new disjoint information into the class hierarchy since an isa between two classes A and B can only be inferred when *all* disjoints present at B are present at A. Thus, it is correct to find isas based on properties (step 3) after finding all disjoints based on properties (step 2) and all isa and disjoint relationships will be found by the Classifier.

5. Conclusions

Whether the object-oriented approach is used primarily during design or is adopted as the underlying model for an actual database implementation, the Classifier is an invaluable support tool. Given any user-supplied schema (at any stage in the development), the Classifier provides complete information concerning the structural relationships in the schema. The relationships discovered by the Classifier are logically correct and thus either exist in the application or indicate that the schema designer has not yet captured the application semantics correctly. The Reporter is intended to provide feedback to the designer so that he can decide if the schema reflects his intentions accurately. If not, the schema can be modified and analyzed iteratively as necessary to capture the application semantics. The Classifier should also be used during schema evolution in order to determine the full impact of any proposed modifications.

Another significance of this research is the precise definition of the static structural aspects of an object-oriented database model. The implementation of a model that directly supports isa, disjoint, constrained properties, and defined classes can now be considered. When coupled with the Classifier any implementation that enforces the structural constructs of this model would correctly enforce *all* structural constraints.

The Classifier is currently being implemented in KEE [KEE86] where the schemas are limited to those structural features supported by an object-oriented data model. Note that KEE is more general than the model described here. The main inferencing steps of the Classifier algorithm are implemented through the KEE rule system.

Future research plans include investigating the possibility that the Classifier will support object-oriented view integration. The Classifier will automatically process the views (one after the other) and produce a complete, correct, integrated schema.

Another future research effort is motivated by the fact that the DDL primitives for specifying classes in the object-oriented model proposed here provide the basis for a rudimentary, object-oriented query language. Since simple queries can be viewed as class definitions, the classifier can be used to find complete information concerning the relationship of the query to the other classes in the schema. The query's superclasses, subclasses, disjoint classes, etc., provide a complete set of structural access paths for the query. A full-featured query language should include additional capabilities but the DDL coupled with the Classifier provide a promising first step.

Finally, research related to the Classifier concerns the formal representation of constraints of an object-oriented model. The *constraint analysis* algorithm [UD88] operates on a general set of constraints that include the structural constraints from the schema. Constraint analysis can be used to construct user views with particular emphasis on the specification of update operations [Urban87]. The Classifier serves as a preprocessor for constraint analysis by ensuring that complete structural information is obtained.

References

[AP86] Atzeni P., and D.S. Parker, Jr., "Formal Properties of Net-Based Knowledge Representation Schemes," *Proceedings of the IEEE International Conference on Data Engineering,* L.A., CA, Feb. 1986.

[Banc88] Bancilhon, F., "Object-Oriented Database Systems," *Proceedings of the Seventh ACM SIGACT-SIGMOD-SIGART Symposium on Principles of Database Systems,* Austin, TX, March 21-23, 1988.

[BCGK87] Banerjee, J., H.T. Chou, J. Garza, W. Kim, D. Woelk, N. Ballou, and H.J. Kim, "Data Model Issues for Object-Oriented Applications," *ACM Transactions on Office Information Systems,* Vol. 5, No. 1, January, 1987.

[BFL83] Brachman, R.J., R.E. Fikes, and H.J. Levesque, "KRYPTON: A Functional Approach to Knowledge Representation," FLAIR Technical Report No. 16, Fairchild Laboratory for Artificial Intelligence Research, Palo Alto, CA, May 1983.

[CDV88] Carey, M.J., D.J. DeWitt, and S.L. Vandenberg, "A Data Model and Query Language for EXODUS," *Proceedings of the 1988 SIGMOD Conference,* Chicago, IL, June, 1988.

[Davis87] Davis, K.C., "The Theoretical Foundation for Inferencing on a Semantic Schema," M.S. Thesis, The Center for Advanced Computer Studies, University of Southwestern Louisiana, Lafayette, LA, June 1987.

[Fish87] Fishman, D., *et al.,* "Iris: an Object-Oriented Database Management System," *ACM Transactions on Office Information Systems,* Vol. 5, No. 1, January, 1987.

[FS84] Finin, T., and D. Silverman, "Interactive Classification as a Knowledge Aquisition Tool," *First International Workshop on Expert Database Systems,* 1984.

[HM81] Hammer, M., and D. McLeod, "Database Description with SDM: A Semantic Database Model," *ACM Transactions on Database Systems,* Vol. 6, No. 3, Sept. 1981.

[KEE86] *KEE Software Development System,* KEE Version 3.0, IntelliCorp, 1986.

[Lipk82] Lipkis, T., "A KL-ONE Classifier," *Proceedings of the 1981 KL-ONE Workshop,* edited by Schmolze, J.G., and R.J. Brachman, BBN Report No. 4842, Bolt Beranek and Newman Inc., 1982.

[MBW80] Mylopoulos, J., P.A. Bernstein, and H.K.T. Wong, "A Language Facility for Designing Interactive Database-Intensive Applications," *ACM Transactions on Database Systems,* Vol. 5, No. 2, June 1980.

[MD86] Manola, F., and U. Dayal, "PDM: An Object-Oriented Data Model," *Proceedings of the 1986 International Workshop on Object-Oriented Database Systems,* Pacific Grove, CA, September 23-26, 1986.

[MSOP86] Maier, D., J. Stein, A. Otis, and A. Purdy, "Development of an Object-Oriented DBMS," in *Proceedings of the First ACM OOPSLA Conference,* Portland, OR, Sept., 1986.

[SI83] Schmolze, J.G., and D. Israel, "KL-ONE: Semantics and Classification," *Research in Knowledge Representation for Natural Language Understanding, Annual Report September 1982 - August 1983,* BBN Report No. 5421, Bolt Beranek and Newman Inc., 1983.

[SL83] Schmolze, J.G., and T.A. Lipkis, "Classification in the KL-ONE Knowledge Representation System," *Proceedings of the Joint International Conference on Artificial Intelligence,* 1983.

[SS77] Smith, J.M., and D.C. Smith, "Database Abstractions: Aggregation and Generalization," *ACM Transactions on Database Systems,* Vol. 2, No. 2, June 1977.

[Urban87] Urban, S.D., "Constraint Analysis for the Design of Semantic Update Operations," Ph.D. Dissertation, The University of Southwestern Louisiana, The Center for Advanced Computer Studies, Lafayette, LA, 70504, September 1987.

[UD88] Urban, S.D., and L.M.L. Delcambre, "Constraint Analysis: A Tool for Explaining the Semantics of Complex Objects," *Proceedings of the Second International Workshop on Object-Oriented Database Systems,* October, 1988.

[Zdon86] Zdonik, S.B., "Why Properties are Objects or Some Refinements of 'is-a'," *Proceedings of the Fall Joint Computer Conference,* Dallas, TX, Nov. 1986.

A Performance Comparison of Object and Relational Databases Using the Sun Benchmark

Joshua Duhl & Craig Damon

Ontologic, Inc.
47 Manning Road
Billerica, MA., 01821

Abstract

A general concern about object-oriented systems has been whether or not they are able to meet the performance demands required to be useful for the development of significant production software systems. Attempts to evaluate this assertion have been hampered by a lack of meaningful performance benchmarks that compare database operations across different kinds of databases.

In this paper, we utilize the Sun Benchmark [Rube87] as a means for assessing the performance of an object database and comparing it with existing relational systems. We discuss the benchmark, and many of the implementation issues involved in introducing a relationally oriented benchmark into an object-oriented paradigm. We demonstrate the performance of an object database using Ontologic's Vbase object database platform as an example of a commercially available object database, and we compare these benchmark results against those of existing relational database systems. The results offer strong evidence that object databases are capable of performing as well as, or better than, existing relational database systems.

1. Introduction

The promise of object-oriented databases has been that they can potentially provide faster performance than traditional database management systems. This promise has made by many people, and while not yet verified, it has often been a focus of discussion. On the one hand, proponents state that object databases will provide higher performance for several reasons: Operations can be performed on individual objects or classes of objects; Sub-components can refer to an object by object identity rather than by state (key); Object references can be cached for in-memory access times; and complex design components can be represented more directly using objects than with relational systems [Maie86]. On the other hand, higher levels of abstraction generally lead to worse performance. Analogously, one would expect a high level language, such as PL/1, to be slower than a lower level language, like Fortran, and Fortran to be slower than assembler. One of the major attractions of object systems is the high conceptual level and abstraction at which users can approach, interact with, and model their problem domains. Implementing this high level of abstraction, following this vein, would lead to poor performance because the overhead incurred in supporting the abstraction model will be too great.

Object databases are an emerging and developing technology. Until last year, object databases existed either in early stages of development or as research prototypes. As such they were basically unsuitable for fair performance comparisons with established relational systems. In the past year, however, several object databases have reached a plateau in their development where they can be deemed suitable for performance comparisons with existing relational systems.

Several benchmarks have been developed for measuring database performance. The common database benchmarks, such as the Wisconsin benchmark [Bitt83] and the TP1 benchmark [Anon85] are closely targeted at relational database usages, which emphasize operations specific to the relational model and high volume transaction processing usages respectively. These are inappropriate measures for the kinds of comparisons of interest to users of object-oriented systems. The Sun benchmark was developed in an attempt to measure fundamental database operations in a usage pattern more typical of engineering applications. This benchmark more closely approaches the kind of benchmark suitable

"A Performance Comparison of Object and Relational Databases Using the Sun Benchmark" from *Object-Oriented Programming Systems, Languages, and Applications (OOPSLA) Proceedings*, 1988, pp. 153-161. Copyright © 1988 by The Association for Computing Machinery, Inc., reprinted by permission.

for comparison of object and relational database systems.

2. The Sun Benchmark

The Sun Benchmark was developed to establish an acceptable metric for measuring the *response time* of simple database operations. While it is strongly influenced by the relational model, it is intended for use across different kinds of database systems, and attempts to provide generic, data model independent definitions and benchmark tests that are suitable for benchmarking databases of any data model.

The benchmark itself consists of a simple schema and a representative set of fundamental database operations. Each of the seven operations is measured in terms of its *response time*, the elapsed time between the invocation and return of the operation. The Sun Benchmark is summarized below. Portions of the summary are taken directly from [Rube87].

The schema consists of 3 *record types*: a person record, a document record and an author record. A *record type* is defined as a group of *records* with the same field types. It is a relation in a relational system and a class or type in an object-oriented system. A *record* is defined as a set of fields. It corresponds to a tuple in a relational system and an object in an object-oriented system. Often the fields of an object may be group or multiple valued. The Sun Benchmark definition allows for this specific variation between an object and a record. It also defines a *key* as a unique field over all records of a type. Examples would be a relational primary key or a unique object identifier (UID).

Each of the three record types consists of a set of fields:

1. A **Person** has three fields: a person ID, a name and a birthdate. All IDs are 4 byte integers, serving as keys. Birthdates are randomly generated 4 byte integers that span a 100 year interval. Names are randomly generated strings of up to 40 bytes.

2. A **Document** has seven fields: a document ID, a title, a page count, a document type, a publication date, a publisher, and a description. Titles, publishers, and descriptions are strings up to 80 bytes. Page count, document type and publication date are integers.

3. An **Author** has two fields: a person ID or key referencing a person and a document ID or key referencing a document. It connects each person to zero or more randomly selected documents and each document to exactly 3 randomly selected people.

The Benchmark specifies constructing two versions of the database: The small database is populated with 20,000 Persons, 15,000 Authors and 5,000 Documents. The large database is a factor of ten larger than the small version (i.e. 200,000 Persons, etc.).

The benchmark is comprised of seven individual benchmark operations, defined as follows:

Name Lookup: Fetch the name of a person with a randomly generated ID.

Range Lookup: Fetch the names of all people with birthdates within a particular randomly generated 10 day range.

Group Lookup: Fetch the author ID's for a given random document ID.

Reference Lookup: Fetch the name and birthdate of a person referenced by a randomly selected author record.

Record Insert: Store a new author record.

Sequential Scan: Serially fetch records from the document table, fetching the title from each, but without performing any pattern match computation on the title.

Database Open: Perform all operations necessary to open files, database schema information, and other data structures and overhead to execute the benchmarks, but not time to load the application program itself.

Each operation is performed 50 times, and the entire set, except for database open, is repeated 10 times to simulate an entire session with an engineering application with a mix of different database operations. The reported results are therefore averaged over the entire 500 iterations of each benchmark operation, or 50 iterations in the case of database open.

3. Overview of Vbase

Vbase [Andr87, Onto87] is the object-oriented database platform developed by Ontologic, Inc. It combines the characteristics of object-oriented languages, as set forth by [Wegn87], i.e., objects, classes (types) and inheritance, with the common DBMS characteristics of persistent storage, i.e., multi-user support, concurrency control, and transactions. Vbase incorporates the notions of data abstraction and strong type checking, notions which are both heavily influenced by the CLU programming language [Lisk81].

Abstract types are specified using the declarative Type Definition Language (TDL). A TDL definition specifies the abstract behavior of an object or class of objects. The behavior of an object, its state (properties) and the set of operations defined on that state, is defined by the object's abstract type, or inherited from the object's supertype. Vbase supports a large hierarchy of kernel types, including a sub-hierarchy of 13 aggregate types. Aggregate types include arrays, dictionaries, stacks, and sets. Vbase also supports user defined types, free operations (operations unassociated with any specific type), storage class information, and representation manager specification through TDL.

Objects are manipulated through a compiled procedural language, COP, which is an extension of the C language and is strongly influenced by CLU. COP extends C by adding iterators (operations which iterate over an aggregate of objects yielding each object in turn), exception handling, and syntactic support for object operation invocation and property access. Currently all Vbase applications are written in COP.

In Vbase the specification of an object is separate from its underlying representation. The operations specified in TDL are performed by methods implemented in COP. This distinction between specification and representation allows for changes to be made to the implementation without altering the abstract model.

4. Sun Benchmark on Vbase

The Sun Benchmark is meant to be data model independent. However, it is evident that its conceptual basis and construction are strongly influenced by the relational paradigm. As such some of the relational constructs or operations do not correspond to equivalent object-oriented counterparts. When introducing this essentially relationally oriented benchmark into an object-

oriented system, we encountered both modeling and implementation differences, some of which have been previously encountered in other similar efforts[Smit87].

4.1 Modeling Differences

One of the greatest variances of object-oriented systems from relational is the object identifier provided in an object system. In a relational system, tuple identification is provided by a fabricated unique key that must be maintained for each record. Most tuple accesses are performed using this key. In object-oriented systems, unique references (UID's) are generated as a part of object creation. They provide object identity and can be freely used at any time (across all time) with safety, independently of the field values of an object. As explicitly allowed by the benchmark definition, we have used the Vbase object reference as the key in all cases where appropriate.

A property that refers to another object usually holds the UID of object it references. As such, UID's allow for *direct connectivity* between objects. However, in Vbase, as in many object systems, an object's UID also contains information about the object's type. This differentiates simple direct connectivity, such as with pointers and as found in the network model, from what could be called typed direct connectivity. This additional type information embedded in the object reference can be used to provide information for semantic validation. Unlike relational systems, object systems inherently support this notion of direct connectivity.

Another variance from relational systems is that object-oriented systems support the notion of aggregates or aggregate objects. Aggregate objects allow a group of similarly typed objects to be referred to and manipulated as a single object. They are container objects. Their behavior may be subtyped and refined so as to support combinations of ordering, keyed access, and allowing for multiple copies of the same instance (i.e.. multisets or bags vs. sets).

A substantial variance from the relational model is the disappearance of the Author record type. In the Sun Benchmark, the Author record type exists solely to provide a connective relation between persons and documents. It serves as a many-to-many connective modeling construct. Vbase inherently supports the notion of *distributed properties*. A distributed property is a multi-valued property, which refers directly to each individual object in the set. When used with inverses, distributed properties provide a direct implementation of a many-to-one mapping, or in the case where the inverse property itself is distributed, a many-to-many mapping. Because distributed properties can provide direct connectivity between a single object and many related objects, the need for an intermediate connective modeling construct vanishes entirely.

Conceptually, a person can be considered having authored a document if the person has in fact written a document. In an object system, this relationship can be modeled in several ways. An Author can be modeled as a subtype of type Person or it can be modeled as an optional property (relationship) on type Person (between the person and the documents authored). If Author is modeled as a subtype of type Person, then when a person writes a document and has it published he or she becomes an author. In an object system this could be modeled with dynamic type acquisition. The type of the Person object is changed and in fact specialized to Author, because the Person object has changed. Since Vbase currently does not support the notion of dynamic type acquisition, we have modeled the notion of an author as an optional property. In this way, the potentiality of becoming an author is maintained.

Another fundamental modeling difference from relational systems is found in an object system's support for operations. Relational systems generally perform well when accessing a field in all tuples of a relation but perform poorly when accessing individual records. Operations in object systems are primarily type specific, and are tailored to the type of object they operate upon, so performance is generally high. In object systems, operations also encapsulate behavior, and as such encapsulate code performing some application function that in relational systems normally resides in the application. In Vbase the abstract specification of an object is separate from its implementation. This is particularly useful for operations whose behavioral implementation (their method) can be refined and optimized without affecting the abstract specification or operation invocation.

4.2 Implementation Differences

The benchmark can be implemented in two ways. It can either use all three types and behave like the table oriented relational model, which we will refer to as the *object-relational* (OR) version, or it can use only two types and can take advantage of the direct relationships inherent in the object-oriented paradigm, which we refer to as object version.

The OR version models the original three types, Person, Author and Document. The Person and Document types link directly to the Author type, which models the intermediate table necessary for the many-to-one, one-to-many and many-to-many relationships in a relational system. Type Author has two properties, personlink and documentlink that are both optional multi-valued inverse properties. The documentlink property, denoted author$documentlink links directly to the Document$authorlink property on type Document. The Author$personlink property links to the Person$authorlink property on type Person. If either property is modified the inversely linked property is also modified automatically by Vbase. The TDL is listed below.

```
define type person
   import Document, Author;
   supertypes = {Entity};
   classtype = $ExplicitClass;
   properties = {
     name : String;
     birthdate: Integer;
         authorlink: distributed Set[Author] inverse
                 Author$personlink;
   };
end Person;

define Type Document
   import Person, Author;
   supertypes = {Entity};
   classtype = $ExplicitClass;

   properties = {
     title : String;
     pages : Integer;
     type : Integer;
     date : Integer;
     publisher : String;
     description : String;
         authorlink: distributed Set[Author] inverse
                 Author$documentlink;
   };
end document;
```

```
define type Author
  import Person, Document;
  supertypes = {Entity};
  classtype = $ExplicitClass;

  properties = {
    documentlink : optional Document inverse
              Document$authorlink;
    personlink : optional Person inverse
              Person$authorlink;
  };
end author;
```

The object version models only two of the three types, Person and Document, taking advantage of distributed properties available in the Vbase object model to eliminate the intermediate Author type. The notion of authorship is fulfilled through an inverse relationship property. The many-to-many mapping is accomplished by a set of direct inverse links between the document's *authors* property, denoted Document$authors, and the *publications* property on Person, Person$publications.

With this combination of modeling constructs, the semantics of authorship can be modeled quite naturally: if it has a value, then the person has authored a document, and if it is empty, then the person has not authored anything. Direct, inverse, and optional properties are modeling features inherent in Vbase that also result in significant performance advantages, both in size and speed. Other than the elimination of the Author type, the object version TDL differs only slightly from the OR version:

```
define type Person
  import Document;
  supertypes = {Entity};
  classtype = $ExplicitClass;

  properties = {
    name : String;
    birthdate: Integer;
    publications : distributed Set[Document] inverse
              Document$authors;
  };
end Person;

  define Type Document
    import Person;
    supertypes = {Entity};
```

```
    classtype = $ExplicitClass;

    properties = {
      title : String;
      pages : Integer;
      type  : Integer;
      date  : Integer;
      publisher : String;
      description : String;
      authors : distributed Set[Person] inverse
                Person$publications;
    };
end Document;
```

Note: The full TDL can be found in Appendix A.

In both versions, optimized implementations of the create operation (the create method) have been written to achieve faster performance. Additionally, a special iterator method has been written to yield people whose birthdays fell within the 10 day range of birthdays as required by the range lookup operation. Birthdates are stored as keys into a B-Tree holding objects of type Person. The iterator made use of a pre-release functional interface to the B-Trees that is to be integrated into the 2.0 release of Vbase.

The aggregate classes containing all People or Documents have been implemented in the small version of the benchmark as Lists. In the large version they will be implemented as B-Trees.

The group lookup is implemented as an iteration over the set of Authors on a given random document.

The name lookup is performed as a property access on the name property on the random people.

The reference lookup is performed as two property accesses on each random Person.

5. Results

5.1 Benchmark Environment

The Benchmark encourages performance optimization. It suggests taking advantage of cache memory, permitting caching of as much of the database as the database system allows, and utilizing the fastest and most efficient data structures and access methods for each benchmark operation. The Vbase cache size is user determinable with a current

207

Sun Benchmark Data [1]

Small (40,000 instances) Database Results Only

DBMS	INGRES	UNIFY	RAD-UNIFY	VBASE	VBASE
Model Type	Relational	Relational	Relational	Relational	Object
Name Lookup	35 ms	60 ms	9 ms	11.4 ms	9.8 ms
Range Lookup	393ms*	358 ms	76 ms	95.9 ms	84.1 ms
Group Lookup	116 ms	85 ms	24 ms	6.0 ms	5.1 ms
Reference Lookup	165 ms	50 ms	6 ms	30.6 ms	9.8 ms
Record Insert	56 ms	230 ms	43 ms	95.44 ms**	24.3 ms****
Sequential Scan	2 ms	11 ms	3 ms	1.53 ms	1.6 ms
Database Open	1300 ms	580 ms	580 ms	1020 ms	1036 ms
Actual Size	6.3 MB	3.8 MB	3.8 MB	12.1 MB****	10.4 MB#

Figure 1.

* These are estimated, not empirical times. See [Rube87] for more detail.

** This is implemented as a Create operation.

*** An alternative implementation of an insert function would involve a Create operation in Vbase. The average time for this is 75.7 ms.

**** This figure represents 5.5 MB of kernel data, and 6.6 MB of benchmark data.

\# This figure represents 5.5 MB of kernel data, and 4.8 MB of benchmark data.

[1] The figures in this table for Ingres, Unify, and RAD-Unify are presented in [Rube87]. Original data for Vbase are added by the authors.

ONTOLOGIC, INC.
June 20, 1988

limit of about 8 megabytes. We found 6 megabytes to be optimal for the small database. At the writing of this paper, the large database benchmark has not yet been completed.

The original Sun benchmark was performed on a Sun 3/160 processor, with 8 megabytes and a local database stored on disk. Our version was executed on a Sun 3/160 processor with 16 megabytes of physical memory, and the database stored on a local disk, using version 1.1 of Vbase.

The difference in the physical memory size affected the ability to cache more of the database in main memory. With more physical memory available, a larger cache size is also possible. Thus physical memory size indirectly affects benchmark performance through the cache size. When the cache size remained constant and the benchmark was executed on machines with different sized physical memories there was no noticeable difference in the benchmark timings.

In implementing the benchmark support code, the most awkward phase is randomly generating the UID references, since they are not simply consecutive integers. Instead, we build an in-memory array containing all of the references to a given type, and randomly chose an entry in this array. To ensure that building this array does not bias the results in any sense, we close the database and flush all remnants of this activity (save these arrays) before running any of the tests. Loading this array is not included in the actual benchmark timings.

5.2 Discussion

The table in Figure 1 summarizes the results of the small database version of the Sun Benchmark, and allows for comparison of both Vbase models to the existing relational versions. The large version has yet to be completed at the time of the writing of this paper. Rad-Unify, developed by Rubenstein, et. al., is an in-memory version of Unify. It caches as much of the database as possible, which in the small benchmark is the entire database. It also utilizes a simplified locking mechanism that allows for only one writer at a time. Vbase also caches the entire database for the small benchmark, as well as providing full multi-user support.

Overall, these numbers indicate that an object system can meet and in many cases exceed the performance of a fast relational system, even in a problem clearly from the relational domain. The results also indicate that an object system can model a relational implementation and achieve response times comparable to the relational systems. Note that it is possible to achieve improvements in performance by using an alternative schema definition.

5.2.1 Trends

For several of these tests, the early timings dominated the averages, themselves being dominated by the disk transfer time of the schema objects as well as the data itself. All the tests show continual improvement in the timings over the course of the benchmark, particularly after the first 100 iterations and even more so after 200 iterations.

The name lookup test drops dramatically over the course of the benchmark coming to a constant 0.8 milliseconds (ms) after 350 iterations. The reference lookup follows a similar trend, dropping to approximately 3.2 ms after 300 iterations. This trend occurs because more of the referenced objects have been brought into the cache and can be found in the cache as the benchmark proceeds. The trend applies, but to a lesser extent, to all of the tests except the Sequential Scan test, which maintains a fairly constant timing after the first 50 iterations. It should be noted that Rad Unify exhibits similar behavior.

For the record insert test, we provided two numbers for the object version. To implement the behavior described in the benchmark using Vbase, no creation was required. Instead, an extra value was placed in the distributed (multi-valued) property on both the selected Person and the selected Document. While this is a meaningful distinction between relational and object systems (many of the tuples created in a relational system exist only to express relationships and would not be required on an object system), creates remain a necessary and important component of any database system. As the timings indicate, this is the one area where the performance of Vbase is relatively slow. This is not a commentary on object databases, but a limitation in the current implementation of Vbase.

Vbase supports a generic create method that is called to create any new entity. The original timing for the alternative record insert, using a create, was

290.6 milliseconds. Rewriting the create method resulted in an average time of 75.7ms. (a peak time of 66.8ms) which is nearly a factor of four improvement in create performance timing. This ability to modify and enhance the implementation without affecting the abstract specification is a capability entirely unavailable in relational systems, and is clearly a significant advantage for object systems.

Like many of the tests, the range lookup showed a trend of steady improvements in performance with each group of 50, reaching a constant plateau of 54.4 milliseconds after 300 iterations. The average time is comparable to the Rad Unify time.

Performance was not significantly affected by using a remote database. The initial 100 iterations were most affected, as they performed the majority of disk access. Later iterations were unaffected as most of the database had been already cached in memory.

6. Sun Benchmark Criticisms

The Sun Benchmark is useful as a performance metric for comparisons between relational systems, and between relational and object systems. However, it is weak when attempting to provide truly meaningful comparisons between object systems.

The *working set* is atypical for object applications. By a *working set* we mean the set of objects touched or used by the application at any given time during the course of application execution. In this Benchmark each individual benchmark strictly called for objects to be randomly selected and operated upon. Objects could only be clustered with objects of a similar type, but could be kept in the cache over the entire benchmark. In many engineering applications closely related objects are accessed successively, with greater frequency and to a much higher degree than are random, disjoint objects. Because of this general usage pattern, semantically related objects are often physically clustered together in the database. This "semantic clustering" usually results in much higher performance because many of the related objects are brought into cache memory at the time a requested object is brought in, thereby improving the overall access times for related objects.

The Benchmark model (i.e. Person, Author, Document) is quite simplistic and does not attempt to approach the complexity or exercise the usual features that an object-oriented application normally includes. One of the promises of object systems is that they provide features for abstractly modeling complex real world objects and their behavior. To this end, these systems provide things like type hierarchies, inheritance models, complex relationships like A-Part-Of (APO), A-Kind-Of (AKO), An-Instance-Of (AIO), aggregates, inverse properties, versions and alternatives, as well as traditional database features such as concurrency control and multi-user support.

In this simple relational benchmark model there is no need for any dynamic behavior. Modeling dynamic behavior, such as in some kind of event simulation application, is something object systems can perform well and are frequently called upon to model.

These initial criticisms begin to give form to the general criticism that while the benchmark allows database assessment and comparison at a low level of fundamental and common database operations, it does not attempt to address what may be more interesting and meaningful comparisons such as the performance at the level of the application. There may be certain kinds of applications such as engineering design, complex modeling, hypermedia and CASE applications, which are better addressed by object databases. The work by Smith and Zdonik on Intermedia [Smit87] points us in this direction.

To this end, we would like to suggest that future benchmarks allow for examination and assessment of databases at a higher, more complex level. Perhaps they can measure performance more at the level of the application. We would like to suggest that such a benchmark include measurements for the access of large and complex data objects such as documents, and images; that it measure graph or associative traversal operations such closure operations; and that it operate in an environment that more closely approximates an engineering environment with remote databases, and possibly distributed data. Furthermore this application benchmark would need to take into account the kinds of complex modeling relationships object databases have been created to model. Work on just such a benchmark is currently being pursued by [Berre].

7. Closing Remarks

The is paper has offered results for a small version of the Sun Benchmark database. At the time of the writing of this paper, the large version is under construction but is not yet complete.

We have found the Sun Benchmark to be a useful benchmark for measuring simple database operations across different kinds of databases. To some degree, this paper stands as "proof of concept", to the benchmark author's intent of developing a benchmark that can be used for measurements across different kinds of databases. Furthermore, it has allowed us to test and give light to the critical assertion that object databases, such as Vbase, are capable of performing at rates comparable to or faster than existing relational systems.

Lastly, it is evident, that benchmarks that more closely address and assess the capabilities of object databases are needed to properly measure this new and developing technology.

References

[Andr87] Andrews, Tim, Harris, Craig, "Combining Language and Database Advances in an Object Oriented Development Environment", *OOPSLA '87 Conference Proceedings*, SigPlan Notices, Volume 22, Number 12, December 1987.

[Anon85] Anon. et al., "A Measure of Transaction Processing Power", *Datamation*, April 1, 1985.

[Berre] Berre, Arne J. Anderson, T. Lougenia, Porter, Harry, Schneider, Bruce, "The HyperModel Benchmark", Unpublished Work. Oregon Graduate Center, Beaverton Oregon.

[Bitt83] Bitton, D., DeWitt, D. J., Turbfill, C., "Benchmarking Database Systems: A Systematic Approach", *Proceedings of the 1983 VLDB*, 1983.

[Codd70] E.F. Codd, "A Relational Model of Data for Large Shared Data Banks", CACM, Vol. 13, 6 (June, 1970) pp 377-387.

[Lisk81] Liskov, B., Atkinson, R., Bloom, T., Moss, E., Schaffert, C., Scheifler, R., Snyder, A., *CLU Reference Manual*, Springer-Verlag 1981.

[Maie86] Maier, David, "Why Object-Oriented Databases Can Succeed Where Others Have Failed", *Proceedings of the 1986 International Workshop on Object-Oriented Database Systems*, 1986.

[Onto87] Vbase Programmer's Guide, Ontologic, Inc., Billerica MA, 1987.

[Rubc87] Rubenstein, W. B., Kubicar, M. S., Cattell, R. G. G., "Benchmarking Simple Database Operations", *SIGMOD '87 Proceedings*, SIGMOD Record, Volume 16, Number 3, December 1987.

[Smit87] Smith, Karen E., Zdonik, Stanley B., Intermedia: A Case Study of the Differences Between Relational and Object-Oriented Database Systems", *OOPSLA '87 Conference Proceedings*, SigPlan Notices, Volume 22, Number 12, December 1987.

[Wegn87] Wegner, Peter, "Dimensions of Object-Based Language Design", *OOPSLA '87 Con-*

ference Proceedings, SigPlan Notices, Volume 22, Number 12, December 1987.

Appendix A

Object Version TDL

```
define type Person
  import Document;
  supertypes = {Entity};
  classtype = $ExplicitClass;

  properties = {
    name : String;
    birthdate: Integer;
    publications : distributed Set[Document] inverse
                          Document$authors;
  };

  operations = {
    refines Delete(e:Person)
    triggers (RemoveFromDates);
  };

  define Iterator BirthRange(low : Integer,
                                   high : Integer )
      yields (Person)
      method (BirthIter)
  end BirthRange;

  define Procedure Create( T: Type,
    keywords
    name : String,
    birthdate : Integer,
    optional publications : Array [Document],
    optional where: Entity,
    optional hownear: Clustering)
    returns (Person)
    raises (BadCreate)
    method (Person_Create)
    triggers (AddToDates)
  end Create;

end Person;

define Variable Birthdays: btree;

define Type Document
  import Person;
  supertypes = {Entity};
  classtype = $ExplicitClass;

  properties = {
    title : String;
    pages : Integer;
    type  : Integer;
```

```
    date  : Integer;
    publisher : String;
    description : String;
    authors : distributed Set[Person] inverse
            Person$publications;
  };
end Document;
```

Relational Version TDL

```
define type person
  import Document, Author;
  supertypes = {Entity};
  classtype = $ExplicitClass;
  properties = {
    name : String;
    birthdate: Integer;
        authorlink: distributed Set[Author] inverse
                Author$personlink;
  };

  operations = {
    refines Delete(e:Person)
    triggers (RemoveFromDates);
  };

  define Iterator BirthRange(low : Integer,
                            high : Integer )
    yields (Person)
    method (BirthIter)
  end BirthRange;


  define Procedure Create( T: Type,
    keywords
    name : String,
    birthdate : Integer,
    optional authorlink : Array [Document],
    optional where: Entity,
    optional hownear: Clustering)
    returns (Person)
    raises (BadCreate)
    method (Person_Create)
    triggers (AddToDates)
  end Create;
end Person;

define Variable Birthdays: btree;

define Type Document
  import Person, Author;
  supertypes = {Entity};
  classtype = $ExplicitClass;
```

```
  properties = {
    title : String;
    pages : Integer;
    type  : Integer;
    date  : Integer;
    publisher : String;
    description : String;
        authorlink: distributed Set[Author] inverse
                Author$documentlink;
  };
end document;


define type Author
  import Person, Document;
  supertypes = {Entity};
  classtype = $ExplicitClass;

  properties = {
    documentlink : optional Document inverse
                Document$authorlink;
    personlink : optional Person inverse
                Person$authorlink;
  };
end author;
```

Reprinted from *IEEE Transactions on Software Engineering*, August 1989, pages 935-946. Copyright © 1989 by The Institute of Electrical and Electronics Engineers, Inc. All rights reserved.

Performance Properties of Vertically Partitioned Object-Oriented Systems

STEPHEN P. HUFNAGEL AND JAMES C. BROWNE

Abstract—It has long been believed that object-oriented system structuring offers advantages for design and implementation of computer software systems with respect to comprehensibility, verifiability, maintainability, etc. The major obstacle to widespread use of object-oriented systems has been that their execution has been intrinsically inefficient due to excessive overhead. This paper contends that much of the execution overhead of object-oriented systems has been due to the implementation structure, that is, the objects are built upon a conventional layered software structure. This paper proposes a vertically partitioned structure for design and implementation of object-oriented systems and demonstrates their performance. We show that the application independent portion of the execution overheads in object-oriented systems can be less than the application independent overheads in conventionally organized systems built upon layered structures.

Vertical partitioning implements objects through extended type managers. An extended type manager not only implements the functionality which defines a type but also implements all state management functions such as storage, access control and consistency management (including concurrency control, error detection, and fault recovery) for the occurrences of that type. Two key design concepts result in performance improvement: object semantics can be used in the state management functions of an object type and atomicity is maintained at the type manager boundaries providing efficient recovery points.

The performance evaluation is based upon a case study of a simple but nontrivial distributed real-time system application. Evaluation of overheads was accomplished by implementing system control, but not implementing application functionality for both conventional layered and vertically partitioned versions of the application. The results show a clear diminution of overhead in the vertically partitioned, object-oriented structured system over the functionally oriented, layered structured system.

Index Terms—Dependability, distributed systems, fault tolerance, object-oriented systems, operating systems, software design methodology, software performance, vertically partitioned systems.

I. INTRODUCTION

THE goal of this research was to evaluate some of the performance consequences of a new vertically partitioned [4], [12] approach applied to the design and implementation of object-oriented systems. Vertical partitioning implements objects through extended type managers. An extended type manager not only imple-

Manuscript received May 14, 1987. This work was supported in part by the Office of Naval Research under Contract N00014-86-K-0763, and in part by the Defense Advanced Research Projects Agency under Contract N00038-86-C-0167.

S. P. Hufnagel is with the Department of Computer Science Engineering, University of Texas at Arlington, Arlington, TX 76019.

J. C. Browne is with the Department of Computer Sciences, University of Texas at Austin, Austin, TX 78712.

IEEE Log Number 8928901.

ments the functionality which defines a type but also implements all state management functions such as storage, access control, and consistency management (including concurrency control, error detection, and fault recovery) for the occurrences of that type.

It is commonly believed that the modularity of object-oriented system structures leads to "good" software systems which are comprehensible and maintainable. It is also commonly believed that these virtues can only be obtained on conventional computer architectures at the cost of performance and efficient use of resources. There is reason to believe that these inefficiencies and performance problems have historically arisen largely because past object-oriented systems have been built upon the inappropriate foundation provided by the conventional layered operating system and database system execution environment.

System structure affects the performance cost of satisfying interdata and interfunctional dependencies and controlling the execution of a computation. Past object-oriented system structures systems (i.e., SMALLTALK [10], [17] and EDEN [1]) which have been embedded in conventional software environments (i.e., UNIX) have typically incurred increased execution control and recovery dependency satisfaction performance "overhead" costs, i.e., they are not practical for many actual uses.

A highly modular object-oriented program structure in the traditional implementation will incur an execution cost increasing rapidly with degree of modularity because the separation of object defining and state management functions requires a large number of expensive context switches to execute state management and execution control functions. The vertically partitioned structure integrates implementation of type functionality and state management in a single execution context in order to reduce total cost. Vertical partitioning also encourages the exploitation of an object's individual semantic properties to minimize the execution of both the functions on data and system overhead functions, such as consistency management and recovery.

This paper first defines and describes an object-oriented system structuring technique based upon "vertical partitioning" which extends object definitions to a low level abstract machine. The experiment shows that the vertically partitioned object-oriented system is more efficient in its execution of the application independent portions of the computation than the conventionally designed and implemented system. The experiment is too limited in scope and too complex to yield a definitive result, but a consistent and straightforward interpretation of the results strongly suggests that vertically partitioned system structures give good performance while retaining the virtues of object-oriented structuring.

II. Definitions of Object-Structuring

Objects and object-structured systems are, like pornography, difficult to define but readily recognizable when in view. Meyers [14], Danforth [8], and others have given extensive definition of objects and object structuring. This section gives only that background necessary to put the definitions herein in perspective.

Each of our objects are a triple ⟨Unique-Name, Type, Representation⟩. The *unique-name* of an object distinguishes it from all other objects. The *type* of the object defines the properties of the object (e.g., program, stack, process, etc.) by defining the operations which may be applied to the object. The representation of an object is hidden from the users view within a type manager which implements the operations of the type definition.

There are two schools of thought and practice concerning the definition of complex objects, abstract data type-based definition, and inheritance-based definition. Danforth [8] discusses the alternatives and conflicts of models provided by type theory for abstract data types and inheritance.

A. Abstract Data Type-Based Object-Structuring

An *object-oriented* software system is an assembly of objects [14]. Each object will satisfy the Parnas [16] module criteria. That is, a *module* (e.g., the type manager of an object) implements an abstract data type and performs all of the required actions on its data, and specifies the necessary pre- and postconditions for acceptance of the results of those actions. The functions of a module are made available to other modules as procedure calls, and these procedure calls constitute the only access to the functions of the module. In particular, the data manipulated by the module is only made available to other modules by *prodedure invocations*; other modules have no direct access to the location or the representation of any data used by the module. Modules detect conditions which violate their specifications and prevent application of functions upon the module's data when the necessary conditions are not met [20].

B. Inheritance-Based Object-Oriented Structuring

In inheritance-based object-oriented system structures types are defined as extensions of existing types [14]. A type definition begins with functions inherited from parent types. Complex types are defined through multiple inheritance. Inheritance is to receive properties or characteristics of another, normally as a result of some special relationship between the giver and the receiver. Frequently this is referred to as a class hierarchy. When using inheritance in this way, an object is specified as what is new about the new object in reference to a class or subclass object definition. As an example, in Smalltalk, a subclass inherits and may extend both the state representation and the operations of the superclass.

C. Abstract Data-Type Inheritance and Vertical Partitioning

Inheritance is not compatible with vertical partitioning for several reasons. It tends to inhibit definition of type specific semantics for state management functions and to blur the concept of strong atomicity at manager boundaries required by vertical partitioning. Abstract data type definitions of objects, on the other hand, provide a natural framework for implementation of both of these requirements for vertical partitioning. We have, therefore, chosen the abstract data type-based definition and structure as the implementation framework for vertical partitioning. America [2] has made a similar argument in justification of his choice for the design and implementation of the POOL-T system.

III. Vertical Partitioning Concepts

Vertical partitioning is an end point of abstract data-typed based object-oriented system structuring in which the state and the total functionality of the system is partitioned by object type. A vertically partitioned system is defined by specification of a set of object types. A vertically partitioned system type manager extends beyond the traditional type manager definition [5]. An extended type manager not only implements the functionality which defines each type but also implements all state management functions such as access control, data storage, concurrency management, error detection, and fault management (i.e., recovery and restart). Thus, the functions implemented by the database and operating system layers in a traditional layered system structure are incorporated as needed in the extended type managers. Extended type managers are implemented on a low level abstract machine, the principal function of which is to provide virtualization of and access control to physical resources. Each type manager maintains the property of atomicity for its functions to provide for safe fault recovery points at its boundaries.

Vertical partitioning simply carries type manager structuring of systems to its logical extreme. Operating systems and database systems, as we now know them, largely disappear as separate entities since most of their functions are incorporated in the extended type managers.

We are presenting a radical alternative for system structuring. The hypotheses we put foward are:

1) that object-oriented systems implemented in the vertically partitioned framework are more efficient than a system of the same functionality implemented in the conventional layered system framework,

2) that this sytem structuring technique yields a partitioning of state and functionality that results in effective and efficient distributed and parallel systems, and

3) that this system structuring framework leads to verifiable robust systems with respect to fault tolerance.

Note that the first hypothesis is stronger than the statement that "an object-oriented system implemented in the vertically partitioned structure is more efficient than an object-oriented system of the same functionality implemented in a conventional framework." The basis for this claim is that special case state management algorithms are almost always more efficient where they apply them than are general algorithms and that partitioning by type establishes a basis for locality and specialization of both state management and computational operations. Both type-specific functions and state maintenance functions can take advantage of the semantics of the typed objects. Hypotheses 2) and 3) are justified herein only by plausibility arguments. They will be the subject of future publications. The simulation experiment which will be presented, in a subsequent section, is a partial validation of hypothesis 1).

IV. VERTICALLY PARTITIONED SYSTEM STRUCTURES

This section will describe how a collection of extended type managers are created by a type-type manager and are executed on an abstract machine. Distributed and concurrent processing is supported by our paradigm.

A. Extended Type Managers

An extended type manager defines all of the properties of an object by defining the functions that can be applied to occurrences of the object. This definition of a type manager is parallel to the programming language definition of a manager [18] which was derived from the definition of a monitor [11]. The extended type managers defined herein carry over all of the properties of conventional type managers. Its extensions implement generic type specific algorithms for the management of the state of the occurrences of the object type they implement. In particular, such extended type managers implement 1) storage of and access to the occurrences of the type it implements, 2) atomicity of its type-defining operations including fault-tolerance and control of internal concurrency as necessary.

Complex object types are defined by definition of extended type managers which define the more complex object types in terms of functions provided by the extended type managers for simpler objects.

B. System Structure

Extended type managers are typed object occurrences defined by a special system extended type manager whose name is "type" and whose "type" is type [6]. For brevity we will refer to this special type manager as "type-type." Type-type has, for type managers, all of the responsibilities of an extended type manager. Fig. 1 illustrates the type-type concept.

This system structure is a natural one for definition of distributed systems [3], [19]. Type-type can, for exam-

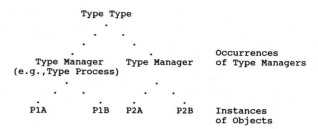

Fig. 1. Object type manager hierarchy.

ple, create multiple instances of an extended type manager whose implementation utilizes distributed algorithms for state management and install them (the equivalent of storage for a data object) at multiple sites of a distributed resource set.

A vertically partitioned system thus consists of type-type, a set of system and application-specific type managers and the occurrences of the types defined by these type managers. A distributed vertically partitioned system consists of an occurrence of type-type at each site together with such system and application specific type managers that are required to attain system-level specifications.

C. Model of Execution

The model of execution in a vertically partitioned system-structured is a tree of invocations of procedures defined by extended type managers. The system is initialized from type-type. The execution of an application is begun at some procedure of the external interface of an application-specific type manager.

D. System Type Managers

The functions of distributed operating and database systems are subsumed in the type specific state management algorithms of the extended type managers. A given implementation of type-type may itself be distributed. It will be convenient to provide a library of extended type managers which define commonly needed object types, as will be described.

1) Communications: A name manager and a switchboard (circuit) manager are used in establishing communications. A name manager establishes a path to the present location of the object but does not guarantee that the object will remain at that location. Migratory objects may be tracked by either a forwarding address or a call to the name manager.

A switchboard manager establishes a two-way communications path. A switchboard manager is analogous to a two-way circuit. Both ends of the circuit must be updated or have the information available to update if there is a change in the connectivity.

2) Process: A process is a declared type that makes a program object, address space, and a processor to execute. A process is an object to which the function *execute* applies. A process is created (defined) by giving a process type manager a program and an address space, and a processor. The process type manager is responsible for the installation and control of the program.

Informally, a *process* may be defined as a schedulable stream of instructions with a program counter (PC) imbedded in some address space where names have been resolved. A process may invoke procedures defined by type managers. The process' locus of computation may flow from execution in one object's address space to execution in another object's address space.

E. Abstract Machine

We are generating a distributed system that integrates the normal operating system and database system functions. The abstract machine which provides the execution environment for vertically partitioned systems can be very simple, since the functions are subsumed into the extended type managers and by a selected set of system type managers.

The abstract machine has a scheduler that multiplexes the processor among the type managers and schedules the type manager's requests for memory and communications resources. The abstract machine will provide the processor number upon which the software is running. The abstract machine interface consists of requests for resources (i.e., CPU, local area network, and memory), linkage between type managers, and requests for CPU identification (ID). The abstract machine is also responsible for restarting the system and the startup of the type-type manager.

V. Performance and Dependability in Vertically Partitioned Systems

The motivation for vertical partitioning of an object-oriented system design is to attain high performance and high dependability. Performance will be enhanced by use of the semantics of the objects. Object-oriented systems traditionally result in a workload that contains a great deal of context switching and data movement, thereby reducing performance. This increased workload arises because of the smaller granularity of system structures resulting from object-oriented design. Much data movement is among related object data structures. Vertical partitioning lowers the flow of data across domain boundaries. (Intra-domain context switches are typically less expensive than interdomain switches.) Also, traditional object-oriented designs have not taken full advantage of semantic information available about the object's functions and storage.

All mechanisms for monitoring integrity in the presence of faults are based upon redundancy [13]. By vertical partitioning of composite objects, we allow the use of the semantic properties of object data by the type managers that act on the data. Semantic properties of data and data structures can be used to improve overall system performance [9]. Type manager implementation of functions often allows compile-time binding of consistency and fault management functions to their associated data structures, instead of run-time interpretation of generic operating system or database system functions. Compile-time binding typically results in improved system efficiency [9]. Decomposition of total processing on the basis of application-based structures cuts down the data flow and inter-domain context switches. Performance may also be improved due to the locality of functions and data within the object boundaries.

The use of the semantic properties of object data results in type-specific fault localization, fault recovery, "operating system" support routines, and "database" routines. Hence, system-wide operating systems and system-wide database systems are no longer required. Simplicity of recovery results from atomicity at object boundaries and from use of type-specific fault detection and recovery mechanisms. Vertical partitioning limits the propagation of faults, localizes data, limits the interdependencies among objects for fault recovery, and enhances overall system security.

VI. Design of Vertically Partitioned Systems

This section will consolidate the concepts and definitions given preceding into a vertically partitioned object-oriented design approach. Justification for the specifications and design options will be discussed.

A. System Partitioning

The approach is to develop an object-oriented system design that "vertically partitions" the state and the functionality of the system by type. The concept of composite objects is included. Decomposition of total processing is done on the basis of application type definition rather than on software system layers.

B. Hierarchical Structuring

The hierarchical definition of composite objects in terms of other objects subsumes the concept of nested transactions [15]. Composite objects provide a variable granularity of definitions that provides design control over data consistency, software integrity, and fault recovery.

C. Exploiting Semantics

The algorithms implementing the functions defining an object should exploit the object's individual semantic properties in order to provide application-specific fault localization, fault recovery, and the necessary "operating system" and "database" routines.

D. Hierarchical Atomicity and Fault-Tolerance

Atomicity must be maintained by the type manager's procedures. Atomicity implies that the invoking of an object's type manager will have one of two outcomes: a new state will be created and be committed to or there will be no change to the object's state. Each externally accessible function or procedure of the type manager will return, as a minimum, an exception flag that will indicate a completed or aborted execution. A temporary state of pending commitments is possible while waiting for higher level objects to commit. Once an object's new state is committed, its state can only be altered by invoking a compensating action. During a temporary state of pending either the object's original state (i.e., possibly with a time lag) may be used for additional accesses, or access to the object's state information may be blocked, awaiting either the indication to commit to a new state or the indication to return to an earlier state.

The hierarchical definition of composite objects in terms of other objects must in each case guarantee the atomicity, consistency, and durability of its objects. Each type manager must implement correct concurrent access to the data of the object controlled by its procedures to maintain data consistency both during normal execution and when recovering from faults.

Since objects are hierarchically structured, commitment of higher level (ancestor) objects must wait until all lower level (descendant) object calls have completed and tentatively committed. Should the higher level object decide to abort execution, all lower level objects must also abort execution and return to a previous safe state. The results of this hierarchical definition of composite objects are intrinsic to the structure of the system. The type managers of the various objects in the system must each contain the recovery and/or control procedures necessary for overall safe state recovery.

E. Relationship to Transaction-Oriented Design

The intrinsic structure of composite objects subsumes transaction and nested transaction concepts. The basic difference between the transaction and object view is the time at which the sequence of elementary operations is bound to the set of data objects. The object view allows binding of a sequence of operations to a set of data items at compile time or load time while the transaction view can only support binding of the operational sequence at run time.

If the need for indivisible actions on logical data objects can be foreseen then early binding can be provided and a resultant increase in efficiency is possible. Specificity in the choice of localized recovery mechanisms allows specific fault recovery that aids in overall system efficiency. For example, in forward recovery [7] the semantics of logical operations are used to allow programmed exception handling. Finally, partitioning at object boundaries limits the effect (e.g., access range) of functions, reduces the propagation of faults, and enhances overall system security.

VII. Performance Evaluation of Vertical Partitioning

This section first presents the goal, scope, and approach of the methodology evaluation effort. Then the requirements and specifications for a sample application are given. A description of the techniques of design, implementation, and execution of the experiment are reviewed. Next, a definition of the specific types of metric data which were collected during the experiments is given. Finally, the overall analysis of the methodology evaluation results is given. A case by case representation of some of the experimental results are presented in the Appendix.

A. Introduction

The goal is to evaluate the performance properties of a vertically partitioned object-oriented structured system and to compare these properties to similar properties of a functionally structured, conventionally layered system. The scope of this study is confined to comparison of the costs of executing the system overhead functions of state management and execution control for both an object-oriented system structure and a functionally layered system structure in an otherwise fixed execution environment. No advantage was taken of the possibilities of the vertically partitioned object-oriented system for using the properties of functions on objects to make the processing more efficient except for the case of fault localization and fault recovery, which is a function required by the application. The experiment thus does not take into account a potential major advantage of vertical partitioning; performance may often be improved by taking advantage of the semantics of the application. The results will thus be pessimistic with respect to the potential performance of the vertically partitioned implementation.

B. Approach

The evaluation of the methodology was done by discrete event simulation modeling. Two programs were written to evaluate execution behavior. The requirements for a sample application are given in Section VII-C. The first program met the design specifications of the functional layered approach (Section VII-D), and the second program met the design specifications of the vertically partitioned object-oriented approach (Section VII-E).

Both hardware and software were simulated. The programming language Pascal was used. The simulation software was executed on a DEC 2060 computer. Transaction-based modeling was used. That is, sets of identical states (e.g., a CPU crashed, two CPU's were operational, etc.) were defined in the two simulator programs and identical sequences of transactions were executed by the simulators. Each simulation program incorporated measurement data gathering for analysis of the designs.

The functionally designed model was developed first. When the program was completed and working to the author's satisfaction, the program was "frozen." A copy of the program was made and used as the basis to start the object design. The complete hardware simulation portions and metric collection portions of the original simulator were kept intact. The operating system code, database code, and application code were repartitioned and augmented to create object structures. Then the code was modified as needed to work within the object structures. Finally fault localization and fault recovery portions of the code were optimized as appropriate, to take advantage of the individual semantic properties of the object structures. No functional capability was introduced nor was any functional capability lost in creating the object designed program from the functionally designed program. Only the structures were changed.

C. Application Requirements

We will now describe the application requirements that were used to generate the system software specifications. The system requirements are a simplified abstraction of a real system [19].

The hardware configuration will consist of three computers connected to two local area networks that are also attached to two disks, two operator displays, two communications (message) receivers, and a system command unit. Communications between the hardware units will be by passing messages on one of the local area networks. The application programs will support external message reception of track update messages by the communications units. One of the communications units will be enabled by the software program to format each track update message for transmission to the communications processing function on one of the computers. There will be three software processing functions: 1) the communications processing function, which will receive track update messages from a communications unit on the local area network, decode each message to create a track report message, and send each track report message to the track processing function; when the system is initialized the communications processing function will send a message to one of the communications units to make it the active unit, the other unit will stay in standby; 2) the track processing function will receive track report messages from the communications processing function, will perform track update processing, will create display update messages, and will pass the display update message to the display processing function; 3) the display processing function will receive display update messages from the track processing function, will create two display command messages, and will send the display commands messages to both of the display units; when the system is initialized the display processing function will send an initialization command message to each of the display units.

The system will provide for continued operation after, and recovery from, a single point of failure. That is, the system will automatically reconfigure itself to bypass a nonoperational hardware unit and continue receiving and processing external track update messages. If a nonoperational hardware unit becomes operational the system will reconfigure itself to include the operational unit.

When all hardware units are operational the following system configuration will be used. 1) Communications unit 1 will be active and communications unit 2 will be in standby. 2) Local area network 1 will be exclusively used for communications among hardware units. 3) The communications processing function will be located in computer 1, the tracking function will be located in computer 2, and the display processing function will be located in computer 3. 4) Duplicate information will be placed on disk units 1 and 2. 5) Duplicate information will be displayed on display units 1 and 2.

If a computer becomes nonoperational, the system will detect the failure and reconfigure itself to redistribute the processing function of the nonoperational computer to the next higher numbered computer, modulo three (i.e., if computer 1 fails then computer 2 will configure itself to do both the communications function and the tracking function). If a computer becomes operational, after having been nonoperational, the system will reconfigure itself to the fully operational configuration just described.

The following assumptions are made. 1) Messages are reliably passed and messages will be passed in the order that they are sent. 2) The hardware units are "fail stop," that is, they will stop and provide an indication when a hardware failure occurs.

D. Functional Software Specifications

Each computer has a kernel operating system. Each operating system is responsible for local configuration based upon the operability of the system hardware units. It maintains a local and global status of the system configuration and exchange status between processors whenever a software reconfiguration occurs. The operating system provides local area network access routines and passes messages among processes and the local area network. Interprocess communication is done by message passing. A database system is provided to allow uniform access to disk data structures.

The application software is partitioned into three processes: a communications process, a track process, and a display process. The default system configuration has the communications process on CPU 1, the track process on CPU 2, and the display process on CPU 3.

E. Object Design Specifications

This subsection details the design specifications for a vertically partitioned object-oriented design to meet the requirements given earlier in this section. The program contains a type-type manager, switchboard manager, process manager, and three application managers. The application managers are a communications manager, a track processing manager, and a display manager.

F. Performance Metrics

The metrics for evaluation of the "overhead" processing costs described in Section VII-A are those which measure the amount of computational work done to compose "primitive" elements of computation into logical computation structures. These overhead costs result from the satisfaction of dependencies and from the control of flow. They also include system related functions such as fault recovery. These processing overhead costs include the flow of data between units of computation and the costs for invocation of units of computation. The specific metrics which we chose include the number of CPU context switches, flow of data and control between software modules, number of switches, flow of data and control between software modules, number of changes of execution scope, and flow of data among CPU's and I/O units. These metrics will be further described in Section VII-J.

G. Design and Implementation

Each execution model included three components: a hardware configuration, the definition of a software system structure, and a workload. In addition each software model was equipped with an execution path trace capability and performance measurement software. The hardware structure, software instrumentation package, and the workload were identical for both the functional simulation and the object-oriented simulation. The only thing that was changed and evaluated was the two software system structures (vertically partitioned object-oriented structure versus functionally layered structure).

H. Hardware Testbed

The hardware testbed was designed to meet the requirements given in Section VII-C. For each simulation program the same hardware testbed was simulated. In each case three CPU's were connected by two communications local area networks (LAN's). Attached to the networks were two disks, two message communications (COMMS) units, two operator display consoles, and a control console. Duplicate units of each type of failure critical node (i.e., CPU, Comms, disk, network, display) were identical except for address. Identical units were specified to allow automatic software reconfiguration to provide for continued system operation in the event of the failure of a single hardware unit. Two interface design specifications (IDS) were written, one for each simulator. The hardware description and usage in each IDS was identical. The interprocess versus intertype manager message formats differed between both simulator programs as a result of the different software structures. Fig. 2 illustrates the hardware testbed design.

1) Workload: Twelve test cases were defined to evaluate the two software designs. A test case was composed of a set of system states and a set of transactions. For evaluation, each test condition was set and the test transactions were executed on both simulator programs and identical types of metric data were collected from each program for analysis.

A case-by-case study was performed on the data from each of the simulation models. The details of this study are reported by Hufnagel [12]. For each test case, the reference defines the test conditions, provide the data from both simulation programs, and discuss the test case results.

2) Software System Structures: The application software included the hierarchy of modules required to meet the system specification and the control logic necessary to drive the computation flow and detect and recover from selected faults. The modules executed the control logic necessary to allow an execution flow but the modules did not contain actual processing logic (i.e., tracking algorithms or graphic software, etc.). An execution of a transaction by one of the simulation models represents a traversal of the computation graph. Fault management was explicitly modeled. In the case of the functional layered

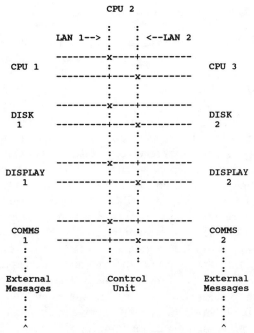

Fig. 2. Hardware testbed.

structure, all of the data which can be reached in a particular layer could be destroyed.

I. Execution

In each case the execution of the simulation model was accomplished by defining the paths through the computation graph defined for each of the system methodologies and then traversing the graphs summing the metric values. The vertices of this dependency graph are the functions of the type managers in the case of the object-oriented system, and the functions embedded in the layers in the case of the functional system. Thus, evaluation by computation graph traversal allows one to gather data about each of the methods which we have defined. Each procedure call implies a context switch. When the procedure call was across type managers or across processes there was a larger cost than for internal (i.e., internal to a type manager or process) context switch. The flow of data between modules is measured by evaluating the data carried on each arc; intermodule transfers of data was distinguished from an intertype manager or interprocess flow of data.

J. Metric Data Description

This subsection will give a description of the specific metric sums that were kept by each of the simulation programs during the execution of a test case. There were two classes of metric measures. The primary metrics were CPU context switching, CPU control flow, and CPU data flow. These metrics were direct measures of the structural workload. The other secondary metric measures to be discussed are components of the structural workload and are useful in explaining the primary metric measures.

CPU Context Switches is the performance cost metric sum that was associated with changes in any computer execution domain during the processing of a transaction. The context switch metric was set to 1 for a computer subroutine call. The context switch metric was set to 10 for a message received by a process (in the functional system) or by a type manager (in the object system) from a process, from a type manager, or from a communications, disk, or display hardware unit. This function was chosen because message context switching generally has a much higher performance cost in real systems. Within the simulating programs, the CPU context switch metric was set to zero for processing within any of the noncomputer units.

CPU 1 messages, CPU 2 messages, and CPU 3 messages are a special class of context switches. They are measures of the number of messages sent to each respective CPU during the execution of a test case. These metric sums are separate and distinct from the CPU context switches sum. The respective metric sum was increased by 1 whenever a message was sent to computer 1, 2, or 3.

Proc/TM switches are a special class of context switches. For the functional system this is a count of the number of times that a process domain was entered and for the object system the number of times that a type manager domain was entered. These metric sums are separate and distinct from the CPU context switches sum.

CPU Control Flow and CPU Data Flow are the performance cost metric sums that were associated with the passing of control information and data into any computer execution domain. For each computer subroutine, process, or type manager invocation, processing domain-specific metric values were added to the respective sums.

VIII. Performance Analysis

This section will first give a quantitative analysis of the performance of the two program structures based upon the experiments described in Section VII, partially reported in the Appendix, and further reported by Hufnagel [12]. Then a qualitative analysis will be given based upon the inherent properties of the methodologies. Finally, the conclusions will be presented.

A. Quantitative Analysis

Execution of the vertically partitioned object structured system yielded from 33 to 59 percent fewer context switches than execution of the functional system. Within the range, the difference was lower during cases that require system configuration, and higher during cases that were exclusively message processing.

The control flow metric sums were consistently (i.e., generally between 19 and 30 percent) higher for the functional system. The object system's data flow metric sums showed a typical four or five percent improvement over the functional system's metric sums.

The display data flow and disk data flow metric sums were always the same between systems and, except for the initialization case, always the same between cases. For each case these results confirm that the same application task was always being done by both systems. For all cases link data flow was similar between systems but CPU 1, 2, and 3 messages and CPU 1, 2, and 3 data varied greatly between systems.

The vertically partitioned object system recovery processing from system failure had significant performance improvement over the equivalent functionally designed system. Notably, there was a 36 percent difference in context switches and a 20 percent difference in CPU control flow. This improvement is due to the use of semantic knowledge about the objects in designing the recovery mechanisms.

One might intuitively expect in comparing a layered functional system to a traditional (i.e., nonvertically partitioned) object system design: 1) a higher context switching in the object case because of the greater granularity of the computation domains, 2) equivalent or increased data flow in the object design due to the passing of data to layered general purpose system wide processing routines to perform operations on the data, 3) equivalent or higher control flow, because in passing data, control information to command operations on the data also needs to be passed.

In the experiments the observed performance (see the Appendix) advantage of the vertically partitioned object design was predominantly due to 1) the type managers performing all operations on their own data, 2) there was no operating system and hence no operating system process switching, 3) intertype manager data access synchronization was not required because each type manager had exclusive control of its data.

Because type managers perform all operations on their data there was a reduction (ranging from 5 to an excess of 300 percent) in data flow. In the experiments, the functional system passed output data to an operating system routine that performed the output. The object system requested access to the network and performed its own output. Hence, the object system did not incur a data flow penalty.

Operating system process switching was a significant performance cost contributor in the functional system. In the object system, messages were sent directly between type managers. The distributed switchboard type manager provided routing information to local type managers, as was needed. In the functional system all interprocess messages were first decoded by the operating system and then passed to the appropriate process. This affected the context switches, data flow, and control flow metric sums. Another significant contributor to the control flow metric was the fact than an interprocess context switch had a higher control flow cost than an intertype manager context switch. This occurred because a type manager context switch required less passing of control information than a process switch.

Profound differences in message passing, ranging to 300 percent reduction in message passing within the vertically partitioned object system were seen. In the object system intertype manager data access synchronization was not needed because type managers are solely responsible for storage of the occurrences of their data object types. Other type managers do not have access to their data. Consequently, file locking and unlocking were not needed when data were being written by the object system. In the functional system, as a part of the disk data write protocol, the writing CPU had to send both file lock and file unlock messages to the other CPU's. The effect of this design difference was a contributing factor to the results of all the cases except the initialization case which did not have disk write operations. The functional system's file lock/unlock protocol had a significant impact on the context switching and control flow metrics because file lock/unlock messages had to be constructed, sent, received, decoded, and processed.

B. Qualitative Analysis

The motivation for an object-oriented system design is increased comprehensibility and reduced software complexity. It has been "folklore" that these virtues can be brought only at the cost of efficiency. A vertically partitioned object program structure was shown to provide a mechanism by which we may compose elementary (primitive) operations on primitive data objects to form logical data structures and logical operations which retain efficiency.

Many fault recovery concepts from transaction-oriented software systems can be transformed to the object-oriented structure proposed here (discussed in Section V). The vertically partitioned object design approach has been shown to avoid many of the previous complications in implementing fault recovery. These complications arise when transactions are used to provide atomicity.

In Section III it was shown that a hierarchy of composite objects (i.e., composed of objects) provides a simple means for fault recovery. An important concept is that a hierarchical structure must be maintained within composite objects. In a typical layered hierarchical system a hierarchical view is taken of the entire system, whereas the vertical partition method results in a hierarchical view of each object type.

The concept needed to provide efficient and manageable fault recovery is that actions should be composed into atomic steps that meet invariant conditions before entering and/or leaving the object type manager's boundaries. Atomicity must be maintained within each type manager's domain. In the object-oriented design approach, when a fault is detected, each object's type manager may either correct or compensate for the fault, thereby masking the fault or signaling to a higher level object to possibly act on the fault indication. As such, hierarchical vertical partitioning at the object level provides a limitation on fault propagation.

Well-designed type managers will minimize the flow of data between object modules because they are designed around their data structures and all operations on the data are done locally. The resultant passing of controls and names helps system performance and is a very good security feature.

The choice of recovery mechanisms within each type manager is an important factor with regard to efficiency and performance. Section III discussed how the semantics of the object can be used to allow programmed exception handling resulting in compile time binding. Efficiency is enhanced by compile time binding of the sequence of elementary operations to a set of data items. As an example, forward recovery is a more efficient technique then recovery by rollback to a previous system state. In the case of the object structure, it can be observed that software faults within a type manager can only affect objects of that type.

The classical objection to object-oriented designs is that they are not efficient. The results given here suggest that this lack of efficiency is due to building objects on top of a traditional layered structure. Vertical partitioning within the objects encourages the use of the semantics by the type manager of each object. The keys to the performance improvement are type managers designed around data structures, compile time binding of functions to data, and the ability of the type managers to use the object's semantic properties to optimize data processing, execution control, fault location, and recovery.

It was one author's (SPH) observation that the object program was easier to code, modify and debug because changes or problems could generally be localized to one or more specific type managers. Control logic changes and problems in the functional system typically involved complex interactions between the operating system and the application program.

C. Conclusion

The results of the performance evaluation experiments have established that a vertically partitioned object program can have competitive performance efficiency with a layered functional program. This was achieved without taking advantage of the potential additional performance enhancements to be made through explicit use of application semantics. Performance efficiency was quantified by the software metrics of context switches, CPU control flow, and CPU data flow.

In summary, the system structuring approach proposed in this paper can result in software that is an improvement over previous attempts to balance dependability and performance while maintaining high software comprehensibility and low software complexity.

APPENDIX
EXPERIMENTAL RESULTS

This Appendix contains the results from two important cases obtained from the methodology evaluation experiments. The design, implementation, and execution of the experiments was presented in Section VI. For these test cases we will present 1) the initial conditions, 2) selected metric data sums (that were defined in Section VI) from both the function and object programs, and a percentage difference ("Functional Program data"/"Object Program data − 100") of the individual metric data sums, and 3) a discussion of the test case's results. The full set of experimental results are reported by Hufnagel [12]. An overall experimental analysis is presented in Section VIII.

The context switches, CPU control flow, and CPU data flow were the primary metrics selected for system evaluation. Other metrics were collected and will be used, as needed, to help explain differences in the primary metrics.

Two test cases will now be discussed.

A. Fully Operational Processing

Initial Conditions: The system was fully operational (i.e., CPU 1 was configured to do communications processing, CPU 2 was configured to do track processing, and CPU 3 was configured to do display processing), inter-CPU status had been passed, and two separate external target update messages were received by the communications hardware units.

Results:	Functional System	Object System	Percentage Difference
Context Switches:	1414	888	59
CPU Control Flow:	25700	20512	25
CPU Data Flow:	71246	67894	4
Link Data Flow:	5660	5340	5
Disk Data Flow:	264	264	0
Display Data Flow:	3200	3200	0
CPU 1 Messages:	34	26	30
CPU 2 Messages:	6	2	300
CPU 3 Messages:	6	2	300
CPU 1 Data Flow:	1484	1404	5
CPU 2 Data Flow:	152	32	375
CPU 3 Data Flow:	260	140	85
Proc/TM Switches:	46	36	27

Discussion: Communications hardware unit 1 reformatted the target update messages and individually put the reformatted target update messages on LAN 1, addressed to CPU 1. First, CPU 1 received the track update message and executed the disk write protocol to write a copy of the message to the input message log on both disk 1 and disk 2. CPU 1 then executed the communications message decoder function that resulted in a track update report.

CPU 1 put the resultant track update report message on LAN 1, addressed to CPU 2. CPU 2 received and decoded the message and executed the track update function that resulted in a display update message.

CPU 2 put the display update message on LAN 1, addressed to CPU 3. CPU 3 received and decoded the display update message and performed the display data preparation function and sent two display command messages to each of the two display units (i.e., for a total of four messages). Display units 1 and 2 received the messages and updated the operator displays.

Next, CPU 1 received the second track update message and executed the disk write protocol to write a copy of the message to the input message log on both disk 1 and disk 2. CPU 1 then executed the communications message decoded function that resulted in a track update report. CPU 1 put the resultant track update report message on LAN 1, addressed to CPU 2. CPU 2 received and decoded the message and executed the track update function that resulted in a display update message. CPU 2 put the display update message on LAN 1, addressed to CPU 3. CPU 3 received and decoded the display update message and performed the display data preparation function and sent two display command messages to each of the two display units (i.e., for a total of four messages). Display units 1 and 2 received the messages and updated the operator displays.

In the functional system CPU 1 was sent 34 messages; (24) messages were disk replies (i.e., either read data or write acknowledgment messages), (2) were track update messages from communications unit 1, and (8) were file lock/unlock acknowledgments from CPU's 2 and 3. In the object system CPU 1 was sent 26 messages, (24) messages were disk replies, and (2) were track update messages from communications unit 1.

In the functional system CPU 2 was sent (6) messages, (4) were file lock/unlock messages from CPU 1, and (2) were track report messages from CPU 1. In the object system CPU 2 was sent (2) track report messages from CPU 1.

In the functional system CPU 3 was sent (6) messages; (4) were file lock/unlock messages from CPU 1 and (2) were display update messages from CPU 2. In the object system CPU 3 was sent (2) display update messages from CPU 2.

This case represents the fully operational steady state system computation workload. The overall results are encouraging because in all metric categories the object system's metric sums indicate the same or lower performance costs than in the functional system. That is, the results from this case can be interpreted to say that the object system, as quantified by the performance metric sums, was as good as or better than the functional system.

The object approach had less overall context switching (about 50 percent difference) within the system CPU's. The dependency graph analysis revealed that context switching was reduced in the object system design because 1) the object system did not lock files before writing data to disk and 2) the object system had 36 type manager calls while the functional system had 46 process switches of which 40 were kernel operating system calls. A vertically partitioned object system design only requires file read/write synchronization for concurrent operations within a type manager. This is because type managers are assigned storage blocks by their abstract machine and they are solely responsible for the contents of the storage blocks. Hence, the need to maintain data consistency does not require system wide intertype manager synchronization. Due to the file directory structure of the functional system an inter-CPU file lockout mechanism was incorporated in the design for disk write operations. A file lock/unlock operation requires a significant amount of context switching due to the construction of the required messages, sending of the messages, decoding of the messages, and processing of the message commands. This also explains why there were six CPU 2 and six CPU 3 messages in the functional system's results and only two respective messages in the object system's results. In both designs, there were two data transfer messages from CPU 1 to CPU 2 and two data transfer messages from CPU 2 to CPU 3. The additional messages at CPU 2 and CPU 3 in the functional system are attributable to the file lock/unlock messages from CPU 1 to CPU 2 and CPU 3. The difference in CPU 1 messages of 34 versus 26 for the functional system and object system, respectively, is due to the four pairs of file lock command acknowledgments and file unlock acknowledgments from CPU 2 and CPU 3 to CPU 1.

The object system shows an information flow improvement (25 percent for CPU control flow, 4 percent for CPU data flow, and 5 percent for link data flow). Control flow improvement in the object system partially results from not having the file lock/unlock protocol discussed in the previous paragraph. The object system's data flow improvement resulted from the type manager's direct output control of the two display command messages of 400 words of display hardware commands each. The predominant contributor to the control flow difference was 46 process switches by the functional system, as compared to 36 type manager invocations by the object system. Each process switch had a control flow cost of 92 words while each type manager invocation had a control flow cost of 10 words. Consequently, it was concluded that a significant portion of the functional system's control flow was due to operating system process switching.

In this case, the disk and display data flow were identical because identical application tasks were performed. There was a system difference in CPU 1, 2, and 3 (i.e., interprocessor) data flow because of the respective difference in CPU 1, 2, and 3 message numbers, as discussed earlier.

B. CPU 1 Failure and System Recovery

Initial Conditions: Prior to this case the system had been fully operational. CPU 1 had failed since the processing of the last message of the previous case and was nonoperational and two external target update messages were received by the communications hardware units.

Results:	Functional System	Object System	Percentage Difference
Context Switches:	1282	936	36
CPU Control Flow:	24839	20651	20
CPU Data Flow:	71272	67882	4
Link Data Flow:	5508	53284	3
Disk Data Flow:	264	264	0
Display Data Flow:	3200	3200	0
CPU 1 Messages:	1	1	0
CPU 2 Messages:	29	25	16

Results:	Functional System	Object System	Percentage Difference
CPU 3 Messages:	7	3	133
CPU 1 Data Flow:	110	110	0
CPU 2 Data Flow:	1334	1294	3
CPU 3 Data Flow:	290	150	93
Proc/TM Switches:	41	38	7

Discussion: For this case, each system (i.e., functional and object) first had to recognize the failure of CPU, and as then each system had to reconfigure itself to bypass the nonoperational CPU and relocate the processing functions of the nonoperational CPU. Finally, each system had to process the two target update messages.

Communications hardware unit 1 reformatted the target update messages and put the first reformatted message on LAN 1, addressed to CPU 1. CPU 2 was monitoring the LAN activity, had captured a copy of the message addressed to CPU 1, and had recognized that CPU 1 had not ACKed the track update message from the communications unit. CPU 2 reconfigured its software to add the communications processing function that had been previously assigned to CPU 1. CPU 2 sent a message to communications unit 1, commanding it to send future track update messages directly to CPU 2. Then CPU 2 executed the communications function on the captured message and passed a track report message to the tracking function, also on CPU 2. CPU 2 executed the tracking function and sent a display update message to CPU 3 for display processing. CPU 3 received and decoded the display update message and performed the display data preparation function and sent two display command messages to each of the two display units (i.e., for a total of four messages); the display units updated the operator displays.

Next, communications unit 1 sent the second track update message to CPU 2. CPU 2 performed the communications and track processing functions and sent a display update message to CPU 3. Finally, CPU 3 performed the display data preparation function and sent two display command messages to each of the two display units; the display units updated the operator displays.

In both the functional and object systems CPU 1 was sent (1) track update message from communications unit 1. Then, the systems reconfigured and CPU 1 was excluded from the system processing.

In both systems: 1) CPU 2 captured a copy of the track update message sent to CPU 1, 2) CPU 2 recognized the failure of CPU 1 by the absence of a message ACK on the network, 3) CPU 2 reconfigured to perform the communications and track functions, and 4) CPU 2 processed the captured message. Then, in the functional system CPU 2 was sent (29) messages; (24) were disk read or write replay-messages, (1) was a track update message from communications unit 1, and (4) were file lock/unlock acknowledgment-messages from CPU 3. In the object system CPU 2 was sent 25 messages; (24) messages were disk replies, (1) was a track update message from communications unit 1. In the functional system CPU 3 was sent (7) messages; (1) was a status message from CPU 2,

(4) were file lock/unlock messages from CPU 2, and (2) were display update messages from CPU 2. In the object system CPU 3 was sent (3) messages; (1) was an advisory message that CPU 1 was down from CPU 2 and (2) were display update messages from CPU 2.

This is a complex case to interpret because the metric data sums include performance cost data for system reconfiguration and message data processing. The metric sums resemble a combination of (re)configuration and the fully operational system message processing.

This case has a 36 percent context switching difference, as compared to 59 percent in the previous case. In this case the functional system had a reduced file lock/unlock workload because of the nonoperational CPU. This reduced workload resulted in reduced context switching and control flow metric sums as compared to the object system. Specifically, the functional system number of messages was 8 less in this case due to file locking/unlocking in the functional system design. This file lock/unlock protocol is considered the primary reason that the functional system had an increased context switch metric sum.

The control flow metric sums differed by 20 percent. The dependency graphs revealed that in this case there were 38 object system's type manager invocations and 41 functional system's operation system invocations. The object system's superior performance, indicated by the control flow metric, is attributable to the greater control flow cost of an operating system process switch.

The object system had a slightly reduced overall data flow of 4 percent. This is attributed to the direct output of the display command messages (i.e., in this case each of 400 data words).

The functional systems provided intercomputer statusing during the reconfiguration while the object system updated status as a part of processing the first message.

ACKNOWLEDGMENT

The authors wish to thank Applied Research Laboratories and the Department of Computer Sciences, The University of Texas at Austin, for the use of their facilities in support of this research.

REFERENCES

[1] G. T. Almes, A. P. Black, E. D. Lazowska, and J. D. Noe, "The EDEN system: A technical review," *IEEE Trans. Software Eng.*, vol. SE-11, pp. 43–49, Jan. 1985.

[2] P. America, "POOL-T: A parallel object-oriented language," in *Object-Oriented Concurrent Programming*, A. Yonezawa and M. Kokoro, Eds. Cambridge, MA: MIT Press, 1987.

[3] J. C. Browne, J. Dutton, V. Fernandes, J. Silverman, A. Tripathi, and P. Wang, "Zeus: An object-oriented distributed operating system," in *Proc. ACM Nat. Conf.*, San Francisco, CA, 1984.

[4] J. C. Browne, "Vertically partitioned object-oriented system architecture for reliable high performance parallel distributed systems," in *Proc. XP 7.52 Workshop Data Base Theory*, Austin, TX, IEEE & ACM, Aug. 1986.

[5] L. Cardelli and P. Wegner, "On understanding types, data abstraction, and polymorphism," *Comput. Surveys*, vol. 17, no. 4, pp. 471–522, Dec. 1985.

[6] E. Cohen and D. Jefferson, "Protection in the Hydra operating system," in *Proc. Fifth Symp. Operating Systems Principles*, ACM, 1975, pp. 141–160.

[7] F. Cristian, "Exception handling and software fault tolerance," *IEEE Trans. Comput.*, vol. C-31, no. 6, pp. 531–540, June 1982.

[8] S. Danforth and C. Tomlinson, "Type theories and object-oriented programming," *ACM Comput. Surveys*, vol. 20, no. 1, Mar. 1988.

[9] H. Garcia-Molina, "Using semantic knowledge for transaction processing in a distributed system," *ACM Trans. Database Syst.*, vol. 8, no. 2, pp. 186–213, June 1983.

[10] A. Goldberg, *Smalltalk-80: The Language and Its Implementation*. Reading, MA: Addison-Wesley, 1984.

[11] C. A. R. Hoare, "Monitors: An operating system structuring concept," *Commun. ACM*, vol. 17, no. 10, pp. 549–557, Oct. 1974.

[12] S. P. Hufnagel, "Vertically partitioned object-oriented software design for high dependability and good performance," Ph.D. dissertation, Univ. Texas at Austin, May 1987; also Tech. Rep. TR-87-02, Dep. Comput. Sci., Univ. Texas at Austin, Jan. 1987.

[13] J. C. Laprie, "Dependable computing and fault tolerance: Concepts and terminology," in *Proc. FTCS-15*, IEEE, 1985, pp. 2–11.

[14] B. Meyer, *Object-Oriented Software Construction*. Englewood Cliffs, NJ: Prentice-Hall, 1988.

[15] E. B. Moss, "Nested transactions and reliable distributed computing," in *Proc. Second Conf. Reliability in Distributed Systems*, IEEE, 1982, pp. 33–39.

[16] D. L. Parnas, "A technique for software module specification with examples," *Commun. ACM*, vol. 15, pp. 330–336, May 1972.

[17] G. A. Pascoe, "Elements of object-oriented programming," *Byte*, pp. 139–144, Aug. 1986.

[18] A. Silberschatz, R. B. Kieburtz, and A. J. Bernstein, "Extending concurrent Pascal to allow dynamic resource management," *IEEE Trans. Software Eng.*, vol. SE-3, no. 3, pp. 210–217, May 1977.

[19] A. R. Tripathi and J. O. Richard, "C2 environment and functional requirements," in *Scientific Rep. to Rome Air Development Center Distributed C**2 System Recovery Mechanism*, Honeywell, Inc., Contract F30602-82-C-0154, 1983.

[20] W. A. Wulf, "Overview of the Hydra operating system," in *Proc. 5th Symp. Operating System Principles*, ACM, Nov. 1975, pp. 122–131.

Stephen P. Hufnagel received the B.A. degree in mathematics and psychology in 1978 and the Ph.D. degree in computer science from the University of Texas at Austin in 1987.

He is an Assistant Professor with the Department of Computer Science Engineering at the University of Texas at Arlington (UTA). Before he joined UTA, he was with The Applied Research Laboratories, University of Texas at Austin. His work included the design, fabrication, and testing of real time data acquisition, processing, and display systems. His current research interests include architectures for an object-oriented approach to high performance and dependable systems design.

Dr. Hufnagel is an affiliate member of the IEEE Computer Society and a member of the Association for Computing Machinery.

James C. Browne was born in Conway, AR, on January 16, 1935. He received the B.A. degree from Hendrix College, Conway, AR, in 1956 and the Ph.D. degree in physical chemistry from the University of Texas at Austin in 1960.

He worked from 1960 to 1964 as an Assistant Professor of Physics, the University of Texas at Austin, carrying out quantum mechanical calculations of small molecules, and doing research development work on operating systems. He was, from 1964 to 1965, at the Queen's University of Belfast, Belfast, Northern Ireland, on a National Science Foundation Postdoctoral Fellowship. He was, from 1965 to 1968, Professor of Computer Science and Director of the Computation Laboratory at the Queen's University of Belfast. In 1968 he rejoined The University of Texas at Austin as Professor of Computer Science and Physics. He has served three terms as Chairman of the Department of Computer Sciences, 1968–1969, 1971–1975, and 1985–1987. He holds the Regents Chair #2. His research interests include operating systems, systems modeling and design, performance evaluation of computer systems, and parallel computation structures. He has published about 145 refereed papers on technical subjects. He serves on numerous government committees, advisory panels, etc.

Dr. Browne is a Fellow of the American Physical Society and the British Computer Society, and a member of the Association for Computing Machinery.

Reprinted from *IEEE Transactions on Knowledge and Data Engineering*, June 1989, pages 196-214. Copyright © 1989 by The Institute of Electrical and Electronics Engineers, Inc. All rights reserved.

Indexing Techniques for Queries on Nested Objects

ELISA BERTINO, MEMBER, IEEE, AND WON KIM

Abstract—In relational databases, an attribute of a relation may only have a single primitive value, making it cumbersome to model complex artifacts of interest to a wide variety of applications. An object-oriented and nested relational model of data removes this difficulty by introducing the notion of nested objects, that is, by allowing the value of an object to be another object or a set of other objects. This means that a class (relation) consists of a set of attributes, and the values of the attributes are objects that belong to other classes (relations); that is, the definition of a class (relation) forms a hierarchy of classes (relations). All attributes of the nested classes are nested attributes of the root of the hierarchy. Just as a secondary index on an attribute or a combination of attributes is useful for expediting the evaluation of a query on a relation, a secondary index is useful for evaluating queries on a nested class in an object-oriented database or a nested relation in a nested relational database. In this paper, we introduce three index organizations for use in the evaluation of a query in an object-oriented or nested relational database. We develop detailed models of the three indexes. Using the models, we evaluate the storage cost, retrieval cost, and update cost of these indexes, and make a number of observations about the use of these indexes for evaluating queries for object-oriented or nested relational databases.

Index Terms—Access methods, complex objects, database performance and measurement, index selection, nested relations, object-oriented databases, query optimization.

I. INTRODUCTION

THE normalized relational model of data restricts the value of an attribute to a single primitive value, such as an integer, a real, a string, or a boolean. Users and researchers of databases have found that this restriction poses a serious problem in modeling complex artifacts, such as a design object or a multimedia document. The current research into object-oriented databases [2], [3], [9], [16] and nested relational databases [1], [7], [8], [11], [17] is partially motivated by the need to remove this problem with the relational model of data. One important element common to object-oriented databases and nested relational databases is the view that the value of an attribute of an object is an object or a set of objects. A class C (or a relation R) consists of a number of attributes, and the value of an attribute A of an object belonging to the class C (or the relation R) is an object or a set of objects belonging to some other class C' (or a relation R'). The class C' (relation R') is called the domain of the attribute A of the class C (or relation R). The class C' (relation R') in turn consists of a number of attributes, and their domains are other classes (relations). In other words, in ob-

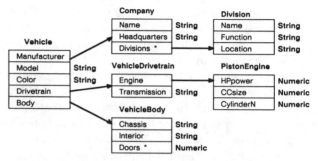

Fig. 1. A class-attribute hierarchy.

ject-oriented databases and nested relational databases, a class or a relation is in general a hierarchy of classes or relations. This hierarchy is called a *class-attribute hierarchy* in [13]. Fig. 1 is an example of a class-attribute hierarchy; the hierarchy is rooted at the class Vehicle, and the * symbol next to an attribute indicates that the value of the attribute is multivalued. An attribute of any class on a class-attribute hierarchy is logically an attribute of the root of the hierarchy, that is, the attribute is a *nested attribute* of the root class. For example, in Fig. 1, the Location attribute of the class Division is a nested attribute of the class Vehicle.

In normalized relational databases, the search conditions in a query are expressed as a boolean combination of predicates of the form < attribute operator value >. The query is directed to one or more relations, and the attribute specified in a predicate is an attribute of one of the relations. The nested structure of the definition of a class or a relation in object-oriented or nested relational databases requires an important generalization of the notion of a predicate. In object-oriented or nested relational databases, the search conditions in a query on a class or relation can still be expressed as a boolean combination of predicates of the form < attribute operator value >. However, the attribute may be a nested attribute of the class or the relation. For example, the following is a query that may be issued against the class Vehicle as defined in the class-attribute hierarchy of Fig. 1.

Retrieve all red vehicles manufactured by Fiat.

The query consists of a predicate against the nonnested attribute Color and a predicate against the nested attribute Name. We will call a predicate on a nested attribute a *nested predicate* and a predicate on a nonnested attribute a *simple predicate*. An important issue in supporting queries in object-oriented or nested relational databases is

Manuscript received March 22, 1989; revised May 12, 1989.
The authors are with the Microelectronics and Computer Technology Corporation, Austin, TX 78759.
IEEE Log Number 8930115.

226

the efficient evaluation of queries involving nested predicates.

To expedite the evaluation of queries, relational database systems typically provide a secondary index using some variation of the B-tree structure [4], [6] or some hashing technique. An index is maintained on an attribute or a combination of attributes of a relation. Since object-oriented and nested relational databases require the notion of an attribute to be generalized to a nested attribute, the notion of secondary indexing must also be generalized to indexing on a nested attribute. The class (relation) in which the attribute is defined may be different from the class on which the index is maintained.

References [15] and [13] first provided preliminary discussions of the notion of secondary indexing on a sequence of nested attributes. In this paper, we introduce three index organizations for evaluating queries that involve nested predicates, and compare them in terms of storage cost, retrieval cost, and update cost. Largely for presentational simplicity, we will cast the discussions in the context of object-oriented databases; however, the results of this paper are clearly applicable to nested relational databases.

The remainder of this paper is organized as follows. Section II defines some terms and introduces three index organizations for evaluating nested predicates. Section III describes the data structures and operations on the indexes. Section IV summarizes the parameters, and assumptions, of the index models that will be developed in subsequent sections. Sections V–VII develop the models for the storage cost, retrieval cost, and update cost, respectively, and compare the costs for the three indexes. Section VIII provides a comparison of the combined retrieval and update costs for the three indexes. Section IX concludes the paper.

II. Three Index Organizations

In this section, after defining several terms we will use throughout this paper, we will introduce three basic index organizations for evaluating nested predicates.

A. Definitions

Definition 1: Given a class-attribute hierarchy $\mathcal{H}$, a *path* $\mathcal{P}$ is defined as $C(1).A(1).A(2) \ldots A(n)$ $(n \geq 1)$ where
- $C(1)$ is a class in $\mathcal{H}$;
- $A(1)$ is an attribute of class $C(1)$;
- $A(i)$ is an attribute of a class $C(i)$ in $\mathcal{H}$, such that $C(i)$ is the domain of attribute $A(i-1)$ of class $C(i-1)$, $1 < i \leq n$;

  $len(\mathcal{P}) = n$ denotes the length of path $\mathcal{P}$;

  the number of classes along path $\mathcal{P}$ is equal to $len(\mathcal{P})$;

  $class(\mathcal{P}) = C(1) \cup \{C(i)$ such that $C(i)$ is the domain of attribute $A(i-1)$ of class $C(i-1)$, $1 < i \leq n\}$.

The path length indicates the number of classes, including $C(1)$, that must be traversed to reach the nested attribute $A(n)$. Note that all classes along a path must be

nonprimitive classes, while the domain of the last attribute in the path can be either primitive or nonprimitive.

A class can have several paths starting from it. The following are example paths for the class-attribute hierarchy in Fig. 1:

P1: Vehicle.Manufacturer.Name	len(P1) = 2
P2: Vehicle.Manufacturer.Headquarters	len(P2) = 2
P3: Vehicle.Body.Chassis	len(P3) = 2
P4: Vehicle.Color	len(P4) = 1.

We assume that each nonprimitive object is identified by an object identifier, which consists of the class identifier of the object class concatenated with the identifier of the object within the class. For example, Vehicle[i] denotes the i-th instance of the class Vehicle. Different object identification schemes are possible, as discussed in [13]. Further, we assume that basic objects are identified by their value.

Definition 2: Given a path $\mathcal{P} = C(1).A(1).A(2) \ldots A(n)$, an *instantiation* of $\mathcal{P}$ is defined as a sequence of $n + 1$ objects, denoted as $O(1).O(2) \ldots O(n + 1)$, where:
- $O(1)$ is an instance of class $C(1)$; and
- $O(i)$ is the value of the attribute $A(i - 1)$ of object $O(i - 1)$, $1 < i \leq n + 1$.

Note that each object $O(i)$, $1 < i \leq n + 1$, in an instantiation is an instance of the class $C(i)$, the domain of attribute $A(i - 1)$ in class $C(i - 1)$, or of any subclass of $C(i)$.

The objects shown in Fig. 2 are instances of some of the classes shown in Fig. 1. The following are example instantiations of the path P1 = Vehicle.Manufacturer.Name:
- Vehicle[i].Company[j].Renault
- Vehicle[j].Company[j].Renault
- Vehicle[k].Company[i].Fiat.

Given a path $\mathcal{P} = C(1).A(1).A(2) \ldots A(n)$, and an object $O(i)$ of a class $C(i)$ along the path, we will use the term *forward traversal* to denote access of objects $O(i + 1), \ldots, O(n)$ such that $O(i + 1)$ is referenced by object $O(i)$ through attribute $A(i), \ldots, O(n)$ is referenced by object $O(n - 1)$ through attribute $A(n - 1)$. Objects on a path may be traversed in a reverse direction of the path, that is, $O(i - 1), \ldots, O(2)$, such that $O(i - 1)$ references object $O(i)$ through attribute $A(i - 1), \ldots, O(1)$ references object $O(2)$ through attribute $A(1)$. It may not be possible to support a *backward traversal*, unless it is possible to directly determine the objects that reference a given object O. For example, in GemStone and ORION a reference from an object to another is unidirectional.

Definition 3: Given a path $\mathcal{P} = C(1).A(1).A(2) \ldots A(n)$, a *partial instantiation* of $\mathcal{P}$ is defined as a sequence of objects $O(1).O(2) \ldots O(j)$, $j < n + 1$ where
- $O(1)$ is an instance of a class $C(k)$ in $class(\mathcal{P})$ where $k = n - j + 2$; and
- $O(i)$ is the value of the attribute $A(i - 1)$ of object $O(i - 1)$, $1 < i \leq j$.

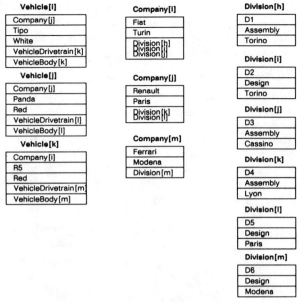

Vehicle[i]

Company[j]
Tipo
White
VehicleDrivetrain[k]
VehicleBody[k]

Vehicle[j]

Company[j]
Panda
Red
VehicleDrivetrain[l]
VehicleBody[l]

Vehicle[k]

Company[i]
R5
Red
VehicleDrivetrain[m]
VehicleBody[m]

Company[i]

Fiat
Turin
Division[h] Division[i] Division[j]

Company[j]

Renault
Paris
Division[k] Division[l]

Company[m]

Ferrari
Modena
Division[m]

Division[h]

D1
Assembly
Torino

Division[i]

D2
Design
Torino

Division[j]

D3
Assembly
Cassino

Division[k]

D4
Assembly
Lyon

Division[l]

D5
Design
Paris

Division[m]

D6
Design
Modena

Fig. 2. Instances of classes of Fig. 1.

Examples of a partial instantiation of the path P1 = Vehicle . Manufacturer . Name are:

- Company [m] . Ferrari
- Company [i] . Fiat.

Definition 4: Given a partial instantiation p = O(1).O(2) ... O(j) of $\mathcal{P}$, p is *nonredundant* if no instantiation p' = O'(1).O'(2) ... O'(k), k > j exists such that O(i) = O'(k − j + i), 1 ≤ i ≤ j.

Of the example partial instantiations, Company[m]. Ferrari is nonredundant, since there are no instances of the class Vehicle having Ferrari as manufacturer. Company[i].Fiat is redundant since there are two instantiations of which Company[j].Fiat is part.

B. Index Organizations

In the following we will refer to the first object and the last object in an instantiation as the *starting object* and the *ending object*, respectively.

Definition 5: Given a path $\mathcal{P}$ = C(1).A(1).A(2) ... A(n), a *nested index* (NX) on $\mathcal{P}$ is defined as a set of pairs (O, S), where S = {O' such that O(1).O(2) ... O(n + 1) instantiation of $\mathcal{P}$ exists, where O' = O(1) and O = O(n + 1)}. The first element of the pair (O, S) is the index key.

A nested index provides a direct association between an ending object and corresponding starting objects along a path. A nested index can be implemented using some variation of the B-tree structure or some hashing algorithm.

Example 1: Let us consider the class-attribute hierarchy in Fig. 1. A nested index on the path P1 = Vehicle.Manufacturer.Name will associate a distinct value of the Name attribute with a list of object identifiers of Vehicle whose Manufacturer is an instance of the Company class whose Name is the key value. For the objects shown in Fig. 2, the nested index will contain the following pairs:

- (Fiat, { Vehicle[k] })
- (Renault, { Vehicle[i] Vehicle[j] }).

Definition 6: Given a path $\mathcal{P}$ = C(1).A(1).A(2) ... A(n), and p = O(1).O(2) ... O(j) instantiation of $\mathcal{P}$, j ≤ n + 1, π<m> (p) = O(1).O(2) ... O(m), m < j denotes the projection of p on the first m elements.

For example π < 2 > (Vehicle[i].Company[j].Renault)

= Vehicle[i].Company[j].

Definition 7: Given a path $\mathcal{P}$ = C(1).A(1).A(2) ... A(n), a *path index* (PX) on $\mathcal{P}$ is defined as a set of pairs (O, S) where S = { π < j − 1 > (p(i)) such that:

- p(i) = O(1).O(2) ... O(j) is a nonredundant instantiation (either partial or not) of $\mathcal{P}$;
- O(j) = O (that is O is the ending object of p(i))}.

The first element of the pair (O, S) is the index key.

Given an index key, a path index records all instantiations ending with the key; in a nested index only the starting objects of the path instantiations are recorded. Note that when n = 1, the nested index and path index are identical and they reduce to the indexes used in most relational database systems.

Example 2: Let us consider the objects shown in Fig. 2. The path index will contain the following pairs:

- (Fiat, { Vehicle[k].Company[i] })
- (Renault, { Vehicle[i].Company[j], Vehicle[j]. Company[j] })
- (Ferrari, { Company[m] }).

Note that a path index can be used to evaluate nested predicates on all classes along the path. In the current example, we could use the index to retrieve the company with a specified name or to retrieve vehicles whose manufacturer has a specified name.

In both the nested index and the path index, the key values can be instances of a primitive class or a nonprimitive class, depending on the domain of the last attribute in the path. In the latter case, the key values are object identifiers, while in the former case they are primitive values. An index whose key values are object identifiers is called an *identity index* in [16]. The only meaningful operator for an identity index is identity equality [12]. For an index whose keys are primitive values, equality is based on value and additional operators may be meaningful, such as ≤ or ≥.

A path may be split into several subpaths, and a different index may be used for each subpath. A special case is when each subpath has length 1; in fact, this is the way GemStone supports nested indexing [15]. This is equivalent to the conventional technique of intersecting a combination of separate indexes.

Definition 8: Given a path $\mathcal{P}$ = C(1).A(1).A(2) ... A(n), a *multiindex* (MX) is defined as a set of n nested indexes NX.1, NX.2, ... , NX.n, where NX.i is a nested index defined on the path C(i).A(i), 1 ≤ i ≤ n.

Example 3: For the path P1 = Vehicle.Manufacturer.Name, the multiindex consists of two indexes. The first index is on the subpath Vehicle. Manufacturer and would contain the following pairs:

- (Company[i], {Vehicle[k]})
- (Company[j], {Vehicle[i], Vehicle[j]}).

The second index is on the subpath Company. Name and would contain the following pairs:

- (Fiat, {Company[i]})
- (Renault, {Company[j]})
- (Ferrari, {Company[m]}).

III. INDEX STRUCTURE AND OPERATIONS

The data structure that we will use to model the various indexes is based on a B-tree. A B-tree organization is used, for example, in ORION [14] and in the relational system SQL/DS [10].

A. Index Structure

The format of the nonleaf node is identical in all the indexes. A nonleaf node consists of f records, where a record is a triple (key-length, key, pointer). The pointer contains the physical address of the next-level index node. The fanout, f, is between d and 2d, where d is the order of the B-tree. The fanout of the root node can be between 2 and 2d records.

The format of the leaf node is identical in the nested and multiindexes; it is similar to the leaf node of that used in [14]. An index record in a leaf node consists of the record-length, key-length, key-value, the number of elements in the list of unique identifiers (UID's) of the objects which hold the key value in the indexed attribute, and the list of UID's. Fig. 3(a) shows the format of a leaf node. In the case of a nested index the UID's are not those of the objects in the class that directly contains the indexed attribute, but they are of objects that indirectly contain the indexed attribute. We assume that the list of UID's is ordered. Also we assume that when the record size is larger than the page size a directory is kept at the beginning of the record recording for each page storing the record, the page address, and the highest UID stored in that page. In this way, when deleting or adding a UID in the record, it is possible to determine directly the page to be updated.

A leaf-node record in a path index consists of the record-length, key-length, key-value, the number of elements in the list of instantiations having as ending object the key value, and the list of instantiations. Each instantiation is implemented as an array of dimension equal to the number of classes along the path. Therefore, given a path $\mathcal{P} = C(1).A(1).A(2) \ldots A(n)$, if $C(1), C(2) \ldots, C(n)$ are the classes along the path, the number of elements in the array is n. The 1st element in the array is the UID of an instance of class $C(1)$, the 2nd element is the UID of the instance of class $C(2)$ referenced by attribute $A(1)$ of the instance identified by the 1st element of the array, and so on. Fig. 3(b) shows the format of a leaf node. Fig. 4 provides examples of leaf-node records in a path index for the objects shown in Fig. 2. We as-

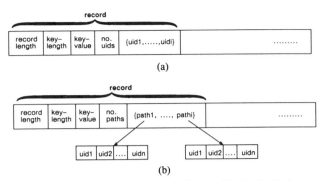

Fig. 3. (a) A leaf node in a nested or multiindex. (b) A leaf node in a path index.

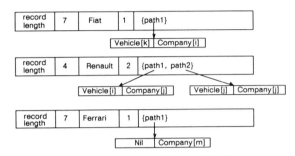

Fig. 4. Leaf-node records in a path index.

sume that when the record size is larger than the page size, the elements of the array are ordered and a directory is kept at the beginning of the record.

B. Index Operations

1) Nested Index: Given a path $\mathcal{P} = C(1).A(1).A(2) \ldots A(n)$ and a nested index defined on this path, the evaluation of a predicate against the nested attribute $A(n)$ of class $C(1)$ requires a lookup of a single index. Therefore, the cost of evaluating a nested predicate is the same as if the attribute $A(n)$ were a direct attribute of class $C(1)$. This index also has the lowest storage overhead.

However, updates to a nested index are costly. Let us consider a path $\mathcal{P} = C(1).A(1).A(2) \ldots A(n)$, and an object $O(i)$, $1 \le i \le n$, which is an instance of a class $C(i)$ along the path. Suppose that $O(i)$ has an object $O(i + 1)$ as the value of the attribute $A(i)$ and that $O(i)$ is updated to assign to $A(i)$ a new object $O'(i + 1)$. An update to a nested index proceeds as follows.

1) Determine the set $S.old$ of the value(s) of the nested attribute $A(n)$ with respect to $O(i + 1)$; a forward traversal of the path is done starting from object $O(i + 1)$. Usually $S.old$ contains only one element, unless some attribute along the path after $A(i)$ is multivalued.

2) Determine the set $S.new$ of the values(s) of the nested attribute $A(n)$ with respect to $O'(i + 1)$; to do this, the path must be forward traversed from object $O'(i + 1)$. If $S.old = S.new$, no updates to the index are required. Otherwise, step 3) is executed.

3) Determine the set R of the UID(s) of object(s) of class $C(1)$ that contains direct or indirect references to

O(i); the path is reverse traversed from object O(i). If i = 1, $R = \{O(i)\}$.

4) The index must be updated as follows:

i) if $S.new \subset S.old$, then $\Delta = S.old - S.new$; for each key value K in Δ, the leaf-node record of K is updated by eliminating from the set of UID's the UID's in the set R.

ii) if $S.old \subset S.new$, then $\Delta = S.new - S.old$ for each key value K in Δ, the leaf-node record of K is updated by adding to the set of UID's the UID's in the set R.

iii) otherwise $\Delta.1 = S.old - S.new$ and $\Delta.2 = S.new - S.old$; for each key value K in $\Delta.1$, the leaf-node record of K is updated by eliminating from the set of UID's the UID's in the set R; and for each key value K in $\Delta.2$, the leaf-node record of K is updated by adding to the set of UID's the UID's in the set R.

Let us consider the path P1 = Vehicle.Manufacturer.Name and the nested index of Example 1. Suppose that Vehicle[i] changes the Manufacturer from Company[j] to Company[i]. We need two forward traversals of length 1, but no backward traversal. We have to access the object Company[j] and determine the value of the attribute Name, which yields $S.old = \{\text{Renault}\}$. Then we have to access the object Company[i] and determine the value of the attribute Name, which yields $S.new = \{\text{Fiat}\}$. $R = \{\text{Vehicle}[i]\}$. Then updates to the nested index involve the following:

• Vehicle[i] is eliminated from the set of UID's associated with the key value Renault;

• Vehicle[i] is added to the set of UID's associated with the key value Fiat.

If O(i) is the updated object, the forward traversal has length $lf = n - i$, where n is the path length. The backward traversal has length $lb = i - 2$ if $i > 2$, and $lb = 0$ if $i \leq 2$. If no reverse references are kept in objects, the nested index cannot be used, unless updates are very infrequent. If objects along the path are clustered, the number of accesses to secondary storage may be lower than the number of object accesses.

Note that when the updated object belongs to the last class along the path (i.e., $i = n$) and the key values are unique with respect to the instances of class C(n) [i.e., there are no two instances of C(n) having the same values for A(n)], no forward or backward path traversal is needed. Suppose that all instances of the class Company have different names, and that the name of Company[i] is changed from Fiat to Toyota. The index update is performed simply by looking up the key value Fiat; saving the list of UID's associated with this key; removing this key from the index; and finally inserting the new name, associating with it the saved list of UID's. In this case, the update cost is the same as if the index were not nested, since there are no additional costs due to object traversal.

Insertion and deletion are similar to update, except that they require only one forward traversal.

2) Path Index: Given a path $\mathcal{P} = C(1).A(1).A(2) \dots A(n)$ and a path index defined on it, the evaluation of a predicate against the nested attribute A(n) of a class C(i), $1 \leq i \leq n$, takes a lookup of a single index. Once the set of instantiations associated with the key value is determined, the i-th elements are extracted from the arrays representing these instantiations. However, a greater number of pages may need to be accessed than with a corresponding nested index because leaf-node records in a path index contain more information than those in a nested index.

Again, let us assume that an object O(i), $1 \leq i \leq n$, which is an instance of a class C(i) along the path, is updated by replacing object O(i + 1), the value of attribute A(i), with a new object O'(i + 1). To update the index, the following steps must be performed.

1) Determine a set $S.old$ of the value(s) of the nested attribute A(n) with respect to O(i + 1); the path is forward traversed from object O(i + 1). $S.old$ contains only one element, unless some attribute along the path after A(i) is multivalued.

2) Determine a set $SP.new$ of partial instantiations from O'(i + 1) to the attribute A(n), and a set $S.new$ of the value(s) of A(n) with respect to O'(i + 1) by a forward traversal of the path from O'(i + 1).

3) For each key value K in $S.old$, access the leaf-node record of K, and for each instantiation p such that the i-th element of the array is equal to O(i) and the (i + 1)-th element of the array is equal to O(i + 1), execute the following steps:

• save in a temporary set T the portion of p from the 1st element to the (i − 1)-th element of the array;

• eliminate p from the set of instantiations associated with K.

4) Generate the new instantiations having O(i) at the i-th position and O'(i + 1) at the (i + 1)-th position. Let us denote the set of new instantiations as P. The i-th element of P is generated by concatenating the i-th element in T, O(i), O'(i + 1), and the 1st element in $SP.new$; the (i + 1)-th element of P is generated by concatenating the (i + 1)-th element in T, O(i), O'(i + 1), and the 1st element in $SP.new$; ... The $(c(1) \times c(2))$-th element of P is generated by concatenating the c(1)-th element in T, O(i), O'(i + 1), the c(2)-th element in $SP.new$, where c(1) and c(2) are the cardinalities of the sets T and $SP.new$, respectively.

5) For each key value K in $S.new$, access the leaf-node record of K and modify the set of instantiations associated with K by adding the instantiations in the set P.

Note that unlike the nested index, a path index does not require a backward traversal, since the paths are stored in the leaf-node records. Therefore, this index can be used even if backward references are not kept in objects. Further, when updates are performed on objects of the last class on the path [i.e., C(n)], no forward traversal is needed.

As an example, let us consider a path $\mathcal{P} = C(1).A(1).A(2).A(3).A(4)$, and an instantiation $p = O(1).O(2).O(3).O(4).O(5)$. The set of instantiations in the leaf-node record for the key value O(5) will contain the instantiation O(1).O(2).O(3).O(4). Let us assume that we modify object O(2) by replacing a reference to object O(3) with a reference to object O'(3); the value of attribute A(3) in object O'(3) is an object O'(4); and the value of attribute A(4) in object O'(4) is an object O'(5). The path index on the path P is updated as follows.

1) Starting from O(3), execute a forward traversal of length 2; that is, access object O(3) and determine O(4), the value of attribute A(3). Then access object O(4) and determine the value of its attribute A(4). We have *S.old* = {O(5)}.

2) Starting from O'(3), execute a forward traversal, keeping track of all objects found along the path. We have *S.new* = {O'(5)} and *SP.new* = {O'(4)}.

3) Access the leaf-node record with a key value equal to O(5). We have:
- T = {O(1)};
- eliminate the instantiation O(1).O(2).O(3). O(4).O(5) from the set of instantiations in this record.

4) Generate the new instantiations by concatenating each element of T [i.e., O(1)], O(2), O'(3), and each element of *SP.new* [i.e., O'(4)]. We now have

$$P = \{O(1).O(2).O'(3).O'(4)\}.$$

5) Access the leaf-node record with a key value equal to O'(5) and add the instantiations in the set P to the set of instantiations associated with O'(5).

3) Multiindex: Given a path $\mathcal{P}$ = C(1).A(1).A(2) ... A(n), a multiindex requires a lookup of (n − i + 1) indexes to evaluate a predicate against a nested attribute A(n) of a class C(i), 1 ≤ i ≤ n. As described in [15], the index NX(n) is scanned first and the list of UID's obtained is sorted. Then the index NX(n − 1) is accessed, performing a lookup with the sorted list, and so forth until the index NX(i) is accessed. In particular, to evaluate a predicate with respect to class C(1), n indexes must be accessed. Therefore, the multiindex has lower performance than a nested index. It may have lower or higher performance than the path indexing, depending on the patterns of reference among objects. We will provide a more precise comparison in Section V.

Let us consider the multiindex in Example 3. Suppose that we wish to retrieve all vehicles manufactured by Fiat. The multiindex can be used as follows. First, the index on the subpath Company.Name is accessed looking up for Fiat. The set of UID's retrieved is {Company[i]}. Then, the index on the subpath Vehicle.Manufacturer is accessed for the UID's in the set retrieved by the previous index lookup. Since the set contains only one element, a single index lookup is needed. The lookup of Company[i] in the index on the subpath Vehicle.Manufacturer returns the set of UID's {Vehicle[k]}. This set is the answer to the query.

The primary advantages of multiindexing is the efficiency in updates, since neither forward or backward traversals are required. Suppose that an object O(i), 1 ≤ i ≤ n, which is an instance of a class C(i) along the path,

is updated by replacing object O(i + 1), the value of attribute A(i), with an object O'(i + 1). Index NX.i is updated by removing the UID of object O(i) from the set of UID's associated with O(i + 1), and adding it to the set of UID's associated with O'(i + 1).

IV. PARAMETERS OF THE INDEX COST MODELS

In this section we summarize the parameters used and assumptions we make in the cost models of index we will develop in Sections V–VII.

The parameters that we consider in the model have been grouped as follows. Some of these parameters are provided as input, while others are derived from the input parameters. All lengths and sizes are in bytes.

Logical Data Parameters: Given a path $\mathcal{P}$ = C(1).A(1).A(2) ... A(n), we have the following parameters that describe characteristics of the classes and attributes.

$D(i)$	Number of distinct values for attribute A(i), 1 ≤ i ≤ n. In particular, when 1 ≤ i < n, this parameter defines the number of distinct references from instances of class C(i) to instances of class C(i + 1) through attribute A(i).
$N(i)$	Cardinality of class C(i), 1 ≤ i ≤ n.
$k(i)$	Average number of instances of class C(i), assuming the same value for attribute A(i). As pointed out in [14], $k(i)$ = $\lceil N(i)/D(i) \rceil$.
UIDL	Length of the object-identifier.

System Parameters:

IO	Time needed to fetch a page.
P	Page size.

Index Parameters:

d	Order of a nonleaf node.
f	Average fanout from a nonleaf node. $d \le f \le 2d$, for nonleaf nodes other than the root node. $2 \le f \le 2d$, for the root node.
pp	Length of a page pointer.
kl	Average length of a key value for the indexed attribute, [i.e., A(n)], for a nested index, for a path index, and for the n-th index in a multiindex.
kll	Size of the key-length field.
rl	Size of the record-length field.
nuid	Size of the no. uids (n. paths) field.
ol	Sum of *kll*, *rl*, and *nuid*.
L	Average length of a nonleaf-node index record for a nested index, for a path index, and for the n-th index in a multiindex; $L = kl + kll + pp$.
L'	Average length of a nonleaf-node index record for the i-th (1 ≤ i ≤ n) index a multiindex; $L' = UIDL + kll + pp$.
DS	Length of the directory at the beginning of the record, when the record size is greater than the page size.

TABLE I

| UIDL = 8 | kl = 8 | kll = 2 | rl = 2 | nuid = 2 | ol = 6 | pp = 4 |
| L = 14 | L' = 14 | f = 218 | d = 146 | P = 4096 | | |

XN — Average length of a leaf-node index record for a nested index.

XP — Average length of a leaf-node index record for a path index.

$XM(i)$ — Average length of a leaf-node index record for the i-th ($1 \leq i \leq n$) index the multiindex.

LP — Number of leaf level index pages.

NLP — Number of nonleaf level index pages.

np — Number of pages occupied by a record when the record size is larger than the page size.

In Sections V–VII we will compare the three indexes with respect to the storage, retrieval, and update costs. The parameters $k(i)$ ($1 \leq i \leq n$) model the degree of reference sharing, which impacts the costs most significantly. Two objects share a reference if they reference the same object.

Assumptions: To simplify our model, we make a number of assumptions.

1) There are no partial instantiations. This implies that $D(i) = N(i + 1)$; that is, each instance of a class $C(i)$ is referenced by instances of class $C(i - 1)$, $1 < i \leq n$. Without this assumption, we would have to introduce additional parameters to take into account object reference topologies.

2) All key values have the same length. As discussed in [14], this implies that all nonleaf node index records have the same length in all indexes.

3) The values of attributes are uniformly distributed among instances of the class defining the attributes.

4) All attributes are single-valued.

As in [14], for some parameters we have adopted values from the B-tree implementation of indexes in ORION. Also we have assumed that the average length of a key value is equal to the size of a UID. The values for these parameters are listed in Table I.

V. Storage Cost

In formulating the storage costs of the three indexes, we use a model similar to that developed in [14]. We first provide the cost formulas for the three indexes, and then compare them using these formulas.

A. Cost Model

1) Nested Index: $k(1, n)$ is the average number of instances of class $C(1)$ having the same value for the nested attribute $A(n)$.

$$k(1, n) = \prod_{i=1}^{n} k(i) = \frac{N(1)}{D(n)}$$

The number of leaf pages is

$$LP = \lceil D(n) / \lfloor P/XN \rfloor \rceil, \quad \text{where}$$

$$XN = k(1, n) * UIDL + kl + ol \quad \text{if } XN \leq P$$

$$LP = D(n) * \lceil XN/P \rceil, \quad \text{where}$$

$$XN = k(1, n) * UIDL + kl + ol + DS \quad \text{and}$$

$$DS = \lceil [k(1, n) * UIDL + kl + ol]/P \rceil$$

$$* (UIDL + pp) \quad \text{if } XN > P.$$

The estimation of parameters $k(1, n)$ and LP is valid under the assumption that there are no partial instantiations. If there were partial instantiations, this estimation represents the upper bound.

The number of nonleaf pages is evaluated as follows. Let $LO = \min(D(n), LP)$. Then the number of nonleaf pages is

$$NLP = \lceil LO/f \rceil + \lceil \lceil LO/f \rceil /f \rceil + \cdots + X$$

where each term is successively divided by f until the last term X is less than f. If the last term X is not 1, 1 is added to the total (for the root node).

The number of terms in the expression for NLP represents the number of nonleaf nodes that must be accessed when scanning the index. We denote it by h and we will use it in evaluating the retrieval cost in Section VI. The *height* of the index is therefore equal to $h + 1$.

2) Path Index: PN is the average number of path instantiations ending with the same value for the nested attribute $A(n)$.

$$PN = \prod_{i=1}^{n} k(i)$$

The number of leaf pages is

$$LP = \lceil D(n) / \lfloor P/XP \rfloor \rceil, \quad \text{where}$$

$$XP = PN * UIDL * n + kl + ol \quad \text{if } XP \leq P$$

(each instantiation is implemented as an array of UID's of length n)

$$LP = D(n) * \lceil XP/P \rceil, \quad \text{where}$$

$$XP = PN * UIDL * n + kl + ol + DS \quad \text{and}$$

$$DS = \lceil [PN * UIDL * n + kl + ol]/P \rceil$$

$$* (UIDL * n + pp) \quad \text{if } XN > P.$$

The number of nonleaf pages is evaluated as in the previous case.

3) Multiindex: We first express $S(n)$, the storage size of the n-th index in a multiindex. The number of leaf pages in the n-th index is obtained as follows:

$$XM(n) = k(n) * UIDL + kl + ol$$

$$LP(n) = \lceil D(n) / \lfloor P/XM(n) \rfloor \rceil$$

$$\text{if } XM(n) \leq P$$

$$LP(n) = D(n) * \lceil XM(n)/P \rceil$$

$$\text{if } XM(n) > P.$$

The number of nonleaf pages is formulated as in the case of the nested index or the path index.

The storage size $S(i)$ of the i-th index $(1 \leq i < n)$ is given by formulating the number of leaf pages as follows:

$$XM(i) = (k(i) + 1) * UIDL + ol$$

(the key values for the intermediate indexes along the path are object identifiers)

$$LP(i) = \lceil D(i) / \lfloor P/XM(i) \rfloor \rceil$$
$$\text{if } XM(i) \leq P \quad 1 \leq i < n$$
$$LP(i) = D(i) * \lceil XM(i)/P \rceil$$
$$\text{if } XM(i) > P \quad 1 \leq i < n.$$

The number of nonleaf pages is expressed as in the other two types of index.

Therefore, the total size of the multiindex is the sum of $S(i)$, $1 \leq i \leq n$. In the following we will denote by $h(i)$, $1 \leq i \leq n$, the number of nonleaf pages that must be accessed when scanning the i-th index. It is evaluated as in the previous cases.

B. Comparison

Using the above formulations, we evaluated the index sizes for the three types of index. It is quite obvious that the nested index has the lowest size, independently of the object-reference topology. However, which is the better between the path index and the multiindex depends on the degree of reference sharing among objects.

The cost formulas were evaluated for the case of path length 2 (a path involving two classes). The reason is that for greater path lengths, it is in general preferable to split the path in several subpaths of lengths 1, 2, or 3 and allocate either a nested index or a path index on each subpath. In order to model different degrees of reference among objects, we have fixed the cardinality $N(1)$ to 200 000 and varied the parameters $D(1)$ and $D(2)$ so that the parameter $k(1)$ would assume values in the set $\{1, 5, 10, 50, 100\}$ and $k(2)$ would assume values in the set $\{1, 5, 10, 50\}$. Table II in the Appendix shows the values for these parameters and the computed value of $k(1, 2)$ (significant only for the nested and path indexes). Note that when $k(1)$ and $k(2)$ assume value 1, there is no sharing of references.

We compared the three indexes with respect to different values of parameters $k(i)$. For the storage cost, we note that the path index has a certain degree of redundancy with respect to the multiindex. Some instantiations may share some references. In this case, the referenced objects (and all objects following in the instantiations) are replicated in the arrays implementing the instantiations. This degree of redundancy is modeled by the parameters $k(i)$.

Fig. 5(a) and (b) shows the storage requirements for the three indexes for different values of $k(1)$ and $k(2)$ equal to 1 and 5. The graphs for $k(2)$ equal to 10 and 50 exhibit a similar behavior. It can be seen from the figure that when there is no sharing of references among objects of class

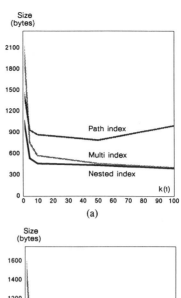

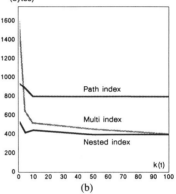

Fig. 5. (a) Storage overhead $k(2) = 1$. (b) Storage overhead $k(2) = 5$.

$C(1)$, the path index has less storage overhead than the multiindex. However, when the degree of reference sharing increases, the same information is replicated several times in the path index, increasing the storage overhead relative to the multiindex. Also note that when the degree of reference sharing increases, the multiindex and the nested index have almost the same storage overhead. This is due to Assumption 1) (cf. Section IV). Under this assumption, an increase in the degree of reference sharing of class $C(1)$ implies that the size of class $C(2)$ decreases.

VI. Retrieval Cost

In this section we compare the retrieval cost of the three types of index, for both single-key queries and range-key queries. A *single-key query* is a query with a single predicate of the form: key = value. A *range-key query* has a single predicate of the form (key < value), or (key > value), or (key between value-1 and value-2).

A. Single-Key Queries

1) Cost Model: For both the nested index and the path index, predicate evaluation requires scanning only one index, while for the multiindex n indexes must be accessed. In the following, we will formulate A, the number of index pages to be accessed to evaluate a single-key predicate.

(1) Nested Index and (2) Path Index: Let X be the size of a leaf-node record.

The number of index pages accessed is

$$A = h + 1 \qquad \text{if } X \leq P$$

$$A = h + \lceil X/P \rceil \qquad \text{if } X > P$$

(h is the number of nonleaf nodes that must be accessed; cf. Section V-A) where $X = XN$ for the nested index, and $X = XP$ for the path index.

(3) Multiindex: We first formulate the number of index pages accessed for the n-th index, and then for the i-th index $1 \leq i < n$.

The number of pages accessed in the n-th index is

$$A(n) = h(n) + 1 \qquad \text{if } XM(n) \leq P$$

$$A = h(n) + \lceil XM(n)/P \rceil \qquad \text{if } XM(n) > P.$$

To determine the number of pages accessed for an i-th index, we have to determine the number of UID's retrieved by a scan of the $(i + 1)$-th index. This number, denoted as $NUID(i)$, is determined as follows:

$$NUID(n - 1) = k(n)$$

$$NUID(i) = k(i + 1) * k(i + 2) * \cdots k(n - 1)$$

$$* k(n), \qquad 1 \leq i < n - 1.$$

To evaluate the number of leaf pages that must be accessed given $NUID(i)$ UID's, we use a formula developed in [19]. This formula determines the number of pages hit when accessing k records randomly selected from a file containing n records grouped into m pages:

$$H(k, m, n) = m * \left[1 - \prod_{i=1}^{k} \frac{n - (n/m) - i + 1}{n - i + 1} \right].$$

Applying this formula, we obtain the number of index leaf pages accessed (denoted by $AL.i$) in scanning the i-th index

$$AL(i) = H(NUID(i), LP(i), D(i)) \qquad \text{if } XM(i) \leq P$$

$$AL(i) = NUID(i) * \lceil XM(i)/P \rceil \qquad \text{if } XM(i) > P.$$

To determine the number of nonleaf pages to be accessed, we can again use the formula of [19] to determine the pages hit at level $h(i)$ in a B-tree, where k is equal to $AL(i)$, m is the number of index pages at level $h(i)$, and n is the number of index records at level $h(i)$. To determine the pages hit at level $h(i) - 1$ in the B-tree, the same reasoning can be applied, until the root is reached. However, to simplify the model we assume that the number of nonleaf pages accessed is equal to $h(i)$. This value is the lower limit. Therefore, the number of pages accessed in the i-th index is

$$A(i) = H(NUID(i), LP(i), D(i)) + h(i)$$

$$\text{if } XM(i) \leq P$$

$$A(i) = NUID(i) * \lceil XM(i)/P \rceil + h(i)$$

$$\text{if } XM(i) > P.$$

2) Comparison: Using the cost formulas derived above, we computed the number of pages accessed to evaluate a single-key query for the three indexes. The cost formulas were first evaluated for the case of path length 2, and the other parameters assume the same values as those used for the storage cost.

We evaluated the retrieval cost with respect to the parameters $k(i)$, as for the storage cost. The product of these parameters determines the size of the leaf-node record for the nested index and path index, and therefore it may have a nonnegligible impact on the retrieval cost when the size exceeds the page size. For the multiindex the values of the parameters $k(i)$ are even more crucial. In fact, after the $(i + 1)$-th index is scanned, the product $k(n) * k(n - 1) * \cdots * k(i + 1)$ determines the number of UID's that must be looked up in the i-th index. Unless the number of UID's is very large, each of these UID's causes an index lookup. Therefore, the number of index lookups in the i-th index is proportional to this product.

Fig. 6(a) and (b) shows the retrieval costs for the three indexes for different values of $k(1)$, and for values of $k(2)$ equal to 1 and 50. We also evaluated the retrieval costs for values of $k(2)$ equal to 5 and 10. The retrieval cost in the case of $k(2)$ equal to 5 and 10 is the same as the case of $k(2)$ equal to 1 for the nested index, and equal in most cases for the path index, while it goes down for the multiindex.

When the degree of reference sharing of class $C(2)$ is low ($k(2)$ equal to 1), the number of pages accessed for the multiindex is not much higher than that for the other two indexes. However, when $k(2)$ has higher values, the difference increases. This happens because the number of UID's of instances of class $C(2)$ that are retrieved from the second index is given by $k(2)$. For each one of these UID's, the first index must be accessed to determine the UID's of instances of class $C(1)$ associated with that UID. This factor affects significantly the retrieval cost of the multiindex. Therefore, as $k(2)$ increases, the number of accesses to the first index increases; while in the other indexes a single index scan is needed.

Note that the retrieval cost of the nested index and path index is the same for varying values of $k(1)$ and $k(2)$, as long as the record size does not exceed the page size. The retrieval cost of the two indexes becomes different once the record size exceeds the page size; this is because the record size increases faster for the path index than the nested index. Therefore, in Fig. 6(b) we see that for values of $k(1)$ between 10 and 20, the number of page accesses for the nested index is still stable, while it increases for the path index for $k(1)$ greater than 10.

An overall conclusion that can be drawn is that the factor which most significantly affects the retrieval cost of the multiindex is the value of $k(2)$. The access cost increases linearly with the value of $k(2)$. For the other two indexes, the factor that affects the retrieval cost most significantly is the value of the product $k(1) * k(2)$ when it exceeds a certain threshold value. In particular, the ac-

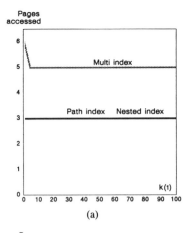

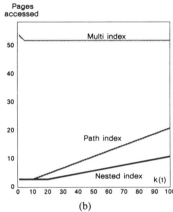

Fig. 6. (a) Performance of single-key queries for $k(2) = 1$ and number of classes = 2. (b) Performance of single-key queries for $k(2) = 50$ and number of classes = 2.

cess cost is constant for

$$k(1) * k(2) \leq 1000 \text{ for the nested index; and}$$

$$k(1) * k(2) \leq 500 \text{ for the path index.}$$

When $k(1) * k(2)$ is greater than the above thresholds, the access cost increases with the product. However, we note that this increase is less than a linear increase as in the case of the multiindex. The cost for the nested index and path index increases when the leaf-record size is larger than the page size. When record size is smaller than the page size, the access cost is constant.

The above thresholds for the nested index and the path index are explained as follows. For $k(1) * k(2) \leq 500$ (cf. expression for XN in Section V-A), the record size in the nested index is smaller than the page size. Therefore, only one leaf page access is needed to access a leaf-node record. For $500 < k(1) * k(2) \leq 1000$, a leaf-node record occupies two pages. However, the index height decreases by 1, offsetting the increase in the number of leaf-page accesses, and keeping the access cost constant. However, when $k(1) * k(2) > 1000$, the leaf node record occupies more than two pages. The decrease in the index height is not enough to offset this, and the cost starts increasing. The same discussion applies to the path index when the record size is greater than the page size for $k(1) * k(2) > 250$.

On the basis of all the experiments we did, we generalize the above discussion to the case of a path length n. As we discussed before, the nested index and the path index have constant access times when the leaf-record size does not exceed a certain threshold value. In particular, on the basis of the expressions given for XN and XP in Section V-A, we have the following.

1) The nested index has a constant access time, if $k(1) * k(2) * \cdots * k(n) \leq 500$; otherwise the access time grows linearly with $(k(1) * k(2) * \cdots * k(n))/500$.

2) The path index has a constant access time, if $k(1) * k(2) * \cdots * k(n) \leq (500/n)$; otherwise the access time grows linearly with $(k(1) * k(2) * \cdots * k(n))/(500/n)$.

Now let us see how the above threshold is obtained for the nested index. (The derivation for the path index is similar.) Let us consider the expression for XN (when XN is smaller than the page size) given in Section V-A:

$$XN = k(1) * k(2) * \cdots * k(n) * UIDL + kl + ol.$$

Assuming that the terms kl and ol are negligible, we have that $XN \leq 4096$ (page size) if

$$k(1) * k(2) * \cdots * k(n) \leq (4096/UIDL).$$

Since $UIDL$ is equal to 8, we see that the threshold is 500.

As we discussed in Section VI-A-1), the multiindex requires a lookup of n indexes for a path length n. For the i-th index, the number of keys that must be looked up is given by $k(i + 1) * k(i + 2) * \cdots * k(n)$. If we consider only the accesses to the leaf pages and assume that for each key a page must be accessed (the real number is slightly smaller and it is given by Yao's formula), we have the following conclusion.

3) The multiindex has an access time that grows linearly with

$$1 + k(n) + k(n - 1) * k(n) + k(n - 2)$$
$$* k(n - 1) * k(n) + \cdots + k(2)$$
$$* k(3) * \cdots * k(n - 1) k(n).$$

B. Range-Key Queries

In formulating range-key queries, we will make use of the following additional parameters:

$NREC$ number of records per leaf-node, if X is the record size then $NREC = \lfloor P/X \rfloor$ if $X \leq P$; $NREC = 1$ otherwise.

NRQ number of key values in the range specified for a given query.

We assume that in a range search, the index is traversed to determine the leaf node containing the lowest value in the range. Then a sequential search is performed on the leaf nodes until the node containing the highest value in the range is determined. That is, we assume that the leaf nodes of the index are linked.

1) Cost Model: As in the case of single-key queries, for both the nested index and the path index, predicate evaluation requires scanning only one index, while for the multiindex n indexes must be accessed.

(1) Nested Index and (2) Path Index: Let X be the size of a leaf-node record.

The number of index pages accessed is

$$A = h + \lceil NRQ/NREC \rceil \qquad \text{if } X \le P$$
$$A = h + NRQ * \lceil X/P \rceil \qquad \text{if } X > P$$

where $X = XN$ for the nested index, and $X = XP$ for the path index.

When the record size is smaller than the page size, the expression $\lceil NRQ/NREC \rceil$ determines the number of leaf pages to be accessed to retrieve all records associated with the keys in the range.

(3) Multiindex: The expression for the number of index pages accessed in the n-th index is similar to that for the nested and path indexes

$$A(n) = h(n) + \lceil NRQ/NREC \rceil \qquad \text{if } XM(n) \le P$$
$$A(n) = h(n) + NRQ * \lceil XM(n)/P \rceil \qquad \text{if } XM(n) > P.$$

To determine the number of pages accessed for an i-th index, we use the approach used for single-key queries. The number of UID's retrieved by the scan of the $(i + 1)$-th index is as follows:

$$NUID(n - 1) = NRQ * k(n)$$
$$NUID(i) = NRQ * k(n) * k(n - 1)$$
$$* \cdots * k(i + 1)$$
$$1 \le i < n - 1.$$

In fact, when accessing the n-th index (i.e., the last index), NRQ keys are searched. For each of these keys, $k(n)$ UID's are retrieved. Therefore, when accessing the $(n - 1)$-th index $NRQ * k(n)$ keys are searched. For each of these keys, $k(n - 1)$ UID's are retrieved. Therefore, the total number of UID's retrieved by searching the $(n - 1)$-th index is given by $NRQ * k(n) * k(n - 1)$, which is the number of keys to be searched in the $(n - 2)$-th index, and so forth, until the 1st index is scanned.

2) Comparison: We studied the case of path length 2, using the same values for the parameters as those used for the storage cost. The parameter NRQ assumes the value 10 or 20.

Fig. 7(a) shows the retrieval cost of the three indexes for different values of $k(1)$, for $k(2)$ equal to 10, and for $NRQ = 10$; while Fig. 7(b) is for $NRQ = 20$. The multiindex has the worst retrieval cost, since the number of UID's retrieved in each index lookup increases in the case of range queries compared to the case of single-key queries. The path index has better retrieval cost than the multiindex, but worse than the nested index. This is due to the greater size of the leaf-node records in the path index compared to that in the nested index.

VII. Update Cost

Given a path $\mathcal{P} = C(1).A(1).A(2) \ldots A(n)$, and an object $O(i)$, $1 \le i \le n$, an index on the path may have to be updated when the current value of attribute

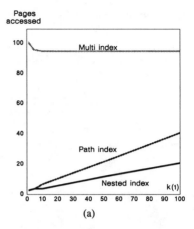

(a)

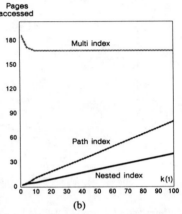

(b)

Fig. 7. (a) Performance of range queries for $k(2) = 10$ and $NRQ = 10$. (b) Performance of range queries for $k(2) = 10$ and $NRQ = 20$.

$A(i)$ [i.e., object $O(i + 1)$] is replaced with an object $O'(i + 1)$. In this section we will derive the cost formulas for update operations. The cost for update, delete, and instance creation will be denoted by U, D, and I, respectively. We will not include the cost of updating, deleting, or creating the object itself, since this cost is common to all indexes. We only account for the cost related to updating the index. Further, to simplify the analysis, as in [18], we do not include the costs due to index page splits; that is, we only consider the cost of leaf-page update.

A. Cost Model

We will use the following additional parameters.

CFT   Cost of a forward traversal.
CBT   Cost of a backward traversal.
CBM   Cost of a B-tree update.

1) Nested Index: We will assume that reverse references are supported. If reverse references are not supported, the nested index cannot be used (if there are updates). We also assume that reverse references from object O to object O' are stored in O. As discussed already, to update the nested index it is necessary to execute two forward traversals, one backward traversal, and one B-tree update. Of course, the backward traversal and the B-tree update are necessary only if the value of A(n) for O(i + 1) is different from the value for O'(i + 1). We use *pdiff* to denote the probability that the value of A(n) for O(i + 1) is different from the value for O'(i + 1). Therefore, U is on average

$$U = 2 * CFT + pdiff * (CBT + CBM).$$

To formulate *CFT*, we use the fact that the number of objects that must be accessed is $n - i$. For each object, the physical address of the object must be determined first, and then the object itself must be fetched. Therefore,

$$CFT = 2 * (n - i).$$

The formulation of *CBT* is based on the fact that the number of objects that must be accessed in the backward traversal is

$$NO = \sum_{j=2}^{i-1} \left(\prod_{i=j}^{i-1} k(i) \right) \quad \text{if } i > 2$$

$$NO = 0 \quad \text{otherwise.}$$

Since for each object two I/O operations are necessary, we obtain

$$CBT = 2 * NO \quad \text{if } i > 2$$

$$CBT = 0 \quad \text{otherwise.}$$

Note that if the length of the path is two (i.e., $n = 2$) and the updated object belongs to the second class in the path (i.e., $i = 2$), $CFT = 0$ and $CBT = 0$.

The probability *pdiff* is given by the following expression:

$$pdiff = 1 \quad \text{if } i = n;$$

$$pdiff = 1 - \left[\frac{\left(\prod_{j=i+1}^{n} k(j) \right) - 1}{D(i) - 1} \right] \quad \text{if } i < n.$$

The cost of a B-tree update is the cost of removing the UID of object O(i) from the record associated with the old value of A(n) and the cost of adding it to the new value. Therefore, the cost of each of these operations is the cost of finding the leaf node containing the record and the cost of reading and writing the leaf node. We denote the cost of each such operation as *CO*. The average value of *CBM* is formulated as follows:

$$CBM = CO * (1 + pl)$$

where *pl* is the probability that the old and new values of A(n) are on different leaf nodes.

$$CO = h + 2 \quad \text{if } XN \leq P$$

when modifying a leaf page, a page is accessed to read the leaf page containing the updated record, and another to write this page; in addition, *h* pages are accessed to determine the leaf node containing the record to be updated.

$$CO = h + 2 + (np - 1)/np \quad \text{if } XN > P \quad (1)$$

when the record size is larger than the page size and *np* is the number of leaf pages needed to store a record ($np = \lceil XN/P \rceil$), $h + 1$ of I/O's are necessary to access the leaf page that contains the header of the record. From the header of the record, it is possible to determine the page from which a UID must be deleted or to which a UID must be added. If this page is different from the page containing the header of the record, a further access must be performed. The probability of this is given by $(np - 1)/np$.

The probability that the current and new value of A(n) are on different leaf nodes is

$$pl = 1 \quad \text{if } XN > P$$

when the record size is larger than the page size, each record is stored in different pages;

$$pl = 1 - \left[(NREC - 1)/(D(n) - 1) \right] \quad \text{if } XN \leq P$$
$$(2)$$

where *NREC* is the number of index records per leaf page.

The costs of index updates for object deletion and creation are equal, and are evaluated similarly. The major difference is that only one forward traversal is necessary and the cost of a B-tree update includes only the removal (or insertion) of a UID from a leaf-node record. Therefore, $D = I = CFT + CBT + CBM$, where *CFT* and *CBT* are the same as in the case of object update, while $CBM = CO$.

(2) Path Index: As we have seen already, to update a path index it is necessary to execute two forward traversals to determine the values of A(n) for O(i + 1) and for O'(i + 1), and one B-tree update. Note that unlike the previous case, the B-tree update is necessary even if the value of A(n) for O(i + 1) is equal to the value of O'(i + 1). In fact, even if the value of A(n) is the same, we have to modify the leaf-node record associated with A(n) to modify the instantiations affected by the update. However, no backward traversal is necessary. Therefore, $U = 2 * CFT + CBM$.

The expression for *CFT* is the same as that for the nested index.

The expression for *CBM* is slightly different from that for the nested index. In fact, two different leaf nodes are updated when the old and new values of A(n) for O(i) are different, and the records associated with the old and new values are stored in different leaf nodes. Therefore,

$$CBM = CO * (1 + pdiff * pl),$$

where *CO* is the same as expression (1) in which *XP* is substituted for *XN*.

The cost of index updates for object deletion and creation is similar to that for the nested index. Therefore, $D = I = CFT + CBM$, where the expressions for *CFT* and *CBM* are the same as the nested index.

(3) Multiindex: Only the i-th B-tree must be updated. Therefore,

$$U = CBM = CO * (1 + pl),$$

where *CO* is given by expression (1) in which $XM(i)$ is substituted for *XN*, and by expression (2) in which $D(i)$ is substituted for $D(n)$.

The cost of index updates for object deletion and creation is given by

$$D = I = CO.$$

B. Comparison

Using the cost formulas developed in the previous section, we compared the update costs of the three indexes. We considered updates to both C(1) and C(2). Again, we compared the three indexes on the basis of the values of parameters $k(i)$. These parameters are relevant for the nested index and path index for the following reasons. First, the record size depends on the product of parameters $k(i)$, and therefore it may influence the update costs when the record size exceeds the page size. Second, for the nested index these parameters determine how many objects must be accessed in a backward traversal.

Fig. 8(a)–(d) shows the update costs for the case when class C(1) is updated. Note that when the degree of object sharing of class C(2) is low [Fig. 8(a)], the update costs for the nested index and path index are constant. When the value of $k(1) * k(2)$ is equal to 500, the cost of update increases for the path index. This increase results from the increased size of the leaf-node record. The record size in the first index for the multiindex depends only on $k(1)$; when class C(1) is updated, only the first index is updated. In the path index, the record size depends on the product $k(1) * k(2)$, and therefore the cost of update increases in general by 1 when the product increases. Note, however, that in Fig. 8(c) the cost for the nested index and the path index decreases. This happens because the number of nonleaf nodes that must be scanned to determine the records to be updated (parameter h in the cost equations) decreases from 2 ($k(1) < 50$) to 1 ($k(1) > 50$). There is a corresponding increase in the number of leaf pages needed to store a record: for $k(1) \leq 50$ this number is 1 for the nested index and 2 for the path index, and for $k(1) > 50$ it is 2 for the nested index and 3 for the path index. However, for $k(1) > 50$, the probability of an additional page access is 0.5 for the nested index and 0.7 for the path index (cf. expression (1) for *CO*). As such:

$CO = 4$ for $k(1) < 50$ and $U = 12$ for both the nested index and the path index;

$CO = 3.5$ for $k(1) > 50$ and $U = 11$ for the nested index; and

$CO = 3.7$ for $k(1) > 50$ and $U = 11.4$ for the path index.

However, when the record size increases so that the record occupies more than three pages, the probability of an additional page access starts to increase, offsetting the gain

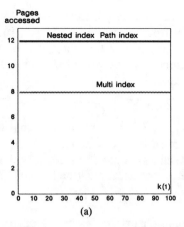

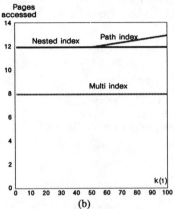

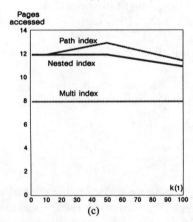

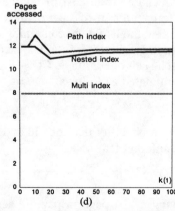

Fig. 8. (a) Update cost $k(2) = 1$, class modified is C(1), number of classes = 2. (b) Update cost $k(2) = 5$, class modified is C(1), number of classes = 2. (c) Update cost $k(2) = 10$, class modified is C(1), number of classes = 2. (d) Update cost $k(2) = 50$, class modified is C(1), number of classes = 2.

due to the reduced tree height. This explains the initial decrease and the subsequent increase in the costs for the nested index and path index in Fig. 8(d). Therefore, for values of the product $k(1) * k(2)$ greater than 1000, we can expect the cost function assumes values that are closer to 12.

When class $C(2)$ is updated, instead of $C(1)$, no forward or backward traversals are needed. When there is no reference sharing ($k(1) = 1$ and $k(2) = 1$), all three indexes have the same update costs. When object sharing increases, the update cost of the multiindex decreases. The decrease in the multiindex is due to the fact that the size of the second index [i.e., the index on class $C(2)$] decreases as the value of $k(1)$ increases. In fact, when $k(1)$ increases, the cardinality of class $C(2)$ decreases (because we assume no partial instantiations). The update cost for the nested index and path index has a trend similar to that observed for the case of updates on class $C(1)$. The cost is constant, then decreases and then increases again. This is explained in the same way.

An important point is that when the path has length 2 and reverse references are stored in the objects, the nested index can be as effective as the multiindex. In fact, when the indexed attribute $A(2)$ in an object $O(2)$ of the second class is updated, we do not need to access the objects of the first class to determine the objects that reference O, since O contains reverse references to these objects. Therefore, once O is accessed for an update, the reverse references can be determined. When an object $O(1)$ of the first class is updated by assigning to attribute $A(1)$ a different instance of the second class, as we discussed earlier, two forward traversals are necessary to access the objects O′ and O″, the old and new values of $A(1)$, respectively. But these two objects must be accessed anyway to update the reverse references to $O(1)$ (i.e., removing it from O′ and adding to O″). When they are accessed, the value of $A(2)$ can be determined. If a multiindex were used in such a situation, the overhead of accessing objects O′ and O″ would be unavoidable, without the benefit of a faster predicate evaluation.

When the path length is greater than 2, a backward traversal is required for the nested index, thereby increasing the update cost relative to the path index. To assess the effect of the backward traversal, let us consider the case of path length 3. The values for $k(1)$, $k(2)$, and $k(3)$ are the same as those assumed for the cost of single-key queries (Section VI-A). Fig. 9(a)–(d) shows the update costs for some values of $k(2)$ and $k(3)$ when class $C(3)$ (last class in the path) is updated. We can see that for the nested index, the dominant factor is the backward traversal, since $k(3) * k(2)$ objects must be accessed (see the expression for *CBT* in the previous section). For example, when $k(3) = 1$ and $k(2) = 10$ [Fig. 9(b)], ten objects must be accessed. Since for each object two accesses are necessary, the backward traversal costs 20 accesses. Thus, the costs for the nested index are constant in Fig. 9(a) and (b) for fixed combinations of $k(3)$ and $k(2)$, and are almost independent of the values of $k(1)$.

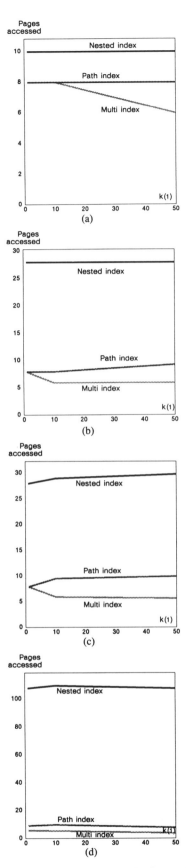

Fig. 9. (a) Update cost $k(2) = 1$, $k(3) = 1$, class modified is $C(3)$, number of classes = 3. (b) Update cost $k(2) = 10$, $k(3) = 1$, class modified is $C(3)$, number of classes = 3. (c) Update cost $k(2) = 10$, $k(3) = 10$, class modified is $C(3)$, number of classes = 3. (d) Update cost $k(2) = 50$, $k(3) = 10$, class modified is $C(3)$, number of classes = 3.

Fig. 9(c) shows that the costs for the nested index also increase for increasing values of $k(1)$. This happens because, for the combinations of values for $k(1)$, $k(2)$, and $k(3)$, the leaf-record size exceeds the page size; therefore, the probability of an additional page access increases. The same consideration explains the increases in the update cost of the path index. The path index incurs a lower cost than the nested index when the third class is updated, because it does not require the backward traversal. However, the costs of updating the classes $C(1)$ or $C(2)$ are almost equal for both the nested index and path index.

An overall conclusion about the update cost for the nested index and the path index is as follows:
- for path length 2, the nested index is preferable, if reverse references are supported;
- for path length 3, the nested index is preferable if reverse references are supported and updates are only on the first or second class in the path; otherwise the path index is preferable.

We now generalize the discussion to the case of path length n to determine the cost trend for updates (the trends for delete and insert are obtained in similar ways). The update cost for the multiindex is almost constant and it is independent of the path length. For the other two indexes, the dominant cost factors are the forward and backward traversals. The costs of forward and backward traversals depend on the class updated.

The update cost for the path index depends on the path length, while for the nested index it depends on the path length and on the product of the parameters $k(i)$. To see this, let us determine the average update cost, denoted as $\mathcal{Y}$, assuming that updates are equally likely on all classes along the path.

The path index requires two forward traversals. From the expression for *CFT*, the average update cost is

$$\mathcal{Y} = \left[4 * \sum_{i=1}^{n} (n-i) \right] \Big/ n = 2*(n-1).$$

We see that the average update cost grows linearly with $2*(n-1)$.

The nested index requires a backward traversal in addition to the forward traversal. By using the expression for *CBT*, we obtain the average cost of the backward traversal

$$\left[2 * \left(k(n-1) * k(n-2) * \cdots * k(2) \right. \right.$$
$$+ k(n-2) * k(n-3) * \cdots * k(2) + \cdots$$
$$\left. \left. + k(3) * k(2) + k(2) \right) \right] \Big/ n.$$

By adding this cost to the cost of forward traversal which is the same as the path index, we obtain the average update cost as follows:

$$\mathcal{Y} = 2 * (n-1) + \left[2 * \left(k(n-1) * k(n-2) \right. \right.$$
$$* \cdots * k(2) + k(n-2)$$
$$* k(n-3) * \cdots * k(2)$$
$$\left. \left. + \cdots + k(3) * k(2) + k(2) \right) \right] \Big/ n.$$

VIII. Combined Retrieval and Update Cost

In this section we compare the three indexes on the basis of the combined cost of retrieval and update. As we have seen in the previous sections, the nested and path indexes have lower retrieval costs, but higher update costs. The multiindex incurs lower update costs and higher retrieval costs.

To compare the overall costs, we considered the following mix of retrieval (R), update (U), and delete/create operations (D/I). The overall cost is computed as the average of the costs of the three types of operations multiplied by their relative frequencies.

$$(90\%R, 5\%U, 5\%D/I), (80\%R, 10\%U, 10\%D/I),$$

$$(70\%R, 15\%U, 15\%D/I),$$
$$(60\%R, 20\%U, 20\%D/I),$$
$$(50\%R, 25\%U, 25\%D/I),$$
$$(40\%R, 30\%U, 30\%D/I),$$
$$(30\%R, 35\%U, 35\%D/I),$$
$$(20\%R, 40\%U, 40\%D/I),$$
$$(10\%R, 45\%U, 45\%D/I).$$

For retrieval, we used only single-key queries with predicates on the first class of the path [i.e., $C(1)$]. We assumed that updates apply equally to all classes along the path. For example, if the mix is $(80\%R, 10\%U, 10\%D/I)$ and the number of classes along the path is 2, 5 percent of the update operations and 5 percent of delete/insert operations are performed on each class.

First let us consider a path length 2. The nested index performs better than the other indexes when the retrieval percentage is 60 percent or more. However, the differences between the nested index and the multiindex are not very high for $k(2) = 1$. When the retrieval percentage is between 50 and 30 percent, the nested index costs slightly higher than the multiindex for $k(2) = 1$ and $k(1) > 1$. This is because for these values of $k(1)$ and $k(2)$, the gain in query performance is not high enough to offset the increased update cost. However, for values of $k(2)$ greater than 1, the nested index has a lower overall cost than the other indexes. Finally, when the retrieval percentage is 20 percent or less, the multiindex has the lowest overall cost if $k(2) \leq 10$. When $k(2)$ has values greater than 10, queries become expensive (cf. Section VI), and the lower update cost cannot offset the increased query cost.

A simple rule for determining which index to use in the case of path length 2 when the overall cost must be minimized is the following:
1) choose the multiindex if

$k(2) = 1$ or (the operations are mainly updates

and $k(2) \leq 10$); otherwise

2) choose the nested index

if there are reverse references from class $C(2)$

to class $C(1)$; otherwise

3) choose the path index.

This rule is based on the fact that when there is no sharing of references in the second class ($k(2) = 1$), the overall cost of the multiindex is not much higher (only one page access more, even for the case of retrieval 80 percent or more) than the other two indexes, even when the operations are mainly retrieval. In fact, in this case the performance of queries is good (cf. Section VI). However, the retrieval cost increases as the degree of reference sharing for class $C(2)$ increases. Therefore, even when most of the operations are updates, the increased retrieval cost may outweigh the reduced update cost. The nested index is chosen if there are reverse references from the class $C(2)$ to class $C(1)$; otherwise the path index is chosen. If it is not possible to determine the degree of reference sharing and the frequency of retrieval and update operations, a nested index represents a good choice in most cases, provided of course that reverse references are supported.

Next, we consider a path length 3. Fig. 10(a)–(d) shows some selected results for the overall costs for the three mixes for some values of $k(2)$ and $k(3)$. The path index performs better on the average than the other indexes for all access patterns. In fact, the path index incurs a retrieval cost that is comparable to that of the nested index, while it has on the average a lower update cost than the nested index. However, for high values of the product $k(1) * k(2) * k(3)$ the overall cost of the path index increases [see, for example, Fig. 10(a)] because the retrieval cost that is comparable to that of the nested index, larger than the page size. Therefore, when the record occupies several pages, the increased retrieval cost outweighs the reduced update cost, especially when the percentage of retrieval is high (80 percent or more). Further, when the operations are mainly update (70 percent or more), the multiindex performs better for low values of $k(2)$ and $k(3)$ [compare Fig. 10(c), (d)]. When the values of $k(2)$ and $k(3)$ start increasing, the decrease in the update cost is not enough to offset the increased retrieval cost. When $k(2)$ and $k(3)$ are equal to 1, the overall cost of the mulitiindex is not much higher than the cost of the other indexes.

A simple rule for determining which index to use in the case of path length 3 when the overall cost must be minimized is the following:

1) choose the multiindex if

$$\big(k(2) = 1 \text{ and } k(3) = 1\big)$$

or (the operations are mainly

updates and $k(2) * k(3) \le 10$);

otherwise

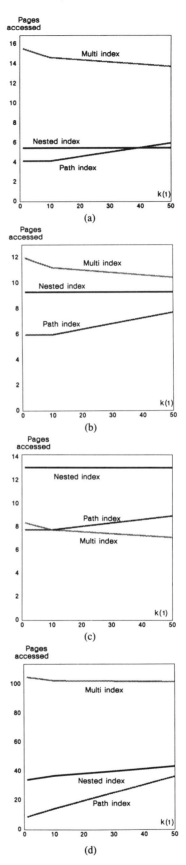

Fig. 10. (a) Overall cost $k(2) = 10$, $k(3) = 1$, mix $= (80\%R, 10\%U, 10\%D/I)$, number of classes $= 3$. (b) Overall cost $k(2) = 10$, $k(3) = 1$, mix $= (50\%R, 25\%U, 25\%D/I)$, number of classes $= 3$. (c) Overall cost $k(2) = 10$, $k(3) = 1$, mix $= (20\%R, 40\%U, 40\%D/I)$, number of classes $= 3$. (d) Overall cost $k(2) = 50$, $k(3) = 10$, mix $= (20\%R, 40\%U, 40\%D/I)$, number of classes $= 3$.

241

2) choose the nested index

    if there are reverse references from class $C(2)$

    to class $C(1)$, and the operations are mainly

    retrieval and $k(1) * k(2) * k(3) > 100$;

        otherwise

3) choose the path index.

This rule is explained in a way similar to the case of path length 2. When the degree of reference sharing of class $C(2)$ and $C(3)$ is 1, the overall cost of the multiindex is not much higher than the other two indexes. However, as the product of $k(2) * k(3)$ goes above 10, the increase in the query cost is not offset by the lower update cost. In the other cases, the nested index is chosen if reverse references are supported, the operations are mainly retrieval, and $k(1) * k(2) * k(3) > 100$. In fact, in this case the nested index may outperform the path index, since the query cost of the path index increases faster than the nested index when $k(1) * k(2) * k(3) > 100$. This increase in the query cost for the path index has a major impact on the overall cost, if most of the operations are retrieval. If, however, this product is less than or equal to 100, or the percentage of retrieval is less than 80 percent, the path index is chosen. If it is not possible to determine the degree of reference sharing and the frequency of retrieval and update operations, a path index represents a good choice in most cases.

We now discuss briefly how our results can be generalized to the case of path length greater than 3. The nested index has a high update cost mostly due to the backward traversal. This cost increases as the degree of reference sharing increases. Therefore, this index cannot be used unless either there are few updates or the degree of reference sharing is very low (equal to 1). The path index does not require backward traversal when executing updates, and therefore has a lower overall cost in most cases. However, the leaf-record size tends to become very large when the degree of reference sharing increases, thereby increasing the query cost.

In general, the best solution for a path of length greater than 3 is to split the path into several subpaths of lengths 1, 2 or 3 and to allocate on each subpath either a nested index or a path index. This approach requires fewer index lookups than with the multiindex. Further, an update on a class requires accesses to only objects of the classes belonging to the subpath of the updated class; that is, it limits any forward and backward traversals to the subpath.

Reference [5] provides an algorithm that determines the most efficient configuration of indexes on the basis of the access patterns and logical data characteristics. In particular, the algorithm determines whether the path must be split, how many subpaths the path should be split into, and the type of index to use for each subpath. As an example, let us consider the path $P = C(1).A(1).A(2).A(3).A(4).A(5)$.

This path may be split into the subpaths

$$P(1) = C(1).A(1)$$
$$P(2) = C(2).A(2).A(3)$$
$$P(3) = C(4).A(4).A(5).$$

A possible configuration consists of a conventional index on $P(1)$, a path index on $P(2)$, and a nested index on $P(3)$.

IX. CONCLUDING REMARKS

A nested object is an object which recursively consists of other objects. Nested objects arise naturally in object-oriented and nested relational databases as a consequence of allowing the value of an attribute of an object to be an object or a set of objects. A nested object in an object-oriented and nested relational database is an instance of a class or a relation which is the root of a nested hierarchy of classes or relations. In normalized relational database systems, a secondary index is a useful data structure for expediting the evaluation of queries involving predicates on the indexed attribute. In object-oriented and nested relational databases, the nested definition of a class or a relation requires the notion of secondary indexing to be generalized to predicates on the nested attributes of the target class or relation of a query. A nested attribute is an indirect attribute of a class or a relation that is the root of a nested hierarchy of classes or relations.

In this paper, we introduced three index organizations for use in evaluating queries on nested objects in object-oriented and nested relational databases. For each of the index organizations, we developed a detailed cost model for computing the storage cost, retrieval cost, and update cost. Using these models, we computed and compared the costs of the three indexes under a range of values for key parameters. The most important parameter is the degree of reference sharing among objects for the various classes in the path. As we have shown in the paper, this parameter influences both the retrieval and update costs.

Our general conclusion about retrieval performance is that the nested index has the best retrieval performance, followed by the path index, and then the multiindex. The nested and path index have a constant cost if the product of degrees of reference sharing among the classes does not exceed a certain threshold value. However, the cost of the multiindex is independent of the index-record size and increases linearly with the product of degrees of reference sharing.

Our general conclusion about update performance is that the multiindex is the best. For path length 2, the nested index has a slightly lower cost than the path index. For path length 3, the performance depends on how updates are distributed on the classes on the path. If updates are primarily on the first and second classes, the nested index has a slightly lower cost than the path index. If, however, updates are largely on the last class on the path, the path index costs significantly less than the nested index.

TABLE II					
N(1)	D(1) = N(2)	D(2)	k(1)	k(2)	k(1,2)
200,000	200,000	200,000	1	1	1
200,000	40,000	40,000	5	1	5
200,000	20,000	20,000	10	1	10
200,000	4,000	4,000	50	1	50
200,000	2,000	2,000	100	1	100
200,000	200,000	40,000	1	5	5
200,000	40,000	8,000	5	5	25
200,000	20,000	4,000	10	5	50
200,000	4,000	800	50	5	250
200,000	2,000	400	100	5	500
200,000	200,000	20,000	1	10	10
200,000	40,000	4,000	5	10	50
200,000	20,000	2,000	10	10	100
200,000	4,000	400	50	10	500
200,000	2,000	200	100	10	1000
200,000	200,000	4,000	1	50	50
200,000	40,000	800	5	50	250
200,000	20,000	400	10	50	500
200,000	4,000	80	50	50	2500
200,000	2,000	40	100	50	5000

TABLE III							
N(1)	D(1)=N(2)	D(2)=N(3)	D(3)	k(1)	k(2)	k(3)	k(1,3)
2,000,000	2,000,000	2,000,000	2,000,000	1	1	1	1
2,000,000	200,000	200,000	200,000	10	1	1	10
2,000,000	40,000	40,000	40,000	50	1	1	50
2,000,000	2,000,000	200,000	200,000	1	10	1	10
2,000,000	200,000	20,000	20,000	10	10	1	100
2,000,000	40,000	4,000	4,000	50	10	1	500
2,000,000	2,000,000	40,000	40,000	1	50	1	50
2,000,000	200,000	4,000	4,000	10	50	1	500
2,000,000	40,000	800	800	50	50	1	2,500
2,000,000	2,000,000	2,000,000	200,000	1	1	10	10
2,000,000	200,000	200,000	20,000	10	1	10	100
2,000,000	40,000	40,000	4,000	50	1	10	500
2,000,000	2,000,000	200,000	20,000	1	10	10	100
2,000,000	200,000	20,000	2,000	10	10	10	1,000
2,000,000	40,000	4,000	400	50	10	10	5,000
2,000,000	2,000,000	40,000	4,000	1	50	10	500
2,000,000	200,000	4,000	400	10	50	10	5,000
2,000,000	40,000	800	80	50	50	10	25,000

We also evaluated the combined retrieval and update cost for various mixes of retrieval, update, delete, and insert operations. Based on these evaluations, we derived some simple rules for the cases of path length 2 and 3; these rules allow us to determine the optimal index organization for most of the cases. If statistics about frequencies of operations and degrees of reference sharing are not available, the general rule is that for path length 2 the nested index should be used, provided that reverse references exist, while for path length 3 the path index should be used. For path lengths greater than 3, the best solution is to split the path into several subpaths of lengths 1, 2, or 3 and to allocate on each subpath either a nested index or a path index. Reference [5] provides an algorithm for defining the optimal configuration of indexes for paths of length greater than 3.

Throughout this paper, we assumed a query with only one predicate on a nested attribute. In general, however, a query can have a boolean combination of predicates. We offer as a topic of future research a detailed quantitative analysis of query processing strategies based on the indexing techniques presented in this paper for queries containing several predicates on both nested and simple attributes.

Appendix

Tables II and III are a list of the values for some of the parameters used in our experiments. Table II shows the values of parameters $N(1)$, $N(2)$, $k(1)$, $k(2)$, and $k(1, 2)$ used in the index evaluations in Sections V–VIII for a path of length 2.

Table III shows the values of the parameters $N(1)$, $N(2)$, $N(3)$, $k(1)$, $k(2)$, $k(3)$, and $k(1, 3)$ used in the index evaluations in Section VIII for a path of length 3.

References

[1] S. Abiteboul and N. Bidoit, "Non first normal form relations to represent hierarchically organized data," in *Proc. ACM SIGACT-SIGMOND Symp. Principles of Database Syst.*, 1984, pp. 191–200.

[2] T. Andrews and C. Harris, "Combining language and database advances in an object-oriented development environment," in *Proc. 2nd Int. Conf. Object-Oriented Programming Syst. Languages, Appl.*, Orlando, FL, Oct. 1987, pp. 430–440.

[3] J. Banerjee, H. T. Chou, J. Garza, W. Kim, D. Woelk, N. Ballou, and H. J. Kim, "Data model issues for object-oriented applications," *ACM Trans. Office Inform. Syst.*, vol. 5, pp. 3–26, Jan. 1987.

[4] R. Bayer and E. McCreight, "Organization and maintenance of large ordered indexes," *Acta Inform.*, vol. 1, pp. 173–189, 1972.

[5] E. Bertino, "On index configurations in object-oriented databases," document in preparation, 1989.

[6] D. Comer, "The ubiquitous B-tree," *ACM Comput. Surveys*, vol. 11, pp. 121–137, June 1979.

[7] P. Dadam *et al.*, "A DBMS prototype to support extended NF2 relations: An integrated view on flat tables and hierarchies," in *Proc. ACM SIGMOD Int. Conf. Management of Data*, Washington, DC, May 1986, pp. 356–366.

[8] D. Deshpande and D. Van Gucht, "An implementation for nested relational databases," in *Proc. Int. Conf. Very Large Data Bases*, Los Angeles, CA, Aug. 1988, pp. 76–87.

[9] D. H. Fishman *et al.*, "IRIS: An object-oriented database management system," *ACM Trans. Office Inform. Syst.*, vol. 5, pp. 48–69, Jan. 1987.

[10] SQL/Data System: Concepts and Facilities. GH24-5013-0, File No. S370-50, IBM Corp., Jan. 1981.

[11] IEEE Computer Society, *Database Engineering* (Special Issue on Non-First Normal Form Relational Databases), Z. M. Ozsoyoglu, Ed., Sept. 1988.

[12] S. Khoshafian and G. Copeland, "Object identity," in *Proc. 1st Int. Conf. Object-Oriented Programming Syst., Languages Appl.*, Portland, OR, Oct. 1986.

[13] W. Kim, "A foundation for object-oriented databases," MCC Tech. Rep., ACA-ST-248-88, Aug. 1988.

[14] W. Kim, K. C. Kim, and A. Dale, "Indexing techniques for object-oriented databases," in *Object-Oriented Concepts, Applications, and Databases*, W. Kim and F. Lochovsky, Eds. Reading, MA: Addison-Wesley, 1989.

[15] D. Maier and J. Stein, "Indexing in an object-oriented DBMS," in *Proc. Int. Workshop Object-Oriented Database Syst.*, Asilomar, CA, Sept. 23–26, 1986, pp. 171–182.

[16] D. Maier *et al.*, "Development of an object-oriented DBMS," in *Proc. 1st Int. Conf. Object-Oriented Programming Syst. Languages, Appl.*, Portland, OR, Oct. 1986, pp. 472–482.

[17] A. Makinouchi, "A consideration of normal form of not-necessarily normalized relations in the relational data model," in *Proc. Int. Conf. Very Large Data Bases*, 1977, pp. 447–453.

[18] M. Schkolnick and P. Tiberio, "Estimating the cost of updates in a relational database," *ACM Trans. Database Syst.*, vol. 10, pp. 163–179, June 1985.

[19] S. B. Yao, "Approximating block accesses in database organizations," *ACM Commun.*, vol. 20, pp. 260–261, Apr. 1977.

Elisa Bertino (M'83) received the doctorate degree in computer science from the University of Pisa, Pisa, Italy, in 1980 with full marks and honors.

Since 1980 she has been a Researcher at the Institute for Information Processing (IEI) of the Italian National Research Council, Pisa. From July 1982 to July 1983, and during the summer of 1984, she was a Visiting Researcher at the IBM Research Laboratory, San Jose, CA, where she worked on the R* project. Since July 1988 she has been a Visiting Researcher at the Microelectronics and Computer Technology Corporation (MCC), Austin, TX, where she is currently working on several issues concerning object-oriented database management systems.

Won Kim received the B.S. and M.S. degrees in physics from the Massachusetts Institute of Technology, Cambridge, and the Ph.D. degree in computer science from the University of Illinois at Urbana–Champaign. His Ph.D. dissertation was on query processing in relational database systems.

He joined the Microelectronics and Computer Technology Corporation (MCC), the research consortium of U.S. computer companies, in its early days (1984) and is currently Director of the Object-Oriented and Distributed Systems Laboratory in the Advanced Computing Technology Program of MCC, Austin, TX. He is also a Principal Scientist at MCC. He is the chief architect of the ORION object-oriented database system, intended for applications in the artificial intelligence, computer-aided design, and office systems domains. Prior to joining MCC, he was a Research Staff member for four years at IBM Almaden Research Center, where he participated in a number of database systems research projects, including distributed systems, highly available systems, and engineering design database systems.

Dr. Kim is currently an Associate Editor of the *ACM Transactions on Database Systems*, and for six years has been the Chief Editor of *Data Engineering*, the quarterly bulletin of the IEEE Technical Committee on Data Engineering. He has organized international conferences on Databases for Parallel and Distributed Systems, Deductive and Object-Oriented Databases, and Databases for Advanced Applications.

About the Editor

Frederick E. Petry is currently Professor of Computer Science and Director of Graduate Studies in the Computer Science department of Tulane University. He is also co-director of the Center for Intelligent and Knowledge-Based Systems (CIAKS) at Tulane. Previously he was a faculty member in the Computer Science department at the University of Alabama at Huntsville and Ohio State University. He received the B.S. and M.S. degrees in physics and a PhD in Computer Science from Ohio State in 1975.

Mr. Petry's research areas currently include integration of AI systems and databases, models of uncertainty in databases including fuzzy databases, genetic algorithms, and computer arithmetic. He has published over 80 research papers in journals, conference proceedings, and books and has directed over a half-dozen PhD students. His research has been supported by the National Science Foundation (NSF), numerous Department of Defense (DoD) agencies, private companies, and state agencies. He has been a frequent consultant for the government and the private sector.

He is currently editor for a series of volumes: *Advances in Databases* and *Artificial Intelligence* and is an associate editor-in-chief for IEEE Computer Society Press. Professional activities have included several positions in the IEEE Computer Society at the local and national level. He is a senior member of IEEE, and a member of ACM, AAAI, and IFSA.

About the Editor

Ez Nauouraii is a Senior Instructor at the System Research Education Center, IBM US Education in Thornwood, New York. He was formerly a staff member in the Computer Science Department of IBM T.J. Watson Research Center, Yorktown Heights, New York. He was a member of the advanced technology group in San Jose, California. He has been a lecturer on behalf of IBM at universities in Japan, South East Asia, South America, at the University of California at Los Angeles, and Santa Clara University. He has authored or co-authored 10 technical publications and several technical disclosures. He has edited five IBM Proceedings on Productivity Tools Symposiums, and served as the Program Chair for IBM US and European Tools Symposiums.

He received a Master's Degree in Statistics from New York University. His interests and contributions have been primarily in the areas of databases, operating systems, and productivity tools.

He is a Senior Member of the IEEE Computer Society and was formerly Editor-in-Chief of the Computer Society Press, Computer Society Editorial Press Activities Board, and the Educational Activity Board.

IEEE Computer Society

IEEE Computer Society Press Publications

Monographs: A monograph is an authored book consisting of 100-percent original material.

Tutorials: A tutorial is a collection of original materials prepared by the editors, and reprints of the best articles published in a subject area. Tutorials must contain at least five percent of original material (although we recommend 15 to 20 percent of original material).

Reprint Collections: A reprint collection contains reprints (divided into sections) with a preface, table of contents, and section introductions discussing the reprints and why they were selected. Reprint collections contain less than five percent of original material.

Technology Series: Each technology series is a brief reprint collection — approximately 126-136 pages and containing 12 to 13 papers, each paper focusing on a subset of a specific discipline, such as networks, architecture, software, or robotics.

Submission of proposals: For guidelines on preparing CS Press books, write the Editorial Director, IEEE Computer Society Press, PO Box 3014, 10662 Los Vaqueros Circle, Los Alamitos, CA 90720-1264, or telephone (714) 821-8380.

Purpose

The IEEE Computer Society advances the theory and practice of computer science and engineering, promotes the exchange of technical information among 100,000 members worldwide, and provides a wide range of services to members and nonmembers.

Membership

All members receive the acclaimed monthly magazine *IEEE Computer*, discounts, and opportunities to serve (all activities are led by volunteer members). Membership is open to all IEEE members, affiliate society members, and others seriously interested in the computer field.

Publications and Activities

IEEE Computer. An authoritative, easy-to-read magazine containing tutorials and in-depth articles on topics across the computer field, plus news, conference reports, book reviews, calendars, calls for papers, interviews, and new products.

Periodicals. The society publishes six magazines and five research transactions. For more details, refer to our membership application or request information as noted above.

Conference proceedings, tutorial texts, and standards documents. The IEEE Computer Society Press publishes more than 100 titles every year.

Standards Working Groups. Over 100 of these groups produce IEEE standards used throughout the industrial world.

Technical Committees. Over 30 TCs publish newsletters, provide interaction with peers in specialty areas, and directly influence standards, conferences, and education.

Conferences/Education. The society holds about 100 conferences each year and sponsors many educational activities, including computing science accreditation.

Chapters. Regular and student chapters worldwide provide the opportunity to interact with colleagues, hear technical experts, and serve the local professional community.

OTHER IEEE COMPUTER SOCIETY PRESS TITLES

Monographs

Analyzing Computer Architectures
Written by J.C. Huck and M.J. Flynn
(ISBN 0-8186-8857-2); 206 pages

Desktop Publishing for the Writer: Designing, Writing, and Developing
Written by Richard Ziegfeld and John Tarp
(ISBN 0-8186-8840-8); 380 pages

Digital Image Warping
Written by George Wolberg
(ISBN 0-8186-8944-7); 340 pages

Integrating Design and Test—CAE Tools for ATE Programming
Written by K.P. Parker
(ISBN 0-8186-8788-6); 160 pages

JSP and JSD—The Jackson Approach to Software Development (Second Edition)
Written by J.R. Cameron
(ISBN 0-8186-8858-0); 560 pages

National Computer Policies
Written by Ben G. Matley and Thomas A. McDannold
(ISBN 0-8186-8784-3); 192 pages

Physical Level Interfaces and Protocols
Written by Uyless Black
(ISBN 0-8186-8824-2); 240 pages

Protecting Your Proprietary Rights in Computer and Hi-Tech Industries
Written by Tobey B. Marzook, Esq.
(ISBN 0-8186-8754-1); 224 pages

Tutorials

Ada Programming Language
Edited by S.H. Saib and R.E. Fritz
(ISBN 0-8186-0456-5); 548 pages

Advanced Computer Architecture
Edited by D.P. Agrawal
(ISBN 0-8186-0667-3); 400 pages

Advanced Microprocessors and Hi-Level Language Computer Architectures
Edited by V. Mulutinovic
(ISBN 0-8186-0623-1); 608 pages

Advances in Distributed System Reliability
Edited by Suresh Rai an Dharma P. Agrawal
(ISBN 0-8186-8907-2); 352 pages

Computer Architecture
Edited by D.D. Gajski, V.M. Multinovic, H. Siegel, and B.P. Furht
(ISBN 0-8186-0704-1); 602 pages

Computer Arithmetic I
Edited by Earl E. Swartzlander, Jr.
(ISBN 0-8186-8931-5); 398 pages

Computer Arithmetic II
Edited by Earl E. Swartzlander, Jr.
(ISBN 0-8186-8945-5); 412 pages

Computer Communications: Architectures, Protocols and Standards (Second Edition)
Edited by William Stallings
(ISBN 0-8186-0790-4); 448 pages

Computer Graphics (Second Edition)
Edited by J.C. Beatty and K.S. Booth
(ISBN 0-8186-0425-5); 576 pages

Computer Graphics Hardware: Image Generation and Display
Edited by H.K. Reghbati and A.Y.C. Lee
(ISBN 0-8186-0753-X); 384 pages

Computer Graphics: Image Synthesis
Edited by Kenneth Joy, Max Nelson, Charles Grant, and Lansing Hatfield
(ISBN 0-8186-8854-8); 380.4 pages

Computer and Network Security
Edited by M.D. Abrams and H.J. Podell
(ISBN 0-8186-0756-4); 448 pages

Computer Networks (Fourth Edition)
Edited by M.D. Abrams and I.W. Cotton
(ISBN 0-8186-0568-5); 512 pages

Computer Text Recognition and Error Correction
Edited by S.N. Srihari
(ISBN 0-8186-0579-0); 364 pages

Computers for Artificial Intelligence Applications
Edited by B. Wah and G.J. Li
(ISBN 0-8186-0706-8); 656 pages

Database Management
Edited by J.A. Larson
(ISBN 0-8186-0714-9); 448 pages

Digital Image Processing and Analysis: Vol 1—Digital Image Processing
Edited by R. Chellappa and A.A. Sawchuk
(ISBN 0-8186-0665-7); 736 pages

Digital Image Processing and Analysis: Vol 2—Digital Image Analysis
Edited by H.A. Freeman and K.J. Thurber
(ISBN 0-8186-0605-3); 384 pages

Local Network Technology (Third Edition)
Edited by William Stallings
(ISBN 0-8186-0825-0); 512 pages

Microprogramming and Firmware Engineering
Edited by V. Milutinovic
(ISBN 0-8186-0839-0); 416 pages

Modeling and Control of Automated Manufacturing Systems
Edited by A. A. Desrochers
(ISBN 0-8186-8916-1); 384 pages

Modern Design and Analysis of Discrete-Event Computer Simulation
Edited by E.J. Dudewicz and Z. Karian
(ISBN 0-8186-0597-9); 486 pages

Nearest Neighbor Pattern Classification Techniques
Edited by Belur V. Dasarathy
(ISBN 0-8186-8930-); 500 pages

New Paradigms for Software Development
Edited by William Agresti
(ISBN 0-8186-0707-6); 304 pages

Object-Oriented Computing, Vol. 1: Concepts
Edited by Gerald E. Petersen
(ISBN 0-8186-0821-8); 214 pages

Object-Oriented Computing, Vol. 2: Implementations
Edited by Gerald E. Petersen
(ISBN 0-8186-0822-6); 324 pages

Office Automation Systems (Second Edition)
Edited by H.A. Freeman and K.J. Thurber
(ISBN 0-8186-0711-4); 324 pages

For Further Information:

IEEE Computer Society, 10662 Los Vaqueros Circle, P.O. Box 3014,
Los Alamitos, CA 90720

IEEE Computer Society, 13, avenue de l'Aquilon, 2
B-1200 Brussels, BELGIUM

IEEE Computer Society, Ooshima Building, 2-19-1 Minami-Aoyama,
Minato-ku, Tokyo 107, JAPAN